The Jews in Medieval Egypt

THE LANDS AND AGES OF THE JEWISH PEOPLE

Series Editor:
Ira Robinson (Concordia University, Montreal)

The Jews in Medieval Egypt

Edited by
Miriam Frenkel

BOSTON
2021

The publication of this book was made possible by grants from the following institutions:

- The Joseph & Racheline Barda Chair for the Study and Research of Jewish Heritage in Egypt
- Misgav Yerushalayim—The Center for Research and Study of Sephardi and Oriental Jewish Heritage
- Mandel Institute for Jewish Studies (The Hebrew University of Jerusalem)

Library of Congress Cataloging-in-Publication Data

Names: Frenkel, Miriam, editor.
Title: The Jews in medieval Egypt / edited by Miriam Frenkel.
Description: Boston : Academic Studies Press, 2021. | Series: The lands and ages of the Jewish people | Includes bibliographical references.
Identifiers: LCCN 2020038768 (print) | LCCN 2020038769 (ebook) | ISBN 9781618117465 (hardback) | ISBN 9781618117472 (paperback) | ISBN 9781618117489 (adobe pdf) | ISBN 9781644695128 (epub)
Subjects: LCSH: Jews--Egypt--History--To 1500. | Egypt--Civilization--Jewish influences. | Egypt--History--1250-1517.
Classification: LCC DS135.E4 J48 2021 (print) | LCC DS135.E4 (ebook) | DDC 962/.00492400902--dc23
LC record available at https://lccn.loc.gov/2020038768
LC ebook record available at https://lccn.loc.gov/2020038769

ISBN 9781618117465 (hardback)
ISBN 9781618117472 (paperback)
ISBN 9781618117489 (adobe pdf)
ISBN 9781644695128 (epub)

Book design by Kryon Publishing Services, Ltd.
www.kryonpublishing.com

Cover design by Ivan Grave

Published by Academic Studies Press
1577 Beacon Street
Brookline, MA 02446, USA
press@academicstudiespress.com
www.academicstudiespress.com

Contents

Introduction vi

1 Between the Hellenistic World and the Cairo Genizah: The Jewish Community in Late Antique Egypt 1
Tal Ilan

2 A Concise History of Islamic Egypt 22
Yehoshua Frenkel

3 The Community's Borders; Converts and Renegades 47
Moshe Yagur

4 Communal Self-Government: The Genizah Period 72
Mark R. Cohen

5 Introduction to the Legal Arena 86
Oded Zinger

6 Jewish Economic Life in Medieval Egypt: Images, Theories, and Research 124
Jessica Goldberg

7 Jewish Family Life in Medieval Egypt 146
Miriam Frenkel

8 Situating Egyptian Pietism 175
Elisha Russ-Fishbane

9 Languages and Language Varieties Used by Medieval Egyptian Jews 191
Esther-Miriam Wagner

10 Hebrew Poetry in Medieval Egypt 209
Joseph Yahalom

11 The Jews in Medieval Egypt under the Mamluks (1250–1517) 244
Amir Mazor

Bibliography 269

Index 301

Introduction

MIRIAM FRENKEL

The Alexandrians turned out in force
to see Cleopatra's children,
Kaisarion and his little brothers,
Alexander and Ptolemy,
who'd been taken out to the Gymnasium for the first time,
to be proclaimed kings there
before a brilliant array of soldiers.

Alexander: they declared him
king of Armenia, Media, and the Parthians.
Ptolemy: they declared him
king of Cilicia, Syria, and Phoenicia.
Kaisarion was standing in front of the others,
dressed in pink silk,
on his chest a bunch of hyacinths,
his belt a double row of amethysts and sapphires,
his shoes tied with white ribbons
prinked with rose-coloured pearls.
They declared him greater than his brothers,
they declared him King of Kings.

The Alexandrians knew of course
that this was all just words, all theatre.

But the day was warm and poetic,
the sky a pale blue,
the Alexandrian Gymnasium
a complete artistic triumph,
the courtiers wonderfully sumptuous,
Kaisarion all grace and beauty
(Cleopatra's son, blood of the Lagids):
and the Alexandrians thronged to the festival,
full of enthusiasm, and shouted acclamations
in Greek, and Egyptian, and some in Hebrew,
charmed by the lovely spectacle—
though they knew of course what all this was worth,
what empty words they really were, these kingships.

—Constantine P. Cavafy

Constantine Cavafy (1863–1933), the well-known Alexandrian poet, describes in this poem the coronation of new kings in Alexandria, Egypt. The native Egyptians, as far as he is concerned, know very well that "these kingships" are nothing but "empty words." Still, they enthusiastically take part in the pompous ceremony and don't mind cheering "in Greek, and Egyptian, and some in Hebrew." They constitute a spectrum of nationalities, creeds, and languages who share the same mother country and enjoy its blue skies, warm weather, and beautiful edifices. The country is theirs while the kings are but artificial ornaments in an amusing spectacle. Jews are an indispensable part of this amalgam of nationalities, creeds, and languages, and Hebrew is heard among the multilingual acclamations.

Jews, indeed, lived in Egypt for many centuries, from biblical times until the middle of the previous century. The existence of the earliest communities is attested by the Bible for the early sixth century BCE, through the Persian period, and especially during the Ptolemaic and Roman periods, for which there is much archaeological and literary evidence of extensive Jewish settlement in Egypt.[1] Nevertheless, Jewish life in medieval Islamic Egypt was for many years an obscure and understudied theme. It was not until the discovery of the Cairo Genizah that this period started to be studied and revealed.

The Cairo Genizah is a trove of over a quarter of a million pages of books and documents that accumulated in a back chamber in the Ben Ezra synagogue, designed to serve as a *bet genizah*. A *bet genizah* is a storage place where writings in Hebrew script are deposited when they are no longer in use or in circulation. The discovery of the Genizah by Western scholars during the last third of the nineteenth century and the gradual research done on them since then has illuminated the history and culture of the entirety of Jewish society in the lands of Islam, particularly during the High Middle Ages (tenth–thirteenth centuries), since most of the Genizah manuscripts date from this period.[2] But, more than any other parts of the Muslim world, the Genizah writings tell the story of the Jews of Egypt during the Middle Ages, which was till then unclear and largely ignored.

It was in medieval Egypt that some of the most prominent Jewish leaders and thinkers operated, Moses Maimonides being perhaps the most famous of them. The present book will not focus on them. It is intended to provide a

1 See Tal Ilan's chapter in this volume.

2 Adina Hoffman and Peter Cole, *Sacred Trash: The Lost and Found World of the Cairo Geniza* (New York: Next Book-Schocken, 2011).

broad canvas of Jewish society and culture rather than concentrating on particular persons, influential and famous though they may be. The chapters gathered in this volume venture to offer the reader a wide-ranging picture of Jewish life in medieval Egypt as depicted by the most recent scholarship.

The book opens with two introductory chapters. The first chapter, by Tal Ilan, leads the reader along the road from the Byzantine era of late antiquity into the medieval Islamic period. To use Ilan's words, it is "about the Jewish community of Egypt that gave birth to the Cairo Genizah." Ilan offers a review of the history of the Jews in the Byzantine period and argues that the new Jewish community that was coming into being in Egypt in late antiquity had the identity markers of the Jewish community that produced the Cairo Genizah as of the ninth century CE. The chapter provides an overview of the scanty information available, gathered mainly from papyri, about the geographic dispersion, economic conditions, and legal status of the Jews of Egypt in late antiquity. By reviewing the information about the literary products of this community, which include biblical and liturgical texts, marriage contracts, personal letters, and magical texts, Ilan demonstrates how it was indeed the forerunner of the later medieval community reflected in the Genizah documents. The chapter ends with a discussion of the puzzling absence of contemporary rabbinic texts from Egypt in spite of the well-documented rabbinical activities in Palestine and Babylonia at this time. Ilan provides three possible explanations for this silence.

Yehoshua Frenkel's introductory chapter provides a concise chronological history of Islamic Egypt. It starts with the abrupt Arab-Islamic conquest of Egypt (639–42), goes on to describe the gradual incorporation of the Nile valley into the Islamic Caliphate during the Umayyad period (657–749), and continues to the turbulent Abbasid period (750–868), which marks a turning point in the transformation of the Nile valley from a Christian land to an Islamic territory. It then turns to describe the Tulunid (868–905) and Ikhshidid (935–68) periods, during which Egypt renewed its Mediterranean maritime trade and became a regional power; actually, the strongest land in the eastern Mediterranean basin, a position it retained for many centuries to come. Special attention is given to the Fatimid (969–1171) and Ayyubid (1171–1250) periods, which are also termed "the classical Genizah period," since most Genizah writings originate from that time. It ends with a description of the Mamluk Sultanate (1250–1516), followed by a discussion of its frequent portrayal as a regime of continuous decay. Frenkel's introduction is not merely a chronological survey of events. The economic, demographic, cultural, social, and political aspects of the various epochs of medieval Egypt are broadly referred to, with special attention given to interreligious relations. It thus supplies the reader with the required background for the Jewish history of this country throughout the Middle Ages.

After these two introductory chapters, the volume goes on to delineate the contours of the Jewish community in medieval Egypt, and to find out where the border stones, which defined the Jewish community of Egypt, were positioned.

This is the task upon which Moshe Yagur embarks in his article. Yagur tries to outline the community's boundaries by focusing on those people who crossed them: apostates, converts, and manumitted slaves who converted to Judaism. He tries to find out, how and when the boundaries were crossed, who crossed them, and what the varying attitudes of members and leaders of the Jewish community towards were these crossings. By examining these three groups of converts, and comparing them, the chapter arrives at the startling conclusion that the movement across religious boundaries was not necessarily one-way, but rather a varied and overlapping movement. Converts to Judaism included European Christians, local Copts, and even local Muslims; many of the converts were manumitted slaves previously purchased by Jews; while Jews themselves converted not only to Islam but also to Christianity. The chapter points at ongoing contacts between converts and their families and former communities. In some cases, Jews remained married to their convert spouses, or even married converts. Moreover, in many cases religious identity could be molded, erased, or reinvented to the extent that one's religious identity was not always clear to other community members. Yagur's conclusion is that communal boundaries were far from being firm and clear, but rather were porous and blurred.

The next chapter, by Mark Cohen, concerns the organizational features of Jewish life in medieval Egypt. It ventures to describe the functioning of Jewish self-government of this time. As in other parts of the Islamic Caliphate, the Jews of Egypt were also allowed to govern themselves in accordance with their ancestral laws, and to elect their own leaders. The chapter describes the governing Jewish institutions, namely the Palestinian *yeshivah* and its head, the *ga'on*, who governed the Jewish communities of Egypt and other countries of the Levant until the end of the eleventh century, as well as the local Nagidate of Egypt, which succeeded them. It then proceeds to describe the local community, which Cohen considers to be "the fundamental cell of organized Jewish communal life in Egypt." The chapter offers a comprehensive description of the community's heads, officials, and judiciary, discusses its financial infrastructures and ends with a discussion of the local community's internal politics. The chapter takes a double comparative approach, which parallels the Jewish communal life of medieval Egypt to that of the surrounding Muslim society and to that of medieval Europe.

A central feature of Jewish self-government in Egypt was the maintenance of a Jewish judiciary, which implemented Jewish law. This is the topic of Oded Zinger's chapter. By treating the judiciary as a dynamic arena with a lively, dramatic and competitive nature, Zinger offers here a new approach, which aims at discovering "how legal institutions were integrated within the broader social fabric and what people did outside of court with the intention to affect legal action." The chapter starts with a review of past research on Jewish legal institutions in medieval Egypt, and of the various approaches used in their study. Then it describes the Jewish legal arena, which consisted of the local Jewish court and the documents it produced as well as of other, Jewish and Islamic, legal institutions. Special attention is given to the legal act of acquisition (*qinyan*) that forms the basis of most legal activity in Genizah courts. Next, it discusses the social embeddedness of the legal arena, by surveying the ways litigants influenced the legal process by actions outside of legal institutions. Zinger pleads for the social embeddedness of the Jewish legal arena in medieval Egypt not to be considered as corruption, but rather as a major aspect of its dynamic legal culture and as a central component of its strength and vitality. The chapter ends with a description of the different sources of authority of the local Jewish court in medieval Egypt.

The next chapter, by Jessica Goldberg, discusses the economic life of the medieval Jews of Egypt. The chapter starts with a survey of the state of the art in which Goldberg demonstrates the crucial importance of the Cairo Genizah for the study of economic life, not only of medieval Egypt and its Jews but also of Egypt's economic connections with the Islamic Mediterranean and Indian Ocean. At the same time, she also points out the limitations of the Genizah as source material, which can only reflect a partial economic reality. Goldberg discusses the involvement of Jews in the Egyptian economy, and states that "Jews could be found in nearly every economic circumstance possible in medieval Islamic society and in most kinds of work." Contradicting the traditional postulation of Jewish merchants as "cross-cultural" brokers, Goldberg shows that Egyptian Jewish merchants of the eleventh century, as a part of a larger Islamic merchant community, tended rather to be the opposite, namely brokers of the products of their home region into the "international" markets of the Islamic

Mediterranean, and later—to the market centers of the Indian Ocean trade. Although Jews constituted a far more urban segment of Egyptian society than other confessional groups, they were an indispensable part of the Egyptian economy, being deeply embedded not only in trade, but in almost every other profession. Goldberg relates the deep embeddedness of Egyptian Jews in the larger economy to the absence of guilds in the Islamicate world, to the organization of most production into small partnership workshops, and to the lack of special status distinctions among professions. It is these conditions, she claims, which made it possible for Jews, as well as for other minority groups, to work in the same industries: "sometimes in competition, sometimes developing the solidarity of profession." In spite of this deep integration of Jews in the Egyptian economic system, the chapter also notes the particular ways their religious identity affected their economic identity. This was mainly due to the poll tax, which was heavy enough to hinder their economic mobility and also to shape social hierarchy within the community.

The seventh chapter, by Miriam Frenkel, concerns Jewish family life in medieval Egypt. It starts with a short survey of the ways family, kinship, and pedigree were conceived in this society, then goes on to speak about the functions expected and fulfilled by family members. As it turns out that the family's borders were not confined to blood kin alone, special attention is given to the role of domestic slaves in the family. The chapter discusses at length the institution of marriage: its roles, the legal processes required to establish and to end it, and its structure, including a short discussion of polygyny, which was prevalent and legal in this society, albeit frequently frowned upon. The chapter ends with a description of the relations between family members as they surface in Genizah documents: spousal relations, relations between parents and children and among siblings.

After presenting the main infrastructures of Jewish life in medieval Egypt: the community, the judiciary, the economic frameworks, and the family, the next two chapters are devoted to Jewish literary and spiritual activities. In the eighth chapter, Elisha Russ-Fishbane discusses the mystical movement of thirteenth-century Egypt known as *Ḥasidut Mitzraim.* This movement, also labeled "Jewish Sufism," marks a unique chapter in the history of Jewish-Muslim relations. The movement, led by no other than the "head of the Jews" himself, Abraham b. Moses Maimonides (Abraham Maimuni, 1186–1237), aspired at cultivating an inner attachment to God, with the ultimate goal of generating a broad religious revival as the harbinger of messianic redemption. Its devotees, who originated from all parts of the socio-economic spectrum, adopted a harsh spiritual regimen, which had clear parallels to Sufi rites. Russ-Fishbane considers the movement to be "the richest historical engagement of any known Jewish group with the religious heritage of Islam." The chapter introduces the reader to Abraham Maimuni's theological outlook, and discusses his reform project and its consequences. Russ-Fishbane estimates that this episode marks a critical transition from a Jewish dialogue with Sufi and Near Eastern models of piety to "a concrete pietist movement embedded within the fabric of Jewish communal life."

The next chapter, by Joseph Yahalom, deals with one of the most creative literary genres composed by Egyptian Jews during the Middle Ages, namely, Hebrew poetry. Not only did Hebrew poetry occupy a central place in the spiritual and social life of Egyptian Jewry of this period, writing poetry was also a central medium through which the leadership, and those attached to it, expressed themselves. In this chapter, Yahalom provides a detailed survey of the poetic works of thirteen writers, who lived for certain periods of time in Egypt, and were engaged in writing Hebrew poetry. Some of them, like Moses Maimonides, were among the most prominent Jewish leaders of their time. The survey combines literary analysis of the poems with biographical data about their writers. The poets surveyed are Samuel b. Hoshaʿna, Abraham ha-Kohen, Yeshuʿah b. Nathan, Eli b. Amram, Solomon ha-Kohen b. Joseph, Joseph ibn Abitur, Judah ha-Levi and Aharon ibn al-ʿAmmānī, Eleʿazar ha-Kohen ben Khalfūn, Moses Darʿī, Moses Maimonides, Anatoli b. Joseph, Joseph ha-Maʿaravi, and Joseph b. Tanḥum the Jerusalemite. By way of conclusion, the chapter ends with the harsh critiques written by Judah al-Ḥarīzī on the local poets of Egypt. Nevertheless, Yahalom contests Judah al-Ḥarīzī's stance and praises the unique path of Egyptian poets, who continued the old Eastern tradition of poetry.

Egyptian pietism and Egyptian poetry were two central manifestations of Jewish literary activities in medieval Egypt. The literary products of *Ḥasidut Mitzraim* were articulated in Judeo-Arabic, while most Judeo-Egyptian poetry was written in Hebrew. The next chapter, by Esther-Miriam Wagner, deals with the topic of languages and language varieties used by medieval Egyptian Jews. Her chapter starts with an overview of the variety of languages used by medieval Egyptian Jewry: Judeo-Arabic, Arabic, Hebrew, and Aramaic, and the different function ascribed to each of them, as attested by Genizah manuscripts. An important methodological distinction is made between three different entities: the written language, the spoken language, and the reading tradition. In order to understand the writing habits of this society, Wagner examines the education system, paying special attention to the training of professional scribes. Most of the chapter is naturally devoted to Judeo-Arabic, which is the most prevalent language used in the Genizah writings. Wagner examines habits of code switching and script switching among several individual Genizah writers, and finds that they demonstrate the Arabic/Judeo-Arabic/Hebrew linguistic continuum that was a feature of medieval Egypt. By examining private and traders' letters, and by using parallels from comparative modern examples and from sociolinguistic theory, she tries to trace certain features of the spoken language. Finally, Wagner arrives at the conclusion that the mixing of the languages used by medieval Egyptian Jews "created particular registers, with the Aramaic and Hebrew content varying decidedly between more religious and more secular genres." In spoken medieval Judeo-Arabic, she assumes a diversity of different registers, bound to particular circumstances.

The volume ends with Amir Mazor's chapter about the Mamluk era, which constituted the last phase in the history of Egyptian Jewry in the Middle Ages. After a comprehensive political and military survey of the era, Mazor turns to describing economic and demographic trends during the Mamluk epoch, and their implications for the Jewish population of Egypt. He shows that although the social, cultural, and intellectual integration of Jews in Mamluk society was limited compared to previous periods, they still were far from being isolated, especially in comparison with the status of the Jews in Latin Europe at the same time. They continued to take part in public and intellectual life, especially during the first century of the Mamluk sultanate. The chapter describes the system of Jewish self-government embodied at this time in the office of the Nagidate, and also discusses at length the state's policy towards the Jews, which was characterized by a stricter enforcement of the Pact of ʿUmar.[3] Mazor shows that while some of the most discriminatory and humiliating anti-*dhimmī* laws were promulgated during this time, most of them were enforced for limited periods or never enforced at all. Moreover, in most cases Jews received the protection of the authorities against intolerant actions of the mob. All in all, Mazor cautions that Mamluk state policy should be examined in the social, legal, and economical contexts of the Islamicate society of the Mamluk sultanate. The chapter ends with a description of the economic, social, and cultural revival of the Egyptian Jewish communities toward the end of the fifteenth century, after the expulsion from Spain and the arrival of the Sephardi exiles. This very

3 See Mark Cohen's chapter in this volume.

last phase may serve as an introduction to the next chapter in the history of the Jews of Egypt, that of Ottoman rule.

The eleven chapters gathered in this volume reveal the rich texture of Jewish life in medieval Egypt. The medieval community, which was the direct successor of the late antique one, did not build high walls to separate itself from its surrounding Islamicate society, yet managed to maintain its particularity and uniqueness. This particularity was anchored in its efficient communal apparatus, based on the right to self-government granted by Muslim rule. Its judicial system was flexible and deeply influenced by the wider society, but this was part of its strength and vitality. Its family life resembled that of the neighboring communities and so did the economic and occupational patterns it assumed. It was in Egypt that "the richest historical engagement of any known Jewish group with the religious heritage of Islam" occurred, through the pietist movement led by Abraham Maimuni, but the same community also produced unique Hebrew poetry, which continued and preserved the old Eastern tradition. The Jews of medieval Egypt used several languages, but clearly preferred Judeo-Arabic, the language that demonstrates more than anything else the singular blend of embeddedness along particularity that describes this society.

1

Between the Hellenistic World and the Cairo Genizah: The Jewish Community in Late Antique Egypt

TAL ILAN

This chapter is about the Jewish community of Egypt that gave birth to the Cairo Genizah. In looking for the history of this community one has to start with the dramatic event that effectively killed the previous, thriving Jewish community in Egypt—the Hellenistic-Jewish one that spoke Greek, initiated the first translation of the Bible (into Greek—the Septuagint), hosted a competing Temple to the one in Jerusalem (the Onias Temple), and whose model was Philo of Alexandria. All this came to an end in 117 CE. Since Egypt is also the cradle of (pre-Christian) anti-Semitism,[1] for some time before 116–17 CE tensions between the ruling Romans with their accomplices—the indigenous Egyptian and Greek population—and the Jews had been brewing. In 115 CE the Jews rebelled. What they hoped to achieve, and how the rebellion developed, is mostly unknown,[2] but the meager historical evidence that is at our disposal shows that there were few Jews left in Egypt after this event, and that

1 P. Schäfer, *Judeophobia: Attitudes toward the Jews in the Ancient World* (Cambridge, MA: Harvard University Press, 1997).

2 For an updated discussion, see M. Pucci Ben Zeev, *Diaspora Judaism in Turmoil, 116/117 CE: Ancient Sources and Modern Insights* (Leuven: Peeters, 2005).

virtually nothing of the ancient thriving Hellenistic Jewish community survived the revolt.

If one is looking for a good overview of the history of the Jews in Egypt between the crushing of the Jewish Revolt in 116–17 CE and the first documents deposited in the Cairo Genizah, the best work to consult is still Victor Tcherikover's Prolegomenon to his *Corpus Papyrorum Judaicarum* (henceforth *CPJ*) that appeared in 1957.[3] The following review is in constant dialogue with that work, since it is impossible to tell the story of this community without recourse to it. After bewailing the destruction of Hellenistic Judaism in 117 CE, and stating categorically that for many decades, perhaps centuries, Jewish life did not succeed in achieving any significant revival in Egypt, Tcherikover took his timeline for describing major events regarding the Jews of Egypt in late antiquity from the writings of Christian church fathers and chronographers. One could argue that he had no choice, since no comparable Jewish reports have survived from the same period. However, by doing so, Tcherikover enslaved himself to the approach the church fathers themselves wanted him to adopt, which is that the Jews were bitter enemies of Christianity, who used every opportunity to attack it and collaborated with all its manifest and hidden enemies.

This is how he told the story: In 335 CE, according to the Bishop of Alexandria, Athenaios, Jews and pagans broke into churches, plundered sanctuaries, and insulted monks and nuns (Athanasios, *Epist. encycl.* 3). In the events after the death of Athenaios in 378 CE, when the Arians were contesting the Catholic Church for supremacy in Alexandria, the Jews, according to another Christian scholar, took part in acts of violence directed against Catholic sanctuaries (Theodoret, *Hist. eccl.* 4. 18). Sometime later, in 415 CE, according to the Church historian Sokrates (*Hist. eccl.* 7. 13) the Jews were expelled from Alexandria, after a showdown between the secular Byzantine governor of the city and Kyrillos, its bishop. When they returned to the city thereafter is impossible to say, but return they did because a number of influential Jews (like Domnos the physician, 474–91 CE)[4] are mentioned in later Christian sources. Finally, during the Sasanian invasion of Egypt in

3 V. Tcherikover (ed.), "Prolegomena: The Late Roman and the Byzantine Period," in *Corpus Papyrorum Judaicarum*, vol. 1, ed. A. Fuks and M. Stern (Cambridge, MA: Harvard University Press, 1957), 93–111. Henceforth *CPJ* I.

4 Damascaius, in M. Stern, *Greek and Latin Authors on Jews and Judaism*, vol. 2 (Jerusalem: Israel Academy of Sciences and Humanities, 1980), no. 551.

616–27 CE, according to Eutychios (Ibn Batrik, *Ann.* 2. 245–7), the Jews welcomed the new (non-Christian) invaders.[5]

All these observers are Christian and see in the Jews collaborators with the enemies of Christianity. There is no doubt that all three events—clashes between Catholics and Arians in the fourth century, between the Monophysite Alexandrian church and the Orthodox Roman governor in the fifth century, and the invasion of Christian Egypt by the Zoroastrian Sasanians at the beginning of the seventh century—were major events for the history of Christianity in Egypt, and that the Jews were indeed expelled from Alexandria in the fifth century, but they probably touch only marginally on Jewish interests or political choices. It would be much more plausible to see the Jews in all these instances as victims of these politics than as active parties in them. Their mention in them is often far more a rhetorical tool of Christian theologians than a reflection of real events.

Rightly, Tcherikover placed his history of the Jews of Egypt in his introduction to a collection of Jewish papyri from the Hellenistic, Roman, and Byzantine periods. Much of what we know about the Jews of Egypt from these periods derives from papyri—perishable material that has miraculously survived the ravages of time in Egypt because of the dry climate. Papyri become progressively more important for telling this story as time goes by, since for the Hellenistic period we have more external information about the Jews of Egypt than for the early Roman period, and for the early Roman period we have more information about the Jews than for the late Roman and Byzantine periods. Tcherikover and his *CPJ* team, however, concentrated on Greek papyri, and ironically, these also become less informative with the passage of time. There are more Greek papyri on the Jews of Egypt for the Hellenistic period than for the Roman period, and more such papyri for the Roman period than for the Byzantine period.

Better sources for Jewish history in this period are papyri in the native languages of the Jews—Hebrew and Aramaic. Toward the end of the nineteenth century, papyri in these languages began to be published by European scholars.[6] From these papyri, Tcherikover drew conclusions about the

5 *CPJ* I, 96–100.

6 In 1879 Moritz Steinschneider published Hebrew and Aramaic papyrus fragments housed in the Egyptian Museum in Berlin, apparently hailing from the Fayyum: M. Steinschneider, "Hebräische Papyrus-Fragmente aus dem Fayyûm," *Magazin für die Wissenschaft des Judenthums* 6 (1879): 250–4. In 1886 David Müller and David Kaufmann published such papyri housed in Vienna, also apparently from the Fayyum: D. H. Müller and D. Kaufmann,

introduction of Hebrew into the post-117 CE Jewish community, which in its previous incarnation had not a scrap of this language in its vocabulary. He rightly claimed that the source of influence and inspiration for this new Jewish community was neighboring Palestine, from where one may assume most of the newly settled Jews in Egypt had migrated. Tcherikover addressed these papyri very briefly and did not publish them in the third volume of *CPJ*, because of his concentration on Greek papyri. This review will pay much more attention to these Hebrew and Aramaic papyri.

For more internal evidence on the Jews in Egypt at this time Tcherikover searched rabbinic literature. This was an important move, because only the story told by the authors of this literature was eventually incorporated into the story of post-Temple Judaism, until the arrival of Islam. However, what Tcherikover found was very disappointing. He found in it some Egyptian rabbis, but only two (a certain Rabbi Zakkai of Alexandria—for example, *yKet* 4:6, 28d—and perhaps also a Tanḥum son of Papa—*yQid* 3:12, 64d) could really be dated to the time he was researching. Both appear in dialogue with the rabbinic community in Palestine. Tcherikover took this to support his thesis on the close relationship between the Jews of Egypt and those of rabbinic Palestine. However, as we will see below, rabbinic influence on Egyptian Jews at the time is virtually non-existent.

In the last sixty years no up-to-date overview has been written on the subject of the Jews in Egypt in late antiquity, either because it has been assumed that there is no new evidence to consult, or because the area of research has not come under review, or both. However, in light of the editorial work underway[7] for the collection and redaction of a new *Corpus Papyrorum Judaicarum* (henceforth *N.CPJ*), which incorporates papyri that have been published since the completion of the old *CPJ*, there is new evidence, and a review of the history of the Jews in the Byzantine period can now be offered.[8] It will be argued

"Über die hebräischen Papyri," in *Mittheilungen aus der Sammlung der Papyrus Erzherzog Rainer*, vol. 1, ed. J. Karabaček (Vienna: Verlag der k.k. Hof- und Staatsdruckerei, 1886), 38–44. In 1905 scraps of such papyri were found by the British Bernard Grenfell and Arthur Hunt in their excavations at Oxyrhynchos, and Cowley, who edited them, dates them to about 400 CE: A. E. Cowley, "Hebrew and Aramaic Papyri," *JQR* 16 (1904): 1–8; idem, "Notes on Hebrew Papyrus Fragments from Oxyrhynchus," *Journal of Egypt Archaeology* 2 (1915): 209–13.

7 N. Hacham and T. Ilan, *Corpus Papyrorum Judaicarum* vol. IV (Jerusalem and Berlin: De Magnes and De Gruyter, 2020); vol. V, in press, vol. VI, in preparation.

8 For more on Tcherikover's attitude, see now T. Ilan, "The Jewish Community in Egypt before and after 117 CE in Light of Old and New Papyri," in *Jewish and Christian Communal*

that the new Jewish community that was coming into being in Egypt in late antiquity had the identity markers of the Jewish community that produced the Cairo Genizah as of the ninth century CE. The chapter begins with a short overview of what we know from this period (especially from papyri) about the Jews in Egypt, about their geographic dispersion, about their economic conditions, and about their legal status. As we will see, this is meager. It will end with a review of what we know of the Jewish community and their literary output, mostly in Hebrew and Aramaic, and demonstrate how these constitute evidence that this community was indeed the forerunner and the matrix of the Genizah community.

The geographic distribution of the Jewish settlement in Byzantine Egypt

The most important city of settlement for Jews in late antiquity, as also of the earlier Hellenistic Jewish community, was the great metropolis, Alexandria. Papyri are no good for telling anything about the Jews of Alexandria, because the humid climate of that city has not allowed for their preservation. Thus, the papyri tell us about the Jews of Egypt who lived upriver. Sometimes, however, these were in touch with the Jews of Alexandria. *CPJ* 505, a fragmentary letter, tells of a Jew coming to some unknown location up-river from Alexandria. It is unlikely, though, that the papyrus was written by a Jew or to a Jew, and it tells little about the connection between Jews of the *chora* (that is, rural Egypt) and those of Alexandria. On the other hand, among the new papyri a *ketubbah* from Antinoopolis dated to 417 CE, written in Aramaic and housed today in the papyri collection of Cologne, records the marriage of Samuel son of Sympti (or Sambati, שמואל בר סמפטי) with a Mitra daughter of Lazar (מיטרא ברת לעזר) from Alexandria.[9] This papyrus clearly furnishes evidence for a relationship between the metropolis and the hinterland, although with the state of knowledge at our disposal now, not much importance can be attached to it.

Identities in the Roman World, ed. Y. Furstenberg (Leiden: Brill, 2016), 201–24. See also idem, "Julia Crispina of the Babatha Archive Revisited: A Woman between the Judean Desert and the Fayum in Egypt, between the Diaspora Revolt and the Bar Kokhba War," in *Gender and Social Norms in Ancient Israel, Early Judaism and Early Christianity: Texts and Material Culture*, ed. Michaela Bauks, Katharina Galor, and Judith Hartenstein (Göttingen: Vandenhoeck and Ruprecht, 2019), 269–76.

9 C. Sirat, P. Cauderlier, M. Dukan, and M. A. Friedman, *La Ketouba de Cologne: Un contrat de mariage juif à Antinopolis*, vol. 12 of *Papyrologica Coloniensia* (Opladen: Westdeutschen Verlag, 1986).

The ancient Jewish community in Upper Egypt, which Tcherikover dated to as early as the Ptolemaic period, but which, we argue in *N.CPJ*, should actually be dated back even further, to the Jewish settlement at Elephantine in the Persian period, seems to have been hit hardest by the Jewish Revolt.[10] Tcherikover notes the complete silence of this region about Jews after 117 CE.[11] Only one new document may change this picture slightly: an ostracon from Edfu, dated paleographically to the seventh century, listing payments of the *annona* tax by three separate groups: captives, carpet-weavers, and the Hebrews (*SB* XIV 11844). In the Byzantine period the term "Hebrew" was used side-by-side with, or even replacing, *Ioudaios* for Jews.[12] This indicates perhaps that some Jews had recently come to reside in Edfu. However, they seem just as foreign in the region as the "captives" mentioned next to them (although obviously the third group, the carpet-weavers, were hardly foreign). Most Jewish papyri of clear provenance are from the Fayyum,[13] from Oxyrhynchos,[14] and from Hermopolis/Antinoopolis.[15] This distribution of Jewish papyri is confirmed in the new documents collected since *CPJ*. However, we may wonder whether Jews chose to live in Oxyrhynchos and Hermopolis because they were such great metropoles, or whether we know about the Jewish community in these locations because they are both sites of great papyri excavations and publications. Volume 3 of *CPJ* counted nine papyri from Oxyrhynchos. In 1964, when the corpus appeared in print, only twenty-nine Oxyrhynchos papyri volumes had been published. In the intervening years, another fifty-three volumes have appeared. It is rather disappointing that they have only yielded another seven relevant documentary papyri,[16] indicating perhaps not a major presence of Jews at the site, but rather a major presence of Oxyrhynchos in the papyri record. These Greek papyri, however, are not the only evidence for a Jewish presence in

---

10 *N.CPJ* IV, 21-5.

11 *CPJ*, vol. 1, 94.

12 Hacham and Ilan, "Introduction."

13 *CPJ*, nos. 451, 455, 459, 460, 461, 466, 474, all from the Late Roman period, but also no. 512, from the Byzantine period.

14 *CPJ*, nos. 452b, 465, 473, 475, 477, 516, from the Late Roman period; nos. 503, 509, 510, from the Byzantine period.

15 *CPJ*, nos. 453, 506 (Hermopolis), 508 and 511 (Antinoopolis).

16 (1) P.Oxy. XLIII 3125; (2) XLIV 3203; (3) XLVI 3314; (4) L 3574; (5) LV 3805; (6) LXI 4123; (7) LXXVII 5119; (8) LXXXIII 5364; and see also published elsewhere (9) *SB* XVI 12553; (10) P.CtYBR inv. 154 v; (11) P. CtYBR inv. 760.

Oxyrhynchos. The majority of the Hebrew and Aramaic papyri of this period were also excavated at Oxyrhynchos.

The economic status of the Jews in Byzantine Egypt

In order to describe the economic life of the Jews in the period after the Jewish Revolt, Tcherikover used evidence found in Greek papyri that mention Jewish peasants (*CPJ* 470, 471, 474), a donkey-driver (*CPJ* 472), a guard (*CPJ* 475), and even a higher-ranking labor-manager (*CPJ* 477), all from the third and the fourth centuries. After the rise of Christianity, the papyri he collected revealed Jews engaging in herding or tanning (*CPJ* 509), wine-trading (*CPJ* 508, 512), and cloth-dying (*CPJ* 511). The meagerness of this evidence led him back to his thesis about the importance of Christian anti-Judaism for defining the status of the Jews in this period: "Their economic activity was seriously hampered by the harsh conditions created in Egypt, as elsewhere in the Empire, by the new epoch, especially by the hostile attitude of the Church, perceptible in the economic field as in every other."[17] Even when he did find one Jewish landowner in the Oxyrhinchite nome from the sixth century (*CPJ* 510), he refused to believe it, stating:

> [T]hese Jews, consequently, were legally regarded as being in independent possession of some land, but it is doubtful whether they were in fact independent landowners. The close vicinity of the mighty family of the Apiones, representatives of Egyptian early-medieval feudalism, would hardly leave the small landowners of the neighborhood any considerable degree of independence.[18]

We find Tcherikover voicing surprise at the fact that "a hundred years after their expulsion we find the Jews of Alexandria again rich and influential."[19] It should be noted, however, that he has moved here not just from poor to rich but from one source to another. Tcherikover found poor Jews in the papyri. All that Tcherikover knows about rich Jews derives from tendentious anti-Jewish Christian literary compositions.

New papyri only produce more of the same sort of evidence. From the second and third centuries we have a peasant (P.Wisc. II 57) and two landowners

17 *CPJ* I, 104.

18 *CPJ* I, 104–5.

19 *CPJ* I, 104.

(one of them a woman: P.Petaus 126; SB XVI 12553); in the fourth century we have two wine dealers (one of them from Palestine—P.Oxy. LXI 4123; L, 3574) and a purple dealer (P. Herm. Rees 52). From the fifth century we have one merchant (*pragmateus*—*BGU* XII, 2161); and from the sixth century a woman who rents a bakery—she must have been a baker (P.Brooklyn 15). All these together add up to eighteen persons mentioned in papyri, whose economic circumstances can be glimpsed. For a time period of over 500 years (117–640 CE), this is a negligible number, and this has been interpreted by Tcherikover to mean that the Jewish community in Egypt, which had been decimated in 117 CE, did not really recover until the Arab conquest.

However, it is much more likely that we know of many more Jews and their economic circumstances, especially from the later centuries in the papyri, but we simply cannot identify them as Jewish. In the early Roman period, Jewish papyri have been identified as such based on biblical names. However, once Christians begin to make extensive use of these names, distinguishing between Jew and Christian becomes almost impossible. In the Byzantine period Greek papyri become ever less useful for telling the story of Judaism in Egypt.

The legal status of the Jews

Did the laws applicable to the Egyptians in Egypt apply to Jews? Were they singled out after the revolt for special treatment—first as punishment for the uprising and later, with the rise of Christianity, out of mere hostility? Due to lack of information, Tcherikover could not really answer any of these questions. He wrote:

> In A.D. 212 the famous *Constitutio Antoniniana* of Caracalla bestowed Roman rights upon the inhabitants of the entire Roman Empire, and Jews were no exception to the rule. In the documents the new citizens are styled Aurelii, and some papyri mention Jewish Aurelii (Nos. 473, 474, 477, 503, 508). Jurists have long debated whether the promulgation of *Constitutio Antoniniana* meant that the local laws and customs were replaced by the Roman law. It is now commonly accepted that the local civic units continued their functions even under Roman law. Thus the Jewish communities and the right of their members "to live according to their ancestral laws" remained untouched.[20]

20 *CPJ* I, 100.

Yet this observation had its problems. In vol. 2 of *CPJ* the largest single group of documents that inform us of the Jews' legal status were receipts on ostraca from Edfu, given to Jews for having paid the Jewish tax (*ioudaikos telesma*). The Romans imposed this tax on the Jews of the entire Empire after the destruction of the Temple in 70 CE, and it was still being collected in Egypt before 116 CE. When did it stop? The editors of vol. 3 could point to *CPJ* 460, a document from Karanis in the Fayyum (from 145–46 CE or 167–68 CE) as evidence that in the middle of the second century it was still being collected. In the prolegomenon Tcherikover wrote on this question:

> It remains an open question whether Jews in the early Byzantine age had to pay a special tax. All taxes imposed on Jews by previous Emperors were abolished by Julian. It is generally agreed that the Christian Emperors after Julian re-enforced payment of all such taxes, and although no adequate evidence has been offered in support of this supposition, it seems to be reasonable. We do not know when the "Jewish tax," established by Vespasian, was abolished . . . but we can hardly believe that it was abolished without being replaced by the imposition of other financial obligations upon the Jews: neither the state of the Imperial *fiscus* nor the attitude of the Christian rulers towards the Jews are likely to have permitted such benevolence. It is probable that theological justifications were found for the new taxes imposed on Jews.[21]

Was there a Jewish tax constantly collected from the Jews of Egypt throughout the entire Byzantine era? The editors of *CPJ* III thought they identified a unique Jewish tax. They based this assumption on four additional documents. Two of them are dated paleographically to the second century, one from the Fayyum (no. 452b—mentioning an *emporias Ioudaion*) and one from Oxyrhynchos (no. 516—mentioning *prokeim[enon] Ioudaion*); and two are dated to the fifth or sixth century, one from Hermopolis (no. 506—a receipt for the head of the Jews for something) and one of unknown provenance (no. 504—mentioning *Ioudaeikos*). All four, clearly administrative documents, are not precisely dated, and to three the description "fragmentary" is attached (nos. 504, 506, 516). All four documents have certainly something to say about

21 *CPJ* I, 103.

Jews in the administration, but it is still doubtful whether they point at a Jewish tax, or taxes.

We have seen so far that the sort of documentation one could use to study the Hellenistic Jews of Ptolemaic and early Roman Egypt fails when we come to the Late Roman and Byzantine periods. Geographically, the distribution of the papyri may not really reflect a distribution of the Jewish settlement pattern; economically, the papyri do not reveal who among the persons featuring in them is really a Jew; and legally, there is simply no information to make an educated guess about the Jews of Egypt at this time. When we turn to the Jewish community and the Hebrew and Aramaic papyri that it produced, the data at our disposal becomes varied and informative. It is here that the Genizah-like character of this community becomes evident.

The Jewish community in Egypt

The title of *kephalaiotes Ioudaion* (head of the Jews) is mentioned in one Greek papyrus in the old *CPJ* from the Fayyum.[22] This Greek term in the Byzantine period could mean both tax-collector and president of a guild or a corporation. The same title is also mentioned in two new papyri from Oxyrhynchos, and Karanis,[23] from which it transpires that this was the title of an official, whose job it was to collect taxes on behalf of the government from the Jewish community. Obviously, such a person represented a collective of people who were recognized as having a common interest—a guild, or a community. Many scholars have argued that the legal form the Jewish community took in this period was that of a Roman *collegium*.[24]

The most important papyrus for attesting the existence of an organized Jewish community already at the end of the third century CE is from Oxyrhynchos and is dated to 291 CE.[25] In it we read that the Jewish synagogue of the city manumitted a Jewish slave woman and her two children. The institute that is a party to the manumission of the slave is *tes synagoges ton Ioudaion*. The editors of *CPJ* translated this term as "the community of the Jews" and explained that "the Jewish community of Oxyrhynchos is meant,

22 *CPJ*, no. 506.

23 P.Oxy. LXXXIII 5364, in which the editor also refers to an unpublished papyrus mentioning the same title: P.Mich. inv. 6036.2.

24 See recently C. Balamoshev, "The Jews of Oxyrhynchos Address the *Strategos* of the Nome: An Early Fourth Century Document," *Journal of Juristic Papyrology* 47 (2017): 27–43, esp. 28–32.

25 *CPJ*, no. 473.

not the 'synagogue' in the narrow sense of the word. The synagogue in Egypt is always called *proseuche*, not *synagogue*."[26] It seems, however, that they are protesting too much. We only know of Jewish houses of prayer in Egypt from before 117 CE. If the Jewish community of Egypt in the Late Roman-Byzantine period was indeed as different from its predecessor as the editors of *CPJ* would like us to think, it could very well have used for its prayer-house the Greek term used throughout the Roman Empire for the institution. Another papyrus from Oxyrhynchos, albeit from almost 300 years later (566 CE) mentions a certain Lazar, a Jew, who rents a building for a synagogue (P.Oxy. LV 3805). Like elsewhere, the term synagogue could in both papyri apply both to the structure and to the community that patronized it.

CPJ 473 also demonstrates the close relationship of the new Jewish community in Egypt with its sister community in Palestine. It specifically mentions as involved in the manumission transaction that takes place in the synagogue of Oxyrhynchos "Aurelius Justus, senator of Ono in Syrian Palestine, father of the community." Obviously, this Aurelius Justus is a Palestinian Jew who came to Egypt to assist local Jews in redeeming and freeing Jewish slaves. The Jewish value of redeeming (Jewish) captives (פדיון שבויים), so often mentioned in rabbinic literature, is manifested in this papyrus.

The Hebrew and Aramaic papyri also tell us something about the new synagogue communities of Byzantine Egypt and of their leadership. Four Hebrew letters found among these papyri are addressed to the head or heads of the synagogue (ראשי הכנסת).[27] This title is mentioned in contemporary rabbinic literature (for example, *mYoma* 7:1; *mSotah* 7:7). The Greek title for the head of the synagogue (*archisynagogos*) was also a title common throughout the Roman world for the local leaders of the Jews.[28] In addition to this title, one letter mentions another title for a group of Jewish leaders—פרוסטטין (*prostatin*; see MS Heb. d. 83). This is the plural of the Greek title *prostates*, accorded occasionally to leaders of the ancient synagogue, though it is much less frequent.[29] Unfortunately, the papyri in which these titles appear are much

26 *CPJ* III, 35.

27 See M. Mishor, "Papyrus Fragments of Hebrew Letters," *Leshonenu* 55 (1991): 281–8 [in Hebrew].

28 For a summation of the topic see T. Rajak and D. Noy, "*Archisynagogoi*: Office, Title and Social Status in the Greco-Jewish Synagogue," *Journal of Roman Studies* 83 (1993): 75–93.

29 For a summation of all the evidence see Bernadette J. Brooten, "Iael Prostates in the Jewish Donative Inscription from Aphrodisias," in *The Future of Early Christianity: Essays in Honor of Helmut Koester*, ed. A. T. Kraabel, G. W. E. Nickelsburg, N. R. Peterson (Minneapolis: Fortress Press, 1991), 153–4.

too fragmentary to give us any idea of what the heads of the synagogue or the *prostatin* were required to do.

One may assume that in the synagogue, religious services were held and Jewish religious texts were studied. The Hebrew texts discovered in Egypt give circumstantial support to this assertion, since their provenance is usually unknown, and not one of them was found in a structure that could be identified as a synagogue.

Religious and literary production

In the following section, the Hebrew and Aramaic texts discovered in Byzantine Egypt will be reviewed. It begins with the texts that provide evidence for the existence of Jewish synagogal prayers and services, and continues with texts that attest to other Jewish activities in the community. As will be shown, each of these texts is in fact a forerunner to a genre that is well attested in the Cairo Genizah.

Biblical texts

During the Hellenistic period, Jews used exclusively the Greek translation of the Hebrew Bible.[30] Only one papyrus with a Hebrew biblical text has been discovered from this entire epoch.[31] Not many Hebrew biblical texts have survived from Byzantine Egypt at all: the excavations at Antinoopolis have produced one quite large piece of parchment with parts of 1 Kgs 22 written on it, two smaller parchment fragments preserving the remains of Job 21, and a tiny bit of 2 Kgs 21:8–9.[32] The Oxford collection of Hebrew papyri from Oxyrhynchos includes one with traces of Exod 2[33] and the Berlin collection, apparently hailing from the Fayyum, includes a mysterious-looking piece of parchment with holes bored through, perhaps for use as an amulet, on which

30 For a list of Jewish Septuagint papyri, including several from the Hellenistic and Early Roman period, see R. A. Kraft, "The 'Textual Mechanics' of Early Jewish LXX/OG Papyri and Fragments," in *The Bible as Book: The Transmission of the Greek Text*, ed. S. McKendrick and O. A. O'Sullivan (London: British Library and Oak Knoll Press, 2003), 51–68.

31 The famous Nash papyrus, see now *N.CPJ* IV, 207-12.

32 See now Jelle Verburg, Tal Ilan, and Jan Joosten, "Four Fragments of the Hebrew Bible from Antinoopolis, *P.Ant.* 47—50*," *Journal of Egypt Archaeology* 106 (2020) 1-8.

33 See C. Sirat, *Les papyrus en charactères hébraïques trouvés en Égypte* (Paris: Éditions du CNRS, 1985), 32, pl. 83.

Exod 4 is etched.[34] It has recently been revealed that this parchment actually hails from the Cairo Genizah and so we must update the present article. Between the finds from Qumran and other locations in the Judaean Desert from the last two centuries BCE-first two centuries CE and the earliest biblical texts from the Cairo Genizah, dated to not before the ninth century, these small papyrus and parchment fragments are the only extant witnesses of the Hebrew Bible. They more or less conform to the *Masoretic* biblical text, indicating that the fixed form of the Hebrew Bible, as we know it today, and as is generally attested in the Cairo Genizah, was well under way in late antiquity. Paleographically, the biblical texts from Byzantine Egypt have been shown to bear a much closer resemblance to the texts of the Cairo Genizah than to those from Qumran.

Thus, unlike the Jews of Hellenistic Egypt, who read the Bible in Greek, the Jews of Byzantine Egypt possessed Torah scrolls and other biblical books in Hebrew. In this they were definitely closer to their decedents, the Cairo Genizah Jews, than to their predecessors, the Hellenistic Jews. Of special interest is the question, what did Jews in Antinoopolis in the sixth and seventh centuries do with the biblical books of Kings and Job, which were not regularly read in the synagogue? Perhaps they are an indication that there was a Jewish study-house in Antinoopolis, where additional biblical texts were discussed and studied. More cannot be said.

Piyyut

The second literary genre attested in the papyri in Hebrew and Aramaic is *piyyut*—Jewish liturgical poems composed for synagogal services, especially for the festivals. *Piyyut* is a recognized devotional literary genre in use in Jewish prayer even today, and recorded in Jewish prayer books from the Cairo Genizah onwards. No recorded *piyyutim* have been preserved from a period earlier than the Cairo Genizah, except the papyri under discussion here, although it has always been assumed by scholars that *piyyut* is considerably older than its earliest attestation in manuscripts. Sa῾adia Ga᾿on (882/892–942), who was himself born in the Fayyum, Egypt, lists in his early composition, the *Igron*, several *paytanim* (authors of the *piyyut*), whom he describes as "early poets" (אלשערא

34 For a drawing of the papyrus by Ada Yardeni see Sirat, *Les papyrus*, 34. No photograph is attached but I have seen the original.

(אלאולין),[35] obviously implying that they were considerably older than the poets of his day. The presence of *piyyutim* among the Hebrew and Aramaic papyri of late antiquity in Egypt serves as a major turning point in the study of this genre, as it partly confirms what had up to their discovery been only a working hypothesis. Collecting all the publications of these fragments to date (from Oxford, Berlin, Vienna, the British Library in London, Cologne, and Yale), we can now boast fifteen *piyyutim* on papyri, thirteen in Hebrew[36] and two in Aramaic.[37]

There is still a major debate raging about the exact date and provenance of the earliest poets who produced the *piyyut*. In his introduction to his anthology of Yosi ben Yosi's *piyyutim* (being considered the earliest of all the *paytanim*), Mirsky showed that the range of dates offered for him was from before the destruction of the Second Temple to the foundation of a Jewish Diaspora in medieval Spain. He, however, settles for the fifth century, because he sees in Yosi ben Yosi's poetry some (but not much) evidence of an acquaintance with rabbinic literature.[38] This dating principle is, however, not very sound, because recently it has become common to view the *paytanim* as active outside of rabbinic circles, on which see more below.

In his recent article about a papyrus *piyyut*, which was found in the old cemetery of Cairo and is now housed in the Beinicke Library in Yale, Yahalom argued for a seventh-century date of composition,[39] but his arguments are not based on any more solid evidence. Paleography is not very

---

35 R. Sa῾adia Ga᾿on, *Ha-᾿Egron: Kitāb ᾿Uṣul al-Shi῾r al-῾Ibrānī*, ed. N. Allony (Jerusalem: Academy of Hebrew Language, 1969), 155.

36 From Oxford see Cowley, "Notes on Hebrew Papyrus Fragments," 211; Cowley, "Hebrew and Aramaic Papyri," 3, 3–4; from Berlin: Steinschneider, "Hebräische Papyrus-Fragmente," 250–2; from Vienna: Müller and Kauffmann, "Über die hebräischen Papyrus," 40; from London: H. Loewe, "The Petrie-Hirschfeld Papyri," *Journal of Theological Studies* 24 (1923): 126–41; P. A. H. de Boer, "Notes on an Oxyrhynchus Papyrus in Hebrew: Brit. Mus. Or. 9180 A," *Vetus Testamentum* (1951): 49–57; from Cologne: F. Klein-Franke, "A Hebrew Lamentation from Roman Egypt," *ZPE* 51 (1983): 80–84; from Yale: Y. Yahalom, "A *Piyyut*-Papyrus for the Winter Holidays: And Its Significance for the History of the Settlement at the End of the Byzantine Period," *Cathedra* 162 (2017): 8–34 [in Hebrew].

37 From Berlin: J. Yahalom, "'Ezel Moshe'—According to the Berlin Papyrus," *Tarbiz* 47 (1978): 173–84 [in Hebrew]; from Vienna: Müller and Kauffmann, "Über die hebräischen Papyrus," 38–9. Both were republished in M. Sokoloff and J. Yahalom, *Jewish Palestinian Aramaic Poetry from Late Antiquity: Critical Edition with Introduction and Commentary* (Jerusalem: Israel Academy of Sciences and Humanities, 1999), 82–7, 100–3.

38 A. Mirsky, *Yosse ben Yosse: Poems Edited with an Introduction, Commentary and Notes* (Jerusalem: Mossad Bialik, 1991), 15–16.

39 Yahalom, "A *Piyyut*-Papyrus for the Winter Holidays," 9–10.

useful, in light of the dearth of dated documents from this period written in Hebrew or Aramaic (the *ketubbah* from Antinoopilis from 417 CE being the only one). Considering this state of affairs, a dating argument based on archaeological data may not seem so out of place. There are four *piyyut* fragments housed in the British Library, all found together by the archaeologist and Egyptologist Flinders Petrie in Oxyrhynchos, who reported that "the papyri come from an untouched mound that was finally closed, . . . in the days of Severus, thus before 211 C.E."[40] This conclusion is based on the latest coins that were found, sealed in the same mound with the papyri. If there is any truth in this dating, the conclusions required are revolutionary. First of all, it pushes back the date of the *piyyutim* to the beginning of the third century. Secondly, it allows for the existence of a Hebrew-speaking, ritually active Jewish community in Oxyrhynchos already at the end of the second century, less than a century after the crushing of the Jewish revolt in 117 CE. This evidence of early twentieth-century archaeology should not be pushed too far, but the information is at least worth noting, and certainly worth checking with Carbon 14 dating methods.

Hundreds of *piyyutim* were found in the Cairo Genizah. At least one of our papyri *piyyutim*—in Aramaic about an argument between Moses and the Red Sea before it consented to part—was also found in the Cairo Genizah (Ox 2701/9—Ms Heb e 25), and Yahalom reconstructed the papyrus text based on the Genizah specimen. The connection between the corpus presented here and the text from the Cairo Genizah is evidently very tight.

Ketubbot

Next to the synagogue service, Jewish marriage is one of the most important markers of Jewishness. Gradually over the centuries, the Jewish marriage contract—the *ketubbah*—developed from a universal document to a very Jewish one. As already mentioned above, an Aramaic *ketubbah* on a papyrus from Antinoopolis, dated to 417 CE, is housed today in the papyri collection of Cologne.[41] The contract includes a very precise date (in Greek in Hebrew letters) a location (Antinoopolis), a specification that the marriage is according to the law (*nomos*) of all the house of Israel (כנימוס כל בית ישראל) and it then lists all the items included in the marriage contract. The contract ends with

40 de Boer, "Notes on an Oxyrhynchus Papyrus," 4.

41 Sirat et al., *La Ketouba de Cologne*.

the husband pledging all his possessions to pay his bride this price, should the occasion arise.

The importance of this document is enormous. Jewish marriage contracts in Aramaic survive from fifth-century BCE Elephantine (Egypt)[42] and then from the second-century CE Judaean Desert.[43] Finally, many Jewish marriage contracts were found in the Cairo Genizah.[44] The papyrus described here can be considered the missing link that bridges a void of 1400 years in Egypt or a void of 800 years in the Jewish world at large.

Another papyrus, P 8497 from Berlin, formerly interpreted as a contract, could in fact be another *ketubbah*.[45] The text is very fragmentary but it begins by mentioning a man (תאוומסי—Thaumasios) and a woman (מטרונה—Matrona) and the extant end includes a list of goods and prices. If it was a contract signed between the two, it could have been a marriage agreement.

If both extant contracts in a Jewish language from Egypt are marriage contracts, this may suggest that in Christian Egypt a limited self-rule was accorded the Jews with relation to personal law. They could marry (and probably also divorce) according to their own laws. We have no evidence that they could practice any other form of law, independent of the state.

Personal letters

In late antiquity personal letters became an ever more popular means of communication. This was as true for the Jews as for their non-Jewish neighbors. Among the Aramaic and Hebrew papyri there survive fragments

42 B. Porten and A. Yardeni, *Textbook of Aramaic Documents from Ancient Egypt*, vol. 2, *Contracts* (Winona Lake, IN: Eisenbrauns, 1989), 30–3, 60–3, 78–81, 132–40.

43 P. Benoit, J. T. Milik, and R. de Vaux, *Les Grottes de Murabbaʿat*, vol. 2 of *DJD* (Oxford: Clarendon, 1961), 109–17; 243–56; N. Lewis (with Y. Yadin), *The Documents from the Bar-Kokhba Period in the Cave of Letters: Greek Papyri* (Jerusalem: Israel Exploration Society, 1989), 76–82, 130–3; A. Yardeni and B. Levine (with Y. Yadin and J. Greenfield), *The Documents from the Bar-Kokhba Period in the Cave of Letters: Hebrew, Aramaic and Nabatean-Aramaic Papyri* (Jerusalem: Israel Exploration Society, 2002), 118–41; H. M. Cotton and A. Yardeni, *Aramaic, Hebrew and Greek Documentary Texts from Nahal Hever and Other Sites*, vol. 27 of *DJD* (Oxford: Clarendon, 1997), 57–9, 224–37, 250–74.

44 M. A. Friedman, *Jewish Marriage in Palestine: A Cairo Geniza Study* (Tel Aviv: Tel Aviv University Press, 1980).

45 See Sirat, *Les papyrus*, 11; for a picture of the document see pl. 46. For the forthcoming publication, see Tal Ilan, "Another Ketubbah on a Papyrus from Byzantine Egypt?", *Eretz Israel: Ada Yardeni Memorial Volume* [in Hebrew].

of ten letters—eight written by men[46] and two by women.[47] The majority of the letters written by men are in Hebrew (five), two are in Aramaic and one is too fragmentary to decide. Both letters written by women are in Aramaic. Of the eight letters written by men, four are directed to the heads of the synagogue. Both letters written by women are private—one to a brother and the other to two sons. This find alerts us to the fact that the Jews of Egypt, like their non-Jewish neighbors at this time, were writing and sending letters, and they often did so in their native languages. The fact that women wrote letters in Aramaic says something about the language that some Jews even spoke at home in these new communities, and not only conducted services, or wrote religious poetry, or studied religious texts in. That some Jews wrote letters to family members in Greek (and thus evidently also spoke it among themselves) is proven by a papyrus (P.Oxy. XLVI 331) from the fourth century, in which a certain Judah is writing to his wife and his father Iose, telling them of a riding accident in which he was involved, which landed him injured in Babylon (Fusṭāṭ) and he is asking them to come from Oxyrhynchos to his assistance.

---

46 From Oxford: 1. MS Heb. d. 69 (P), to Ya῾aqov ben Yitzhaq from Lazar ben Yosah (in Hebrew)—Cowley, "Hebrew and Aramaic Papyri," 4–7; M. Mishor, "A Hebrew Letter from Oxford," *Leshonenu* 54 (1989): 215–64 [in Hebrew]; 2. MS Heb. f. 114 (P) to Yitzhaq (in Aramaic)—Cowley, "Hebrew and Aramaic Papyri," 7–8; 3. MS Heb. d. 83 (P) fragment b from Oshayah to the Heads of the synagogue (in Hebrew)—Cowley, "Notes on Hebrew Papyrus Fragments," 212; Mishor, "Papyrus Fragments," 285–6; 4. MS Heb. 57a from Anina to the Heads of the Synagogue (Hebrew)—Cowley, "Notes on Hebrew Papyrus Fragments," 210–11; Mishor, "Papyrus Fragments," 283–4. From Florence: 5. PSI inv. 26018 + 26019 from Reuven (in Hebrew)—Mishor, "Papyrus Fragments," 286–7. From Manchester: 6. Ryland Library Box 5 14/25 to Suma bar Huna head of the synagogue (Aramaic?)—Mishor, "Papyrus Fragments," 285; 7. From Vienna: H 36 to the heads of the Synagogue (language unclear)—Mishor, "Papyrus Fragments," 285; 8. H 49, too fragmentary to comment (in Hebrew)—Mishor, "Papyrus Fragments," 288. Another letter perhaps from a father (Pantos—פנטוס) to a son (קירים סמבטי—*kyrios* Sambati) from the Berlin collection is P 8149, which was never published, see Sirat *Les papyrus*, pl. 38.

47 1. From Oxford: Ms heb. e.120 from Harqan to her brother Eleazar—Cowley, "Hebrew and Aramaic Papyri," 7; M. Mishor, "Oxford Bodleian Library Ms Heb e. 120," *Leshonenu* 63 (2001): 53–9; 2. From Berlin P8282, from Sarah to her sons Yiẓḥaq and Tanḥum. On both see T. Ilan, "An Addendum to Bagnall and Cribiore, *Women's Letters from Ancient Egypt*: Two Aramaic Letters from Jewish Women," in *Israel in Egypt: The Land of Egypt as Concept and Reality for Jews in Antiquity and the Early Medieval Period*, edited by Alison Salvesen, Sarah Pearce, and Miriam Frenkel, 397-416. Leiden: Brill, 2020.

Thousands of personal letters were found in the Genizah, from all times, most of them written in the local language of the writers, both by men and by women. Our papyri are the forerunners of these documents.

Magic papyri

Magic was rife in late antiquity—pagans wrote magical texts, Christians wrote magical texts and Jews wrote magical texts. In Egypt they were written in Greek, in Coptic, in Hebrew, and in Aramaic. They were a syncretistic bag of pagan, Jewish, and Christian elements, but there is no doubt that Jewish elements were considered very effective by Christians and pagans. Of special interest are five Aramaic papyri fragments found together with Coptic and Greek magical artifacts, in two cases actually on the verso of Greek texts. This find has suggested to scholars that the fragments hail from a multilingual workshop producing amulets for customers of different ethnicities and religions, emphasizing the fluid boundaries between religions when it came to magic.[48]

Hebrew and Aramaic documents from late antiquity are certainly Jewish. Magical texts from Egypt that have come down to us in these languages can be divided into two sorts: amulets and recipes. A leaf from a magical recipe-book housed in Oxford[49] lists cures for and spells against several ailments, like a dog-bite. Amulets on metal surfaces from Oxyrhynchos[50] and Tel el-Amarna[51] inscribed in Hebrew and Aramaic have been found and published.

Other, Greek magical texts may also be of Jewish provenance, but this is harder to prove and more difficult to defend. One of them is a silver amulet, which was found in Carnarvon, Wales. It was probably in the possession of a Roman soldier who dropped it in that location when his unit was stationed

---

48 P. Marassini, "I frammenti aramaici," *Studi Classici ed Orientali* 29: *Nuovi papiri magici in Copto, Greco e Aramaico*, ed. E. Bresciani, S. Pernigotti, F. Maltomini, and P. Marrassini (1979): 125–30.

49 First published by Cowley and then republished by Geller. Cowley, "Notes on Hebrew Papyrus Fragments," 212; M. J. Geller, "An Aramaic Incantation from Oxyrhynchos," *ZPE* 58 (1985): 96–8. For other possible magical recipes housed in Oxford see MS Heb. e. 84 (P) (Cowley, "Hebrew and Aramaic Papyri," 8); MS Heb. d. 86 (P), fragment b (Cowley, "Notes on Hebrew Papyrus Fragments," 213).

50 F. Klein-Franke, "Eine aramäische tabella devotionis (T. Colon. inv. nr. 6)," *ZPE* 7 (1971): 47–52; and see also A. Yardeni and G. Bohak, "A Pregnancy Amulet for Marian, Daughter of Esther," *Eretz-Israel* 32: *The Joseph Naveh Memorial Volume* (2016): 100–7 [in Hebrew], written for the same client and so presumably also from Oxyrhynchos.

51 R. Kotansky, J. Naveh, and S. Shaked, "A Greek-Aramaic Silver Amulet from Egypt in the Ashmolean Museum," *Le Muséon* 105 (1992): 5–25.

there. The soldier, named Alphaios (Aramaic חלפי), seems to have been Jewish, because although the amulet is inscribed in Greek characters, aside from a word or two it is completely in Hebrew. There is no doubt that the amulet's author was a Jew, and the name of the client may imply that he, too, was one. Its Egyptian provenance is indicated by a date inscribed on it: XIII Toth. XIII is the Latin 13 and Toth is the name of an Egyptian month. It was only ever used in an Egyptian calendar.[52]

In the Cairo Genizah a very large number of magical texts have been found,[53] all in Hebrew and Aramaic. Of special interest is one of them (T-S K 1.157: 1a/12–21),[54] which is a translation of a Greek magical papyrus—an incantation in the category of uterine magic, for the purpose of curing the condition known in antiquity as the "wandering womb." In Greek the text is found on a papyrus that lists a large collection of magical texts, so syncretistic that they were clearly recorded by a pagan magician.[55] However, the religious framework of this particular spell is Jewish. It alludes to a string of biblical quotations and expresses ideas rooted in biblical creation theology. A direct link between the magical papyri of late antiquity and the magical texts of the Genizah is thereby established.

By way of conclusion

We have patiently followed the papyrological evidence of a Jewish existence in Egypt from after the crushing of the Jewish revolt in 117 CE to the death of the papyrus in the eighth and the ninth centuries. We had to rely on the papyri for the reconstruction of this Jewish community because the Jews themselves have left us no narrative on which we can fall back to tell us the story. The only narrative we have that the Jews preserved through the ages of their late antique story is found in rabbinic literature, and it has next to nothing to say about the Jews of Egypt.

Despite this near silence on the part of the rabbis, this survey has tried to show that, while there is little doubt that the 116–17 CE revolt had devastating

52 For this find see R. Kotansky, *Greek Magical Amulets. The Inscribed Gold, Silver, Copper, and Bronze Lamellae*, part 1: *Published Texts of Known Provenance. Text and Commentary* (Opladen: Westdeutscher Verlag, 1994), 3–12.

53 For the publication project of these texts see first and foremost P. Schäfer and S. Shaked (eds.), *Magische Texte aus der Kairoer Geniza*, 3 vols. (Tübingen: Mohr Siebeck, 1994–9),

54 See ibid., 1:112–13.

55 P. Lond. 1, 121, and see also K. Preisendanz, *Papyri Graecae Magicae: Die griechischen Zauberpapyri*, vol. 7, 2nd ed. (Stuttgart: Teubner, 1973–4), , 260–71.

consequences for the Jews, these were not as long-lasting as previous scholarship had assumed. If we apply our analysis to documents that had been ignored by previous scholars, we encounter a much richer and varied picture of the Jews in Late Antique Egypt. The nascent Jewish community we have been following may be called a "proto-Genizah" community. The Cairo Genizah includes tens of thousands of documents from over a thousand years, and it has supplied evidence for several major genres that define Judaism for the best part of the Middle Ages. It includes documentary texts such as personal letters and contracts, primarily *ketubbot*; it boasts a huge array of biblical scrolls and codices and an enormous repository of religious poetry; scores of magical texts have also surfaced among its treasures.[56] If we look at the modest catalogue of papyri from Late Antiquity presented in this article, we see that all these genres have their antecedents within it. In this respect the papyri of Late Antiquity answer the definition of a "proto-Genizah" community.

Yet, having documented the presence, it is no less pertinent to observe the absence. The oldest and most reliable collection of rabbinic texts is found among the papers of the Genizah.[57] The papyri to date have not yielded even one scrap of rabbinic text. The rabbis were active in Palestine and Babylonia at the same time that the proto-Genizah Jewish community of Egypt was coming into existence. What is the meaning of this silence? A prevalent explanation concerning the absence of a common language between the rabbis and the Jews of Egypt,[58] could work well for the pre-115 CE Hellenistic-Jewish community of Egypt, where all knowledge of Hebrew had been lost, but cannot be used for the post-117 CE community, where Hebrew and Aramaic were the languages of liturgy and seem also to have been the major languages of communication. We need to offer alternative explanations. There are three possible ones:

The first suggestion is that the Jewish community in Egypt was a non-rabbinic community. Scholars have recently emphasized the breach that apparently existed between synagogue-based communities and rabbinic-

56 For *ketubbot* see Friedman, *Jewish Marriage*; for Torah scrolls, see M. C. Davies and B. Outhwaite, *Hebrew Bible Manuscripts in the Cambridge Genizah Collections* (Cambridge: Cambridge University Press, 1978–2003), 4 vols.; for *piyyut* see, for example, J. Yahalom, *Palestinian Vocalised Piyyut Manuscripts in the Cambridge Genizah Collections* (Cambridge: Cambridge University Press, 1997); for a publication of magical papyri see Schäfer and Shaked, *Magische Texte aus der Kairoer Geniza*.

57 R. Brody and E. J. Weisenberg, *A Hand-List of Rabbinic Manuscripts in the Cambridge Genizah* (Cambridge: Cambridge University Press, 1998).

58 D. Mendels and A. Edrei, *Zweierlei Diaspora: Zur Spaltung der antiken jüdischen Welt* (Göttingen: Vandenhoeck & Ruprecht, 2010).

based communities, and described this division with a distinction between halakhah and midrash, or midrash and Targum, or rabbinic texts and *piyyut*, or between the somber text-centered rabbis and the colorful mosaic world of ancient synagogues.[59] Perhaps the Jewish community of Egypt was a non-rabbinic, synagogue-based community; hence the dramatic presence of *piyyut* among the papyri from Egypt and the total absence of rabbinic texts.

The second explanation touches on the very nature of rabbinic literature. By their own admission, theirs is an oral Torah, an oral law. If the rabbis indeed refrained from putting their teachings down in writing,[60] while liturgical poets had no such compunctions, it should come as no surprise that none of their teachings were discovered among the papyri of Egypt. Perhaps rabbinic literature was studied in Egypt long before it was committed to writing in the age of the Cairo Genizah, but the fact that it was an oral transmission made it invisible.

The third and last explanation touches on the nature of the evidence at hand. As we saw throughout, the number of texts at our disposal is still very small and limited. In the last century, very few additional texts in Hebrew and Aramaic from Egypt have shown up. This says little, though, about what is still preserved under the sands of Egypt or in the storehouses of European museums. Perhaps the evidence for a rabbinic Judaism in late antique Egypt has simply not yet been discovered.

---

59 See in L. I. Levine, *The Ancient Synagogue: The First Thousand Years* (New Haven: Yale University Press, 2000), 440–70.

60 Y. Sussmann, "Oral Law Literally," in *Talmudic Studies Dedicated to the Memory of Professor Ephraim E. Urbach*, ed. Y. Sussmann and D. Rosenthal (Jerusalem: Magness Press, 2005), 209–384 [in Hebrew].

2

A Concise History of Islamic Egypt

YEHOSHUA FRENKEL

The End of the Byzantine Era and the Emergence of the Islamic State

The province of Egypt was an important part of the vast lands controlled by the Byzantine emperors. For almost 300 years it supplied Constantinople with grain. Alexandria was an important center of Christian theology, although after the post-Council of Chalcedon schism (451) the influence of the local Egyptian Monophysite Copts was limited primarily to the Nile Valley.

In the early years of the seventh century, the Byzantine Empire was unable to maintain its defenses against external pressure. Within a few years, invading tribes had overrun much of the Balkans, while the Persians occupied and set up their own provincial governments in Syria and Egypt (614–18), before the Byzantine emperor Heraclius was able to launch a counter-offensive (628) and defeat the Persian armies. Our knowledge of Egypt's history between the departure of the Sasanian-Persians and the arrival of the Arab-Islamic conquerors is very fragmented. Yet, we can surely conclude that the province's defense was feeble and that its social cohesion weakened.

The Arab-Islamic conquest of Egypt subjected an ancient land explosively and rapidly (639–42). It shifted the deeply rooted political and cultural alignment of the Nile Valley from the Mediterranean Sea to Western Asia and North Africa, from Greek and Latin centers of learning to the Arabic and Islamic heartlands of a new world religion. Rome and Constantinople were replaced by Damascus and Baghdad. Wheat was exported to support the holy cities in Arabia, rather than to the maritime hubs of the Mediterranean.[1]

Geopolitical considerations led the emerging caliphate to place its administrative headquarters far from the Mediterranean city-ports. Facing Byzantine naval operations, the new regime removed its headquarters from the port city of Alexandria, the former Byzantine capital of Egypt, and constructed a new administrative center near Babylon, named Fusṭāṭ. The new town developed and became the political, economic and cultural hub known from the tenth century as al-Qāhira (Cairo). It served as the headquarters of dozens of governors and rulers.[2]

The Incorporation of the Nile Valley into the Islamic Caliphate

In the decades that followed the Islamic conquest of Egypt, South Arabian tribes were the backbone of the Islamic army that controlled the Nile Valley. A clear majority of Egypt's population during the Umayyad period (657–749) adhered to the Coptic Church. The few Muslim inhabitants of the urban centers were still named "Saracens," or "Mōagaritai" (*muhājirūn*, "emigrants"), in contemporary local documents and the caliph in Damascus was designated *amīr al-mu'minīn* (Gk. *tōn pistōn*; "the commander of the faithful").[3]

Contemporary Umayyad papyri shed light on taxation, social life, and the state apparatus. They convey the impression that the hierarchic bureaucratic mechanism still maintained many aspects of the Byzantine system. Umayyad Egypt was ruled by a general commissioner, who was stationed in the new capital of Fusṭāṭ. The land was divided, in line with the traditional division of Egypt, into five provinces, each headed by an administrator (*'āmil*; *amīr*), who had full control over the province's finances. Each province was divided, in turn, into territories grouped around a town. The heads (*sāḥib*) of these territories passed the orders to a headman (Gk. *meizōn*) in charge of the villages' affairs.

1 Hugh Kennedy, "Egypt as a Province in the Islamic Caliphate, 641–868," in *The Cambridge History of Egypt*, vol. 1, *Islamic Egypt 640–1517*, ed. Carl F. Petry (Cambridge: Cambridge University Press, 1998), 62–85.

2 Abu 'Umar Muḥammad ibn Yūsuf ibn Ya'qūb al-Kindi, *Wulah misr*, ed. Rhuvon Guest (London: Luzac, 1912); ibid., ed. Ali Umar (Cairo: Maktabat al-thaqāfa al-diniyya, 1428/2008); Shihāb al-Dīn Ahmad ibn 'Ali ibn Ḥajar al-'Asqalani al-Shafi'i, *Raf' al-iṣr 'an quḍat miṣr* (Cairo: Maktabat al-Khanji, 1418/1998).

3 Robert G. Hoyland, *Seeing Islam as Others Saw It: A Survey and Evaluation of Christian, Jewish and Zoroastrian Writing on Early Islam* (Princeton, NJ: Princeton University Press, 1997), 548–50.

Two other important administrative positions were the supreme judge (*qāḍī*) and the officer in charge of public order (*ṣāḥib al-shurṭa*). During the Umayyad period, they were manned by local Arabs-Muslims, and backed by a standing army. The new Arabo-Islamic caliphate depended totally on local officials (Gk. *pagarchs*), who were required to provide revenues and manpower.

The conquered population was subjected to paying a yearly tax composed of money, foodstuffs, and textiles.[4] In order to facilitate administration and taxation, the Umayyad government carried out a census (*taʿdīl*) of Egypt. This was a necessary tool in line with the government's efforts to control farming communities and to monitor villagers' movement. A special officer was nominated by the caliph in order to keep the Arab records, registering daily births and deaths, the collection of revenues and the monthly payment to the army.[5] Later on, a separate head of the department of cultivators' taxes (*kharāj*, annual taxation based on produce) was appointed.

This is well demonstrated in the following letter, dated 91/710, in which the governor of Egypt instructs Basil (Basīla), the Christian administrator of the province of Aphrodito (Ishquwa) in Upper Egypt (between Asyut and Suhaj):

> In the Name of Allah, the Merciful, the Gracious.
> I praise Allah. Beside him there is no God.
> I already had ordered to divide [the support] of the Egyptian and Syrian boats' captains and the food supply of the warriors who sail on board these ships.
> Following the reception of this instruction you shall immediately order the population of the province that is under your jurisdiction to bake high quality bread. Low quality bread will be rejected.[6]

Following the growth of the Muslim community in Egypt during the reign of caliph ʿUmar ibn ʿAbd al-ʿAzīz (fl. 717–20), Muslims were required for the

4 Abū al-ʿAbbās Aḥmad ibn Yaḥya ibn Jābir al-Balādhurī, *Futūḥ al-Buldān*, ed. M. De Goeje (Leiden: Brill, 1866), 214–15.

5 Raif Georges Khoury, "Al-Layth Ibn Saʿd (94–175/713–791), grand maitre et mécène de l'Egypte, vu à travers quelques documents islamiques anciens," *Journal of Near Eastern* Studies 40/3 (1981): 189–202; Abū al-Qāsim ʿAbd al-Raḥman ibn ʿAbd al-Ḥakam, *Futūḥ Miṣr wa-akhbāruhā* [*The History of the Conquest of Egypt, North Africa and Spain*], ed. Ch. Torrey (New Haven: Yale University Press, 1921), 102.

6 Yusuf Ragib, "Lettres nouvelles de Qurra b. Šarīk," *Journal of Near Eastern Studies* 40 (1981): 175–6.

first time to pay taxes.[7] This step provoked an angry reaction from the local Arabic elite and the massive flight of converted indigenous farmers from their villages.

The heavy taxes imposed on the Copts and their conscription to forced labor precipitated the Copts in the eastern Nile Delta into rebellion (106/724). Yet, the revolt evidently failed to reverse the raising of the tax rate. Moreover, the caliph permitted 1500 Arabs to settle on the eastern edge of the Delta, in the same area in which the Copts had rebelled (109/727). The revolt of 724 was only the first in a series of revolts that inflicted heavy blows to the peasants. Nevertheless, the historian al-Muqaddasī is probably right when remarking that on the eve of the Fatimid conquest, a clear majority of the Delta population were still Copts, but the process of the Arabization of Egypt's countryside was underway.[8]

The islamization of Egypt indicates not only changes in the belief system of the country's population, but also the emergence of a community that was engaged in developing new religious rituals and writings and in changing the public sphere. Anti-Islamic Coptic apologetic writings are a clear indicator for the visible and challenging changes that threatened the local Church. Demographic changes created social backlashes even among the Arabs. The transmission of a saying, ascribed to the caliph ʿUmar, to the effect that "Muhammad was sent to spread the call, not to tax the villagers who have converted to Islam," reflects their objection to the assimilation of the Coptic peasants.

Abbasid Egypt—an autonomous power

At the beginning of summer 750, Abbasid troops entered Fusṭāṭ. Continuing their Syrian offensive, they wiped out the old regime and installed a new governing density (Caliphate). The most striking characteristic of the early Abbasid administration in Egypt was its continuity with the Umayyad period. Although Ṣāliḥ ibn ʿAlī al-ʿAbbāsī (d. 769), the commander in chief founded a new encampment, al-ʿAskar, north of Fusṭāṭ, this did not indicate the

7 Shaun O'Sullivan, "Coptic Conversion and the Islamization of Egypt," *Mamluk Studies Review* 10 (2006): 71–4; Stephen J. Davis, Bilal Orfali, and Samuel Noble (eds. and trans.), *A Disputation over a Fragment of the Cross: A Medieval Arabic Text from the History of Christian-Jewish-Muslim relations in Egypt* (Beirut: Dar al-Machreq, 2012), 9–11.

8 Shams al-Din Muhammad al-Muqaddasi, *Ahsan al-taqasim fi maʿrifat al-aqalim*, ed. M. De Goeje, vol. 3 of *BGA* (Leiden: Brill, 1906/1967), 194, 203,

beginning of a new order. As before, the heads of the administration were selected from local Egyptians, while the governor of Egypt was nominated by the caliph, who from 760 resided in Baghdad.

Following the ascension of caliph Hārūn al-Rashīd (786–809), the stability of the regime suffered several setbacks. But with the arrival of a new governor, ʿAbd Allah ibn Ṭāhir (813–29), a new phase opened in the history of Egypt.[9] Like the other Western provinces of the caliphate (that is, the region stretching from the Euphrates to Iberia), Egypt was entrusted to a viceroy, who was often a leading figure in the Turkish military establishment. Therefore, the governor of Egypt ceased to be appointed directly by the Abbasid caliph. From this point onward he was nominated by the commander of the caliphal armies.

In 831, heavy farming taxes instigated the protest of Arabs and Copts, and a general rebellion, known as "the Bashmurite revolt,"[10] threatened Abbasid authority in the Nile Valley. It was only in February 832 that caliph al-Maʾmūn could come to visit Egypt, a gesture indicating that matters were back on track. Al-Maʾmūn was the only Abbasid caliph ever to visit Egypt.

The crushing of the Copt villagers by the Abbasid government during the Bashmurite revolt is considered to be a turning point in the transformation of the Nile valley from a Christian land to an Islamic territory. A prevailing interpretation of this violent event is that the crushing of the rebels symbolizes the waning of the Coptic peasantry's objection to conversion. From this point, Islamization gained speed.

During the years 811–19, following the demise of Hārūn al-Rashīd, the Abbasid dynasty was submerged in a bloody struggle for power between his sons. This civil war, known as the Fourth *Fitna,* increased the political confusion in Egypt. While the two brothers, al-Amin and al-Maʾmun, were engaged in a fierce and destructive war in Baghdad, the local elite and the standing garrisons failed to secure a deal and to ensure stable government in Egypt. In 833, al-Muʿtaṣim, al-Maʾmūn's brother and heir, ended the political-social order implemented in Egypt by the early Muslim caliphs, and abolished the local army. The autonomous provincial elite experienced a serious setback. For the next centuries they would be governed by foreign armies.

9 A member of an important ninth-century family of administrators and provincial governors. Clifford Edmund Bosworth, "The Tahirids and Arabic Culture," *Journal of Semitic Studies* 14/1 (1969): 45–79; Scott Savran, *Arabs and Iranians in the Islamic Conquest Narrative* (London: Routledge, 2016), 40–1.

10 So named after the Bashmuric dialect of Coptic in the Nile Delta. Gawdat Gabra, *The A to Z of the Coptic Church* (Lanham: Scarecrow Press, 2009), 74.

The lack of stability in the province was aggravated by a series of anti-Abbasid revolts. Moreover, the continuing and even deepening crisis of the caliphate opened the gate to the renewal of Byzantine pressure on the Abbasid frontiers. Egypt was again directly threatened by the Byzantine fleet that sailed in the Eastern Mediterranean.

The weakening of the Abbasid administration in Egypt resulted in several peasant revolts. These drove caliph al-Mutawakkil (r. 847–62) to nominate Ibn al-Mudabbir, the director of finance in Damascus, to take charge of Egypt's taxes and revenues, hoping he would be able to furnish him with increasing sums of money.

The Tulunids

In 868, Aḥmad ibn Ṭūlūn, a son of a Turkish slave-soldier, was sent to rule the Nile Valley. Following a direct confrontation with Ibn Mudabbir, the long-time agent of the Abbasid bureaucracy in Egypt, Ibn Ṭūlūn seized the reins of power, thus becoming, *de facto*, the autonomous ruler of Egypt and Syria (868–84).[11] Between Ibn Ṭūlūn's appointment as governor and his death, Egypt emerged as a significant power in the eastern Mediterranean basin.[12]

Ibn Ṭūlūn's ambitions are well reflected in the impressive buildings he constructed in Egypt. North of Fusṭāṭ and al-ʿAskar, he designed a new area, along the lines of Samarra, that served at the time as the seat of the Abbasid caliph. The complex was surrounded by walls and monumental gates led to the inner streets. Ibn Ṭūlūn ordered the construction of a large new palace, a hospital, and a vast plaza (*al-maydān*), which was used for a variety of purposes, including military reviews and sporting events. The central mosque of this new quarter is a large and outstanding edifice, which still impresses visitors today.

Demonstrating leadership and efficiency, Ibn Ṭūlūn succeeded in increasing his government's income. The flow of new taxes allowed the budget to grow. Considerable sums of money were allocated to the recruitment of additional soldiers and the construction of a navy. With these tools, Ibn Ṭūlūn waged war against the Byzantines in Northern Syria, and annexed the Syrian provinces to the Tulunid territory. On contemporary glass weights, his name is rendered accompanied by the title *mawlā amīr al-muʾminīn* (the intimate client of the Commander of the Faithful). In later Muslim historiography, Ibn

11 This is clearly attested in his coins that bear the caliph's name.

12 Luke Treadwell, "The Numismatic Evidence for the Reign of Aḥmad b. Ṭūlūn (254–270/868–883)," *Al-ʿUṣūr al-Wusṭā* 25 (2017): 14–40.

Ṭūlūn is described as a pious Muslim. His occupation of the Syrian territories is termed a holy war (*jihad*) against the infidels.[13]

In 905, the Tulunids were overthrown and Abbasid direct control over Egypt was restored. This was followed by the purge and arrest of agents who served the toppled administration. Yet, Egypt did not remain under the direct control of Iraq for long. The Abbasids were forced once more to give the Nile valley into the hands of an autonomous army commander.

In 935, the anarchy in the heartlands of the Abbasid caliphate enabled a Turkish military commander by the name of Muḥammad ibn Ṭughj to take control of the Nile valley. With loyal soldiers under his command, he declared himself an autonomous ruler. In 939, The Abbasid caliph al-Rāḍī (r. 934–40) acknowledged his limits and awarded Muḥammad ibn Ṭughj the governorship of Egypt and the royal title of *al-Ikhshīd* ("king").[14] Due to their army's qualities, the Ikhshidid dynasty, as it came to be known, succeeded in deterring rival powers who made great efforts to seize Syria. Their achievements fortified Egypt's position as the strongest land in the eastern Mediterranean basin, a position it retained for many centuries to come.

Another significant development recorded during these decades, besides the emergence of Egypt as a regional power, was the renewal of the Mediterranean maritime trade, as is manifested in the renovation of the Syrian coastal port towns. In consequence, Italian merchants from the southern parts of the peninsula started to sail regularly to the ports of Egypt and Syria. The story about the ten Venetian ships that sailed in 828 to Alexandria and returned with St. Mark's relics preserves the memory of a routine journey across the sea. The Jewish chronicle written by the Graeco-Italian poet Ahimaatz ben Paltiel (1017–60) is additional grist to the mill. His "chronicle"[15] narrates sailing between southern Italy and Palestine.

During the last decades of direct Abbasid rule in Egypt and under the Tulunids and the Ikhshidids, Islamic and Arabic cultural production in Egypt emerged and occupied a newly visible position in the history of this civilization.

13 'Abd Allāh ibn Muḥammad al-Madīnī al-Balawī, *Sirat Aḥmad ibn Ṭūlūn*, ed. M. K. 'Ali (Damascus: al-Maktaba al-'Arabiyya, 1939), 34–5.

14 Michael Fedorov, "On the Portraits of the Sogdian Kings (Ikhshīds) of Samarqand," *Iran* 45 (2007): 153–60.

15 Marcus Salzman (trans.), *The Chronicle of Ahimaaz* (New York: Columbia University Press, 1924). On the legendary theft of St. Mark's relics, see Deborah Howard, "Venice and Islam in the Middle Ages: Some Observations on the Question of Architectural Influence," *Architectural History* 34 (1991): 59–74.

This socio-lingual-religious change reflects both the growth in size of Egypt's Muslim population and the spread of the Arabic language at the expense of the declining Coptic.

Migration is one explanation for this growth. Starting with the Arab conquest and during the succeeding centuries, the Nile valley attracted migrants from other regions of the caliphate. Beside Arab tribesmen, the sources report migrants from a wide variety of ethnicities. It seems that during the Abbasid period, the tide of settlers originated predominantly from the East. The causes of this human movement were the growing instability in Iraq and in its adjacent provinces, on the one hand, and the recognition that lucrative opportunities could be found in the Nile Valley, on the other. Some of the emigrants came to play a significant role in the political and administrative apparatus of the Egyptian state[16] and its army.[17]

The cultural transformation of Egypt is manifested in the emergence of an Egyptian Arabic school of historiography. Ibn ʿAbd al-Ḥakam's book on the history of the conquest of Egypt is a prominent example. Ibn ʿAbd al-Ḥakam depicts the Islamic conquest of Egypt as a fulfillment of the Prophet's diplomatic initiative, which is verified by a letter supposedly sent by Muḥammad to the patriarch of Alexandria.[18] Another example is al-Kindī's history of jurists, which reflects Arabo-Islamic self-confidence.[19] Another Egyptian writer, al-Balawī, composed the biography of Aḥmad ibn Ṭūlūn.[20] There were additional biographies of renowned Egyptians written at this time.[21]

Another aspect of the Arabo-Islamic cultural milieu that emerged in medieval Egypt is manifested in lists of Egyptian scholars and transmitters of religious wisdom. Thus, for example, the renowned saint, Layth ibn Saʿd (713-91), whose renovated tomb in Cairo still attracts many visitors,[22] is mentioned

16 The convert Jew Yaʿqub ibn Killis who became a chief administrator is a prominent example.

17 Eliyahu Ashtor, "Un mouvement migratoire au haut Moyen Age: Migrations de l'Irak vers les pays méditerranéens." *Annales: Histoire, Sciences Sociales* 27/1 (1972) : 185–214.

18 Ibn ʿAbd al-Ḥakam, *Futūḥ Miṣr*, 45; David S. Margoliouth, *Mohammed and the Rise of Islam* (New York, and London : Putnam, 1905), 369.

19 al-Kindī, *Wulah misr*; Mathieu Tillier, "The Qāḍīs of Fusṭāṭ-Miṣr under the Ṭūlūnids and the Ikhshīdids: The Judiciary and Egyptian Autonomy," *Journal of the American Oriental Society* 131/2 (2011): 207–22.

20 al-Balawī, *Sirat Aḥmad ibn Ṭūlūn*.

21 Abū Saʿīd ʿAbd al-Raḥmān ibn Aḥmad ibn Yūnus al-Ṣadafī al-Miṣrī, *Taʾrīkh Ibn Yūnus al-Ṣadafī*, ed. A. F. ʿAbd al-Fattāḥ (Beirut: Dār al-Kutub al-ʿIlmīyah, 2000).

22 Khoury, "Al-Layth Ibn Saʿd."

in several chronicles, in which he is presented as a central node in the chains of transmitters of legal traditions.

Dhū al-Nūn al-Miṣrī (d. c. 860), a mystic from Ikhmīm in Upper Egypt, holds a special position in the Sufi biographical dictionaries. No written work of his has survived, but a vast collection of poems, sayings, and aphorisms attributed to him is regularly quoted in Sufi literature. This preponderance is salient evidence for his pre-eminent position in the early circles of Muslim mystics.[23]

The Ikhshidids did not last long. After the rule of ʿAlī, the son of Muḥammad the Ikhshīd (r. 961–66), a black eunuch named Kāfūr served as the *de facto* ruler of Egypt (r. 966–68). During his days, Egypt experienced social discontent, unrest, growing insecurity, and economic crises. This opened the door for an offensive from the West: the only case in Egypt's long history that this land was conquered from that direction.

The Fatimids—Egypt as an international hub

In the ninth century, a branch of the Shīʿa called the Ismāʿīliyya, organized a secret network of missionaries (*al-daʿwa*), which promoted a call for a revolutionary religio-political change in the territories of the Abbasid caliphate. The political importance of the Ismāʿīlī movement surged as a result of this successful propaganda campaign.

By the middle of that century, the Ismāʿīliyya succeeded in establishing several autonomous enclaves ("islands" in their political vocabulary) in various parts of the Abode of Islam. The town of Salāmiyya in Syria was one of these enclaves. It served as the headquarters of ʿAbd Allāh al-Mahdī, the founder of the Fatimid dynasty. Yet, after a short while he was forced to flee (in 902). Accompanied by his young son and future successor, al-Qāʾim, he went to North Africa. Although originating in the east, they succeeded in winning the hearts and swords of Berber tribes in what is now Tunisia and eastern Algeria, and established a new Fatimid center in 910.

ʿAbd Allāh al-Mahdī's enterprise was the first step in the Fatimids' long march to establish a Mediterranean empire. Moreover, their missionaries carried their message to the four corners of the Muslim world and beyond. Ismāʿīlī enclaves popped up in Yemen (as early as 881), India, Iran, and other near and remote lands. Due to the propaganda of these supporting cells, Ismāʿīlī agents

23 Michael Ebstein, "Ḏū l-Nūn al-Miṣrī and Early Islamic Mysticism," *Arabica* 61 (2014): 559–612.

made ground in other parts of the lands of Islam while the Fatimids' navy and army enabled them to become significant players in the Mediterranean arena.

Ideological and practical impulses drove the Fatimid leader (*imām*), whose capital had been located since 921 in al-Mahdiyya, on the Mediterranean coast of Tunisia, to engage in the formidable challenge of crossing the Libyan desert and invading the Nile valley, an intricate military expedition that achieved an unprecedented victory. Heading an army of Berber tribesmen, Jawhar al-Ṣaqlabī (d. 992) departed al-Mahdiyya on February 969 and reached the gates of Alexandria in May.

Using diplomacy rather than force enabled Jawhar to cross the Nile and to seize control of Fusṭāṭ, the capital of Egypt. The white color of the Fatimids replaced the black banners of the Abbasids. Changing the call to prayer symbolized this bloodless victory. North of the old city of Fusṭāṭ, Jawhar laid the foundations for a new city, which he named al-Qāhira (Cairo), meaning "the victorious." Cairo was constructed on the model of the Tunisian port city of al-Mahdiyya. The capital served not only as the administrative heart of Egypt and neighboring Syria, but also a hub of medieval intercontinental commerce that stretched from the Mediterranean to India. Nāṣir-i Khuṣraw (1004–88), a Persian traveler and zealous adherent of the Fatimid imamate, left an eyewitness account of the rich and colorful court and of the spectacular urban ceremonies that were orchestrated by the Fatimid imams, who staged pageantry-filled processions and rituals that broadcasted their image and ideology.

During the opening years of their government, and particularly in the reigns of the three first imams (969–1021), the Fatimids invested in agricultural and industrial production and in commercial activity. Wasteland was reclaimed for the cultivation of the old winter crops and more recent summer crops. Egypt had come to play a significant role in several long-distance trade networks. For many years, the mints of the Imamate cast high-quality golden coins (dīnārs), which were considered reliable currency for use in long-distance international trade. The export of cloth was matched by the import of commodities from across the Mediterranean and the Indian Ocean. Across the Sahara came slaves and gold. Foreign embassies and merchants who traveled to and from Byzantium, India, North Africa, and Spain called at the imam's court. Cairo developed into a rich and vibrant cosmopolitan hub. Among the sources at our disposal for reconstructing this global economic revolution, the Cairo Genizah documents constitute a significant portion.

The long-distance maritime trade that the Fatimids encouraged opened a new chapter in the maritime history of the eastern Mediterranean. Their navy connected the Syrian coast, where old port cities experienced a renascence, with Egypt's ports, the most important of which was Alexandria. Boats that sailed on the Nile linked Cairo with coastal settlements and townships along the river. The renewal of naval trade in the Mediterranean opened the gates to Italian merchants who slowly started to sail from Southern Europe to Syria and Egypt. The risk that accompanied such commercial activity encouraged the development of merchants' institutions and instruments. Partnerships, traders' networks, the employment of agents and remote payments promised to reduce danger and to generate profits.

The Fatimids introduced a new version of Islam. On the basis of pseudo-Aristotelian texts that circulated in the Islamicate world from the eighth century, the Ismāʿīlī mission elaborated a complex metaphysical systems combining Shiʿī theology with a diversity of philosophical traditions, notably Neoplatonism. The Ismāʿīlī missionaries expressed their theology in terms of the most fashionable philosophical themes and vocabulary, maintaining that their interpretation of worldly reality is occult and should be revealed only to a limited number of adherents that will safeguard the secrets.

The Fatimid-Ismāʿīlīs believed that their imams were in possession of a special occult knowledge (*ʿilm*) and had perfect understanding of the exoteric and esoteric meanings of the Qurʾān. The central pillar of their doctrine was the belief in mankind's permanent need for a divinely guided, sinless and infallible leader.

During the early years of the Fatimid caliphs' rule in Cairo, the dynasty showed determined pursuit of the Redeemer's (*al-mahdī*) vision of restoring to the Muslim community its true faith and true government at the hands of the true heirs of the prophet Muḥammad. That this claim was not favorably received by all Sunni inhabitants of the Fatimid Caliphate we can deduct from the story of Ibn al-Nābulsī's martyrdom in 973.[24] The imam al-ʿAzīz ordered him to be flayed publicly at the gate of his capital in response to this Sunni zealot's declaration: "Had I ten arrows, I would fire nine of them against you, the North Africans [that is, the Fatimids], and only the remaining one towards the Byzantines."[25]

24 Thierry Bianquis, "Ibn al-Nabulusi, un martyr sunnite au IVe siecle de l'Hegire," *Ann. Islam* 12 (1974): 45–66.

25 Abū Muḥammad ʿAbd al-ʿAzīz al-Kattānī al-Dimashqī, *Dhayl tahrikh mawlid al-ulama* (Riyad: Dar al-ʿAsima, 1988), 97 (47); Abu al-Qāsim ʿAli Ibn ʿAsākir, *Taʾrikh madinat Dimashq*, ed. M. al-ʿAmrawi (Damascus: Dar al-Fikr, 1415/1995), 51 (no. 5906)

During the reign of the imam al-Ḥākim bi-Amr Allah (996–1020), violent persecutions of non-Muslim subjects took place. A Druze epistle reports of a dramatic council that took place on a dark night in Cairo's cemetery. Jewish and Christian delegations asked al-Ḥākim to grant them security and to extend their status as protected people (*dhimmah*). In response, al-Ḥākim blamed them for rejecting the true religion and announced that after four hundred years of Muḥammad's revelation their protected status has come to an end.[26] The persecution of non-Muslims by al-Ḥākim are described in Muslim, Christian, and Jewish sources as well. A long Jewish liturgical oeuvre known as "the Egyptian Scroll," which describes the hardships endured by the Jewish communities in Egypt and their miraculous salvation, was found in the Cairo Genizah.

During the Fatimid period, Egypt's state apparatus was deeply militarized. A growing number of military slaves, recruited from various non-Arab ethnic groups, manned the army barracks and played an increasing role in the administration. While the early Fatimid army was based on Berber North-African tribesmen, who adhered to the imams, after the conquest of Egypt this underwent a deep change. The routinization of the imam's charisma was accompanied by the conscription of alien military slaves. Cairo's barracks housed Black African slave soldiers, Turkish cavalrymen, Armenians and others non-Arab ethnic groups. A considerable portion of the agricultural land was assigned to maintain these army units.

A typical characteristic of the Fatimid imamate was the state bureaucracy. Under the guidance of the first imam, a multi-religious corpus of clerks manned the various administrative departments (*dīwān*). Sunnī Muslims, Jews, and Christians were recruited from the local population and administrated the tax revenues, finance, state properties, and internal affairs. This machinery demonstrated a great degree of continuation with earlier Egyptian practices. The administration of justice was handed to Ismāʿīlī adherents of the imam. They were trained in institutions of learning that attracted Ismāʿīlīs from every part of the Muslim world, near and far. The role of the state in the administration of justice explains the considerable number of petitions found in the Cairo Genizah.

The long Fatimid years left two contradicting memories. While Genizah documents and archaeological finds transmit a picture of affluence, of

26 D. de Smet (ed. and trans.), *Les Épîtres sacrées des Druzes*, vol. 3 of *Récit sur les juifs et les chrétiens* (Leuven: Peeters, 2007), 143–53.

flourishing material culture, imported goods, and luxury textiles, chronicles report deep dynastic crises, natural calamities, and shortages.

An example illuminating this complicated reality is furnished by a Genizah document regarding legal claims that followed the journey of the Jewish merchant Joseph al-Lebdī, to India in 1094–97. This voyage started in al-Mahdiyya and continued towards Gujarat, the country of lac, textiles, steel, and beads.[27] The Genizah documents display the wealth of luxurious and exotic goods that were imported from this remote land to Egypt. Another example is provided by an anecdote in Ibn al-Zubayr's *Book of Gifts and Rarities*.[28] It tells of the estate of Rashīda, the daughter of imam al-Muʿizz (r. 953–75), who passed away and left 30,000 robe lengths of silk and 12,000 pieces of colored plain cloth.[29] The religious architecture, which can still be visited today in Cairo, reflects the extensive investment by the Fatimid dynasty in magnificent buildings that convey messages of grandeur and affluence.[30]

At the same time, as mentioned previously, the Fatimid period also witnessed deep calamities. During the rule of Imam al-Ẓāhir (1020–35), the Nile Valley experienced a low rising of the Nile water at the end of the summer. The failure to water the fields caused bad harvests and famines that generated social unrest. The suffering and the high death toll recorded during the long crisis that devastated Egypt in the years 1062–73 was even gloomier. The failure of Imam al-Mustanṣir to address the disaster and supply the market with food caused immense suffering and an unmeasured number of deaths. No wonder that these years were recorded in Egypt's collective memory as "the great catastrophe."

The supply shortage that resulted in an escalating social crisis did not occur in a political or military vacuum. During the second and third quarters of the eleventh century, Western Asia experienced profound changes. Turkish tribes advanced from the Eurasian steppe and headed towards the Mediterranean, conquering Iran, Iraq, Syria, Palestine and vast lands in Asia Minor. Baghdad,

27 S. D. Goitein and Mordechai A. Friedman, *India Traders of the Middle Ages: Documents from the Cairo Geniza ("India Book")* (Leiden: Brill, 2008), 28.

28 Ghāda al-Qaddūmī (trans.), *Book of Gifts and Rarities [Kitab al-hadāyā wa al-tuḥaf]: Selections Compiled in the Fifteenth Century from an Eleventh-Century Manuscript on Gifts and Treasures* (Cambridge, MA: Harvard University Press, 1996).

29 Rashīd ibn al-Zubayr, *al-Dhakhāʾir wal-tuḥaf*, ed. M. Hamid Allah (Kuwait: Daʾirat al-matbuʿat, 1959), 241 (n. 355).

30 Doris Behrens-Abouseif, *Islamic Architecture in Cairo: An Introduction* (Leiden: Brill, 1989), 58.

the capital of the Abbasids, the arch-nemesis of the Fatimids, was conquered by the Seljuqs in 1055. Tughril Bak (Beg), their leader, declared himself *sulṭān,* a title that will appear again and again in the following pages. Although his people's efforts to invade Egypt failed, they took Damascus and Jerusalem from the hands of the Egyptians and incorporated Syria into the domains of the Saljuq Sultanate.

The continuing deterioration of Egypt's economy, and the failure of the Cairene administration to address the deep managerial crisis, forced Imam al-Mustanṣir to ask Badr al-Jamālī, the Armenian governor of Acre, to report to the court (1073). Commanding his loyal Armenian soldiers, the new vizier crushed his opponents and restored order. He received the title of *amīr al-juyūsh* (the commander of the armies), which reveals that his authority did not rest upon a mandate delegated to him by the charismatic head of the Fatimid state. He rather gained his power from his private troops and personal managerial capabilities. The Fatimid dynasty had come full circle. From a charismatic community, it had turned into an army slaves' state.

In 1094, towards the closing days of al-Mustanṣir's long reign, the court in Cairo was caught up in an internal race for power. One camp supported Abū Manṣūr Nizār (1095–97), while the other one sought to nominate his younger brother Abū al-Qāsim al-Mustaʿalī (1094–1101), splitting the Ismāʿīlī community. At the same time, the Fatimids faced a completely new and revolutionary situation, when the Frankish armies known as the Crusaders established the Latin Kingdom of Jerusalem in 1099. They would be defeated only after the imamate's final disappearance from Egypt.

The Fatimids left deep marks on the history of Egypt. *Longue durée* social developments, which originated centuries earlier, culminated during their rule. Cairo, in which only one mosque, named after ʿAmr ibn al-ʿĀṣ, the victorious conqueror of Egypt, was recorded, had become in the mid-twelfth century a giant Islamic metropolis. A new Arabo-Islamic civilization encompassed all components of Egyptian society. Arabic became the *lingua franca* used by all, including Jews. The translation of Coptic liturgical texts and of Jewish writings into Arabic illustrate this cultural turn. Coptic and Aramaic were no longer used in daily life, but were replaced by an Arabic vernacular. Middle Arabic, a diglossia of high and low varieties of Arabic, served as the major linguistic tool to record the collective memory of Muslims and non-Muslims alike and to maintain communal communication.

The Crusaders

In summer 1099, the Crusaders stormed the walls of Jerusalem. An army that had departed from Europe now fought to conquer the Holy Land. A bloody massacre inaugurated the emergence of the first Latin kingdom. The port city of Ascalon/ʿAsaqlān (Ashqelon in Hebrew) was the only place throughout the Palestinian coast and the Sinai desert that resisted the invaders. For the next fifty years, the Fatimid army and navy repelled the Latins' attacks on it.

Cairo was torn by a political conflict amongst the Fatimid elite. All the last three Fatimid caliphs (1149–71) were children, and the last few years of Fatimid rule were essentially a contest for power between army commanders and secretaries. This inner circle crisis in the declining court invited foreign interference in the Cairene political arena, where Frankish and Damascene expeditions collided. Egypt was forced to pay tribute to the Kingdom of Jerusalem. In 1162, Nūr al-Dīn (1146–74), the suzerain of Aleppo and Damascus, decided to interfere in the game, by dispatching several expeditionary forces to Egypt (1164, 1167, 1168).

Saladin and the establishment of a new geo-political map

Nūr al-Dīn's army, commanded by Asad al-Dīn Shīrkūh (d. 1169), came to rescue the Fatimid imam as Frankish troops operated in the Delta. Shīrkūh took with him his nephew Yusūf ibn Ayyūb, better known as Ṣalāḥ al-Dīn, or Saladin, in European sources. Following Shīrkūh's death, Saladin was nominated commander of the Syrian expedition forces, which entitled him the rank of *wazīr*. He was the last vizier of the Fatimid caliphs and the one to end this Ismāʿīlī dynasty, which ruled Egypt for two centuries. After becoming vizier, Saladin arrested the last members of the Fatimid family and swore allegiance to Baghdad. The call to prayer was changed, and in 1171, the muezzins, dressed in black once more, again called the name of the Abbasid caliph.

Saladin felt strong enough now to enter Damascus and ascend the throne of the sultanate, declaring himself the sultan of Egypt and Syria. Practical unification took place only after his victory over the Franks and their departure from Jerusalem in 1187. Securing his hold over Upper Egypt, Saladin turned to the Red Sea region. His men took control over the Holy Cities of Arabia and Yemen. This was crucial to ensuring Egypt's continuing role in the maritime trade between India and the Mediterranean. These achievements, accompanied by a vibrant propaganda campaign, provided Saladin with everlasting worldwide fame. Even medieval European writings present him as the epitome of the ideal knight.

Saladin and his family ruled Egypt for only a few decades. Yet, despite their limited years at the helm of the ship of state, they succeeded in implementing far-reaching changes in Egypt's bureaucratic organization and land tenure that opened a new chapter in Egypt's taxes administration and agrarian history. Saladin had a cadastral survey undertaken. He allocated revenue sources to his clients and allies. He turned the military *iqṭā*ʿ farming allocations into a central administrative tool and a major instrument of military payment. This shaped the history of pious endowments (*waqf*, pl. *awqāf*) for centuries. From his time on, growing portions of Egypt's farming lands and village communities were bequeathed to support and maintain urban religio-social institutions.

The geo-strategic position of Egypt and the Ayyubid presence in Yemen, combined with the internal markets' economic strength, made Egypt a key player in twelfth- and thirteenth-century global trade and international politics. Indian cotton textiles, nowadays on display in Western museums, are supporting evidence for this dynamic cross-ocean maritime commerce.[31] Accounts of shipments of musk and other fragrances from India to Egypt in hundreds of Genizah documents provide additional support to this chapter in the history of medieval long-distance trade.

Several architectural remains shed light on the Ayyubid contribution to Egypt`s military planning. It was Saladin himself who started this building initiative. His projects can be still visited today in Sinai and in Cairo, where he laid the foundations for the citadel on al-Muqaṭṭam hill. This was a major change in the city's urban-political scene.[32] Since the old Ismāʿīlī mosques constructed by the Fatimid imams were converted into Sunnī places of prayer, the Ayyubid sultans refrained from constructing new mosques. Instead, they built a number of learning institutions [*madrasa*], Sufi lodges, and shrines—the most famous of which is the shrine dedicated al-Shāfiʿī (767–820), the famous Muslim jurist to whose legal school the dynasty adhered.

Ayyubid rule over the Nile valley proved at its early stages to be resilient and effective. With the passing of time, internal power struggles weakened the administrative apparatus, and affected its efficiency. Yet, despite these

31 Small fragments of cotton of Indian origin have been found at the Red Sea port Quṣayr al-Qadīm.

32 We shall return to this point further in the story of Mamluk Cairo below.

difficulties it maintained a considerable degree of momentum. Thus, the humanitarian crisis following the low flood of the Nile in 1199–1202, which brought about three years of devastating famine throughout the country, did not interrupt Egypt`s political stability and its economic recovery.[33]

Non-Muslims, especially Christians, experienced under the Ayyubid sultanate much pressure that resulted in mass conversions to Islam. This is reflected in the following Christian account from the year 1168–69: "and he [Shīrkūh] proclaimed in Cairo that the Christians should remove the fringes from their turbans and should fasten (their waists) with their girdles, and the Jews (should attach) a piece of yellow cloth to their turbans."[34] Saladin continued these anti-Christian measures

> should not employ Christians as overseers in the treasuries of the State, nor as inspectors, and his word was accepted and his opinion was carried out, and not one of the Christians returned to be employed as overseers and inspectors in the days of the State of Salah ad-Din, nor of those who ruled after him of his sons and his descendants.[35]

On the other hand, we should highlight the crucial role of *dhimmīs* in the state apparatus and in commerce. Even more conspicuous was their role as court physicians.

The recruitment of slave soldiers started prior to Saladin and was continued by his heirs. Their number and importance increased till they became the backbone of the Ayyubid-Egyptian army. The Mamluk historian al-Maqrīzī reports on the structure and importance of Egypt's military at the waning of the Ayyubid period:

> The Ayyubid sultan Najm al-Dīn al-Malik al-Ṣāliḥ (r. 1240–49) was the ruler who created the mamluk battalion of the Baḥriyya in Egypt. The confrontations that he experienced were the reason for this. Due to the events he experienced on the night in which he had

33 Cecilia Martini Bonadeo, *'Abd al-Laṭīf al-Baġdādī's Philosophical Journey from Aristotle's Metaphysics to the "Metaphysical Science"* (Leiden: Brill, 2013), 109, 135.

34 Sawirus ibn Al-Mukaffa, *History of the Patriarchs of the Egyptian Church Known as The History of the Holy Church*, vol. 3, pt. 2, trans. Antoine Khater and O. H. E. KHS-Burmester (Cairo: Imprimérie de l'Institut Français d'Archéologie Orientale, 1943–76), 106.

35 Ibid., 107.

> been deposed, when his Kurdish soldiers and others deserted him and only his slave-soldiers (*mamālīk*) remained with him, he felt a sense of gratitude for their fidelity. After seizing Egypt, he started to buy slave-soldiers in increasing numbers until they became the backbone of his army. He dismissed his father's and his brothers' army commanders and even arrested some of them and discontinued the revenues they received from allowances of land allocations. Instead, he nominated his slave-soldiers to replace them. They were his loyal entourage and faithful guards. Since their barracks were near his pavilion on the island of al-Rawḍa on the Nile, they were named al-Baḥriyya.[36]

The importance of Egypt during the long years of Muslim-Christian struggle over the control of the Eastern Mediterranean was recognized by the Crusaders, who launched two maritime invasions of the Nile Delta (1218, 1249–50). The Baḥriyya were largely responsible for the ultimate defeat of the crusading army during the latter attack, which was led by the French king St. Louis. At that turning point in Egypt's history, they showed no inclination to accept the authority of Sultan al-Muʿaẓẓam Turān Shāh. The conspirators murdered the sultan and proclaimed his concubine Shajar al-Durr queen (1250). Later on, she was also killed by them, and Ayyubid rule in Egypt effectively came to an end. Najm al-Dīn's *mamluks* seized the throne and installed one of their peers as the sultan of Egypt. In 1260, they succeeded in driving the Mongols out of Syria, a victory that opened a new chapter in the history of the Fertile Crescent.

The Mamluk Sultanate

After the initial expulsion of the Mongols from Syria in 1260, and the decisive victory over a Mongolian army in central Syria at the Battle of Homs in 1281, relations between the Mamluk sultanate and the Mongol Il-Khans of Iran (1256–1353) moved from confrontation to coexistence.

On the northern front, the Frankish presence in Syria came to an end with the conquest of Acre in 1294. While European corsairs occasionally raided the sultanate's coast, the conquest of Alexandria in 1365 being the

36 Taqī al-Dīn Aḥmad ibn ʿAlī al-Maqrīzī, *al-Sulūk li-maʿrifat duwal al-mulūk*, vol. 1, ed. M. M. Ziyāda (Cairo: Matbaʿat Dār al-Kutub, 1934-73), 339–40 (647 AH). Translation by the author.

most famous event in this series of violence, they never posed a real threat to Mamluk rule. Although throughout the sultanate's long history it suffered several military defeats, the most significant of which being Tamerlane's (Timur Lang) incursion into Syria in 1400, it seems that during the Mamluk period, Egypt enjoyed centuries of peace. The sultans' strategy was principally defensive, and Egypt's Mediterranean port cities were accordingly defined as safeguarding gates (*thughūr*). Offensive naval expeditions were only very rarely dispatched.

The sultanate profited from the post-Crusader/Mongol new world order. This global pacification enabled embassies and merchants to set up commercial and diplomatic networks that connected Cairo with the Black Sea in the North, the Horn of Africa in the south, and India and China in the East. European merchants and envoys regularly called at the Sultanate's ports and the royal court in Cairo.[37]

Nevertheless, the *Pax Mongolica* exacted an economic cost on the sultanate. The overland traffic that connected Central Asia with Anatolia's ports, where European merchants regularly embarked, competed with the Mamluk trade route that led from India via Yemen, Egypt and across the Mediterranean, to southern Europe. The Venetians did not send a single convoy to Egypt between 1323 and 1345.[38] After the Black Death (1348–52) the tide reversed again.

Cairo was a global metropolis and a hub in which old and new roads intertwined. The sultanate's seaports were called by European sailors and merchants. From Sinai and Egypt's Red Sea harbors boats navigated to Yemen, East Africa, and India. The Fatimid palaces and Ismāʿīlī mission centers at the heart of Cairo were dissolved. The political and administrative premises were moved from downtown Cairo and relocated to the citadel on al-Muqaṭṭam hill, which overlooks the civilian hub. Sultan Qalāwun's building projects constituted a turning point in the development of Mamluk urban and monumental architecture. The accumulated impact of building created a new urban space. The mamluk city was covered by a dense grid of mosques, institutions of learning,

37 Peter B. Golden et al. (eds. and trans.), *The King's Dictionary—The Rasûlid Hexaglot: Fourteenth-Century Vocabularies in Arabic, Persian, Turkic, Greek, Armenian, and Mongol* (Leiden: Brill, 2000).

38 Robert S. Lopez, "Trade in Medieval Europe: the South," in *The Cambridge Economic History of Europe*, vol. 2, *Trade and Industry in the Middle Ages*, ed. M. M. Postan and Edward Miller assisted by Cynthia Postan (2nd edition; Cambridge: Cambridge University Press, 1987), 387.

hospitals and mausoleums. Ibn Khaldun, who arrived in Cairo during February 1383, called the capital of the Mamluk sultanate

> the metropolis of the universe, the garden of the world, the ant heap of the human species, the throne of royalty; a city adorned with palaces and chateaux, convents, monasteries, and colleges, and illumined by the stars of erudition; a paradise so bounteously watered by the Nile that the earth seems here to offer its fruits to men as gifts and salutations.[39]

Slave markets were a salient phenomenon on the human map of the sultanate. Traveling merchants departed from Cairo for the Mongol realm, Africa, India and the Black Sea region and returned with bonded people who were put on the block in the sultanate's slave markets. These slaves were employed in a wide variety of duties and could accordingly gain prestige and social capital. The spectrum of bonded persons included maids and concubines on the one hand, and manumitted slave-soldiers who occupied high ranking administrative and military positions on the other. This opened the way for the dissemination of the legend of the Joseph precedent, according to which the ruler of Egypt must be a prisoner whom a merchants' caravan brought from a distant land. [40]

The Mamluk sultan was an autocrat and the sultanate—a military regime. Theoretically, it was governed by a one-generation military aristocracy, whose promotion reflected values of meritocracy. A newcomer who was born outside the Abode of Islam was supposed to inherit his predecessor's throne. The power of the sultan and his authority rested on his direct command of the army. The chief officers assembled around him, and his rule depended heavily on their support.

Yet, more than one sultan tried to gain the recognition of the regime's elite in proclaiming his son as successor and future sultan. This inevitable tension led to fierce conflicts. Again and again, these heirs were toppled and replaced by a sultan acknowledged by his peers. Measures taken by the military aristocracy were not innocent of desire for materialistic gains, positions and properties

39 Walī al-Dīn ʿAbd al-Raḥman Ibn Khaldūn al-Mālikī, *al-Taʿrīf bi-ibn khaldūn wa-riḥlatih^{i} gharb^{an} washarq^{an}* (Beirut: Dār al-Kutub al-Lubnānī, 1979), 264; Étienne Quatremère, ed., *Les Prolégomènes d'Ebn-Khaldoun*, vol. 1 (original French edition, Paris: Typographie de Firmin Didot, 1858), trans. M. De Slane (Paris: Imprimerie Impériale, 1873), LXXII.

40 Koby Yosef, "Mamluks and Their Relatives in the Period of the Mamluk Sultanate (1250–1517)," *Mamluk Studies Review* 16 (2012): 55–69.

being the most paramount among them. Already Baybars bought the backing of his senior officers by allocating private *iqṭāʿ* farms to them.[41]

Technically, the sultan was not a sovereign. He was bound by the Islamic canonical law (*sharīʿa*) and his position was ratified by the Abbasid caliph. This was followed by the army commanders' ceremonial oath and an official visit by the religious establishment in the citadel. This complex political ritual established the sultan's legitimacy.[42] To this we should add his self-presentation in official documents and monumental inscriptions. To make the point it is sufficient to look at the set of titles borne by Sultan Baybars, who presented himself as the associate of the Abbasid caliph, the king of Jerusalem and Mecca, the guardian of the sacred shrines of Arabia, and as the victorious commander who destroys the enemies of Islam.

The army was the main pillar of the Mamluk political structure. This was in line with the sultanate's ideology, that perceived the protection of the Abode of Islam by jihad as the sultanate's *raison d'être*. This line of reasoning was used by contemporary jurists to explain the division of work and the land tenure. The military aristocracy (*sayfiyya*, "the men of the sword") comprised the ruling echelon. An elaborated bureaucracy (*qalimiyya*, "the men of the pen") monitored the rural lands, the allocation of *iqṭāʿ* farms and taxation, and was in charge of communication and administration. The religious establishment (*mutaʿamimūn*, "the men of the turban") was supposed to ensure that both the above abided by the *sharīʿa*. The judiciary was divided into four religio-legal schools. Each chief judge was represented by deputies who operated in the provinces. Sufis were a salient component of the religious establishment, and played an active role in social life and in popular rituals. This religious establishment served as the third pillar of the regime.

The sultans' economic initiatives during the thirteenth and early fourteenth century increased the volume of agricultural production along the Nile Valley and Delta. These enterprises came to an end with the Black Death (c. 1348–52). Repeated plague epidemics devastated villages and took their tool in human and animal lives. Many areas were left with insufficient labor

41 Y. Frenkel, "The Impact of the Crusades on the Rural Society and Religious Endowments: The Case of Medieval Syria," in *War and Society in the Eastern Mediterranean, 7–15th Centuries*, ed. Y. Lev (Leiden: Brill, 1997), 237–48.

42 The Mamuk jurist Ibn Jamāʿa (1241–1333) justifies the usurpation of by force as a form of rulership by delegation. See his *Tahrir al-ahkam fi tadbir ahl al-islam*, ed. F. A. Ahmad (Qatr: Dar al-Thaqafa, 1988).

to keep the dikes and canals in working order. Depopulation, desolation and the reduction in farming led to agricultural decline. Even Cairo recorded vast regions of demolished buildings. Changes in land tenure affected society, politics, and economy.

During the early Mamluk period, the substantial majority of the farming lands were "state property," namely administrated by the military bureau. In order to preserve Egypt's farmlands, the farmers were bound to their villages and the regime was involved in maintaining the system of canals and dikes that irrigated most of the fields. The yearly autumn festival of breaking the dam in Cairo, which ostentatiously celebrated the rise of the Nile, reflects the importance attributed to the river and to its regulation in Mamluk society.

However, by the end of the thirteenth century the power of the royal Mamluks had increased greatly. The sultans saw it as necessary to strengthening the economic basis of their power and weakening the position of the non-Mamluk battalions. To achieve this objective, the sultanate twice carried out countrywide cadastral surveys (1298, 1313–25). This brought about changes in the organization of the *iqṭāʿ* system. The military aristocracy used the revenues of the land parcels that were allocated to them as a base for strengthening their control over the agricultural communities. This process culminated in the fifteenth century. A large quantity of agricultural land had been sold by the treasury to private parties. During the fifteenth century, landholding in Egypt altered significantly.

Another indicator of the financial pressure is the direct involvement of sultans and army commanders in the markets. The military aristocracy that governed Mamluk Egypt controlled a considerable share of the country's economic resources. In the fifteenth century, as the volume of precious metals in Egypt's markets deteriorated sharply, it became evident that the sultanate was facing a severe crisis. This caused commercial and administrative changes. Moreover, as the financial burden intensified the sultans increased their involvement in the markets. The salient phenomena of this political economy were the monopolization of trade and increasing cases of compulsory purchases and confiscation of fortunes. In the mid-fifteenth century, maritime trade was monopolized by the sultanate.

The role of the military aristocracy in the social-economic arena of Mamluk Egypt can be illuminated by looking closer at its pious charity endowments (*waqf*) and its moral economy. The foundation of a pious endowment was the typical charitable act in the Mamluk domains. It allowed the founders of pious endowments to demonstrate devoutness, to win the support of the religious establishment, and to affect Muslim public opinion. These institutions offered accommodations to Sufis and students of Islamic law, sickbeds to the ill, shelter to travelers, drinking water, and praying halls.

The Mamluk era also witnessed a significant growth of Sufism, as is attested by the numerous Sufi biographies, composed at this time. From a loose network of lodges, this devotional creed developed into vast systems of organized and institutionalized communities of dedicated worshipers.

These Sufi lodges and institutions of legal and traditional learning shaped Cairo's role as an international center of Islamic scholarship and transmission of knowledge. Cairo became a projecting node in worldwide Sufi networks and a magnetic center that attracted novices and shaykhs from all over the Abode of Islam. This was manifested in the city's changing architecture. Numerous Sufi lodges, mausoleums, schools, and other religious institutions spread through Cairo's neighborhoods. The military elite played the role of patrons of architecture and initiated the construction of buildings that housed these Islamic sites.[43] The creation of an Islamic landscape was not limited to the urban space. A central public space that attracted a considerable number of visitors was also Cairo's City of Death (*qarāfa*).[44]

Alongside religious culture, the Mamluk era witnessed a flourishing of what can be called the secular arts. Popular story-telling, popular music and theater characterize the Mamluk culture just as much. The heroes of these performing arts were legendary figures such as Sultan Baybars, and Alexander the Great (*Iskandar*), whose "biographies" were also written down. These heroes' images were kept alive in Mamluk society`s collective memory, and provided it with images about ideal rulers and uncompromising justice. Another popular genre was that of geographical compositions. It consisted of imagined geographies and reflected the way Mamluk-period authors and their audiences imagined their surrounding world and its diverse peoples.

Muslims' animosity towards their Christian and Jewish neighbors gained new momentum in this period. Violent attacks on non-Muslim communities

43 Stephen R. Humphreys, "The Expressive Intent of the Mamluk Architecture of Cairo: a Preliminary Essay," *Studia Islamica* 35 (1972): 69–119.

44 Shams al-Dīn Muḥammad ibn al-Zayyāt, *Kitāb al-Kawākib al-sayyāra fi tartīb al-ziyāra fi al-qarāfatayn al-kubrā wa-al-ṣughraā* (Baghdād: Maktabat al-Muthanná, 1968); R. Guest, "Cairene Topography: El-Qarafa According to Ibn Ez-Zaiyat," *Journal of the Royal Asiatic Society* 1 (1926): 57–61; Christopher S. Taylor, *In the Vicinity of the Righteous: Ziyara and the Veneration of Muslim Saints* (Leiden: Brill, 1999).

within the borders of the sultanate were recorded already during the days of Baybars, who supported the shaykh al-Khāḍir's measures against churches and monasteries.[45] The popular accusation that the local Christians operated as a fifth column while Islam was besieged by the Crusaders and the Mongols provoked physical attacks on churches and monasteries, as well as decrees against the employment of Christian state administrators. During the Mamluk period, the non-Muslims, mainly the indigenous Coptic population of Egypt, shrank significantly, and the country went through a massive process of islamization. The islamization of Egypt's population is also manifested in the many popular religious texts produced at this time, such as hagiographies, like Abū al-Ḥasan al-Bakrī's *Life of the Prophet*.[46]

The Black Death marks a watershed in Mamluk history. Starting in 1347, Egypt was subjected to enormous losses of population and working beasts. Egypt's irrigation system was severely impaired by depopulation, and this heavily reduced the size and the production of the *iqṭāʿ* farms. Overall, agrarian output fell precipitously in this period. The collapse of the Egyptian agricultural system led to the downfall of the central pillar of the Mamluk economy. The deterioration of the Mamluk military system was also manifested in increasing soldiers' riots. A severe breakdown occurred in the army.

Some scholars, Ashtor being the most salient among them, depicted the Mamluk regime as one of continuous decay:

> The flourishing economy of the Near East had been ruined by the rapacious military, and its great civilizing achievements had been destroyed through inability to adopt new methods of production and new ways of life. . . . In the second half of the 15th century Egypt was dominated by European pre-colonialism.[47]

45 On him, see Peter Malcolm Holt, "An Early Source on Shaykh Khadir al-Mihrani," *BSOAS* 46 (1983): 33–9.

46 Boaz Shoshan, *Popular Culture in Medieval Cairo* (Ithaca: Cornell UP, 1993).

47 E. Ashtor, "The Economic Decline of the Middle East during the Later Middle Ages—An Outline," *Asian and African Studies* 15 (Haifa, 1981): 253–286 [reprinted in his *Technology, Industry and Trade: The Levant versus Europe 1250–1500*, ed. B. Z. Kedar (London: Variorum Reprints, 1992), art. II]; idem, "The Venetian Supremacy in Levantine Trade: Monopoly or Pre-Colonialism?," *Journal of European Economic History* 3 (1974): 5–53.

Others, like Garcin, rejected this theory and ascribed the evident economic crisis to political and demographic decline and to lack of resources.[48] Nonetheless, the almost three centuries of the Mamluk regime constitute a significant chapter in the history of Egypt.

In 1516, Ottoman armies, commanded by Sultan Salim advanced toward the northern frontier of the Mamluk sultanate. The decisive battle took place in Marj Dabiq, north of Aleppo. Moving quickly across Syria, the Ottomans reached the gates of Cairo. The hanging of Tūmām Bāy, the last Mamluk sultan, spread the message. Istanbul was the new capital of the Islamic Near East and the Ottoman sultan—the guardian of Jerusalem and the holy cities of Arabia. Egypt lost its privileged status in the realm of Islam.

Concluding Remarks

This chapter aimed at providing a very brief introduction to the early and middle Islamic periods of the history of the Nile valley. Our major concern was with religious, linguistic and social changes over a lengthy period. From a Coptic land, Egypt became an important center of Islamic creativity and intellectual production. From a province governed by alien emperors, it became a regional power, that played a pivotal role in the history of the eastern Mediterranean and the Islamicate world.

48 Jean-Claude Garcin, "The Mamluk Military System and the Blocking of Medieval Moslem Society," in *Europe and the Rise of Capitalism*, ed. J. Baechler, J. A. Hall, and M. Mann (Oxford: Blackwell, 1988), 113–30; Robert Irwin, "Under Western Eyes: A History of Mamluk Studies," *MSR* 4 (2000): 27–51.

3

The Community's Borders; Converts and Renegades

MOSHE YAGUR

Sometime in the last quarter of the twelfth century, Moses ha-Levi b. Levi,[1] the appointed leader (*muqaddam*) of Qalyūb, wrote a short note to the head of the Jews, Sar Shalom ha-Levi, in the Egyptian capital.[2] The note dealt with a girl named ʿAmāʾim, probably a prospective bride, and her "situation," or status:

> And as for the status of ʿAmāʾim ibnat Abū al-Ḥasan, the sister of Khalaf, the freedman's wife. She came to Qalyūb, she and her mother and sister and her sister's husband and their children, and they stayed in Qalyūb for a while. Then, after that, her mother died, and they both buried her in Qalyūb in the presence of a group of people from Israel who reside in Qalyūb. Then, after that, her brother took her and went to al-Manūfiyya and left the community of Israel. The servant [=the writer of this letter] is not aware, in the matter of the said ʿAmāʾim, of any bond (limiting her), not according to the (Muslim) authorities and not according to the (religious) law.[3]

1 On him see recently Amir Ashur, "On the Identification and Biography of the 'Poet for all Seasons' and his Contact with Maimonides: T-S 10K8.3, T-S 8K13.8, T-S NS 264.98," *Fragment of the Month* (November 2016), accessed June 27, 2017, https://www.repository.cam.ac.uk/handle/1810/262866.

2 On him see Mordechai Akiva Friedman, "Maimonides, Zuta, and the *Muqaddams*: A Story of Three Excommunication Bans," *Zion* 70 (2005): 473–528 [in Hebrew].

3 CUL T-S 10J17.16, edited in Moshe Yagur, "Religious Identity and Communal Boundaries in Genizah Society (10th–13th centuries): Proselytes, Slaves, Apostates" (PhD diss., The Hebrew University of Jerusalem, 2017).

This letter sheds some light on conversion and apostasy as markers of the Jewish community`s boundaries. It exemplifies the conversion to Judaism of non-Jewish slaves, who were purchased by Jews, and eventually converted to Judaism, manumitted, and integrated in the Jewish community, like the aforementioned Khalaf, who married ʿAmāʾim's sister, had children with her, and became a part of her family in its wanderings. At the same time, it also raises many questions: Why did ʿAmāʾim's brother take her with him before converting? Why did he choose to convert in a different town? Did he expect ʿAmāʾim to convert with him, and did she convert with him?

This chapter will examine the subject of communal boundaries by looking at the community's religious boundaries, how and when they were crossed, who crossed them, and what the varying attitudes of members and leaders of the Jewish community were towards these crossers—those who crossed in and converted to Judaism, and those who crossed out and converted from Judaism to other religions. This method is based on the assumption that much about a community's identity can be learned from the way it monitors its borders.[4]

The chapter is divided into four sections: the first three will examine the three main groups of converts: converts to Judaism, slaves who were integrated into Jewish society, and Jews who apostatized. The fourth section will indicate some of the similarities and differences of the three interrelated phenomena. Such a study of the varieties of religious conversion amongst medieval Egyptian Jewry can enrich our understanding of Jewish communal and religious identity in the medieval Muslim Near East.

Conversion to Judaism

Conversion between minority religions under Islam

In many studies it is stated, often without references being given, that under Islam conversion was permitted only from the protected religions of the different minorities to Islam. Indeed, this is the prevalent view in the Shāfiʿī school of law, which argues that the protection, *dhimma*, given to a non-Muslim under Islam is limited only to his original religion, and if he converts to any other religion he loses his legal status and must leave Muslim territory, or else convert to Islam.[5] However, this legal opinion is unique to the Shāfiʿī school alone,

4 See Fredrik Barth, "Introduction," in *Ethnic Groups and Boundaries*, ed. F. Barth (Bergen: Universitatsforlaget, 1969), 9–38.

5 See, for example, S. D. Goitein, *A Mediterranean Society: The Jewish Communities of the Arab World as Portrayed in the Documents of the Cairo Geniza*, 5 volumes plus index volume

while the other three main Sunni schools permit conversion between different protected minority religions, for example from Christianity to Judaism and vice versa.[6] In the writings of the Ismāʿīlī al-Qāḍī al-Nuʿmān, whose book became the cornerstone of Fatimid law, no mention is made of a prohibition on conversion between minority religions, and it is reasonable to assume that in this issue, as in many others, Nuʿmān followed Mālikī law, which permitted such conversions.[7]

Taken together, the literary evidence does not support the common scholarly perception of a widely accepted prohibition of conversion between minority religions, in Sunni or Shiʿi medieval law. Moving on from the normative-prescriptive literature to historical evidence of social reality, one can find quite a few examples of conversions between minority religions under medieval Islam.[8] The Cairo Genizah documents also support the claim that conversions from Christianity to Judaism and vice versa did occur under Islam. Indeed, some Genizah documents describe converts who hailed from Christian Europe. However, the scholarly assumption that most, or all, of the converts to Judaism mentioned in Genizah documents originated from Christian Europe was based on a misunderstanding of Muslim law, and should be corrected.[9]

---

by Paula Sanders (Berkeley, Los Angeles, London: University of California Press, 1967–93), 2:305.

6 See the discussion in Yohanan Friedman, *Tolerance and Coercion in Islam: Interfaith Relations in the Muslim Tradition* (New York: Cambridge University Press, 2003), 146–8. And see also Antoine Fattal, *Le Statut Légal des Non-Musulmans en Pays d'Islam* (Beirut: Dar el-Machreq, 1995), 165.

7 See Asaf A. A. Fyzee (trans.), Ismail K. H. Poonawala (rev.), *The Pillars of Islam, Daʿaim al-Islam of al-Qadi al-Nuʿman* (Oxford: Oxford University Press, 2002–4). On Mālikī influence on Fatimid law see I. K. Poonawala, "Al-Qāḍī al-Nuʿmān and Ismaʿili Jurisprudence," in *Medieval Ismaʿili History and Thought*, ed. F. Daftary (Cambridge: Cambridge University Press, 1996), 129.

8 This issue is still understudied, see David Cook, "Apostasy from Islam: A Historical Perspective," *JSAI* 31 (2006): 248–88. This phenomenon is demonstrated, for example, in the biography of Marwan Ibn al-Muqqamas, who converted from Judaism to Christianity and back, see Sarah Stroumsa, "On Jewish Intellectuals who Converted in the Early Middle Ages," in *The Jews of Medieval Islam: Community, Society and Identity*, ed. Daniel Frank (Leiden and Boston: Brill, 1995), 183–5. Another Jewish convert to Christianity in tenth-century Muslim Egypt is ʿAbd al-Masīḥ al-Isrāʾīlī al-Raqqī, see Khalil Samir, "Abd al-Masih al-Israʾili al-Raqqi," *The Coptic Encyclopedia*, 5b–7a.

9 For such an assumption see, for example, Goitein, *Mediterranean Society*, 2:304–5; Mark R. Cohen, *Poverty and Charity in the Jewish Community of Medieval Egypt* (Princeton, NJ: Princeton University Press, 2005), 125; Norman Golb, "Jewish Proselytism—a Phenomenon in the Religious History of Early Medieval Europe" (The Tenth Annual Rabbi Louis Feinberg Memorial Lecture, Judaic Studies Program, University of Cincinnati, March

A few Genizah documents can demonstrate the claim that some of the converts in Genizah society were indeed locals, probably originally Christians, who converted to Judaism. One example is the first-person letter of an anonymous woman from Upper Egypt, who wrote to the *nagid*, the head of the Jews in the capital, wishing to convert:

> I do not desecrate any holiday or the Sabbath [. . . and wish] to die in the Jewish religion[. . . .] They said to me: go up to Atfiḥ; there are Jews [there]; they will convert you. Thus, your maidservant traveled to Atfiḥ, went to the Jews, and made an appeal to the community. They replied: We cannot act except upon the written instruction of the *nagid*. Therefore, your maidservant comes to your auspicious gate and throws herself upon God and upon you, entreating you by your faith in God not to dash my hopes.[10]

This woman, clearly not yet converted but quite enthusiastic, was told by the anonymous people she met, probably Jews, to "go to Atfiḥ," about forty miles south of Cairo, where there was an established Jewish community that could convert her. Indeed, several Genizah documents that mention Jews in Atfiḥ were described in previous literature.[11] However, additional permission, and maybe further instructions, was required from the *nagid* in the capital. It is quite reasonable to assume that this woman was a local Christian from one of the small communities not too far from Atfiḥ, definitely more likely than to hypothesize that she made all the way from Christian Europe to Upper Egypt in order to convert specifically there.

Another person who converted to Judaism in Egypt was "Mevorakh, the righteous proselyte." In a letter of recommendation written for him, Mevorakh is said to have converted in the court of the judge Menaḥem ben Isaac ben Sasson, who resided in Cairo itself, and not in Fusṭāṭ.[12] In the same way, the anonymous "proselyte [*ger*] from Cairo" mentioned as receiving alms from

---

3, 1987), accessed June 27, 2017, https://oi.uchicago.edu/sites/oi.uchicago.edu/files/uploads/shared/docs/jewish_proselytism.pdf.

10 CUL T-S 8J27.3, translated and discussed in Goitein, *Mediterranean Society*, 2:310.

11 On the Jews in medieval Atfiḥ, see Norman Golb, "The Topography of the Jews of Medieval Egypt (VI. Places of Settlement of the Jews of Medieval Egypt)," *JNES* 33 (1974): 119.

12 JTS ENA NS 21.20, published in Alexander Scheiber, "A Letter of Recommendation on behalf of the Proselyte Mevorakh from the Geniza," *American Academy for Jewish Research Proceedings* 2 (1980): 491–4.

the Jewish community of Fusṭāṭ, old Cairo, in the first half of the twelfth century, should be understood as exactly that—a Cairene man who converted to Judaism and found support and maintenance in the well-positioned Jewish community of Fusṭāṭ.[13]

A case in point is the letter sent to Egypt in the early eleventh century, describing the vicissitudes of its bearer, a Christian convert to Judaism, who now asks for support from the Jewish communities of Egypt, and especially from the addressee, the leader of the Babylonian community in Fusṭāṭ.[14] The letter describes the righteous Christian-cum-proselyte:

> From his youth he had recognized that the uncircumcised walk in darkness[. . .] . Thus he sought the religion of Israel and did not veer from it [. . .] . He fled from them towards Damascus in order to be gathered unto the congregation, but they went after him, and he took refuge[. . .] . They (came) with him to their friends, and the elders of the Christians, the important residents, gathered about him—for he is from a great family—and they (attempted to) entice him to return to them [. . .] but he told them that their statutes were vanity and that their god was Bel[. . .] . He desired to go on to Egypt, for the Christians were persecuting him and being spiteful every single hour.[15]

The editor of this interesting letter suggested that this convert is to be identified with a contemporary Bohemian priest who converted to Judaism, according to a Latin polemical treatise. However, it is clear that the letter discusses a case of a local convert, one whose family members and communal leaders can chase after, bring back, and try to persuade, bribe, or harass him.[16]

Genizah documents, then, as well as contemporary Jewish, Christian, and Muslim sources of various genres, testify to the ongoing phenomenon of conversion between minority religions. This should come as no surprise, as such conversions were allowed according to most Muslim legal schools. Even if such conversions were prohibited, one should bear in mind the ever-present gap between normative law and its actual enforcement.[17] Conversion from

13 CUL T-S NS J 41r, left column, line 19.

14 CUL OR 1080 J 115, published by Norman Golb, "A Righteous Proselyte who Fled to Egypt in the Early Eleventh Century," *Sefunot* 8 (1964): 85–104 [in Hebrew].

15 See partial English translation and discussion in Golb, "Proselytism," 5–6.

16 See Goitein, *Mediterranean Society*, 2:593, note 43.

17 On this point, see Cook, "Apostasy."

Christianity to Judaism was prohibited in Christian Europe, yet none would claim that such conversions did not take place, or that Jewish proselytes mentioned in European literature were all Muslims who converted and migrated from Muslim lands to Christendom.

Who were the converts?

Among the converts mentioned in Genizah documents, the one probably best known to modern readers is Obadiah the Norman. The reasons for his fame are manifold: his literary skills and writing fervor; his remarkable life story; the accidental survival of several different writings of his in the Genizah; and modern scholars' fascination with his image, which led to a decades-long race between scholars who have identified, published, and translated more and more pieces of his works.[18] At the heart of Obadiah's literary corpus is his autobiography. It consists today of seven pages, written on both sides, which form only part of the work. This autobiography, as well as a biographical note he made on a prayer book he copied, gives us Obadiah's original name, as well as the names of his father, mother, and brother, his geographical as well as ethnic origin, childhood events leading to his conversion, the exact date of his conversion, and many of his adventures after his conversion, including his wanderings in the turbulent Middle East of the early twelfth century and his memories from the Jewish communities of Damascus, Aleppo, and Baghdad.

Yet this wealth of information is uncharacteristic of the other converts mentioned in Genizah documents. It is doubtful how much can be gleaned from the story of Obadiah, an educated, noble Catholic European man, to enrich our knowledge about anonymous, local women converts in Egypt. One should not be dazzled by the richness of Obadiah's story and draw too far-reaching conclusions regarding "Genizah converts" in general.

What we do know about the previous lives of converts to Judaism from the Genizah is surprisingly little. The converts mentioned in charity lists are usually anonymous, and only in two cases do we get a clue as to their geographic

18 On him, see Joshua Prawer, "The Autobiography of Obadiah the Norman, a Convert to Judaism at the Time of the First Crusade," *Studies in Medieval Jewish History and Literature* 1 (1979): 110–34. For a full English translation of his writings, and discussion, see Norman Golb, "The Autograph Memoirs of Obadiah the Proselyte of Oppido Lucano and the Epistle of Barukh b. Isaac of Aleppo" (prepared for the Convegno Internazionale di Studi Giovanni-Obadiah da Oppido: Proselito, viaggiatore e musicista dell'età normanna), accessed June 27, 2017, https://oi.uchicago.edu/sites/oi.uchicago.edu/files/uploads/shared/docs/autograph_memoirs_obadiah.pdf.

origin: the aforementioned "Cairene proselyte," and another anonymous convert mentioned among other needy persons "from Rum," that is either from Byzantium or from Western Europe.[19] The situation is not much different with the converts who are mentioned by name: most of the documents betray not a single detail of their previous lives. The few documents that do leave a lot to be desired: a certain "Rachel, the *Rūmī* proselyte," writes how "my husband, Joseph from Barcelona, took me from my land and brought me to Alexandria." Why was she taken? Did she convert to marry him? When did the conversion take place? Can we assume that she was originally Christian? All these details remain obscure, like in several similar documents.

The lives of the vast majority of Genizah converts to Judaism remain hidden. For some of them, we know their previous religion, like in the above-quoted letter discussing the convert who fled to Damascus. Yet even such a document is exceptional in its detailing of the previous religion and some of the religious claims made by the convert against his former coreligionists. Similar documents, even when discussing the convert's previous life briefly, remain silent as to his former religion. Such is the case in the letter from Atfiḥ discussed above: although the woman is still not Jewish, not a single word hints at her current identity. A letter of recommendation from the first third of the thirteenth century, which describes the conversion of "Mevorakh, the righteous proselyte," fails to mention the religion he converted from. Another letter, for a woman who married a Jewish man in Narbonne, southern France, also does not hint at her former religion, though it is clear that she was probably originally Christian. In fact, even the letter of recommendation given to Obadiah, the Norman proselyte, says nothing about his geographic or religious origin. If we had only this letter, and not Obadiah's other compositions, we would not be able to say anything about his identity, besides being a convert to Judaism from an unknown religion.

All these missing details give the impression that the various writers of these documents did not see much importance in documenting the converts' previous lives, and even sought to suppress and erase them. Such erasure is compatible with classic Jewish, and other, religious attitudes towards conversion, which see the neophyte as a new-born: his previous identity is gone, dead, and so his previous name, background, original identity, and even reasons for

19 For "Rūm" as referring vaguely to Christian Europe, see Goitein, *Mediterranean Society,* 1:43–4.

conversion are of negligible importance. All that counts is his current status as a convert.[20]

Integration into Jewish society

Once converted to Judaism, from whatever religion and background, how and to what extent were converts integrated into Jewish society? As far as our limited sources can show us, it seems that there was no clear social obstacle in the way of converts' integration. Genizah documents testify to marriages of converts of both sexes to born-Jews.[21] Converts adopt Hebrew, mostly biblical, names. Several converts are known to us from surviving manuscripts of Jewish literature they copied, from prayer books to poems by R. Judah ha-Levi.[22] Converts are to be found both in Fusṭāṭ, the capital, with its developed charity system, and in various smaller towns in the provinces.[23]

Regarding economic activity, the appearance of converts in charity lists show that at least some of them were destitute, though it is not known whether their conversion led to their financial fall, or the other way around, or perhaps there was no connection between the two. In any case, it is clear that there is no necessary link between conversion and poverty: converts are to be found also in lists of donors to charity, and other documents show that some converts were quite successful in their financial activities.[24] From a different direction, the charity lists show that conversion in itself did not merit the convert with special support: converts were given more or less the average of other needy persons on these lists.[25]

---

20 On this concept see discussion and further references in Avi Sagi and Zvi Zohar, *Transforming Identity: The Ritual Transformation from Gentile to Jew—Structure and Meaning* (New York: Continuum, 2007), 271–83.

21 For example, Obadiah b. Eleazar marries "Mubāraka, daughter of Abraham, a proselyte"—CUL T-S K 25.166. And see a bill of divorce dated 1153 CE from "Menashe, the proselyte" to his wife in Fusṭāṭ—CUL T-S 10J2.26. Both documents are yet unpublished.

22 "Abraham, the little proselyte" copied poems by Judah ha-Levi—JTS ENA 2229.5. "Joseph, the righteous proselyte" dealt in Torah books in the town of Malij—CUL T-S 8J36.5. Obadiah, the Norman proselyte discussed above, copied a prayer book, and composed a Hebrew hymn, see Golb, "Obadiah."

23 See Goitein, *Mediterranean Society*, 2:307–8.

24 On the issue of the economic status of proselytes, see Moshe Yagur, "The Donor and the Gravedigger: Converts to Judaism in the Cairo Geniza Documents," in *Contesting Inter-Religious Conversion in the Medieval World*, ed. Yaniv Fox and Yosi Yisraeli (London and New York: Routledge, 2017), 115–35.

25 In general, it is hard to find a clear hierarchy or logic of precedence in charity lists, see Cohen, *Poverty*, 233–5.

This is not to say that integration of converts was always smooth, and that there was no opposition to the act of conversion, and suspicion towards converts.[26] Ambivalent attitudes towards converts and the concept of conversion are discernible in the classical rabbinic compositions of late antiquity, even to the degree of the Talmudic saying "Proselytes are as hard to Israel as a scab is to the skin."[27] Based on rabbinic notions and concepts, we find a responsum of the eleventh-century *ga'on* Solomon b. Judah, refuting an unspecified claim made against a woman convert, that she "married for the sake of a certain man."[28] The *ga'on* ruled, in concordance with rabbinic law, that the motives of the convert are irrelevant once conversion is complete.[29] Another Genizah fragment of an unknown responsum, this time of the Babylonian *ga'on* R. Hayya, discusses the status of "someone who is from the Gibeonites," whether he is allowed to function as a cantor for the community.[30] The biblical Gibeonites contracted a peace treaty with Joshua under false pretense, and hence in rabbinic thought they are perceived as untrustworthy proselytes, who should not be permitted to "join the community."[31] Clearly, then, the questioner who marked someone as "a Gibeonite" meant that he is from a faulty lineage, or maybe an unworthy convert, who should not be integrated. In his response R. Hayya admits that if the person is indeed "a Gibeonite" then he should not join the community, but that such allegation should first be proven beyond doubt, and that cursed is he who besmears ordinary folks without justification.

Conversion was, therefore, sometimes a cause for deliberation—was the conversion initiated for the "right" reasons? Was the convert from a legitimate lineage, or rather, could a Jewish rival in an internal query besmirch him as a

26 On philosophical-theological debates regarding the possibility of conversion, see David Sklare, "Are the Gentiles Obligated to Observe the Torah? The Discussion concerning the Universality of the Torah in the East in the Tenth and Eleventh Centuries," in *Be'erot Yitzhak: Studies in Memory of Isadore Twersky*, ed. J. M. Harris (Cambridge, MA: Harvard University Press, Center for Jewish Studies, 2005), 311–46.

27 *bYevamot* 47b, and other places. See thorough discussion in Moshe Lavee, "'Proselytes Are as Hard to Israel as a Scab is to the Skin': A Babylonian Talmudic Concept," *JJS* 53 (2012): 22–48.

28 CUL T-S G 2.66, published by Mordechai Akiva Friedman, *Jewish Polygyny in the Middle Ages* (Jerusalem: Bialik Institute, 1986), 332–5 [in Hebrew].

29 See quotes in discussion in Menachem Finkelstein, *Conversion:* Halakhah *and Practice* (Ramat-Gan: Bar-Ilan University Press, 2006), 221–6.

30 CUL T-S NS 90.2, published in Mordechai Akiva Friedman, "Responsa of Hai Ga'on—New Fragments from the Genizah," *Te'uda* 3 (1983): 75–81 [in Hebrew].

31 Joshua 9. On the Gibeonites being forbidden in marriage, see *mQiddushin* 4:1; and see *Halakhot Gedolot*, vol. 2, ed. Azriel Hildesheimer (Jerusalem: Mekize Nirdamim, 1972), 523.

"non-legitimate" convert? A similar accusation was lodged against one of the greatest Jewish figures of the Muslim Middle Ages—R. Saʿadia Gaʾon, who hailed from Egypt and rose to glory in the academies of tenth-century Iraq. In two subsequent fierce conflicts he had with other prominent Jewish leaders and institutions—the Palestinian academy in Tiberias and the exilarch in Baghdad—he was faced with strong opposition to his lineage, which, he claimed, was from the House of David.[32] The Palestinian *gaʾon* wrote that "it was testified [. . .] beyond doubt [. . .] that his father was 'striking a hammer' for idolatrous worship in Egypt, and ate non-kosher food, and was kicked out of Egypt." "Striking a hammer" was interpreted as referring to sounding the *nāqūs* before the Christian prayer, however, it probably alludes to a halakhic term meaning that he was producing items for idolatry. Be that as it may, the accusation is clear and harsh.[33] The *gaʾon* refers to Saʿadia elsewhere as "an Egyptian" and "a Canaanite."[34] A Babylonian competitor of Saʿadia used these allegations later, and reminded his readers that "many have testified [. . .] that he is the son of proselytes [and his forefathers have circum]cised and immersed." This same writer calls Saʿadia "a fool, wicked, rude, stranger, foreigner [. . .]. He is as low as his fathers [. . .]. They say that he is the son of proselytes."[35] All these quotes seem to indicate that at least in the minds of their writers, and perhaps also that of their readers, descent from proselytes was a shameful biographical detail. However, one should remember that a significant part of this conflict was about lineage, superiority, and authority, so the claims regarding Saʿadia's origin might had more to do with these questions than with the integrity and integration of converts.

A series of answers by Maimonides to queries sent to him by Obadiah the Proselyte (not to be confused with his earlier Norman namesake), is yet further testimony to the deliberations of converts and others regarding their

32 See discussion on these controversies in the context of lineage importance in the Jewish communities of medieval Islam in Arnold E. Franklin, *This Noble House: Jewish Descendants of King David in the Medieval Islamic East* (Philadelphia: University of Pennsylvania Press, 2013), 108–11.

33 Moshe Gil, *Jews in Islamic Countries in the Middle Ages* (Leiden and Boston: Brill, 2004), 348. For the new interpretation see Yagur, "Boundaries," 67.

34 CUL T-S 13K2(4r) + OX Bodl MS Heb d74.30r, published by A. Guillaume, "Further Documents on the Ben Meir Controversy," *JQR* N.S 5 (1914–15): 543–7.

35 Abraham E. Harkavy, *Zikkaron la-Rishonim*, vol. 5 (St. Petersburg: Mekize Nirdamim, 1891), 229, 233.

religious status.[36] Obadiah wishes to know if he can recite the Jewish blessings and mention "our fathers," or "you delivered us out of Egypt," even though he himself is not a biological descendant of the Patriarchs. In another query he wonders whether Islam is considered idolatry, and reports to Maimonides that his Jewish teacher insulted him when Obadiah claimed that Islam is not idolatrous. Maimonides goes a long way to prove that Obadiah should say the blessings like any other born-Jew, since he is the ideological, if not biological, descendant of Abraham, the first monotheist and convert. This Maimonides does against the Mishnah, but in concordance with the Palestinian Talmud, and contrary to some of his European contemporaries.[37]

Taking a step back in order to look at the larger picture, the quoted queries point to some tensions towards converts and conversion, based on earlier ambivalent attitudes in rabbinic literature. However, considering the vast majority of evidence concerning converts, it seems that they were integrated quite successfully in Jewish society. There is no testimony for ongoing identification as "descendant of converts" for more than one generation after the conversion. One should also take into account that all examples are taken from the legal genre of responsa, and not from other documents of daily life, and also that all of the respondents went out of their way to fend off suspicion and embrace converts.

Integration of manumitted slaves

Legal and social background

In medieval Egypt, as in many other societies, enslavement was legal and acceptable, and this applied also to Jewish society.[38] Jews purchased, sold, and bequeathed slaves to each other, like their Muslim and Christian neighbors. However, in Jewish law slavery was intrinsically connected with religious conversion, unlike in Muslim and Christian law. According to the normative-prescriptive legal literature, from the Mishnah forward,

36 Maimonides, *Responsa*, vol. 2, ed. and trans. Joshua Blau (Jerusalem: Mekize Nirdamim, 1986), nos. 293, 436, 448.

37 For the halakhic discussion in its European context see Rami Reiner, "A Proselyte—Is He Really Your Brother? The Issue of Proselytes' Status in Jewish Communities of Ashkenaz and Zarfat in the 11th–13th Centuries," in *Ta-Shema: Studies in Judaica in Memory of Israel M. Ta-Shema*, vol. 2, ed. Avraham Reiner et al. (Alon Shevut: Tevunot Press, 2012), 747–69.

38 See Goitein, *Mediterranean Society*, 1:130–47. See recently and thoroughly in Craig Perry, "The Daily Life of Slaves and the Global Reach of Slavery in Medieval Egypt, 969–1250 CE" (PhD diss., Emory University, 2014).

non-Jewish slaves had to be immersed in a ritual bath upon purchase, male slaves had to be circumcised beforehand, and following this rite they were obligated in the same commandments as a free Jewish woman, including, for example, observing the Sabbath and eating kosher food.[39] However, they were not considered Jews, and could not marry Jews, until they were manumitted by their Jewish owners, received their bill of manumission, and immersed once again. Their liminal status is captured in the Talmudic dictum, paraphrased by Maimonides in his *Code*: "they are not gentiles any more, but are not yet Israelites."[40]

Genizah documents demonstrate clearly that the concept of enslavement and manumission as a prolonged conversion process was alive and kicking in Fatimid and Ayyubid Egypt. Bills of manumission, bearing exact dates and the names of the owners and the freed persons, testify to the permission granted to these people "to join the community of Israel, to change your name in Israel," and to male freed persons, also "to study Torah, and have your son study Torah."[41] Other documents indicate the ongoing activity of freed persons within the Jewish community, marrying or divorcing free-born Jews of both sexes, forming financial partnerships, writing letters, receiving and giving charity, and so forth. From the Jewish legal point of view, then, these freed persons were exactly like any other convert to Judaism.

The unique social standing of freed persons

Notwithstanding their legal definition, it seems that in Egyptian Jewish society there was a distinction between a "proselyte," *ger*, that is, a convert to Judaism who was free, and a "manumitted person," *meshuḥrar*, that is, an enslaved person who was manumitted and thus converted to Judaism. First, the mere fact that there were two distinct terms in use for converts and for freed persons shows that these were two distinct populations in the minds of Egyptian Jews. Second, attention should be given to the passive tone of the Hebrew term, *meshuḥrar*, as well as to its Arabic equivalents *ʿatīq*, *ʿataqa*, and its Judaeo-Arabic unique synonym *maʿtūq*. The passivity implied in these terms can be contrasted with the activity, indeed religious heroism, in many of the Genizah documents

39 On halakha regarding the religious identity of slaves see generally Finkelstein, *Conversion*, 108–48.

40 Maimonides, *Mishneh Torah*, Book of Holiness, Law of Illicit Intercourse, 12:11. Based on the Talmudic rule in *bSanhedrin* 58b.

41 For an exemplary English translation of one such bill, see Goitein, *Mediterranean Society*, 5:150 (CUL T-S 8J12.2).

describing proselytes. Third, in quite a number of cases the freed person is described as "So-and-so's freedman/woman." A query sent from the Delta town of Minyat Ghamr to Abraham Maimonides discusses the inheritance of "a freed woman who belongs to the Elder *el-hadar* She᾽erit."[42] In a court deposition from Fusṭāṭ, concerning a debt, one of the parties was "Mubārak, the manumitted of Joseph b. Josiah."[43] The court scribe even wrote that Mubārak was the *mawlā* ("client") of the said Joseph, but then erased this word. The use of the term *mawlā*, with its Islamic legal and cultural implications, is telling.[44] This term appears in other documents, written even by the freed persons themselves, like two letters sent from "Faraj, the *mawlā* of Barhūn," to Joseph Ibn ʿAwkal, one of the great Jewish merchants of early eleventh-century Egypt.[45]

In short, the manumitted slaves were considered part of the extended household of their former owners. They were "their" manumitted persons, they were not "proselytes," although as said, they could—and did—marry Jews, be a part of the community, and participate in its activities. The former owners still had interest in "their" manumitted slaves—some of them record in their wills sums of money, dwelling rights and other assets, which they bequeath to "their" freed person. Others tried to take care of their future and organize a Jewish marriage for them.[46] Still others took the liberty of taking a share in their freed person's estate.[47] In all this, the owners act in disagreement with the requirement of normative halakhic literature, as reflected in the language of the bills of manumission themselves, which emphasize that the former owner or his heirs have no claim whatsoever over the freed person, who is free to do whatever he

42 CUL T-S 8J16.4, published by Shimon Shtober, "Questions Posed to R. Abraham b. Maimonides," *Shenaton ha-Mishpat ha-ʿIvri* 14–15 (1988–9): 262–8 [in Hebrew].

43 CUL T-S 20.47.

44 On *mawālī* in Islamic law and culture, see Ulrike Mitter, "Origin and Development of the Islamic Patronate," in *Patronate and Patronage in Early and Classical Islam*, ed. M. Bernards and J. Nawas (Leiden and Boston: Brill, 2005), 70–80. And see also the classical study of Patricia Crone, *Roman, Provincial and Islamic Law* (Cambridge: Cambridge University Press, 1987), 35–8.

45 CUL T-S 8.12, published in Moshe Gil, *In the Kingdom of Ishmael*, vol. 2 (Jerusalem and Tel Aviv: Bialik Institute and Tel Aviv University Press, 1997), text no. 166 (the next one is also by the same *mawlā*) [in Hebrew]. An English translation was published by S. D. Goitein, *Letters of Medieval Jewish Traders* (Princeton, NJ: Princeton University Press, 1973), 82–4.

46 For wills granting property to manumitted slaves see, for example, CUL T-S 13J22.2, and see a recent discussion in both phenomena in Perry, "Daily Lives," 69–75.

47 See the document in note 42 above.

so wishes. But in so doing, the owners were in perfect agreement with Muslim law and with the common norms of the society surrounding them.[48]

"Sociological conversion" of un-manumitted slaves

The legal path towards conversion of slaves to Judaism started, as noted above, with their immersion and circumcision at the beginning of slavery (for which we do not have any evidence in the Genizah documents), and ended with their manumission ceremony and the granting of a formal bill of manumission, the likes of which were found in the Genizah. Some legal authorities, such as Maimonides, deemed it necessary that the manumitted person immerse once again in a ritual bath. Indeed, one of the bills of manumission, from the time of Maimonides and signed by one of the judges in his court, documents the immersion of a freed slave woman "in the Babylonian synagogue" in Fusṭāṭ.[49]

However, Genizah documents and contemporary responsa by Moses Maimonides and his son, Abraham Maimonides, reveal a different, disputed but ultimately useful path into Jewish community and identity: forming conjugal relations, and even family units, between Jewish male owners and their non-Jewish female slaves. Sexual exploitation was a common feature of the lives of slaves, in medieval Egypt as in other places. Egyptian Jewish society was no exception to this sad reality, as Genizah documents show. However, according to Jewish law such relations were forbidden, and if they did happen, the normative legal literature prescribed the selling of the female slave and the flogging of the owner. Additionally, the matrilineal principle prevalent in Judaism, which considers only children born to a Jewish mother as Jewish themselves, was applicable also in the case of children born to slaves. That is, if an owner cohabited with his female slave illegally, and she bore him a son, this child could not be considered the owner's son, or a Jewish boy at all, but was regarded as a non-Jewish slave.

The confluence of these three factors—the use of female slaves as concubines, the matrilineal principle, and the legal concept of manumission as conversion—resulted not infrequently in the manumission, conversion, and

48 For a general survey of Muslim law regarding slaves and freed persons, see Shaun E. Marmon, "Domestic Slavery in the Mamluk Empire: A Preliminary Sketch," in *Slavery in the Islamic Middle East*, ed. S. E. Marmon (Princeton, NJ: Markus Wiener, 1999), 1–23. And see also Bernard Lewis, *Race and Slavery in the Middle East* (New York: Oxford University Press, 1990), 5–9.

49 CUL T-S 12.872, not discussed before. Edited in Yagur, "Boundaries."

marriage of female slaves to male Jews, mostly their former owners. The best example for such a trend is to be found in a responsum of Maimonides, regarding "a bachelor who purchased a beautiful female slave, and he cohabits with her in the same house . . . and the whole city gossiped about him." Maimonides's response reveals the legal and social logic of the leadership in light of such challenges:

> And the court, in light of such bad news, should coerce him to sell her, or to manumit and marry her, although this is somewhat forbidden, since "he who was suspected regarding a female slave, and she was later manumitted"[50] should not marry her. But we have ruled in several similar cases that he should manumit and marry her. And we did so to enable repentance, for we have said "it is better that he should eat the gravy, than the actual forbidden fat" . . . and God Almighty shall amend our corrupted situation.[51]

The prevalence of marriage with former slaves, and its intimate connection with pre-marital sexual relations, or suspicion concerning such possible relations, is also visible in a torn court record of the "high court of our lord, rabbi and master, the great Exilarch, the head of all diasporas, David b. Daniel," which in a session convened in December 1093 tried to confirm or disprove the Jewish identity of Milāḥ, the daughter of the merchant Eli b. Japheth.[52] Eli declared that he had bought a Nubian slave named Akhtara in the city of Ashkelon, who had a daughter at the time. Later the said daughter died, and Eli manumitted Akhtara, married her, and she bore him another daughter, Milāḥ. If Eli's story is correct, then this Milāḥ was a legitimate Jewish daughter, eligible for Jewish marriage. Eli brought with him two witnesses from Ashkelon, who corroborated his story. Yet the court continued to interrogate them: "Do you happen to know how much time elapsed between her marr[iage] . . . so that her conception and birth will both be holy," that is, are the witnesses sure that the slave was not already pregnant from her owner Eli at the time of manumission and marriage. To this, the witnesses responded: "We do not know." The court, so it seems, had reason to suspect that Milāḥ was conceived prior to manumission, and maybe was the cause of manumission and marriage. Eli, for his part,

---

50 A quote from *mYevamot* 2:8.

51 Maimonides, *Responsa*, vol. 2, no. 211.

52 CUL T-S Misc. 27.4.23+29, published in Friedman, *Polygyny*, 314–19.

knew that his daughter's identity was debated, and that he had better arrange for sympathetic witnesses from Ashkelon.

The previous examples indicate a reality of post-factum manumission and conversion of slaves, that is, the communal leadership or rabbinic authority gave its permission and rehabilitated the intimate relations that already existed. In this way, rabbinic authority was restored by fitting the social reality into the legal concepts of manumission and conversion. Other examples suggest that in some cases even this "post-factum conversion" was not deemed necessary by the Jewish owners or their friends and family members. In such cases, it is clear from the behavior of the litigants, or the phrasing of the questioners, that they believed the formal rite of conversion, or bill of manumission, was superfluous in light of conjugal relations, marriages, and even children that were already present. Such is probably the case known from a fragmentary responsum written in the hand of one of the judges in Maimonides's court, concerning a case of a man who married a woman, but the congregation insisted that this woman was the slave of another man, so she needed a bill of manumission first. The alleged owner denied her being his slave, and declared "she was not my slave, and she became Jewish out of her own free will," and the prospective groom said he would refuse to marry her if she received a bill of manumission.[53]

Another complicated case, elaborated in a responsum of Maimonides, concerns "a man who married a slave woman," his own slave, and later adopted her daughters, without ever granting them a bill of manumission, but instead "he saw fit to attribute the girls to himself, and he declared them as his heirs according to Jewish and Muslim law, and issued court deeds in this matter."[54] To make a prolonged legal disputation short—after many years, claims of forgery, several lawsuits in Jewish and Muslim courts, and confiscation of property, the case was brought before Maimonides in a query. By that time, one of the daughters was already married to a Jewish man, and had borne his children, while formally speaking, at least according to the query, she was still half-slave, and hence half-Jewish, and so were her children. Maimonides ruled that unless new, unbiased witnesses were presented, this daughter's status should be considered free, and hence Jewish, as well as her children. By so ruling, Maimonides in practice "manumitted," and converted, the slave mother, her daughter, and the grandchildren.

---

53 CUL T-S Ar. 48.88, published in Friedman, *Polygyny*, 309–14.

54 Maimonides, *Responsa*, vol. 1, no. 106.

This case, as well as several others, some of them described above, are the remnants of a "sociological" conversion, one in which daily interaction, social bonding, and the forming of family units mattered more than court sessions, rabbinic procedures, and the written law. The meaning of the data discussed in this section is that there were in fact several parallel paths of conversion and integration into the Jewish community of medieval Egypt. One was the formal, "normal" religious conversion, described in legal terms and within a theological framework. The other path was the prolonged, fuzzy, social rather than ideological process of conversion, which was the lot of quite a few male and female slaves under Jewish ownership. The second path can also be divided to two options: in the first, this sociological conversion, affected by legal, economical, and personal factors, was molded into the legal language of manumission and conversion. In the second, more elusive option, the facts-on-the-ground of sociological conversion and integration *replaced* legal manumission and conversion, and the result was family units that consisted of Jewish men (often slave-owners), ex-slave women, and their children.

Conversion from Judaism

Some Jews in medieval Egypt chose to convert to other religions. As in other times and places until the modern period, we have no way to quantify how many Jews converted, or what was their percentage out of the total number of Jews. Jewish converts to other religions appear quite infrequently in Arab literature from the period, and are mostly mentioned only in passing. Therefore, our main sources are Jewish ones, and so they give us mainly their Jewish writers' points of view.

As explained in the first section of this article, under Islam conversion was allowed not only to Islam, but also between minority religions, for example from Judaism to Christianity and vice versa. Indeed, we know of a few Jewish converts to Christianity in medieval Egypt. One of them, Abū al-Fakhr Ibn Azhar, is mentioned in two Coptic historiographical compositions from the thirteenth century, and is reported to have converted to Coptic Christianity in the third quarter of the twelfth century.[55] Abū al-Fakhr is said to have been a highly educated Jewish dignitary, who mastered the Coptic language and Christian teachings after his conversion, and polemicized with the Jews. A treatise

55 See Ibn Al-Mukaffa, *History of the Patriarchs*, vol. 2, pt. 1, 53. He is also mentioned in B. T. A Evetts (ed. and trans.), *Churches and Monasteries of Egypt and Some Neighbouring Countries, Attributed to Abu Salih, the Armenian* (Oxford: Clarendon Press, 1895), 44b–45a.

containing epistles of "the Jew Abū al-Fakhr al-Masīḥī, who converted to Christianity" has survived in manuscript form.[56]

Jews who converted to other religions are mentioned using a variety of terms in contemporary Jewish literature: sometimes they are called *meshūmad,* the classic rabbinic term, probably meaning "annihilated."[57] A common term in Genizah documents and other compositions is *poshe ʿa,* Hebrew for "criminal," which also became a verb in Judaeo-Arabic meaning "to apostatize."[58] Other terms and nicknames are "went out of the community" (literally: "out of the rule," "out of the circle"), "out of the religion" (*kharaja ʿan al-dat, kharaja al-dīn, kharaja al-madhhab*) and others.[59] This richness in terms, combined with the varying and contradictory legal attitudes towards such converts, hint at the many facets of conversion "out of" Judaism. The mere definition of conversion as going "out of" Judaism should be questioned, since according to the dominant view in Jewish legal literature, these converts never really "left," and did not change their legal status in a significant way. In what follows we will demonstrate that this was also the prevalent notion reflected in the Genizah documents and in contemporary responsa.

Portrayal of Jewish converts in Genizah documents

Jewish converts, or "criminals," are mentioned in quite a few contemporary Jewish sources. In some of them they are engaged in commercial activity with other Jews, such as in a query to Abraham Maimonides regarding the permissibility of a convert producing wine for Jews.[60] In a private family letter, a

56 MS BNF Arabe 172, fol. 90–167. The quote is from the opening statement of the composition, fol. 90.

57 See briefly Solomon Zeitlin, "Mumar and Meshumad," *JQR* 54 (1963): 84–6. And see recently Mordekhai Arad, *Sabbath Desecrator with* Parresia: *A Talmudic Legal Term and its Historic Context* (New York and Jerusalem: The Jewish Theological Seminary of America, 2009), 238–52.

58 See Goitein, *Mediterranean Society,* 2: 300–1. And see also in Joshua Blau, *A Dictionary of Medieval Judaeo-Arabic Texts* (Jerusalem: The Academy of the Hebrew Language and Israel Academy of Sciences and Humanities, 2006), 504 (فشع).

59 For further discussion and references see Yagur, "Boundaries," chapter 3.2.

60 Abraham Maimonides, *Responsa,* ed. and trans. A. H. Freimann and S. D. Goitein (Jerusalem: Mekize Nirdamim, 1937), no. 56.

"redhead 'criminal'" is transmitting news about family members.[61] A "criminal" is even mentioned offhand as "testifying" as part of a communal dispute.[62]

In these cases, as well as in others, the converts are described in neutral terms, and in fact, besides the varied terms for "apostate," not a single curse is attached to them.[63] This is also true in a pair of appeals to Jewish dignitaries in two different cases, where converts are described in a negative context, as harassing the writers. In one of them, a Jewish weaver complains that another weaver, a "criminal weaver," working with him and with other Muslims in the same workshop, is harassing him. The writer wishes the addressee to persuade the Jewish owner of the workshop to release him from working there, since the writer still owes the latter money.[64] In the second case, a tax collector is complaining against a group of men from Tyre who are trying to take over his job, and one of them is "a criminal."[65] One should note that despite the negative content of the appeals, no curses or excessively negative terms are applied to the converts, and between the lines we actually learn about a social situation of continuing cooperation and mutual existence of Jews and converts.

The single case known so far in which harsh negative terms are applied to converts is the case of Ben al-Baṣri, a Jew-cum-Muslim who claimed that R. Judah ha-Levi tried to persuade him in Alexandria to sail with him to Frankish Palestine, where he should convert back to Judaism, and then would be given a large sum of money sent to him from his brother in al-Andalus.[66] Ben al-Baṣri is called "a mad dog [. . .] a gutter."[67] However, these terms are used only because Ben al-Baṣri complained against the famous rabbi and almost brought harm to him. Before this incident, it seems that Ben al-Baṣri and the Jewish community conducted business as usual, as can be learned from the fact that his brother

---

61 CUL Or 1080 J 113, mentioned in Goitein, *Mediterranean Society*, 2:301.

62 CUL T-S 16.272, published in Miriam Frenkel, *"The Compassionate and the Benevolent": The Leading Elite in the Jewish Community of Alexandria in the Middle Ages* (Jerusalem: Ben Zvi Institute, 2006), 351–8 [in Hebrew].

63 Goitein, *Mediterranean Society*, 2:302.

64 CUL T-S NS J 277.

65 CUL T-S 13J14.14.

66 See the recent discussion in this incident in S. D. Goitein and Mordechai Akiva Friedman, *Ḥalfon the Traveling Merchant Scholar: Cairo Genizah Documents*, vol. 1 (Jerusalem: Ben Zvi Institute, 2013), 320–29 [in Hebrew].

67 Two Genizah letters discuss this incident: CUL T-S 13J14.1, last published in Goitein and Friedman, *Halfon*, no. 81; CUL Or 1080 J 258, last published in Frenkel, *"Compassionate,"* 640–5.

sent him money, and that the writer says that al-Baṣri is known to Jews in Fusṭāṭ and Damietta.

The converts were intimately familiar to the writers of these Genizah documents, as can be learned from the fact that they are mentioned mostly by their personal name or nickname, such as "Ghālib the criminal" or "Abū ʿImrān" or "the redhead criminal," and the like. It is worth pointing out that almost no letter, or legal query, hints at the religion to which the "criminal" converted. This might be a supplementary phenomenon to the one discussed above, of the total silence regarding Jewish proselytes' previous lives and religious identity. In both cases, the details of a religious identity that was not Jewish are seen as unimportant, and so are neglected or even suppressed. Needless to say, the motives of the actual converts are nowhere discussed. Even more so, even in the few instances of sources discussing forced conversion of Jews to Islam, in twelfth-century Yemen and the Maghreb, the writers use the same spectrum of terms—"criminals," "went out of the community"—regardless of their personal view on the events.[68]

Threats and accusations of conversion

A significant phenomenon in Genizah society, according to our documents, was the accusation that someone, or members of his family, had converted to another religion, or, on the other hand, threats made by members of the community that they would convert, as part of a legal, communal, or financial dispute. These incidents were probably quite common, since more than a third of all the Genizah documents known thus far, which mention "apostates," discuss such potential rather than actual conversions and converts.

Such incidents involved men and women, weak and marginal figures as well as communal leaders. Women who were pressed by the court voiced

68 The most famous Genizah letter describing the coercion in the Maghred is Sasson 713. The section of this letter reporting the events in the Maghreb has been discussed extensively in scholarly literature. See recent discussion and further references in Miriam Frenkel, "Genizah Documents as Literary Products," in *"From a Sacred Source": Genizah Studies in Honour of Professor Stefan C. Reif*, ed. Ben Outhwaite and Siam Bhayro (Leiden and Boston: Brill, 2011), 140–6; Maria Angeles Gallego, "The Calamities that Followed the Death of Joseph Ibn Migash: Jewish Views on the Almohad Conquest," in *Judaeo-Arabic Culture in al-Andalus: 13th Conference of the Society for Judaeo-Arabic Studies, Cordoba 2007*, ed. Amir Ashur (Cordoba: Cordoba Near Eastern Research Unit, 2013), 79–98. For a much less known letter from Yemen, describing coerced conversion there in 1199, see Mosseri IV.7, published in Mordechai Akiva Friedman, *Maimonides, The Yemenite Messiah and Apostasy* (Jerusalem: Ben-Zvi Institute, 2002), 160–7 [in Hebrew].

warnings that they would "turn to bad culture" (*tetze le-tarbut ra'ah*), which in this period was understood as conversion. A Jewish dignitary and public figure from Alexandria confessed in a letter to a colleague that at the peak of a local leadership conflict, "I almost converted (literally: "went out of the *madhhab*") with my family, so my sin shall be on the heads of those who sent these wicked men."[69] A man and his three sons, who were embroiled in a fight with their townsfolk in the district town of Malij, cursed and shouted in the court and threatened to appeal to al-Afḍal, the mighty vizier, and to convert.[70]

Alongside such threats of conversion, in other cases people lodged accusations of conversion against their opponents. No one was immune from such accusations, not even a religious figure, like R. Judah ben Joseph, regularly described in eleventh-century letters as "the great rabbi." When a dispute broke out over the leadership of the Palestinian community in Fusṭāṭ in the middle of the eleventh century, his opponents recruited, so it is reported, dozens of people who testified in court and in writing that he "had converted (lit.: 'committed crimes') in al-Shām, and then went to Egypt in order to Judaize."[71] It seems that this rabbi's supporters did not hesitate to use this very same allegation in response. They accused one of the rabbi's opponents, the Egyptian dignitary Surūr ben Sabra, that "he had converted (lit: 'committed crimes') in the Maghreb, and remained a convert (lit.: 'a criminal') for a few years."[72]

We should pause for a moment to elucidate the social and legal implications of such threats and accusations. Theoretically speaking, from the Islamic legal point of view, if someone had converted to Islam, even only outwardly, and had uttered the *shahāda* in the presence of reliable witnesses, he is to be considered a Muslim. Were the accusers not worried that their accusations, if they reached the Muslim authorities, would cause the actual conversion of community members, including dignitaries and rabbis? On the other hand, is it possible that some people did convert, or were thought by others to have converted, but later chose to "Judaize" and blend again quite comfortably in the elite of Egyptian Jewry, with the Muslim authorities ignorant of or indifferent to the events? One should remember that in order for accusations or threats to

69 CUL T-S 13J23.3, published in Frenkel, *"Compassionate,"* 545–51.

70 CUL T-S 20.93.

71 CUL T-S K 25.244, published by Moshe Gil, *Palestine during the First Muslim Period (634–1099)*, 3 vols. (Tel Aviv: Tel Aviv University and the Ministry of Defense, 1983), vol. 2, no. 399 [in Hebrew].

72 CUL T-S NS J 360, published in Moshe Gil, "Palestine during the First Muslim Period (634–1099): Additions, Notes, Corrigenda," *Te'uda* 7 (1991), no. 449a [in Hebrew].

be effective, they had to be considered reliable or plausible by the community. Can we assume, then, that one could not always know for sure if a person was a convert, a relapsed convert, or perhaps a descendant of converts and apostates?

Returning to the Jewish fold

Some Jews who converted to other religions, in medieval Egypt as well as in other times and places, later decided to return to the Jewish fold. In light of the data discussed above, one can ask whether we are really dealing here with a "return," since bonds and cooperation continued, and the legal definition of the convert was never changed. Indeed, nowhere in our sources is it implied that returning converts encountered much difficulty or suspicion from the Jewish community. This is in sharp contradiction to the social reality and to the legal discussions on this issue in medieval Ashkenazi Judaism.[73] Unlike the European tradition, nowhere in our sources can we detect any specific ceremony for returning to Judaism, or any requirements such as a waiting period or the like.

Some of the returning converts were probably forced converts who had fled the Maghreb, Maimonides probably being the most famous among them. It seems that in their case the act of emigration itself, and settling in a Jewish community in another land, was all that was necessary in order to be considered Jewish again.

The relatively smooth passage from the state of "criminal" back to being a regular member of the community can be learned also from possible cases of the repentance of converts' children. One such possible return is suggested in a Judaeo-Arabic letter written by a father in Jerusalem to his daughter in Egypt. It seems that the mother, the writer's wife, had converted and migrated with her daughter, who was now in dire straits. The father asks his daughter directly: "Who are you with, are you with the Jews, your father's people, or with your mother and the gentiles?"[74] He also details his good economic state, and

73 See the extensive bibliography and new material in the studies of Ephraim Kanarfogel: Ephraim Kanarfogel, "Returning to the Jewish Community in Medieval Ashkenaz: History and Halakhah," in *Turim I: Studies in Jewish History and Literature Presented to Dr. Bernard Lander*, ed. Michael A. Schmidman (New York: Touro College Press, 2007–8), 69–97; idem, "Changing Attitudes towards Apostates in Tosafists Literature, Late Twelfth–Early Thirteenth Centuries," in *New Perspectives on Jewish-Christian Relations*, ed. Elisheva Carlebach and Jacob J. Schacter (Leiden and Boston: Brill, 2012), 297–327.

74 CUL Or 1080 J 21, published in Gil, *Palestine*, vol. 2, no. 293. See English translation and discussion, somewhat outdated, in S. D. Goitein, "Parents and Children: A Geniza Study on

writes that her maternal aunt, that is, the sister of the converted mother, can testify to this. The letter is yet another example of the ongoing ties between converts and their Jewish family members, as well as the matter-of-fact nature of re-conversion in the second generation.

This can also be learned from a query sent to Abraham Maimonides, asking whether a man can have sexual intercourse with a convert woman who is married, according to Muslim law, to another convert. The questioner then proceeds to ask about the identity of potential children born out of such a bond. Abraham Maimonides replies that this woman is not considered married, so such a relationship is not considered adultery per se. "Regarding the children," he continues, "their lineage is 'kosher' . . . and as for their religion, this [will be defined] according to their observance of it, or their abandonment of it."[75] Clearly, then, there is no obstacle in the second generation's way back to Judaism, and it seems that they can choose and shape their religious identity freely.

Conclusions: contested identities and ever-changing boundaries

A comparison of the issues and examples briefly discussed throughout this chapter leads to several general conclusions. The first is about directions. A previous perception of Jewish identity and conversion under Islam portrayed it as movement in two opposite directions: in one direction, proselytes who converted *to Judaism* were European Christians who fled to Muslim lands in order to become Jewish; in the opposite direction, Jews who converted *to Islam* joined the majority and rarely looked back.[76] This chapter has shown that in fact the movement across religious boundaries was varied, overlapping, and not necessarily without return. Converts to Judaism were not necessarily European, and not necessarily even Christians. Jews converted not only to Islam but also to Christianity. Converts to Judaism were not only free-born people who had decided to embrace Judaism, but also enslaved men and women who were purchased by Jews, and went through a prolonged religious-social process of integration and adhesion. All of these different cases of conversion overlapped and

the Medieval Jewish Family," *Gratz College Annual of Jewish Studies* 4 (1975): 55–57.

75 Abraham Maimonides, *Responsa*, no. 57.

76 For descriptions of converts as "bridge burners," see, for example, Gerald J. Blidstein, "Who is not a Jew?—The Medieval Discussion," *Israel Law Review* 11 (1976): 376; Maya Shatzmiller, "Marriage, Family, and the Faith: Women's Conversion to Islam," *Journal of Family History* 21 (1996): 257.

even interacted, like in the letter with which we began, where a manumitted slave and an "apostate" are brothers-in-law.

A second conclusion is about contacts. Our sources show that there were ongoing contacts, on various levels, between Jewish converts and their families and communities. This is true also in the other direction, of people who converted to Judaism, once we understand that not all of these converts were European, but some were local. Contacts could have been kept on a "practical" level, as in business initiatives or dwelling in shared courtyards. They could have also been on a personal and even intimate level, as in cases of Jews who remained married to their convert spouses, or even married converts. A similar phenomenon is the formation of relationships and family ties between Jewish men and their non-manumitted, not-converted female slaves. Contacts could also mean polemics, as in the case of Abū al-Fakhr, the convert to Christianity who polemicized with a fellow Jew, or the anonymous Jewish proselyte who fled to Egypt after polemicizing and quarreling with his family and the townspeople in Damascus. Sometime contacts could even mean religious cooperation, as in a query to Abraham Maimonides regarding a couple of converted Jews, who nonetheless are interested in having their son circumcised by Jews, and according to the Jewish tradition.[77]

A third point is about uncertainty. Many of the relevant documents reveal a social reality in which an individual's religious identity was not always clear to community members. This understanding can lead us to significant conclusions about the dress code for non-Muslims in medieval Egypt, and about daily contacts between people from different religions.[78] People might accuse each other of conversion, an accusation that was harsh enough to be voiced in public as part of a conflict, but too vague to be confirmed, or to be refuted successfully. Religious identity could also sometime be molded, or used as a tool. This usually happened under stressful or otherwise unique circumstances: in a legal discussion, a communal dispute, the threat of excommunication, or the like, one could threaten to convert and so use one's religious identity as a final "wild card" against one's opponents. Slavery was also one of these situations where one's identity was erased and molded, not only by slave-traders and slaveholders, but also, occasionally, by the slaves themselves. Migration was yet

77 Abraham Maimonides, *Responsa*, no. 53.

78 On the absence of Genizah evidence for distinctive dress for non-Muslims, see Goitein, *Mediterranean Society*, 2:285–88.

another human condition in which one could chose, shape, or reinvent one's religious identity in a new location.

To conclude, religious identity and communal boundaries were much more varied, much more porous, indeed, much more interesting, than one might initially think. A good way to understand this is by noting the variety of terms assigned to the act of conversion and to the actors, the converts themselves. The sources themselves are inconsistent in their use of different terms and verbs, and the modern scholar is likewise bewildered by the phenomenon under scrutiny. Are we talking about religion? About theology and law? About society and family? About money and social status? Is this more about self-identification or about communal integration? The best way to "solve" these problems is to acknowledge their importance, and their role in the lives of the people and communities discussed in this chapter and in the entire volume. Perhaps the best working assumption might be that several social circles of identification were simultaneously meaningful for each person.[79]

79 See the conclusion of Uriel Simonsohn, *A Common Justice: The Legal Allegiances of Christians and Jews under Early Islam* (Philadelphia: University of Pennsylvania Press, 2011), 214.

4

Communal Self-Government: The Genizah Period[1]

MARK R. COHEN

In theory, the non-Muslim religious minorities were subject to the authority of Islam, expressed by the phrase *ilzām ḥukm al-islām ʿalayhim*, "subjection to the authority [or: law] of Islam."[2] In practice, however, the minorities enjoyed a large measure of communal autonomy, and were allowed to govern themselves in accordance with their ancestral laws. In the case of the Jews, these ancestral practices were enshrined in the Talmud. They included, among other things, ritual practice, moral conduct, social welfare, and, perhaps most importantly, adjudication in Jewish courts according to Jewish law. While the Muslim ruler reserved for himself the prerogative to appoint the leaders of the Jewish (as well as the Christian) community, in practice it was the Jews themselves who selected the candidate they preferred and petitioned the Muslim authority to approve their choice.

The rule of the Palestinian yeshivah

The Genizah sources indicate that, until approximately the last third of the eleventh century, the Jewish community of Egypt was subject to the authority of the Palestinian *yeshivah* and its head, the *gaʾon*. His role in the affairs

1 We know very little about Jewish communal life in Egypt between the Arab conquest in 641 and approximately the beginning of the eleventh century, when we begin to have dated or dateable documents from the Cairo Genizah. Most of what follows is based on the Genizah.

2 Néophyte Edelby, "The Legislative Autonomy of Christians in the Islamic World," in *Muslims and Others in Early Islamic Society*, ed. Robert Hoyland (Aldershot: Aldgate, 2004), 53–8 (17–22).

of Egyptian Jewry probably stemmed from the special relationship between Palestinian Jewry and the Egyptian community in Byzantine times. A petition in Arabic to the Fatimid caliph in the eleventh century, probably around 1036 (a draft found in the Genizah), indicates that the community in Egypt chose a candidate for the Gaonate and submitted their petition to the Fatimid government, which granted him a letter of appointment.[3] The Fatimid decision to support the Palestinian *gaʾon* and his authority over Egyptian Jewry was consistent with the Fatimid strategy of challenging the authority of the Abbasid caliph in Baghdad, who appointed the Exilarch as supreme authority over the Jews of the Abbasid Empire.

The document in question assumes that the Palestinian *gaʾon* (*roʾsh ha-yeshivah* in Hebrew, *raʾs al-mathība* in Arabic) acted as the religious leader of the Rabbanite Jews, expounded religious law in public lectures, supervised marriage and divorce, and monitored the religious and moral conduct of the Rabbanite majority of Jews, including their behavior toward Muslims. He had the right to impose the ban (*ḥerem*) and to appoint or dismiss preachers, cantors, and slaughterers of kosher meat. Moreover, he defined the competence of communal judges and supervised them as well as the trustees of the rabbinical courts.[4] Another document indicates that the Fatimid government supported the *gaʾon*'s authority by paying a stipend to the *yeshivah*, in the same way that it gave financial assistance to Christian religious institutions. The *yeshivah*'s stipend ended sometime in the early part of the eleventh century.[5]

The Palestinian *gaʾon* faced stiff competition from the *yeshivot* and *geʾonim* of Babylonia, many of whose "loyalists" lived in Egypt. The aura of Babylonia even extended to Jews with Palestinian fidelity. While we have thousands of rabbinic responsa from Babylonian *geʾonim*, few exist from their Palestinian counterparts.[6] Solomon b. Judah, the *gaʾon* of the Palestinian *yeshivah* in the

3 The manuscript shelfmark is Halper 354, ed. S. D. Goitein, "New Sources on the Palestinian Gaonate," in *Salo Wittmayer Baron Jubilee Volume*, ed. Saul Lieberman in association with Arthur Hyman (Jerusalem: American Academy for Jewish Research, 1974), English section, 523–25; idem, "The Head of the Palestinian Academy as Head of the Jews in the Fatimid Empire: Arabic Documents on the Palestinian Gaonate," *Eretz-Israel* 10 (1971): 64–75 [in Hebrew]; idem, *Mediterranean Society*, 2:16–17; Moshe Gil, *A History of Palestine, 634–1099*, trans. Ethel Broido (Cambridge: Cambridge University Press, 1992), 508–10.

4 Gil, *Palestine*, 508–27.

5 Ibid., 551.

6 Ibid., 527–39.

second quarter of the eleventh century, had to send his son to Baghdad to complete his rabbinic studies.[7]

It seems that the loosening of the bonds tying Egyptian Jewry to the Palestinian Gaonate almost led to the creation of a new structure of Jewish self-government centered in Egypt during the final decades of the tenth and first quarter of the eleventh centuries. Two Babylonian-educated scholars living in Egypt, Shemarya b. Elḥanan and his son Elḥanan b. Shemarya, introduced practices that nearly undermined the suzerainty of the Gaonate of Jerusalem.[8] With the death of Elḥanan around the year 1025, Egyptian Jewry's groping toward independence from Palestinian control came to a halt. This was during the Gaonate of Solomon b. Judah (1026–51) and that of his successor, Daniel Nasi b. ʿAzarya (1051–62). Significantly, both of these scholars were "outsiders." Solomon hailed from Fez in Morocco and Daniel from Babylonia, where he had studied. The appointment of two outsiders underscores the absence of native Jewish leadership in Palestine at the time. Not surprisingly, the period witnessed political conflict, for instance, when a Palestinian pretender to the Gaonate named Nathan b. Abraham succeeded, with the help of Egyptian Jewish supporters, in establishing a "counter-Gaonate" in Ramla for four years (1038–42).[9]

At the death of Solomon b. Judah in 1051, a family of native Palestinian claimants headed by Elijah ha-Kohen b. Solomon vigorously opposed Daniel b. ʿAzarya's appointment in Solomon's place. Upon Daniel's death in 1062, Elijah ha-Kohen ascended to the Gaonate (1062–83). His period in office was marked by events that weakened the *yeshivah*. Foremost among these was the conquest of Palestine by the Seljuq Turks, which occurred, according to a Genizah document, in 1073. This momentous event resulted a few years later in the transfer of the *yeshivah* to the more secure city of Tyre, a city that had thrown off the

7 Ibid., 528.

8 Mark R. Cohen, "Administrative Relations between Palestinian and Egyptian Jewry during the Fatimid Period," in *Egypt and Palestine: A Millennium of Association (868–1948)*, ed. Amnon Cohen and Gabriel Baer (Jerusalem and New York: Ben Zvi Institute and St. Martin's Press, 1984), 113–35; S. D. Goitein, "Elhanan b. Shemarya as a Communal Leader," in *Joshua Finkel Festschrift*, ed. Sidney B. Hoenig and Leon D. Stitskin (New York: Yeshiva University Press, 1974), Hebrew section, 117–37 [in Hebrew]; Marina Rustow, *Heresy and the Politics of Community: The Jews of the Fatimid Caliphate* (Ithaca and London: Cornell University Press, 2008), 157–62.

9 Mark R. Cohen, "New Light on the Conflict over the Palestinian Gaonate, 1038–1042, and on Daniel b. ʿAzarya: A Pair of Letters to the Nagid of Qayrawan," *AJS (Association for Jewish Studies) Review* 1 (1976): 1–40; Gil, *Palestine*, 691–719.

yoke of Fatimid sovereignty in 1070 and paid tribute to the Seljuqs in return for its independence. By relocating in independent Tyre, the *yeshivah* loosened its ties with both the Fatimid caliphate and Egyptian Jewry.[10]

The Headship of the Jews

During the Palestinian *yeshivah*'s exile in Tyre (and later on, in Damascus), a new office, the office of head of the Jews (*raʾīs al-yahūd*), arose in Egypt and assumed the role that the *gaʾon* of the *yeshivah* had previously played.[11] This coincided with the rise in Egypt of the Armenian general, Badr al-Jamālī, to power as actual ruler of the Fatimid empire (1074–94), and his relocating of the head of the Coptic church in Cairo. The transformation in the Egyptian Jewish community occurred gradually and with the backing of key figures within the Egyptian Jewish community, supporting the leadership of a "dynasty" of court physicians honored with the biblical title *nagid*. This dynasty began with Judah b. Saadya (ca. 1064–78), followed by his brother, Mevorakh b. Saadya (1078–82 and 1094–1111), was interrupted by twelve years of the so-called "usurpation" by the Nasi David, the son of Daniel b. ʿAzarya (1082–94), and continued with the reign of Moses b. Mevorakh (1111–ca. 1126). The replacement of the Gaonate of Palestine by the Egyptian headship of the Jews was confirmed when the *yeshivah* relocated to Fusṭāṭ following the death of Moses b. Mevorakh in 1126, at which time the *gaʾon* Maṣliaḥ ha-Kohen b. Solomon ascended the headship.

The head of the Jews in Egypt exercised the prerogatives that had been jealously guarded by the Palestinian *gaʾon*. He had supreme judicial authority and, through his "high court" (*bet din gadol*) in the Egyptian capital, appointed judges for local communities. Like the *gaʾon*, he served as a court of appeals for petitioners dissatisfied with the conduct of their cases in local tribunals. In

---

10 On the situation in Palestine during and after the Selljuk occupation see Gil, *Palestine*, 414–20. On the transfer of the *yeshivah* to Tyre, ibid., 416.

11 Mark R. Cohen, *Jewish Self-Government in Medieval Egypt: The Origins of the Office of Head of the Jews, ca. 1065–1126* (Princeton, NJ: Princeton University Press, 1980); Goitein, *Mediterranean Society*, 2:25–40. For a dissenting view of when and how this office originated, see Shulamit Sela, "The Head of the Rabbanite, Karaite, and Samaritan Jews: On the History of a Title," *Bulletin of the School of Oriental and African Studies (BSOAS)* 57 (1994): 255–67; Elinoar Bareket, "The Head of the Jews in Egypt under Fatimid Rule (Hebrew)," *Zmanim* 64 (1998): 34–43 [in Hebrew]; eadem, *Fustat on the Nile: The Jewish Elite in Medieval Egypt* (Leiden: Brill, 1999), 23–4. For a reaffirmation of the regnant consensus, see Rustow, *Heresy and the Politics of Community*, 100–8.

the manner of a Muslim potentate, he wielded coercive authority through his *hayba,* the respectful "dread" that Muslims felt toward their ruler. He endeavored to make peace in private and communal conflicts. He played a role in regulating religious affairs and in monitoring synagogue discipline. By responding to petitions from the poor, he protected the weak. He fulfilled the crucial role of intercessor with the Muslim authorities on behalf of Jews throughout the Fatimid realm and he wielded coercive authority in the use of the *ḥerem* (ban).[12] Finally, he extended his control over other Egyptian communities through his *nāʾib* (deputy), who, in turn, exercised leadership locally. We see this most clearly in connection with the community of Alexandria, the second largest Jewish settlement in Egypt and the port serving the capital of Fusṭāṭ.[13]

Under Mevorakh b. Saadya's successors, the Hebrew title of the office of head of the Jews varied. David b. Daniel used the title Nasi and, towards the end of his reign, Exilarch. Maṣliaḥ ha-Kohen b. Solomon held the title *gaʾon.* The title *nagid* and the office of head of the Jews became fused only from the time of Abraham the son of Moses Maimonides (d. 1237). The Nagidate was the most powerful institution of Jewish self-government in the Islamic world in the later Middle Ages. It lasted until the beginning of the sixteenth century, when the office was abolished by the Ottoman conquerors of Egypt.

The local community

The local community, with its roots in late antiquity, was the fundamental cell of organized Jewish communal life in Egypt. The Cairo Genizah documents, especially its rich store of letters and other papers, mention some ninety localities that were home to Jewish residents.[14] The communities for which we have the most abundant evidence are Fusṭāṭ and Alexandria.[15] The Spanish Jewish traveler Benjamin of Tudela reports a figure of 7000 Jewish

12 Cohen, *Jewish Self-Government,* 228–71.

13 Frenkel, *"Compassionate,"* 87–9, 159–63, 169–75.

14 Norman Golb, "The Topography of the Jews in Medieval Egypt: Inductive Studies Based Primarily upon Documents from the Cairo Genizah," *Jounal of Near Eastern Studies (JNES)* 24 (1965): 251–70; 33 (1974): 116–49.

15 Most of the information in Goitein's description of the local community pertains to Fusṭāṭ; when another community is meant he normally identifies it. Elinoar Bareket focuses on Fusṭāṭ alone. Miriam Frenkel studies Alexandria. Both of these books address the leadership of the communities. My own *Poverty and Charity in the Jewish Community of Medieval Egypt* (Princeton: Princeton University Press, 2005) focuses on the lower-class poor and the better-off Jews.

inhabitants for the capital and 3000 for Alexandria—huge numbers compared to most of the Jewish settlements in northern Europe at the time.[16] Organized community life in Islamic Egypt differed not only in size from its northern European counterpart. Its organization was more informal and more fluid than the local Jewish communities in medieval Europe.[17] If the form of Jewish communal organization in Christian Europe paralleled and perhaps was influenced by the model of the Christian commune, with its oath of membership, formal elections, and communal statutes, so, too, the local Jewish community in Egypt had a less corporate and more informal structure, like the Muslim town in which it was situated.

The unity of the community

All of the Rabbanite Jews living in a single town, both Palestinian and Babylonian, formed part of a single community.[18] The Arabic word *jamāʿa* and the Hebrew term *qahal* are used interchangeably in the Genizah documents to refer to what we call "community." A certain ambiguity results, however, from the fact that the words *qahal* and *jamāʿa* also designate a synagogue congregation,[19] and towns of any significant size had a separate synagogue for those following the Palestinian rite and those adhering to the Babylonian ritual. In larger settlements there might also be a Karaite synagogue, for instance, in Fusṭāṭ and in Alexandria. Where two Rabbanite congregations existed, members of the congregations would meet on special occasions under the same roof, at times even joined by Karaites.[20] Leaders of the respective Rabbanite congregations strove to patch up differences.[21] The highest-ranking Jewish *kātibs* (government clerks) in the eleventh century were often Karaites, and, by virtue of their proximity to the Muslim ruler, exploited their government status in the community's interest.[22]

16 *The Itinerary of Benjamin of Tudela,* ed. and trans. Marcus Nathan Adler (London: Henry Frowde, 1907), 62 (Hebrew), 70 (English); 69 (Hebrew), 77 (English).

17 Mark R. Cohen, "Jewish Communal Organization in Medieval Egypt: Research, Results, Prospects," in *Studies in Muslim-Jewish Relations* 3: *Proceedings of the Founding Conference of the Society for Judaeo-Arabic Studies* (1997): 73–86.

18 Goitein, *Mediterranean Society,* 2:53.

19 Bareket, *Fustat,* 102.

20 Goitein, *Mediterranean Society,* 2:54.

21 Gil, *Palestine,* 535–6.

22 Rustow, *Heresy and the Politics of Community,* 176–99.

The officials of the community

Most of the day-to-day affairs of the community were handled by a small group of individuals who, by virtue of status, appointment, or both were competent to perform the necessary tasks. One group mentioned ubiquitously in the Genizah was the "elders" (Heb. *zeqenim*; Arab. *shuyūkh*). Generally speaking, the elders formed a cadre of public servants, whose job it was to assist officials responsible for specific sectors of communal life. An important communal agreement from the first half of the eleventh century appoints ten elders to assist the judge and communal leader in Fusṭāṭ, the *ḥaver* (that is, Palestinian-trained) Ephraim b. Shemarya, listing their duties: (1) to sit with Ephraim as judges; (2) to share with Ephraim the burden of all the needs of the community; (3) to support him in enforcing religious duties; (4) to promote the desirable and prevent the reprehensible; (5) to deal appropriately with those living in a way not approved by religion; (6) to review letters from the *geʾonim* and answer them as agreed upon by the community.[23] Though Ephraim headed the Jerusalemite congregation (as his title *ḥaver* indicates), he exercised leadership over the entire community, and his authority extended over other Egyptian Jewish communities as well.[24] Sometimes the head of the local community in Fusṭāṭ was a member of the Palestinian congregation; at other times he belonged to the Babylonian synagogue.[25]

The communal leader: the muqaddam

In her book, *Fustat on the Nile,* Elinoar Bareket provides detailed portraits of the most prominent local leaders, Palestinian and Babylonian, in the first two-thirds of the eleventh century.[26] Usually chosen from among the *ḥaverim* of the *yeshivah,* they possessed rabbinic training. During the final third of the century, when fortune led to the decline of the *yeshivah* and the rise of the office of head of the Jews, a subtle change took place in the nomenclature of local leadership. The transformation is signaled by the adoption of one or another of the Arabic

23 Goitein, *Mediterranean Society,* 2:58. For a different interpretation of this document see Bareket, *Fustat,* 41–3.

24 Ibid, 87–9.

25 Ibid, 85, and chapters 4 and 5.

26 Ibid., chapters 4 and 5.

terms, *muqaddam, raʾīs,* or *nāʾib,* as the designation for the leader of a local community.[27]

The functions of a *muqaddam* varied with his training and qualifications, as well as with the needs of the community. He was appointed by and reported to the head of the Jews. The head intervened when conflict broke out between a *muqaddam* and his flock; the latter might express their disapproval of their local leader by boycotting synagogue services and lectures that the *muqaddam* regularly offered.[28] On the basis of documents regarding Alexandria, Miriam Frenkel concludes that the "ideal *muqaddam*" was expected to lead religious services, to keep order in the community, to engage in mutual consultations with the notables of the Jewish community, and to repair breaches.[29] She concludes, further, that ultimate leadership of the community rested in the hands of the elite merchants. These merchants belonged to intersecting networks. They were educated in Jewish texts, frequently intermarried, and regularly contributed to charity.[30] The members of this mercantile elite maintained connections through exchange of information, especially letters, and through informal social gatherings.[31]

In addition to the *muqaddam,* whose position in the local community is clearly defined in the Genizah, another titulary, whose function is not at all clear, appears frequently. His title in Hebrew was *rosh ha-qahal* or *rosh ha-qehillot.* Goitein suggested that the title replaced the ancient title of *rosh ha-keneset* ("head of the synagogue") and that it designated the president of a congregation. However, Goitein goes on, since in the Genizah period it

---

27 Goitein, *Mediterranean Society,* 2:68ff.; Cohen, *Jewish Self-Government,* index s.v. *muqaddam;* and for Alexandria, Frenkel, *Alexandria,* 51 and index s.v. *muqaddam.* By far, most of the documents in her corpus specifically showing the word *muqaddam* date from the period of Mevorakh b. Saadya. An earlier use of the term appears, apparently, in a fragment of an Arabic petition to the Fatimid ruler, ca. 1036, requesting confirmation in office of the head of the Jewish community of Alexandria. The word *muqaddam* is torn away in the fragment. Goitein completes the lacuna: [*muqaddam ʿalā al-yahūd al-rabbaniyīn*] (Goitein, "New Sources," 526). As Goitein explains, a distinction should be maintained between *muqaddam* as a title and *muqaddam* as the name of on an appointed office, which could be held by men holding another title, such as *ḥaver; Mediterranean Society,* 2:68–70.

28 Mark R. Cohen, "Geniza Documents Concerning a Conflict in a Provincial Egyptian Jewish Community during the Nagidate of Mevorakh b. Saadya," in *Studies in Judaism and Islam Presented to Shelomo Dov Goitein on the Occasion of his Eightieth Birthday,* ed. S. Morag et al. (Jerusalem: Magness Press, 1981), 123–54.

29 Frenkel, *Alexandria,* 198–204.

30 Ibid., 209–25.

31 Ibid., 227–31.

became customary to appoint a *ḥaver* and later on a *muqaddam* as leader of a congregation or a community, the old title *rosh ha-qahal* became an honorific devoid of administrative significance.[32]

Judges and judiciary

The backbone of local communal life in Egypt was the judiciary. The ideal that a learned professional judge should preside over the court of three judges was upheld wherever possible. Where it was not feasible, especially in small communities, an expert judge, called *dayyan* or (*av*) *bet din*, who received a salary from the community, would constitute a judicial quorum by enlisting the aid of local laymen, often chosen from among the elders.

Until the end of the eleventh century, the *dayyan* (judge) was appointed by the Jerusalem *ga'on*, and later on, by the head of the Jews. He, too, was confirmed in office by the Fatimid government. A draft of a petition to the new Fatimid caliph asking him to reconfirm the appointment of the *dayyan* of Alexandria, apparently from around the year 1036, defines the scope of his authority, encompassing decisions on "their civil cases, the conclusion of marriages, and the enactment of divorces, in accordance with the rite of their denomination (*madhhab*)."[33]

Indeed, the wealth of legal documents from the Genizah confirms that it was mostly business disputes and questions of personal and family status that occupied the attention of Jewish judges. The petition just mentioned adds that the judge of Alexandria controls "the appointment of cantors . . . in their synagogues and persons administering their emoluments and the dismissal of anyone deserving it, in his opinion." The fact that the Alexandrian judge performed administrative functions, such as appointing cantors and supervisors of the social services, should not be surprising. It is indicative of the informality and organizational fluidity within the local Jewish communities of Egypt.

The terminology and substance of judicial organization underwent certain significant changes at the time of the emergence of the office of head of the Jews. During his first term in office as *ra'īs al-yahūd* (ca. 1078–82), Mevorakh b. Saadya appointed judges in Alexandria, initiating a process that undermined that important prerogative of the Palestinian *ga'on*. Mevorakh's successor, the so-called "usurper," David b. Daniel (1082–94), advanced the process further by appointing a "high court" (*bet din gadol*), in the Fatimid capital. During

32 Goitein, *Mediterranean Society*, 2:75–6.

33 Goitein, "New Sources on the Palestinian Gaonate," 525–28.

Mevorakh's second term as head of the Jews (1094–1111), he took the process to the next level by designating a "permanent" (*qavuʿa*) court, a term formerly bestowed by the Palestinian *yeshivah* on judges like Ephraim b. Shemarya during the first half of the eleventh century. Its use by the head of the Jews in Egypt at the end of the eleventh century points to the growth of a new basis of leadership for Egyptian Jewry in its organic evolution from an older structure of Jewish self-government in the Fatimid Empire.

The lure of Islamic courts

Although the Jewish court and judiciary exercised fairly effective control, their jurisdiction was not absolute. Jews in Egypt frequently made use of the Islamic court system. It was common practice to execute business contracts in an Islamic court or before both an Islamic and a Jewish judge. Some Islamic law schools permitted non-Muslims to have their cases adjudicated in the *qāḍī* court, and mixed litigations—between *dhimmī*s and Muslims—*had* to come before the *qāḍī*. Jewish legal authorities recognized the validity of certain Islamic legal documents.[34] Where Islamic law was more favorable to economic interests than Jewish law, there could be not only a duplication of legal instruments, but even the influence of Islamic practice on documents drawn up in the Jewish court. The Babylonian *geʾonim* went out of their way to assimilate Islamic customary law in an effort to provide Jews, especially Jewish merchants, with an alternative and comparable solution to legal issues so that they would not be tempted to seek resolution in an Islamic court.[35]

The rav

The regular judiciary was complemented by another, albeit informal, source of legal authority. These were the rabbinic scholars qualified by their learning to render legal opinions. They were similar to the *muftī* in Islam and they bore the title *rav*, "master," "rabbi."[36] Their chief function was to receive questions and issue legal opinions, *teshuvot*, the equivalent of *fatwā*s in Islam.

Apart from the years when Shemarya b. Ḷlhanan and his son Ḷlhanan were active in Egypt (ca. 970–1025), both of whom came to Egypt from elsewhere,

34 Mark R. Cohen, *Maimonides and the Merchants: Jewish Law and Society in the Islamic Middle Ages* (Philadelphia: University of Pennsylvania Press, 2017), chapter 9.

35 Gideon Libson, *Jewish and Islamic Law: A Comparative Study of Custom during the Geonic Period* (Cambridge, MA: Harvard University Press, 2003).

36 Goitein, *Mediterranean Society*, 2:28; Bareket, *Fustat*, 201.

no rabbinic academy of higher rabbinic leaning was to be found in that country.[37] During the latter half of the eleventh and the beginning of the twelfth centuries, however, three eminent immigrant rabbinic scholars served the community as jurisconsults. They are the merchant-scholar from North Africa, Nahray b. Nissim (dated documents in Egypt: 1045–96);[38] Judah ha-Kohen *ha-rav ha-gadol* ("the great *Rav*") b. Joseph (dated documents: 1055–90);[39] and Isaac b. Samuel "the Spaniard" (dated documents in Egypt: 1091–1127).[40] All three wrote responsa. Isaac b. Samuel also composed commentaries on the Bible and Talmud as well as liturgical poems. Judah ha-Kohen composed commentaries on the Talmud, liturgical poems and philosophy. He was referred to by contemporaries as "the *Rav*."[41] In a Genizah letter he is praised for "reviving Jewish learning [Torah] in Egypt." Apparently, contemporaries considered him to be the first accomplished Talmud scholar in Egypt since the death of Elḥanan b. Shemarya, ca. 1025.

It seems that the presence of these three rabbis in Egypt during the latter part of the eleventh and the first part of the twelfth centuries contributed to the political change taking place at that time. Just at the moment when the influence and leadership of the Palestinian Gaonate was entering an eclipse, these foreign-born scholars brought significant rabbinic authority to Egypt and offered a local alternative to Palestinian hegemony. This, in turn, encouraged Egyptian Jewry to follow an independent path that had its most concrete manifestation in the replacement of the Palestinian Gaonate by the Egyptian office of head of the Jews. By the time Maimonides arrived in Egypt in the 1160s, the personage of the *rav* was firmly entrenched in Egypt. Maimonides is called *muftiī al-milla,* "muftī of our religious community," by one seeker of legal advice.[42] His son Abraham and the dynasty of Maimonidean heads of the Jews (*negidim*) assured that the rabbinic function would be incorporated into the political role.

---

37 Ibid., 192–222.

38 Cohen, *Jewish Self-Government,* 102–4.

39 Ibid., 104–8.

40 Ibid., 119–21.

41 Goitein, *Letters of Medieval Jewish Traders,* (Princeton: Princeton University Press, 1973) 173, note 2.

42 *Teshuvot ha-Rambam,* vol. 1, ed. Joshua Blau (Jerusalem: Mekize Nirdamim, 1957), no. 178.

Revenues and expenditures[43]

Finances to support communal expenses came from diverse sources: fines, bequests, revenues from meat slaughtering, donations for the purchase of loaves of bread for the poor, ready-made loaves, pledges (called *pesiqa*) of money for the poor, and donations of clothing for the needy and for minor community officials. Expenditures included food for the poor, assistance to travelers, subsidization of the poll tax of the poor, education for the poor and orphans, burial expenses, and emoluments for scholars and officials. Unlike the Jewish communities in Europe, however, revenues did not come from internal taxation. In Egypt, where communal organization was less formal and more fluid than in Europe, income derived mostly from voluntary contributions. An exception was rents from communal properties earmarked as pious trust (*qodesh* or *heqdesh*). Similarly, the supervision of finances and services was largely a voluntary function. The task rested in the hands of laymen of integrity, chosen by the communal leader from among the moneyed class. The principal officer in this category was the *parnas*, a title that in later European Jewry designated the lay administrator of a local community. Complementing and at times identical with the *parnas* was the "trustee of the court" (*ne᾿eman bet din*), an auxiliary of the rabbinical court bearing a variety of responsibilities, among them payment of a husband's alimony to women on behalf of their children.

The single most important source of revenue in the local community (of Fusṭāṭ, to which most of the Genizah evidence in this matter applies) was income from houses or other real estate donated to the community as pious trust. This institution was apparently an outgrowth of the ancient Jewish practice of bestowing gifts on the synagogue or on the poor. It had its equivalent in the Islamic *waqf.* In the Genizah documents it is often mentioned by the Arabic terms *waqf* or *ḥabs.* Unlike in Islam, however, the Jews knew only the public type of pious foundation, not the family *waqf.*

Formally, the donation of a Jewish pious trust was made to the Jewish court, which had ultimate control over the management of trust properties. Often properties were earmarked for the perpetual upkeep of a particular needy group, such as the poor of Jerusalem. The properties were usually administered by the *parnasim,* although other officials also assisted in the task. The general broad principle

43 For the following see Goitein, *Mediterranean Society*, 2:91–143; Cohen, *Poverty and Charity*; and Moshe Gil, *Documents of the Jewish Pious Foundations from the Cairo Geniza* (Leiden: Brill, 1976).

of voluntarism that marked the activity of the *parnasim* in general appears to have extended to the administration of the pious foundations. However, documents from the 1150s on show that, by then, the community was compensating the *parnasim* for their efforts, either by allowing them to deduct ten percent of the proceeds or by farming out the rent collections to them. This change, though not explained, correlates with the fact that the number of *qodesh* properties in the eleventh century expanded greatly in the following period, suggesting that the work had become additionally burdensome.

Monies were expended in several ways. A certain amount (Gil estimates 14%) went for the maintenance of synagogues, mainly to purchase oil for lighting. A smaller amount (10%) was used for direct charity. Most of the money for eleemosynary purposes apparently came from the various fundraising methods mentioned earlier. The lion's share of the income from pious trusts (the remaining 76%) was expended on salaries for scholars and other communal officials, like cantors and beadles (*khādim*). It should be noted that these estimates are based on available accounts of the *qodesh*, which date from the latter half of the twelfth century and may not be wholly reflective of the Genizah period.

Politics and political expression in the Jewish communities

Governance is inevitably accompanied by politics and political conflict. Indeed, the medieval Jewish communities of Islamic Egypt engaged in an active political life. The Genizah provides detailed evidence of this, both in the two largest communities of Fusṭāṭ and Alexandria and in smaller communities like the one in al-Maḥalla.[44] One feature of this political expression is factionalism. Arabic words like *ʿaṣabiyya*, "group solidarity," *ḥizb*, "party," and *taḥazzaba*, "to form a faction," are indicative of the phenomenon. Dissension over leadership played a pronounced role in the life of the community. The conflict between Ephraim b. Shemarya and his opposition in the Babylonian congregation in Fusṭāṭ exemplifies these political struggles.[45] Such dissension could lead people to boycott the synagogue, where public affairs were centered. This had its parallel, if not its model, in Islam in the practice of boycotting the Friday service of the mosque to protest against the government.

---

44 Bareket on Fusṭāṭ (cf. Gil, *Palestine*, 513–14); Frenkel on Alexandria (see her discussion of political conflict, pp. 60ff.; also Gil, *Palestine*, 515–16). For political strife in a medium-sized community (al-Maḥalla) see Cohen, "Geniza Documents Concerning a Conflict."

45 Bareket, *Fustat*, 105–15.

Similarly, the community appears to have followed the Muslim example by the manner in which it expressed political loyally. During the Friday sermon in the mosque, the *imām* proclaimed uttered the name of the ruling caliph in his *khuṭba*. This served as an affirmation of loyalty. So, too, the Jews customarily recited a prayer of fealty for the reigning Jewish leader, be it the *ga*ʾ*on* or the Exilarch. The prayer was inserted in the Kaddish prayer with the formula "in the lifetime(*be-ḥayyei*)of our lord the head of the *yeshivah* (or the head of the exile").[46] As in the mosque, the omission of this formula signaled some sort of rebellion or shift of loyalty to a different leader. The custom, or one like it, was eventually instituted for the Egyptian head of the Jews as well, though we do not know what form it took.

Paralleling the Islamic model, too, was the political phenomenon of the so-called "young men." Like the Muslim *aḥdāth* ("young men") of the towns of Syria, the young men of the Jewish community, called in the Genizah *ṣibyān, shabāb,* or *shubbān* in Arabic and *baḥurim* in Hebrew, represented an aggregate of individuals who surfaced, especially during times of strife, making mischief and rebelling against authority; or they appeared as allies of one faction in the community or another.[47] Apparently, the words reflect a political situation in which different malcontents opposed the "establishment," which was largely identified with the respected "elders." They were called "young men" with a pejorative intention, since rebelliousness was viewed as an unsavory characteristic of youth.[48]

---

46 Cohen, *Jewish Self Government*, 224, 268.

47 Cohen, "New Light," 15–16; Rustow, *Heresy and the Politics of Community*, 310–11.

48 Goitein, *Mediterranean Society*, vol. 2, 61–2.

5

Introduction to the Legal Arena[1]

ODED ZINGER

This chapter introduces the legal arena of Egyptian Jews in the so-called classical Genizah period (1000–1250). The "legal arena" is a broad term that includes not only Jewish courts and legal records, but also other legal institutions and the social space constituted through the different ways Jews experienced such institutions and interacted with them.[2] Thus it includes how legal institutions were integrated within the broader social fabric and what people did outside of court with the intention to affect legal action. The use of the word "arena" is meant to stress its lively, dramatic, and competitive nature. By stressing the action that takes place in the legal arena (whether inside legal institutions or outside of them), I try to give due attention to the choices and agency of the litigants and ordinary people, rather than have them overshadowed by the legal tradition and institutions. As is displayed schematically in Fig. 1, the Jewish legal arena includes Jewish institutions and Muslim institutions. As will become abundantly clear below, the study of the Jewish legal arena in medieval Egypt is still in its early stages. Thus, this chapter not only seeks to open a window onto legal practice as evidenced by the Genizah, it is an invitation to come in and join its study.

---

1 The writing of this chapter was supported by the Martin Buber Society of Fellows at the Hebrew University of Jerusalem and by an Urbach fellowship from the Jewish Memorial Foundation.

2 At the same time, the present chapter is constricted to a narrow aspect of law as a way of organizing social relationships. Therefore, realms of Jewish law (halakhah) such as ritual law will not be addressed.

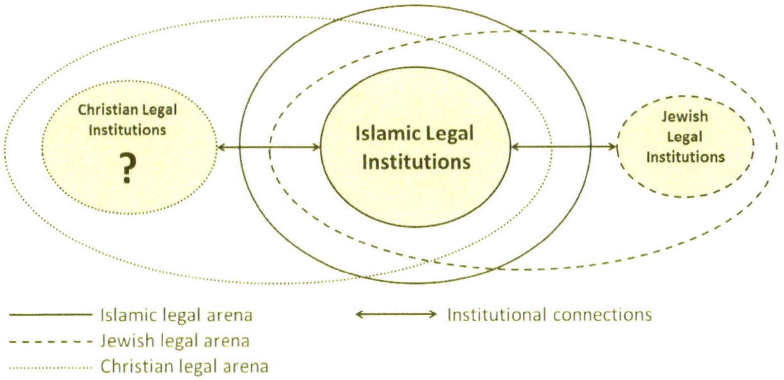

Fig. 1: The legal arenas of medieval Egypt. This figure is an attempt to display schematically the relationships between the different legal institutions and arenas in medieval Egypt. The space covered by the different arenas outside the institutions is not "empty" but consists of the different extra-legal actions available to parties to influence legal institutions (on these see below). The existence and nature of Christian legal institutions in this period is unclear and understudied and this is reflected with the question mark; see the references in Eve Krakowski, *Coming of Age in Medieval Egypt: Female Adolescence, Jewish Law, and Ordinary Culture* (Princeton, NJ: Princeton University Press, 2017), 94, note 72, and Lev E. Weitz, "Islamic Law on the Provincial Margins: Christian Patrons and Muslim Notaries in Upper Egypt, 2nd–5th/8th–11th Centuries," *Islamic Law and Society* 26 (2019): 1–48. One important point that comes out of this diagram is that Jews and Christians may have enjoyed more options in the legal arena than Muslims, as they could use their own communal institutions as well as the Muslim ones.

While it is often stated that the existence of a regular court was the cornerstone of the autonomous Jewish community, we have little direct evidence on these institutions in the premodern period. The Genizah is unique in providing us not only a critical mass of legal documents but also a plethora of personal and communal letters that allow us to situate the legal institutions within the broader social fabric. This chapter will begin by quickly reviewing past and present research on Jewish legal institutions in medieval Egypt. It will then attempt to describe the major characteristics of the Jewish legal arena by starting with the most basic legal act of acquisition (*qinyan*) and then gradually zooming out to look at the local Jewish court and the documents it produced. Next will come other legal institutions, both Jewish and Islamic. The following section will survey some of the ways litigants influenced the legal process by actions outside of legal institutions. The conclusion brings together issues examined throughout the chapter to portray the different sources of authority of the local Jewish court in medieval Egypt.

The study of legal documents in the Genizah began soon after its discovery. In the first stage of Genizah studies, scholars published individual legal documents as curiosities or unique specimens.[3] Later scholars turned to more systematic publication of legal documents and made some initial ventures to describe the legal institutions that produced these documents.[4] Like in so many other topics, it was Shelomo Dov Goitein who provided the first substantial and comprehensive description of Genizah courts in a section titled "Communal Jurisdiction" in the volume on "The Community" in *A Mediterranean Society*.[5] In this section, Goitein provided a synthesis of the judiciary, substantive law, and court procedures.[6] Much of what follows is based on the foundation that Goitein established.

While Goitein laid out the basic features of the Jewish courts in Egypt, at the heart of his work were the letters of long-distance merchants.[7] This secondary

---

3 See, for example, D. S. Margoliouth, "A Jewish-Persian Law Report," *JQR* 11 (1899): 671–5; and David Werner Amram, "An Injunction of a Jewish-Egyptian Court of the Thirteenth Century," *The Green Bag* 13 (1901): 339–43. A similar interest in "curiosities of law" was found in the early days of papyrology, see Leslie S. B. MacCoull, *Coptic Legal Documents: Law as Vernacular Text and Experience in Late Antique Egypt* (Tempe: ACMRS and Brepols, 2009), xix, note 5.

4 See Hartwig Hirschfeld, "Some Judeo Arabic Legal Documents," *JQR* 16 (1925): 279–86; S. Assaf, "Old Genizah Documents from Palestine, Egypt and North Africa," *Tarbiz* 9 (1937–8): 11–34 and 196–218 [in Hebrew]; D. Z. Baneth, "Genizah Documents on Jewish Communal Affairs in Egypt," in *Alexander Marx Jubilee Volume*, Hebrew section (New York: Jewish Theological Seminary of America, 1950), 75*–93* [in Hebrew]; Norman Golb, "Legal Documents from the Cairo Genizah," *JSocS* 20 (1958): 17–46. For early forays on the Jewish courts see Ernest James Worman, "Notes on the Jews in Fustat from Cambridge Genizah Documents," *JQR* 18 (1905): 13–15; and Jacob Mann, *The Jews in Egypt and in Palestine under the Fatimid Caliphs: A Contribution to Their Political and Communal History*, with a Preface and Reader's Guide by Shelomo D. Goitein, 2 vols. (New York: Ktav, 1970), vol. 1, 264–8.

5 Goitein, *Mediterranean Society*, vol. 2, 311–45.

6 It should be noted, however, that Goitein's discussion of legal institutions is not limited to this section. Certain aspects are discussed in different parts of chapter V ("Communal Organization and Institutions"), or in section D ("Communal Autonomy and Government Control") of chapter VII. Many examples of the work of the court, and especially litigation, are presented in the first volume on *Economic Foundations* and the third volume on *The Family* (where the section on "Women in Court" is delegated, see 332–6). See also S. D. Goitein, "The Interplay of Jewish and Islamic Laws," in *Jewish Law in Legal History and the Modern World*, ed. Bernard S. Jackson (Leiden: Brill, 1980), 61–77; idem, "Court Records from the Cairo Genizah in JNUL," *Kiryat Sefer* 41 (1965–66): 263–76 [in Hebrew].

7 This is true even though the trigger for Goitein's *India Book* and interest in the Genizah was the discovery of a dossier of court records; see Goitein and Friedman, *India Traders of the Middle Ages*, xxi. For Goitein and merchants' letters, see Peter N. Miller, "Two Men in

position for legal matters means that less progress has been achieved in the study of legal practice than has been achieved in the study of trade. The result is that the aforementioned section on "Communal Jurisdiction," published in 1971, is still the most comprehensive treatment of legal institutions and procedure.[8]

It is possible to identify three general approaches in which the study of legal matters in the Genizah proceeded after Goitein's pioneering work. The primary one was a legalistic approach that looked at legal practice from the perspective of the rich Jewish legal tradition. By comparing "law in practice" to "law in the books," scholars examined whether everyday practice conformed to the strictures of the legal tradition.[9] In this way, they were able to identify and recover alternative legal traditions that once thrived in Jewish communities but later disappeared from view.[10] Locating occasions in which practice deviated from normative law, it was possible to determine whether such deviations were organic developments from within the Jewish tradition or results of outside influences.[11]

Recently, a diplomatic approach has been proposed for the study of Genizah legal documents.[12] This approach examines the composition of

---

a Boat: The Braudel-Goitein 'Correspondence' and the Beginning of Thalassography," in *The Sea: Thalassography and Historiography*, ed. Peter N. Miller (Ann Arbor: University of Michigan Press, 2013), 31–3. We see the general appeal of merchants' letters to Goitein in the fact he used merchants' letters when he wanted "to make a break in producing large books and turn to writing something short and handy which might be welcome to students, laymen and scholars alike"; see Goitein, *Letters of Medieval Jewish Traders*, vii.

8 Later discussions of the Jewish court can be found in Menahem Ben-Sasson, *Emergence of the Local Jewish Community in the Muslim World: Qayrawan, 800–1057* (Jerusalem: Magness Press, 1997), 293–345 [in Hebrew]; Bareket, *Fustat*, 53–69; and many of the studies cited below.

9 For example, Phillip Ackerman-Lieberman examined legal documents concerning trade and concluded that the practice of Jewish merchants generally adhered to Jewish rather than Islamic law; see his *The Business of Identity: Jews, Muslims, and Economic Life in Medieval Egypt* (Stanford: Stanford University Press, 2014).

10 See, for example, Friedman, *Jewish Marriage*.

11 See the lucid methodological presentation in Amir Ashur, "Engagement and Betrothal Documents from the Cairo Genizah Engagement and Betrothal" (PhD diss., Tel Aviv University, 2006), 2–4 and 7–9 [in Hebrew]. See also Libson, *Jewish and Islamic Law*.

12 A precursor to the recent diplomatic approach can be found in the work of Gershon Weiss. See his "Documents Written by Hillel Ben Eli: A Study in the Diplomatics of the Cairo Geniza Documents" (MA diss., University of Pennsylvania, 1967); "Legal Documents Written by the Court Clerk Halfon Ben Manasse" (PhD diss., University of Pennsylvania, 1970); "Formularies (Shetarot) Reconstructed from the Cairo Geniza," *Gratz College Annual of Jewish Studies* 2 (1973): 29–42, 3 (1974): 63–76, 4 (1975): 69–76.

legal records as a way of studying the institutions that produced them. The figure at the center of the diplomatic approach is the court clerk (also called court scribe) who needed to compose records that would adhere to the legal tradition, satisfy the demands of the people who requested them, and be upheld by other Jewish courts.[13] A systematic diplomatic study of legal documents from urban centers and the periphery, from the tenth to the thirteenth century, promises to give us an institutional history of the Jewish community. Finally, the present writer has been exploring how legal institutions were embedded in the social fabric of the Jewish community. This approach focuses on the agency of the people who used the communal legal services and explores how they maneuvered between different legal institutions, or influenced these institutions by non-legal means. While these three approaches are quite different in orientation, it is important to keep in mind that they seek to recover different aspects of one legal culture of rather small communities. This means that any investigation of the legal culture tends to mix and combine these approaches.

Surveying the legal arena: the act of acquisition, the court, and its records

We begin our survey with the legal act that forms the basis of the great majority of legal activity in Genizah courts. An acquisition (*qinyan*) appears in most legal documents. Basically, acquisition is the act by which legal rights are obtained.[14] Originally used for property rights, acquisition required set physical acts for different types of property (for example "lifting" and "pulling" for objects and animals). However, acquisition was expanded to other contractual rights, such as acknowledgement or release of a debt. In our documents, acquisition is often performed in a symbolic way, most commonly by a transfer of a

13 See Eve Krakowski and Marina Rustow, "Formula as Content: Medieval Jewish Institutions, the Cairo Geniza, and the New Diplomatics," *JSS* 20 (2014): 111–46; Rustow, *Heresy and the Politics of Community*, 266–88. A diplomatic approach is also adopted in Micha Perry, "Communal Scribes and the Rise of a Uniform Hebrew Style around the Mediterranean in the Eleventh Century," *Zion* 82 (2017): 267–308 [in Hebrew].

14 On acquisition, see Shalom Albeck and Menachem Elon, "Acquisition," in *Encyclopedia Judaica*, 1:359–63; Ron S. Kleinman, *Methods of Acquisition and Commercial Customs in Jewish Law: Theory, Practice and History* (Jerusalem: Bar Ilan University Press, 2013) [in Hebrew].

handkerchief or as incidental to land (usually land not actually owned, for example, the four cubits every Jew is supposed to possess in Palestine).[15]

What is important for the present discussion is that acquisition is a private act that requires two witnesses. The majority of Genizah legal documents are thus framed as the testimonies of those who witnessed the act of acquisition. The legal document testifies to the performance of the acquisition, but it is the acquisition and not the document that constitutes the legal act. Thus legal acts could be performed outside of court and not even recorded in writing and theoretically they would still be binding.

Many legal documents in the Genizah state clearly that they were produced in court, but many do not mention a court and it is unclear whether they were produced in one or not. Indeed, there are indications of legal acts being made not only outside of court, but also without being written down (or being written down a substantial time after they were made).[16] While the Jewish courts were at the center of legal life, they did not have a monopoly over legal action or even the writing of legal documents.[17]

Our knowledge about the Jewish courts that operated in different towns in Egypt is spotty. We have abundant information (that has not been studied systematically) about the court that was held in the Palestinian synagogue in Fusṭāṭ in which the Genizah was found. By all accounts, this was the central Jewish court in Egypt. The *gaʾon* of the Palestinian academy (Heb. *yeshivah*) appointed the president of the court (Heb. *av bet din*) as long as the academy resided in Jerusalem. With the decline of the academy following the Seljuq conquest of Palestine (1071), judges in Egypt were appointed by the Head of the Jews in Egypt. The first testimony for such appointment comes from

---

15 In fact, Goitein, *Mediterranean Society*, vol. 2, 329–30, expresses uncertainty whether "the symbolic act itself was always performed."

16 Documents produced outside of court could be brought to the court and the court would add a validation clause (Heb. *qiyyum*) at the bottom. However, many deeds produced in court also contain such a validation clause (on which, more below). Marriage contracts (*ketubbot*) usually did not require a court; see for example Moses Maimonides, *Responsa*, ed. and trans. Joshua Blau (2nd edition; Jerusalem: Rubin Mass-Makhon Moshe, 2014), vol. 2, 637, no. 362 [in Hebrew]. However, other legal acts were also performed outside the court, and occasionally without a deed (or even without a formal acquisition). For a couple of examples, see T-S 13J2.13, T-S NS J30, ENA 4020.26, and Maimonides, *Responsa* [2014], no. 11.

17 This does not mean that at certain times and places the courts or Jewish leadership did not try to assert such a monopoly. For a different view, see Judith Olszowy-Schlanger, "Les archives médiévales dans la genizah du Caire: registres des tribunaux rabbiniques et pratiques d'archivage reconstituées," *Afriques: Débats, méthodes et terrains d'histoire* 7 (2016): 4.

a legal document produced in Alexandria in 1080.[18] The consolidation of the office of the Head of the Jews apparently also ended the occasional setting up of Babylonian and Karaite courts in Fusṭāṭ, for which we have some information until the 1060s but much less afterwards.[19] Outside of Fusṭāṭ, large urban centers like Cairo, Alexandria, and al-Maḥalla could boast of a Jewish court headed by an appointed professional judge (Heb. *dayyan, bet din, ḥaver*), while in smaller centers the court was headed by the local appointed leader (Ar. *muqaddam*), who was not a full-fledged *dayyan* or *ḥaver*.[20] A systematic study of the court records from outside of Fusṭāṭ remains an important desideratum. The danger is that without such a study we may project what we know of the

18 Cohen, *Jewish Self-Government*, 174.

19 On Karaite courts see Oded Zinger, "A Karaite-Rabbanite Court Session in Mid-Eleventh Century Egypt," *Ginzei Qedem: Genizah Research Annual* 13 (2017): 98*–102*, and the literature cited there. On the question of Babylonian courts, Goitein oscillated but seems to have decided that "by the end of the eleventh century it was established that the judges of the Babylonians and the Palestinians will adjudicate together in the Palestinian court," see S. D. Goitein, "The Struggle between the Synagogue and the Community," in *Ḥayyim (Jefim) Schirmann: Jubilee Volume*, ed. Shraga Abramson and Aaron Mirsky (Jerusalem: Schocken Institute, 1970), 70 [in Hebrew]. See further material in S. D. Goitein, "The Public Activity of Rabbi Elḥanan ben Shemarya '*Rosh ha-Seder* of all Israel'," in *Joshua Finkel Festschrift: In honor of Joshua Finkel*, ed. Sidney B. Hoenig and Leon D. Stitskin (New York: Yeshiva University Press, 1974), 117–37 [in Hebrew]; Gil, *Palestine during the First Muslim Period*, docs. 312 and 320–2; T-S 13J1.10, edited in Elinoar Bareket, *The Jewish Leadership in Fusṭāṭ in the First Half of the Eleventh Century* (Tel Aviv: The Diaspora Research Institute, 1995), 244–5, no. 25, and see further 299 (index) [in Hebrew]. Of special note is T-S 8J4.9 2v, edited in S. D. Goitein, "The Synagogue Building and its Furnishings According to the Records of the Cairo Genizah," *Eretz-Israel: Archeological, Historical and Geographical Studies* 7 (1964): 93–4 [in Hebrew], in which the appointment of the caretaker (Ar. *khādim*) of the Babylonian synagogue in 1099 is recorded in the notebook of the court of the Palestinian synagogue. One of the tasks of the caretaker is to write down the speech of the parties at court and be the court's messenger, but the document does not record which court was intended. Apparently, it was obvious that there was only one court (in the Palestinian synagogue). In T-S 13J18.6v (unpublished) there is the beginning of a testimony by Nathan ha-Kohen b. Solomon (a Palestinian judge, see Goitein, *Mediterranean Society*, vol. 2, 513, no. 17) that, while he was about to the leave the Babylonian synagogue after performing a circumcision, he was approached by Nathan he-Ḥaver "the Diadem" (another Palestinian judge, see ibid., 513, no. 18) to make a ruling about a matter of an oath. Again, this document shows that in this period legal activity in the Babylonian synagogue was something unusual. For three leaves from a marriage notebook of the Babylonian synagogue in Damascus from 933 CE, see Friedman, *Jewish Marriage in Palestine*, doc. 53–5. I do not recall seeing an Egyptian court notebook dedicated only to marriage.

20 Goitein, *Mediterranean Society*, vol. 2, 68–75, 215–17, and 314–17. For the title of *shofet*, see ibid., 31, 315–16.

relatively robust and regular court in the Palestinian synagogue in Fusṭāṭ to the workings of other Jewish courts in Egypt.

Jewish courts dealt mainly with issues of personal status, monetary matters, and occasionally with verbal or physical altercations that arose between Jews. Criminal matters were the prerogative of non-Jewish courts, and are practically absent from Jewish legal records. The Jewish court did not just impose Jewish law. It settled disputes, provided legal services by drafting legal records upon demand, supervised the communal endowments and tried to preserve the social fabric of the Jewish community while protecting the socially weak.[21] These goals were usually harmonious, but on occasion tensions arose between them.

The coercive powers of Jewish courts were limited. Physical coercion was in the hands of the Muslim authorities. While Jewish judges could ask them to punish Jewish transgressors, they were reluctant to do so realizing that it would impinge on their legitimacy and autonomy (more on Jewish autonomy below). Jewish courts did not impose fines as punishment.[22] The other means of direct coercion was the ban (Heb. *ḥerem*[23]) or excommunication (Heb. *nidduy*), which usually were also used reluctantly because if they were declared and ignored by even a part of the community, they lost their effectiveness.[24] With these limited direct means of coercion, the court (and communal leaders in general) had to adopt a "softer" approach that employed persuasion and social pressure, which agreed with the courts' goal to settle disputes amicably and preserve the social fabric. For this reason, the courts displayed a strong preference for reaching a mediated compromise over passing verdict. In this they

21 The social commitment of the court can be seen in the expression "the court is the hand of the poor," on which see Gil, *Documents of the Jewish Pious Foundations*, 39, §55. The court was also considered "the father of orphans and judge of widows," see Cohen, *Poverty and Charity*, 142.

22 While we do not find fines as punishments, an obligation to pay a fine for contract breach is quite common. Even in these cases, however, we see that when an agreement was broken, the fine would be either negotiated down or waived altogether. For three examples, see Oded Zinger, "Women, Gender and Law: Marital Disputes according to Documents from the Cairo Geniza" (PhD diss., Princeton University, 2014), 251–4.

23 To be distinguished from the "anonymous ban" (*ḥerem setam*), which was essentially a procedural tool; see Gideon Libson, "The Origin and Development of the Anonymous Ban (*Ḥerem Setam*) during the Geonic Period," *Shenaton ha-Mishpat ha-ʿIvri* 22 (2001–4): 107–232 [in Hebrew].

24 See Goitein, *Mediterranean Society*, vol. 2, 331–3. For Genizah texts of the ban, see Gershom Weiss, "Shetar Herem—Excommunication Formulary: Five Documents from the Cairo Geniza," *Gratz College Annual of Jewish Studies* 6 (1977): 98–120.

were aided by the high value given to reaching a compromise and the general freedom of contact in monetary matters in Jewish law.[25] Such settlements were also less likely to be contested at a later stage by one of the parties, for example, by appealing to a Muslim court.

This emphasis on persuasion and compromise was part of a broader tendency in which the court was not set apart from everyday life, as we often find in modern legal systems.[26] Below, I present aspects of the embeddedness of the legal arena in the social fabric. Here it suffices to draw attention to aspects of the working of the courts that made it accessible to all members of the Jewish community (though not, of course, in equal measure). Court sessions were not steeped in Jewish legal language or halakhic discussions.[27] The members of the court were not taken from a closed list of professional witnesses as was the case with the Muslim *ʿudūl*, and we can assume that many of the male members of the Jewish upper middle class served on the bench at one time or another.[28] Lawyers, that is, legal professionals employed by laymen to represent their case in court in the most beneficial way, did not exist. Occasionally a person would appoint an agent to act on his behalf, but this was done usually when the person could not attend the court in person.[29] Such agents were usually men knowledgeable in Jewish law and in court practice, but they were not specialists, and

25 On *peshara*, see Menachem Elon, "Compromise," in *Encyclopedia Judaica*, vol. 5, 124–9; Itay E. Liphschits, "The Procedural Limits of Compromise (*Pesharah*)," *Shenaton ha-Mishpat ha-ʿIvri* 24 (2007): 63–122 [in Hebrew]. On freedom of contact in monetary matters, see Menachem Elon, *Jewish Law: History, Source, Principles*, trans. Bernard Auerbach and Melvin J. Sykes (Philadelphia: Jewish Publication Society, 1994), vol. 1, 123–7.

26 See Pierre Bourdieu, "The Force of Law: Toward a Sociology of the Juridical Field," *The Hastings Law Journal* 38 (1987): 805–53.

27 This does not mean that the Jewish courts did not uphold Jewish law, but that one did not have to be a scholar in order to participate in the legal proceedings. The same phenomenon has been observed in Islamic courts. See Chibli Mallat, *Introduction to Middle Eastern Law* (Oxford: Oxford University Press, 2007), 83. Goitein went so far as to claim that "it was not so much the content of the law applied as the authority administering it which gave the parties the feeling that they were judged according to the law of the Torah"; Goitein, *Mediterranean Society*, vol. 2, 334. It should be pointed out, however, that the fact that legal records were written in Hebrew characters and utilized a broad range of rabbinic terminology symbolized that the court was upholding Jewish law; see Krakowski, *Coming of Age*, chapter 2.

28 See Goitein, *Mediterranean Society*, vol. 2, 312. On the *udūl*, see Emile Tyan, *Histoire de l'organisation judiciaire en pays d'Islam* (2nd edition, Leiden: Brill, 1960), 239; Farhat J. Ziadeh, "Integrity (*ʿAdālah*) in Classical Islamic Law," in *Islamic Studies and Jurisprudence: Studies in Honor of Farhat J. Ziadeh* (Seattle: University of Washington Press, 1990), 73–93.

29 The significant exception is women, who often appointed a representative even when they were present in the same city.

more importantly, their use did not lead to a professionalization of the judicial process that would hinder others from participating. When the proceedings involved a woman of high social class or one considered particularly modest, the court could send representatives to collect her testimony at her home.[30] The result of these considerations was that Jewish courts were accessible to almost all members of the Jewish community. Being a wealthy educated man certainly provided an advantage, and yet there is no shortage of women and poor men appearing and conducting their affairs in court.[31]

The court was usually held in a synagogue and consisted of three or more members, one of whom was the presiding judge.[32] A source of potential confusion is that the presiding judge is often called "court" (*bet din*) in the legal record, and occasionally all the members of the court were referred to in this way.[33]

While at least in the large urban centers the presiding judge was usually a professional judge, the other members of court were often prominent members of the local Jewish community: welfare officials (Heb. *parnasim*), cantors (Heb. *ḥazzanim*), respectable merchants, and so forth. The court clerk who wrote the legal record is usually one of the signatories (as can be seen by comparing the script of the main text to that of the signatures).[34] However, at other times it was the presiding judge who wrote the record, as can be seen in

30 For an example of a respectable woman, see T-S NS 321.54 and T-S 10J6.11. For a modest woman, see T-S NS 298.38: "since the complaints of the wife of ʿAlī b. Bishr continued repeatedly, necessity required to send representatives to investigate her situation, for she is veiled (*dhāt ḥijāb*)." The topic also features in a famous geonic responsum, see the discussion in Libson, *Jewish and Islamic Law*, 53 and 107–10; Mordechai Akiva Friedman, "The Ethics of Medieval Marriages," in *Religion in a Religious Age*, ed. S. D. Goitein (Cambridge: Association for Jewish Studies, 1974), 93–4; and Krakowski, *Coming of Age*, 198–9.

31 Despite some formal differences, Goitein argued that women appeared freely in Jewish courts on an essentially equal footing to men; see Goitein, *Mediterranean Society*, vol. 3, 332–6. A different position is taken in Zinger, "Women, Gender and Law," 22–72. Children under the age of majority were usually represented by their legal guardians. The only part of the Jewish community that we rarely find acting in court are slaves who were bought and sold, but rarely appear as legal actors.

32 The presiding judge often signed last at the bottom of the legal record, according to the practice of the Palestinian academy. However, at other times it is impossible to tell who the presiding judge was; see Goitein, *Mediterranean Society*, vol. 2, 313. For a list of the Jewish judges active in Fusṭāṭ and Cairo, see ibid., vol. 2, 511–15.

33 Goitein, *Mediterranean Society*, vol. 2, 314; Shelomo Dov Goitein and Mordechai Akiva Friedman, *Ḥalfon the Traveling Merchant Scholar*, 35, note 93 [in Hebrew].

34 For a list of the most prominent Fusṭāṭ court clerks, see Goitein, *Mediterranean Society*, vol. 2, 597, note 39.

many of the documents written by Mevorakh b. Natan.[35] I use the term "court clerk" rather than the commonly used term "scribe," because it seems that his role was broader than merely writing the legal record. As a middleman between the judge and the local community, the clerk was a source of legal expertise to the local community and a source of local knowledge for the judge, who was often, at least in his first years in office, a foreigner appointed from above.[36]

Also present in the court and playing a semi-formal role were the righteous elders (Heb. *ziqne kosher va-yosher*). The identity of these elders is usually not given, but from the few cases that record their names, they seem to have been respectable members of the community and were part of the same pool of people from whom the members of court were taken.[37] These elders represented the local community's interest in preserving the peace and intervened in disputes to bring about an amicable settlement (see more below). They were also used as founts of local knowledge, deciding the required sum of child support or evaluating the price of real estate.

Beyond these functionaries, one also comes across "the trustee of the court" (Heb. *ne'eman bet din*, or simply *ne'eman*) with whom litigants deposited legal documents for safekeeping or funds to be distributed according to the agreement reached in court.[38] While in some legal records there is a clear distinction between the different functionaries, in others we find them used interchangeably. As Goitein observed, "the Jewish judiciary was fluid and variegated, a true mirror of the society whose law it administered."[39]

---

35 A judge in the Fusṭāṭ court active in the years 1151–80, see Goitein, *Mediterranean Society*, vol. 2, 514, note 22.

36 This hypothesis on the court clerk awaits confirmation. The complex role of the court clerk can be seen, for example, in the special relationship that existed between Wuḥsha/Waḥsha, the prominent businesswoman and Hillel b. Eli. See S. D. Goitein, "A Jewish Business Woman of the Eleventh Century," *JQR* 50 (1967): 225–42.

37 On rare occasions we are told the identity of the righteous elders, for example, see Bodl. MS Heb. c 13.20, edited in Friedman, *Jewish Polygyny*, doc. V-2; T-S 18J2.5, ll. 16–18, edited in Oded Zinger, "Jewish Women in Muslim Legal Venues in Medieval Egypt: Seven Documents from the Cairo Geniza," in *Language, Gender and Law in the Judaeo-Islamic Milieu*, ed. Zvi Stampfer and Amir Ashur (Leiden: Brill, 2020), doc. 3; Freer 5 (1908.44E), ll. 14-15 (interestingly, the names of the elders are deleted in the document), edited in Gil, *Palestine during the First Muslim Period*, doc. 54; and the case edited in Zinger, "A Karaite-Rabbanite Court Session." A systematic collection of such examples would be very helpful in trying to characterize these righteous elders.

38 Occasionally the trustee also served as a guardian of orphans. On the trustee, see Goitein, *Mediterranean Society*, vol. 2, 80–2.

39 Ibid., vol. 2, 327.

Generally speaking, we can divide court cases into ones in which there was a prior agreement between the parties and ones involving a dispute.[40] When the parties were in agreement, the court's role was confined to ensuring the agreement did not transgress Jewish law, and if not, to perform the *qinyan* and produce a legal record as testimony.[41] In disputes, the role of the court was naturally more complex. Legal records occasionally present us with a detailed fact-finding process whereby the parties presented their respective claims and the court would question the parties, call on witnesses or request documentation as needed. However, in other cases the claims of the parties and the fact-finding process are truncated, and we are presented only with the legal outcome, usually in the form of an acknowledgment of debt, or a release from previous claims. The altercations in court often involved raised voices, mutual accusations and baseless claims that Goitein famously likened to haggling in the bazaar.[42] As one document describes it: "there were m[any?] words between them and argument, blaming and attacks, some in earnest and some in jest."[43]

Amicable settlement is usually presented as having been reached not by the direct involvement of the members of the court, but through the intervention

40 For general legalist works on Jewish legal procedure, see Eliav Shochetman, *Civil Procedure in Jewish Law* (Jerusalem: Library of Jewish Law, 1988) [in Hebrew]; Yuval Sinai, *The Judge and the Judicial Process in Jewish Law* (n.p.: Nevo, 2010) [in Hebrew].

41 Because Jewish law generally allows for freedom of contract in monetary matters, most agreements did not pose a problem in the eyes of the court. We would certainly like to know what the court did when asked to affirm an agreement that transgressed Jewish law. We do find occasionally a transaction that is problematic from the perspective of Jewish law, for example, one involving hidden interest or when the maintenance of minor children is relinquished by a divorced mother in return for custody. Discussing commercial matters, Philip Ackerman-Liebermann suggested that the court acted as an educator, so when the parties asked the court to record a problematic transaction, it educated the parties about their mistake, but if they persisted the court could go along with them; see Philipp I. Ackermann-Lieberman, "Commercial Forms and Legal Norms in the Jewish Community of Medieval Egypt," *Law and History Review* 30 (2012): 1007–52.

42 See Goitein, *Med. Soc.*, 5:206. For the context, see Zinger, "Women, Gender and Law," 36, note 54.

43 ENA NS 19.14 + ENA 4010.7, ll. 6–7, ed. Mordechai A. Friedman, "The Ransom-Divorce: Divorce Proceedings Initiated by the Wife in Mediaeval Jewish Practice," *IOS* 6 (1976): 289–93 (the translation is Friedman's). For comparison, it is enlightening to read anthropological descriptions of contemporary Islamic courts, see Lawrence Rosen, *Anthropology of Justice: Law as Culture in Islamic Society* (Cambridge: Cambridge University Press, 1989), 7; Anna Würth, "A Sanaʿa Court: The Family and the Ability to Negotiate," *Islamic Law and Society* 2 (1995): 321.

of the above-mentioned "righteous elders."[44] It is possible to see their role as complementary to the work of the court: the court represented the law, and they represented compromise. However, the members of the court were clearly also engaged in mediation, not only in allowing the elders to play their role but in various other ways. For example, we hear of cases being held in private residences and this seems to signify a mode of mediation versus one of adjudication.[45] The court also often postponed the process and procrastinated in order to prod the parties to reach a settlement.[46] Cases of formal arbitration (whereby the parties agree in advance to be bound by the decision of accepted arbitrators) are quite rare.[47]

While Jewish courts preferred and encouraged mediated settlements, they also made decisive rulings. The problem is that, as Goitein observed, "formal judgments, quoting the legal sources and detailing the reasons for the decisions made, are almost entirely lacking." Goitein's solution was that "the countless releases and acknowledgements that do not contain [an explicit remark about mediation] have to be regarded as results of judicial decisions."[48] According to Goitein, judges refrained from giving formal judgements out of religious scruples, so their rulings were given the form of a declaration of acknowledgement or release by one of the parties.[49] In other words, the many examples in which litigants come before the court arguing and then it was settled that one party would release the other or acknowledge a certain debt reflect decisive rulings by the court. Goitein's solution is ingenious and probably true in many cases, yet it appears to be too rigid for a legal culture that Goitein himself described

---

44 On the role of the "elders" in the courtroom, see Goitein, *Mediterranean Society*, vol. 2, 58–61 and 342; Ben-Sasson, *Qayrawan*, 326–9.

45 See, for example, T-S 10J25.3, r. 15-16, ed. Frenkel, "*Compassionate*," doc. 57; T-S 18J2.5, ed. Zinger, "Seven Documents," doc. 3; and NLR Yevr.-Arab. I 1701 (unpublished). Muslim judges also occasionally held court in their private residence.

46 On the procrastination of the courts see Goitein, *Mediterranean Society*, vol. 2, 321–2. On the general issue of time in litigation, see Zinger, "Women, Gender and Law," 231–3.

47 See T-S 8J4.2 2r, edited in Elinoar Bareket, "Books of Records of the Jerusalemite Court from the Cairo Genizah in the First Half of the Eleventh Century," *HUCA* 69 (1998): 12–15 [in Hebrew]. On the distinction between arbitration and mediation see P. Van Minnen and Traianos Gagos, *Settling a Dispute: Toward a Legal Anthropology of Late Antique Egypt* (Ann Arbor: University of Michigan Press, 1994), 30–4; see also Simon Roberts, "The Study of Dispute: Anthropological Perspectives," in *Disputes and Settlements: Law and Human Relations in the West*, ed. John Bossy (Cambridge: Cambridge University Press, 1983), 1–24.

48 Goitein, *Mediterranean Society*, vol. 2, 335.

49 Ibid., 334–5.

as fluid and which, as we have seen, he compared to the bazaar.[50] It is probably best to acknowledge at this stage of the research that Jewish courts in medieval Egypt employed a combination of adjudication and mediation, without asserting that all releases and acknowledgements were a result of judicial rulings.[51] Future research ought to clarify the factors that determined the way a case was presented and when mediation or adjudication would be pursued.

Understanding how what took place in court was translated to a written record is crucial for the way we read legal records, yet we still await a thorough study of this process. Goitein writes that "the presiding judge would recapitulate the statements made by the parties, the recapitulation being taken down verbatim by a clerk or the beadle of the synagogue."[52] From this it appears that while the records in our hand may not quote the speech of the parties, they at least record faithfully the summary made by the judge in the closing of the session. However, there are good reasons to think that the process was less straightforward and probably more diverse than Goitein presents.[53]

If all the court clerk had to do was to write down the judge's oral recapitulation, how come we find so many drafts of legal documents in the Genizah? Similarly, the Genizah preserved numerous pages from court notebooks in which we find short entries in which the court clerk recorded the bare facts of the case (more on these below). This suggests that often the clerk would not write down verbatim a full recapitulation but made notes for himself and wrote the document at a later date. Indeed, the drafting of the final legal record could be delayed and take place weeks and even months after the court session. Goitein's depiction of the process minimizes the role of the court clerk to a mere stenographer. It is more probable that the drafting of the legal records

---

50 Ibid., 327 and vol. 5, 206.

51 This is not the place to go into the various considerations for and against Goitein's solution. For one thing, evidence for judicial rulings is more common than Goitein lets on. See Zinger, "Women, Gender and Law," 31–6, for a preliminary discussion, but the matter clearly awaits a systematic inquiry. This should include a comparison with Islamic courts, on which see Christian Müller, "Settling Litigation without Judgment: The Importance of the *Ḥukm* in Qāḍī Cases from Mamlūk Jerusalem," in *Dispensing Justice in Islam: Qadis and Their Judgments*, ed. Khalid Masud, Rudolph Peters, and David S. Powers (Leiden: Brill, 2006), 47–70; and the articles included in Mathieu Tillier (ed.), *Arbitrage et conciliation dans l'Islam médiéval et modern*, special issue of *Revue des Mondes musulmans et de la Méditerranée* 140 (2016): 13–226.

52 Goitein, *Mediterranean Society*, vol. 2, 336.

53 Goitein points to Maimonides, *Mishneh Torah*, Book of Judges, Laws of Sanhedrin, 21:9 and T-S 8J4.9 2v, ll. 6–7, edited in Goitein, "The Synagogue Building," 93–4. I am not convinced that one can draw such a broad conclusion from these two references.

was a complex process, which changed according to the personalities, expertise, and relationship between the judge and the clerk.[54]

On the one hand, problematizing the relationship between the written record and what took place in court means that we can no longer take them at face value. [55] On the other hand, recognizing that "the legal record is as much an act of forgetting as it is one of remembering" opens a new set of questions on the narrative aspects of legal records: The narrative of which litigant is being adopted by the court? How is the court presenting itself? What drama is enacted and what rhetorical devices are employed?[56]

Legal documents come in many shapes and forms and there are different ways to classify them. One simple and useful classification relates to their role in the judicial process. A *deed* (Heb. *sheṭar*, pl. *sheṭarot*) is a legal document given to one of the parties.[57] For example, in a deed of debt (Heb. *sheṭar ḥov*) the debtor acknowledges a debt to the creditor, who holds on to the deed.[58] In a marriage deed (Heb. *sheṭar ketubbah*), the groom takes on various monetary

---

54 For a casual admittance that the speech recorded in legal documents is not exactly what the parties spoke, see Abraham Maimonides, *Responsa*, no. 68.

55 The study of Genizah legal records can benefit greatly from the advances made in the study of Ottoman legal records. To cite only four examples: Dror Ze᾽evi, "The Use of Ottoman Shari῾a Court Records as a Source for Middle Eastern Social History: A Reappraisal," *Islamic Law and Society* 5 (1998): 35–56; Leslie Peirce, *Morality Tales: Law and Gender in the Ottoman Court of Aintab* (Berkeley: University of California Press, 2003); Bogaç Ergene, *Local Court, Provincial Society and Justice in the Ottoman Empire* (Leiden: Brill, 2003); Ido Shahar, "Theme Issue: Shifting Perspectives in the Study of Shari῾a Courts: Methodologies and Paradigms: Introduction," *Islamic Law and Society* 15 (2008): 1–19.

56 The quote is from Marie A. Kelleher, *The Measure of Woman: Law and Female Identity in the Crown of Aragon* (Philadelphia: University of Pennsylvania Press, 2010), 10. To offer one example, Goitein takes at face value statements to the effect that "X and Y came before the court, many accusations were exchanged the reporting of which would take too long until it was settled that . . . ," suggesting that in these frequent cases judges thought that "the litigants said things that had no actual bearing on the matter"; Goitein, *Mediterranean Society*, vol. 2, 336. While this is certainly possible, it is also possible to read such statements as minimizing conflict (without erasing it—conflict is essential for drama) and highlighting the peace-brokering role of the court. Litigants who enter the stage yelling in disagreement are presented as exiting the court as negotiating members of the community. On the courts' interest in keeping litigants as negotiating members of society, see Rosen, *Anthropology of Justice*, 17.

57 For a historical overview, see Mordechai Akiva Friedman, "Contracts: Rabbinic Literature and Ancient Jewish Documents," in *The Literature of the Sages, Second Part: Midrash and Targum; Liturgy, Poetry, Mysticism, Contracts, Inscriptions, Ancient Science; and the Languages of Rabbinic Literature*, ed. S Safrai et al. (Aspen: Fortress Press, 2007), 421–58.

58 Usually one deed was made, however, in some occasions both parties received a copy. As Ackermann-Liebermann shows, these copies were not necessarily identical, see Philipp Ackerman-Lieberman, "Legal Writing in Medieval Cairo: 'Copy' or 'Likeness' in Jewish

and behavioral commitments and the deed is given to the bride. The *toref* of a deed includes the specific details of the case (names of the parties, date, place, and particulars of the agreement). The *ṭofes* contains the formulaic clauses that constitute the framework of the deed, such as the confirmation of legal capacity,[59] acquisition clause, cancellation of notifications,[60] warranty clause (Ar. *ḍamān al-darak*), [61] and so forth. The earliest legal documents are written in (often beautiful) Hebrew, but by the mid-eleventh century Judeo-Arabic had mostly replaced Hebrew, though Hebrew deeds made a partial come-back in the first half of the thirteenth century.[62] However, even in a Judeo-Arabic deed many of the formulaic clauses employ a mixture of Hebrew, Aramaic and Arabic.[63] Karaite deeds are predominantly in Hebrew.[64] Deeds must be signed by two witnesses, but often more people added their signatures. After the

---

Documentary Formulae," in *"From a Sacred Source": Genizah Studies in Honour of Professor Stefan C. Reif*, ed. Ben Outhwaite and Siam Bhayro (Leiden: Brill, 2011), 1–24.

59 For this clause, see Geoffrey Khan, *Arabic Legal and Administrative Documents in the Cambridge Genizah Collections* (Cambridge: Cambridge University Press, 1993), 204.

60 See Shmuel Shilo and Menachem Elon, "Ones," *Encyclopedia Judaica*, vol. 15, 428–9.

61 Much has been written on this clause, see the bibliography mentioned in S. D. Goitein and Mordechai Akiva Friedman, *Joseph Lebdī: Prominent India Trader*, vol. 1 of *India Book* (Jerusalem: Ben Zvi Institute, 2009), 201, note 70 [in Hebrew].

62 The reasons behind these language shifts are under debate. The standard explanation sees the spread of Judeo-Arabic as a result of the increasing influence of Iraqis in Egypt and the decline of the previous Palestinian tradition (Goitein even went so far as to point out Hillel b. Eli, a Baghdadi cantor who served as a court clerk between 1066–1108, as a crucial figure in this transition). The latter resurgence of Hebrew is usually explained with relation to the immigration of French scholars to Egypt in the first half of the thirteenth century. Recently Ackermann-Lieberman challenged these explanations and offered new ones, see Phillip Ackermann-Lieberman, "Legal Pluralism among the Court Records of Medieval Egypt," *BEO* 63 (2014): 79–112.

63 Putting aside marriage contracts, usually written in either Babylonian or Palestinian Aramaic, the Geniza also preserved occassional deeds in Aramaic and a couple of Judeo-Persian legal documents, see Margoliouth, "A Jewish-Persian Law Report," and Shaul Shaked, "An Early Karaite Document in Judeo-Persian," *Tarbiz* 41 (1971): 49–58 [in Hebrew].

64 On Karaite legal documents, see Jacob Mann, *Texts and Studies in Jewish History and Literature*, with Introduction by Gershon D. Cohen, 2 vols. (New York: Ktav, 1972), vol. 2, 156–68; Judith Olszowy-Schlanger, "Karaite Legal Documents," in *Karaite Judaism: A Guide to its History and Literary Sources*, ed. Meira Polliack (Leiden: Brill, 2003), 255–73. For Karaite legal documents in other languages, see Margoliouth, "A Jewish-Persian Law Report"; Shaked, "An Early Karaite Document in Judeo-Persian"; J. Olszowy-Schlanger, *Karaite Marriage Documents from the Cairo Geniza: Legal Tradition and Community Life in Mediaeval Egypt and Palestine* (Leiden: Brill, 1998), doc. 7; and NLR Yevr.-Arab. I 1701 (unpublished). For later Karaite legal records, see Haggai Ben-Shammai, "New Sources for the History of the Karaites in Sixteenth-Century Egypt (Preliminary Description)," *Ginzei Qedem: Genizah Research Annual* 2 (2006): 11–22 [in Hebrew].

witnesses' signature we occasionally find a signed validation clause which confirms that the signatures are really the witnesses.[65] On the back of some deeds we find, usually confined to the left half of the page, a "follow-up" transaction that relates to the central one on the recto.[66] On the back occasionally an archiving note can also be found. People paid for the writing of the deed and the price increased for larger and more carefully crafted deeds.[67] What all this looks like can be seen in Figs. 2–4:

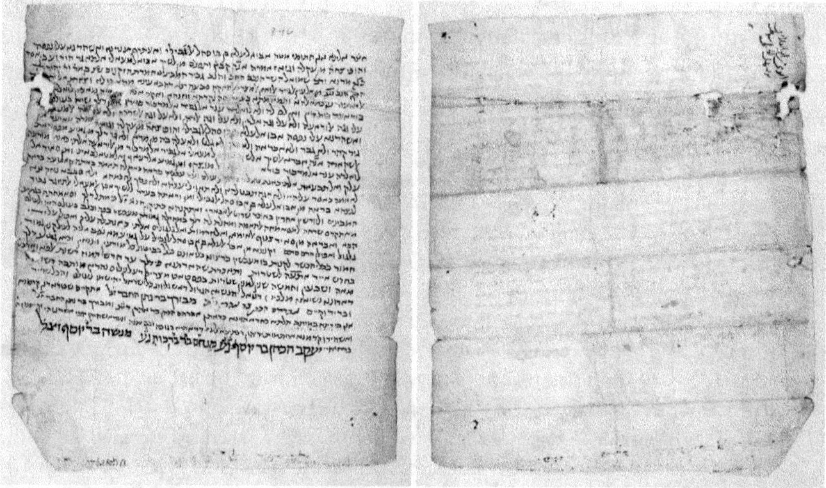

Fig. 2: A deed of quittance from Fustat. The legal act took place in the month of Iyyar 1164, but the writing of the deed was delayed for two months until Tammuz of the same year. After the signing of two witnesses, four lines from the bottom, appears a validation clause (*qiyyum*) signed by three other people. On the verso an archival note in Arabic Script is found in the top right corner. Halper 346. Courtesy of the Library at the Herbert D. Katz Center for Advanced Judaic Studies, Kislak Center for Special Collections, Rare Books and Manuscripts, University of Pennsylvania.

---

65 On the validation clause and why it is needed, see Elon, *Jewish Law*, vol. 2, 610–14.

66 For some examples, see Bodl. MS Heb. a 3.40, Halper 333, T-S 18J1.17, T-S 13J8.31, T-S 12.163, T-S 13J31.6, and Moses Maimonides, *Responsa*, vol. 2, 413, no. 332. Such an entry is called a *faṣl*, see Abraham Maimonides, *Responsa*, 178, no. 106, and Khan, *Arabic Legal and Administrative Documents*, 9.

67 Moses Maimonides, *Mishneh Torah*, Book of Judges, Laws of Sanhedrin, 23:3: "Every judge who sits and augments his honor in order to increase the payments to his cantors and scribes falls under those who incline to greed." We do not have a lot of precise data on court fees, see T-S 13J20.17 (unpublished), T-S 10J25.3, recto 18 (edited in Frenkel, *Alexandria*, doc. 57), and T-S Ar.49.166.2, verso 15 (edited in Gil, *Palestine*, doc. 388).

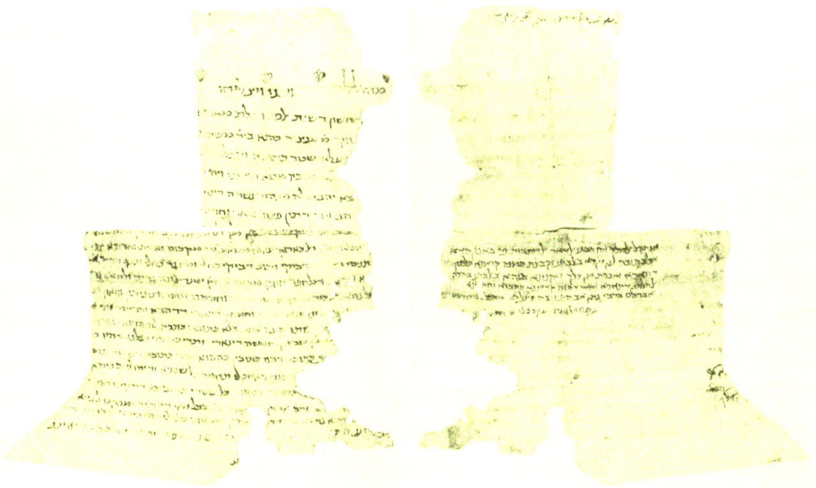

Fig. 3: On the recto, a torn eleventh-century *ketubbah* that was produced after the original ketubbah was lost or destroyed (T-S 16.155 is another piece from this replacement *ketubbah*). On the verso, a note records the sale of real estate mentioned in the *ketubbah* by the wife. Halper 333. Courtesy of the Library at the Herbert D. Katz Center for Advanced Judaic Studies, Kislak Center for Special Collections, Rare Books and Manuscripts, University of Pennsylvania.

While deeds have received the majority of scholars' attention so far, the Genizah also contains many pages from court notebooks.[68] The *court notebook* (also called "book of records"; Heb. *shimush*, Ar. *maḥḍar*) contains the record of the legal proceedings kept by the court. In addition to recording the regular work of the court, people occasionally asked to record in the court notebook a transaction that took place outside the court or in another court. At other times people asked that a copy of a transaction recorded in the court notebook be made for them. While a deed is usually written on a stand-alone piece of parchment or paper, the court notebook was written on paper in a codex form. Since these notebooks came apart with the passing of time, what we usually find in the Genizah are bifolia (a sheet of paper divided in half to form two leaves or four pages) or single leaves of

68 Three studies on Genizah court notebooks are Bareket, "Books of Records," Gideon Libson, "The 'Court Memorandum' (*Maḥḍar*) in Saadiah's Writings and the Genizah and the Muslim *Maḥḍar*," *Ginzei Qedem* 5 (2009): 99–163 [in Hebrew], and Olszowy-Schlanger, "Les archives médiévales dans la genizah du Caire."

the notebook. However, two larger court notebooks have been preserved.[69] Even though the earliest comparable Jewish court notebooks come from sixteenth-century Ashkenaz, these twelfth-century notebooks remain unpublished.[70] It is not always possible to decide whether an item is a deed or a sheet from a court notebook; however, a telltale sign is the existence of unrelated legal entries on the same sheet. The entries can be full-blown records of the proceedings, shorter entries that provide some passages in full but abbreviate or drop others, and bare-bones details upon the basis of which the court clerk will later compose the deed.[71] The fact that we find numerous pages of court notebooks of clerks for whom sizable personal correspondence also survives, suggests that clerks took the notebooks home, reflecting the typical mixture of private and public tendencies in the working of Jewish legal institutions in Egypt.[72] Fig. 4 is an example of a leaft from a court notebooks.[73]

---

69 The largest surviving court notebook is NLR Yevr.-Arab. I 1700. It contains fifty-eight pages and covers the work of the Fusṭāṭ court for three consecutive months in the year 1156. A less well-known court notebook is Bodl. MS Heb. f. 56.43–62, which contains entries from the 1180s. The two notebooks differ in some fundamental ways. For example, the later notebook shows that the court was deeply involved in supervising the communal endowments, which is not evident in the earlier notebook. Also, while the earlier larger notebook contains records from only three months, the later and smaller notebook contains entries from a broader range of years. A systematic study and comparison of the two notebooks thus holds much potential.

70 The observation that "without exception, the corpus of extant *pinkasim* is a product of the early modern period, as no comparable registers remain from the Middle Ages," needs to be revised; see Jay R. Berkovitz, *Protocols of Justice: The Pinkas of the Metz Rabbinic Court 1771–1789* (Leiden: Brill, 2014), 5–6.

71 For an example of the latter, we find an entry stating: "A partnership agreement for 160 dinars will be written. Abū al-Faraj . . . handed over 150 (dinars) to Tamīm . . . who added ten (dinars to the partnership). (Tamīm) will travel with the total to Upper Egypt. He may buy what he wishes. The profit will be divided equally into two halves . . ." (NLR, Evr.-Arab. I 1700.12r, ed. Ackerman-Lieberman, *The Business of Identity*, doc. 8; the translation is Ackerman-Lieberman's with some modifications).

72 Goitein, *Mediterranean Society*, vol. 2, 344. For an interesting testimony, see Mosseri VII 189.2 (unpublished). See also Wael Hallaq, "The Qāḍī's Dīwān (sijill) before the Ottomans," *BSOAS* 61 (1998): 415–36.

73 Several leaves and bifolia of court notebooks were put in chronological order in T-S 8J4 and T-S 8J5. Leafing through these folders gives a very useful impression of the development of the court notebook across time.

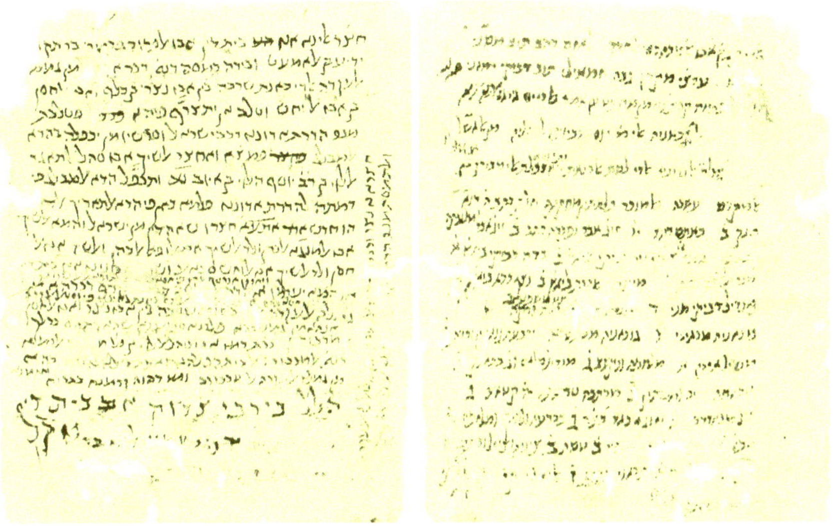

Fig. 4: A leaf from a court notebook. One side records a transaction regarding a commercial partnership that came before the court in 1160 and is signed by the presiding judge and another member of court. On the other side is an unrelated dowry list. Halper 345. Courtesy of the Library at the Herbert D. Katz Center for Advanced Judaic Studies, Kislak Center for Special Collections, Rare Books and Manuscripts, University of Pennsylvania.

Remains of court notebooks are important because whereas a deed gives us information on an individual case, the court notebook supplies not only information about several cases but also about the work of the court in general. A central problem with trying to understand the work of the court from deeds is that the survival of deeds is directly related to their subject matter. For example, when the delayed marriage gift is collected (or relinquished), the *ketubbah* is torn up. For this reason, the vast majority of *ketubbot* found in the Genizah are fragments. The survival of pages from court notebooks, however, seems unrelated to the specific entries recorded in them.[74] Therefore, they provide us with both statistically meaningful and more representative picture of the workings of the court. They allow us to answer question like: how many sessions were held each day (or at least sessions that were recorded)? Was the personnel of

74 However, other problems arise when dealing with court notebooks. For example, marriage records, and especially dowry lists (Ar. *taqwīm*), occupy a central place in court notebooks. However, when it comes to divorce, notebooks contain divorce settlements but do not record mere giving of divorce bills (Heb. *get*). In other words, divorce may be underrepresented in court notebooks.

the court set or did it change from day to day, or even from session to session? What was the breakdown of cases according to topic?

Furthermore, because the notebooks record summaries of cases, probably written during the session or right after it, they allow us to study the process of translation from legal act to writing. Finally, a deed often gives us the final resolution of a case with all the preceding stages telescoped into a single act. With court notebooks it is occasionally possible to follow a single case through several entries made in different court sessions.[75] Plenty of entries from court notebooks have been published over the years due to their specific contents. However, the study of court notebooks *as court notebooks* has barely began.

Formularies and drafts are also important sources for the work of the court. A *formulary* has the frame of a legal record, but some or all of the specific details have been replaced by fillers (the equivalent of John Doe, or "so-and-so"). Writers of legal documents use formularies as a model for how to compose legal documents. When an uncommon legal procedure was conducted, occasionally the court clerk would write down a copy of the record as a formulary for future use. Formularies were often brought together to form collections, several of which were found in the Genizah.[76] Scholars composed more comprehensive collections of formularies as legal monographs.[77] Formularies tell us of cases

75 For example, my impression from the largest surviving court notebook mentioned above is that more than half of the entries are related to other entries in the same notebook.

76 The most important one is Bodl. MS Heb. f. 27.10v–25v, from Lucena in Spain and containing a formulary dated to 1020–21. The collection was edited in Joseph Rivlin, *Bills and Contracts from Lucena (1020-1025 CE)* (Ramat Gan: Bar Ilan University Press, 1994) [in Hebrew].

77 Saʿadya Gaʾon's (d. 942) *Kitāb al-shahāda wa-l-wathāʾiq* (Book of Testimony and Deeds) contains formularies in Aramaic and instructions in Judeo-Arabic. Extensive fragments of this work were found in the Genizah and published in Menahem Ben-Sasson, "Fragments from Saʿadya's Sefer ha-ʿEdut ve-ha-Sheṭarot," *Shenaton ha-Mishpat ha-ʿIvri* 11–12 (1984–6): 135–278 [in Hebrew]. A new and fuller edition is forthcoming: Menahem Ben-Sasson and Robert Brody (eds. and trans.), *Sefer ha-ʿEduyot ve-ha-Sheṭarot le-Rav Saʿadya Gaʾon* (Jerusalem: The Israel Academy for Sciences and Humanities, in press). In Hayya (also Hai) Gaʾon's (d. 1038) *Sefer ha-Sheṭarot* the formularies are in Aramaic, but the instructions are in Hebrew, see Simḥa Assaf, *The Book of Sheṭarot (Formulary) of R. Hai Gaʾon*, supplement to *Tarbiz* 1, no. 3 (1930) [in Hebrew]. Finally, in *Sefer ha-Sheṭarot* of Yehudah ben Barsilai from Barcelona (died at the beginning of the twelfth century) both the instructions and (most) of the deeds are in Hebrew; see S. J. Halberstam, *Sepher Haschetaroth: Dokumentenbuch von R. Jehuda ben Barsilai aus Barcelona* (Berlin: Itzkowski, 1898) [in Hebrew]. A new edition was recently published as Yehudah ha-Barzeloni, *Sefer ha-Sheṭarot*, ed. Joseph Rivlin (Bene Beraq: Sefunim, 2014). See also V. Aptowitzer, "Formularies of Decrees and Documents from a Gaonic Court," *JQR* 4 (1913): 23–51; and Asher Gulak, *ʿOtzar ha-Sheṭarot ha-Nehugim be-Yisraʾel* [*A Treasury of Jewish Deeds*] (Jerusalem: Poʿalim Press, 1926).

that took place, of which a judge or a court clerk thought a similar case might occur again in the future. Formularies also provide another angle for understanding the work of the court clerk in crafting the legal act into a legal record.

Drafts exist for deeds, court notebooks, and formularies. A draft provides us with more than just information about specific cases for which we probably do not have the final product. Not unlike court notebooks and formularies, drafts are intermediary products in the working of the court and thus shed light on the process in which legal records were composed. To give an illustrative example, in November 1091 Muna bt. Samuel sued her husband Jekuthiel for the remainder of her *ketubbah*, according to what was decided in a previous session. A draft of the proceedings reports that "It was settled that [Muna] would take an oath . . . and receive from [Jekuthiel] all of what she deserved and he will write her a bill of divorce." Muna brought to the court various items and said: "This is all that remains of his property with me," and agreed to take an oath on it. The court then made the severity of taking the oath clear to her. A bier and ram horns were brought forth to heighten the dramatic effect of the oath.[78] Next we find in the draft the following deleted: "She said, 'I am not able (to swear).' 'I will swear'," followed by a statement that the elders arranged a compromise: Muna relinquished all her previous claims and whatever she was still owed from the *ketubbah*. In return, Jekuthiel divorced her. Were we to have the final deed, we would be told about the compromise brought about by the elders but not about Muna's fluctuations about taking an oath.[79] Thus the draft reveals what took place but was omitted from the final record.

Surveying the legal arena: Other legal institutions

The local Jewish court was the center of legal life, but there were other venues that constituted what Uriel Simonsohn aptly called "Islam's judicial bazaar."[80] These venues offered litigants ways to bypass, pressure, bolster the local court

---

78 Oaths (Heb. *shevuʿa*, Ar. *yamīn*) are a central component in court procedure in Jewish law. See Haim Hermann Cohn and Menachem Elon, "Oath," *Encyclopedia Judaica*, vol. 15, 360–4.

79 The main document is ENA 4020.47, partially edited in Yeḥezkel David, "Divorce among the Jews according to Cairo Genizah Documents and Other Sources" (PhD diss., Tel Aviv University, 2000), 101–4 [in Hebrew]. Other related documents are T-S 8.184 and ENA NS 30.8. My reconstruction is different from the one offered in Goitein, *Mediterranean Society*, vol. 3, 266.

80 Simonsohn, *A Common Justice*, 63. See also Ben Sasson, *Qayrawan*, 306–16.

or appeal its decisions.[81] Recent scholarship has examined at length the relationship between legal pluralism and communal autonomy.[82] Less attention has been dedicated to the nuts and bolts of how this legal pluralism played out in practice and what legal culture it fostered.

Responsa (singular: responsum, Heb. *she'elot u-teshuvot*, Ar. *fatāwā*) are the answers of legal authorities to queries posed to them.[83] The answers and occasionally the queries can then be gathered and edited into literary collections. All these stages are found in the Genizah, together with many letters that deal with obtaining or using responsa. The common understanding of responsa is that queries were drafted by judges who needed either the expertise or the authority of well-known respondents.[84] The answers were meant to guide the court to make a correct ruling by clarifying what Jewish law says on a specific scenario. However, in the so-called classical Genizah period, many queries were formulated by litigants and their associates who planned to present them in court to bolster their position.[85] We see how obtaining a favorable responsum could be used by a litigant in a letter written by a woman in Alexandria to her son in Fusṭāṭ, in which she tells him: "I have delayed the giving of

81 I believe it is more helpful to define these alternatives to the court according to the authority on which they rely and what is asked from them, than by the characteristics of their documents like physical layout, certain vocabulary, or structure. First, there is a good deal of overlap and exchange in terms of layout and formula between responsa, petitions, and legal records. Second, within each genre there is a spectrum between formal layout and structure and more informal ones. Thus, we find legal queries in personal letters as well as in a formal format with "what does our lord say regarding" and the like. Similarly, we find interested parties talking to the head of the Jews, writing a personal letter or submitting a formal petition.

82 Beyond Simonsohn, *A Common Justice*, see Marina Rustow, "At the Limits of Communal Autonomy: Jewish Bids for Intervention from the Mamluk State," *MSR* 13 (2009): 133–59; and Ackermann-Lieberman, "Legal Pluralism."

83 See Elon, *Jewish Law*, vol. 3, 1453–1528; Y. Zvi Stampfer, "Responsa," in *Encyclopedia of Jews in the Islamic World*, ed. Norman Stillman (Leiden: Brill, 2010), vol. 4, 159–67; Haym Soloveitchik, *The Use of Responsa as Historical Source: A Methodological Introduction* (Jerusalem: Zalman Shazar Center, 1990) [in Hebrew].

84 Thus, when we find in the Genizah a query about a trivial point of law, we should not rush to conclude that the questioner was ignorant of the law. He or she may have known the law, but needed the authoritative weight of the respondent behind them; see Goitein, *Mediterranean Society*, vol. 2, 339.

85 See Blau's comment in Maimonides, *Responsa*, 3:13, note 1. Compare with Islamic law in which the basic fatwa is the one presented by laymen, rather than by a person in a judicial or administrative capacity; see Norman Calder, "The Social Function of Fatwas," in *Islamic Jurisprudence in the Classical Era*, ed. Colin Imber (Cambridge: Cambridge University Press, 2010), 167–74.

judgement (that is, in court) until you bring me the *fatwā* from the Rayyis about what should be done."[86]

To obtain a favorable responsum, litigants could send similar queries to different respondents in the hope of getting a beneficial answer.[87] Another way was to frame the question in such a way that it would enlist a favorable response.[88] Respondents were aware of such manipulations and often began their answers with statements such as "If this is indeed the case."[89] The practices of querying and responding were fluid and exhibited a significant degree of variation. Responsa could play a major role in legal proceedings, however, it was not clear who may formulate questions, who can answer them, what weight these answers carry, from where they draw their authority, and where they should fit in the legal procedure. This fluidity allowed social factors to play a significant role in the process of obtaining responsa.[90] Fig. 7 shows an example of a query (containing three separate sections), with an autograph answer of Abraham Maimonides.

86 Halper 400, recto 13–14 (unpublished).

87 Mordechai Akiva Friedman, "Responsa of Abraham Maimonides on a Debtor's Travails," in *Genizah Research after Ninety Years: The Case of Judaeo-Arabic*, ed. J. Blau and S. C. Reif (Cambridge: Cambridge University Press, 1992), 82–92. Sending similar queries to different authorities is known already from the geonic period.

88 Mordechai Akiva Friedman, "New Fragments from the Responsa of Maimonides," in *Studies in Geniza and Sephardic Heritage Presented to Shelomo Dov Goitein on the Occasion of his Eightieth Birthday*, ed. S. Morag et al. (Jerusalem: Magness Press, 1981), 115–20 [in Hebrew].

89 Such statements are also common in Islamic responsa.

90 I explore this in depth in my "Toward a Social History of Responsa in Medieval Egypt" (in preparation). For the time being, see Berachyahu Lifshitz, "The Legal Status of the Responsa Literature," in *Authority, Process and Method: Studies in Jewish Law*, ed. Hanina Ben Menahem and Neil S. Hecht (Amsterdam: Harwood Academic Publishers, 1998), 59–100, esp. 85 and 98–100; Gerald J. Blidstein, "The License to Teach and its Social Implications in Maimonides," *Tarbiz* 51 (1982): 577–87 [in Hebrew]; idem, "On the Freedom of Instruction and the Authority to Rule: A Study of Two Maimonidean Responsa," in *Study and Knowledge in Jewish Thought*, ed. Howard Kreisel (Beer Sheva: Ben Gurion University Press, 2006), 147–55.

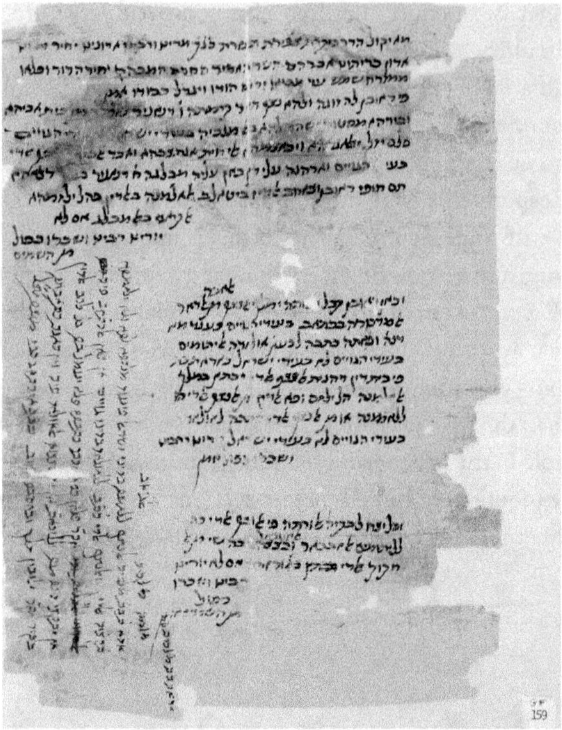

Fig. 5: An autograph responsum of Abraham Maimonides. Halper 159. Courtesy of the Library at the Herbert D. Katz Center for Advanced Judaic Studies, Kislak Center for Special Collections, Rare Books and Manuscripts, University of Pennsylvania.

Petitioning is appealing to a social superior who holds a political position (or has the ear of one) asking him (or rarely her) for assistance. In some cases, petitioning was directed not to an individual but to the Jewish community, congregation or the members of the court.[91] This is the case in the much-discussed institution of "delaying the prayer" (Heb. *'iqquv ha-tefilah*), whereby a Jew would delay or stop the communal prayer to protest the treatment he received from a fellow Jew or a communal institution.[92]

91 This is often the case with women's petitions; see T-S NS J430, CUL Or. 1081 J8, T-S 13J18.10 and T-S 13 J 18.18. The last two are edited in Mark R. Cohen, *The Voice of the Poor in the Middle Ages: An Anthology of Documents from the Cairo Geniza* (Princeton, NJ: Princeton University Press, 2005), nos. 43 and 45.

92 See Avraham Grossman, "The Origins and Essence of the Custom of 'Stopping-the-Service'," *Milet* 1 (1983): 199–220 [in Hebrew]; Menahem Ben-Sasson, "Appeal to the Congregation in Islamic Countries in the Early Middle Ages," in *Knesset Ezra: Literature and Life in the Synagogue Presented to Ezra Fleischer*, ed. S. Elizur et al. (Jerusalem: Ben

The Islamic bureaucracy had an elaborate procedure for petitions; however, in Jewish circles it seems that the procedure was more fluid.[93] We find petitions with formal structure and layout, but also letters of request that lack these features (and, of course, a whole range of in-between).[94] There were also probably numerous cases in which people petitioned a superior orally, without any written trace. Many petitions involve requests for charity, but others are of a legal nature, like a wife protesting her husband's violence to the Head of the Jews and requesting a divorce.[95] Petitions often employ a mixture of claims on the basis of mercy and justice. For example, a widow claims that she and her orphaned children are suffering greatly after they have been deprived of her husbands' estate due to trickery and threats on the part of his creditors and the local Alexandrian court.[96]

Formally speaking, the head of the Jews (or any Jewish legal authority) could not pass judgement without hearing both sides. Thus, the response to a petition was usually procedural. For example, the head of the Jews could order a local court to examine the matter (so petitions were a good way to start litigation with an advantage). In cases where petitions protested the treatment that a party received from a local court, the head

Zvi, 1994), 327–50 [in Hebrew]; Robert Bonfil, "The Right to Cry Aloud: A Note on the Medieval Custom of 'Interrupting the Prayer'," in *From Sages to Savants: Studies Presented to Avraham Grossman*, ed. Joseph R. Hacker et al. (Jerusalem: Zalman Shazar, 2010), 145–56 [in Hebrew]. In *Mediterranean Society*, vol. 2, 323–5, Goitein claims that the technical term for this procedure was *istighātha* (*mustaghīth* is the active participle), a very common term in the Genizah. While occasionally this term is used in the context of this procedure, in most other occasions this term has a more general meaning of petitioning a higher authority (Jewish or Muslim) for assistance and/or protesting against someone; see Mordechai Akiva Friedman, "Abraham Maimonides on his Leadership, Reforms and Spiritual Imperfection," *JQR* 104 (2014): 504–5.

93 See Samuel Miklós Stern, *Fāṭimid Decrees: Original Documents from the Fatimid Chancery* (London: Faber and Faber, 1964). Marina Rustow is currently finishing a large project that will shed much new light on the petitioning process.

94 On the structure of formal petitions, see Geoffrey Khan, "The Historical Development of the Structure of Medieval Arabic Petitions," *BSOAS* 53 (1990): 8–30; Mark R. Cohen, "Four Judaeo-Arabic Petitions of the Poor from the Cairo Geniza," *JSAI* 24 (2000): 446–71. On the physical layout, see Marina Rustow, "The Diplomatics of Leadership: Administrative Documents in Hebrew Scripts from the Geniza," in *Jews, Christians and Muslims in Medieval and Early Modern Times: A Festschrift in Honor of Mark R. Cohen*, ed. Arnold Franklin et al. (Leiden: Brill, 2014), 306–51.

95 For example, see ENA NS 31.21; Mosseri V.355 and T-S 13J13.30, edited in Zinger, "Women, Gender and Law," docs. 3, 4 and 13 respectively.

96 See T-S 28.19, edited in Frenkel, *Alexandria*, doc. 42. For an example in English translation, see T-S 10J16.4 and T-S 13J13.6, edited in Cohen, *The Voice of the Poor*, nos. 47 and 48.

of the Jews could turn the case to the central court in Fusṭāṭ or contact the local judge or *muqaddam* demanding an explanation. However, as we have encountered often in the legal arena, the relationship between the court and the head of the Jews could be quite diverse and fluid. This fluidity provided an opportunity for well-connected litigants to influence the process in court. While we usually do not hear of involvement from above in legal records, this seems to be more to do with how they were crafted than with reluctance on the part of the political leadership to interfere.[97]

Beyond the Jewish venues, Jews could turn to a variety of Muslim venues. As long as they recognized the domination of Islam and paid the poll tax, the non-Muslim communities in the medieval Islamic world usually enjoyed autonomy to run their communal affairs, especially those concerning matters of personal status.[98] However, non-Muslim individuals could avail themselves of Islamic legal venues as well.

The old scholarly consensus was that Jews adhered faithfully to their communal courts and made use of Muslim courts only in exceptional cases. However, a series of studies has proved conclusively that Jewish use of Muslim courts was pervasive.[99] Occasionally Islamic law offered an advantage over Jewish law, for example, in women's inheritance and ability to obtain a divorce. At other times, Jews sought the greater enforceability of Muslim institutions. Jews also used or threatened to use Muslim venues when they were unhappy with the process or outcome of their case in Jewish venues. The Jewish communal leadership saw the use of Muslim legal forums by their flock as a threat both to their authority and to the autonomy and integrity of Jewish communal life. When possible, they imposed a ban over transgressors. However, since the effectivity of the ban decreases if it is overused, they often had to resort to softer means such as requiring parties to receive permission before turning to a legal venue outside the community or adding clauses to legal agreements forbidding the use of Muslim venues.[100]

---

97 The same is true for responsa. While we have numerous queries involving legal disputes, we rarely hear of them in legal records. Yet they clearly influenced legal procedure, otherwise litigants would not try to obtain them.

98 Much has been written on Jewish autonomy under Islam. For a lucid introduction, see Mark R. Cohen, *Under Crescent and Cross: The Jews in the Middle Ages* (2nd edition; Princeton, NJ: Princeton University Press, 2008), 52–74.

99 See Simonsohn, *A Common Justice*, and the studies mentioned in Cohen, *Maimonides and the Merchants*, 203, note 60.

100 The nature of the clause usually depended on the type of deed. In a deed of debt, the debtor often proclaims that that the debt will be collectible "whether in Jewish or gentile courts."

Remarkably, the variety of Jewish legal venues surveyed above (court, responsa, petitioning) is closely paralleled by Islamic legal venues.[101] Muslim courts were headed by *qāḍīs* and produced legal records in Arabic script.[102] Islamic responsa are called *fatāwā* (sing. *fatwā*) and were given by *muftis*.[103] A third venue appears often in Genizah documents under the somewhat perplexing term *sulṭān* (or in Heb. *shilṭon, malkhut*).[104] Several of these documents make a clear distinction between *sulṭān* and Muslim courts. For example, in a 1052 divorce settlement, a Jewish woman undertakes that "she will not harass (her former husband), sue him in Muslim courts (*be-mishpate ha-goyyim*) nor bring him before the government (*shilṭon*)."[105] *Sulṭān* seems to be an umbrella term for various state authorities combining judicial and administrative features, from the Fatimid caliph and the Ayyubid sultan at the top, to their

---

In a release of debt, the former creditor will occasionally declare that they will sue for the debt neither in a Jewish nor gentile court; see more in Friedman, *Jewish Marriage in Palestine*, 474–77. For giving formal permission see, for example, ENA 4010.67 and, from a later date, ENA 2559.1, edited in Mark R. Cohen, "Correspondence and Social Control in the Jewish Communities of the Islamic World: A Letter of the Nagid Joshua Maimonides," *Jewish History* 1 (1986): 39–48.

101 The basic work on Islamic administration of justice is Tyan, *Histoire de l'organisation judiciaire en pays d'Islam*. An English summary can be found in his "Juridical Organization," in *Law in the Middle East*, ed. Majid Khadduri and Herbert J. Liebesny (Washington: The Middle East Institute, 1955), 236–78. The recent study of Yaacov Lev, *The Administration of Justice in Medieval Egypt from the Seventh to the Twelfth Century* (Edinburgh: Edinburgh University Press, 2020), explores the administration of justice in non-Muslim communities within its broader context.

102 Mathieu Tillier, *L'invention du cadi: la justice des musulmans, des juifs et des chrétiens aux premiers siécles de l'Islam* (Paris: Publication de la Sorbonne, 2017). In English, see Mohammad Fadel, "al-Qaḍi," in *The Oxford Handbook of Islamic Law*, ed. Anver M. Emon and Rumee Ahmed. On Muslim legal documents in the Genizah, see Khan, *Arabic Legal and Administrative Documents*, docs. 1–69. Many more such documents await study.

103 For examples of Jews turning to muftis, see T-S Ar. 40.96; Khan, *Arabic Legal and Administrative Documents*, doc. 64–6 and 68; Maimonides, *Responsa*, no. 9 and 90. On Islamic responsa, see the articles in Muhammad Khalid Masud, Brinkley Messick, and David Powers (eds.), *Islamic Legal Interpretation: Muftis and Their Fatwas* (Oxford: Oxford University Press, 1996).

104 On *sulṭān*, see S. D. Goitein, *Studies in Islamic History and Institutions* (Leiden: Brill, 1966), 197, and the latter reference in the next note.

105 T-S 13J8.1, ed. Zinger, "Seven Documents," doc. 4. For more information and examples, see Oded Zinger, "'She Aims to Harass Him': Jewish Women in Muslim Legal Venues in Medieval Egypt," *AJS Review* 42 (2018): 168–9.

viziers, military governors (Ar. *amir*, *wālī*), their deputies (*nāʾib*), the police (*shurtā*) and the guard of the quarter (*ṣāḥib al-rubʿ*) at the bottom.[106]

It seems misguided to expect precise and stable definitions, procedures, and division of labor of these state institutions, as structural flexibility and fluidity of terminology are essential features of the state's operation in the period. At the same time, more work on documentary material in combination with Arabic literary sources will probably help elucidate the contours, nature and functions of this flexibility.[107] To give one example, in a letter written during the reign of Saladin, a Jewish communal leader from Alexandria reports how he contemplated the best way to punish a Jew from his flock. According to his testimony, because he did not know the Muslim governor (*wālī*) or his delegate (*nāʾib*), he wrote down a petition (*waraqat al-mam[lūk] fulān yuqabbil al-arḍ*) but did not know whether to send it to the Muslim judge or to the governor. Then it occurred to him to send it to the supervisor of the markets (*al-muḥtasib*) whose punishment would probably be light.[108] However, the letter reports that the supervisor of the markets passed the matter to the governor, who ruled that the man should be flogged and publicly denounced around the Jewish neighborhood.[109]

---

106 This list is by no way exhaustive and one constantly comes across a bewildering plethora of titles and offices. For an example of trying to interrogate one such title (*ṣāḥib al-ḥarb*), see Zinger, "Women, Gender and Law," 374, note 47.

107 For instance, the term *maẓālim* (a special venue of justice meant to redress wrongs), on which so much ink has been spilled by historians, is rarely mentioned explicitly in Genizah documents. However, the function of turning to the ruler or his representatives for justice is certainly contained in the numerous references to *sulṭān* and Arabic-script petitions found in the Genizah. For example, important information on the *maẓālim* and how it was perceived by a Jew is revealed in a passage from a letter by Mevorakh b. Nathan: "My brother, know that after you left, the Sultan (probably Saladin), may God make his reign eternal, sat and wrote rescripts to the general public. Anyone could come to him and he (the Sultan) examined the injustice done to any oppressed"; ENA NS 19.31 (unpublished). *Maẓālim* is also mentioned in T-S 18J1.10, ed. Khan, *Arabic Legal and Administrative Documents*, doc. 32. On the many studies of *maẓālim* see Mathieu Tillier, "The Mazalim in Historiography," in *The Oxford Handbook of Islamic Law*, ed. Anver M. Emon and Rumee Ahmed (Oxford: Oxford University Press, 2018), 357–80.

108 On the *ḥisba* see Kristen Stilt, *Islamic Law in Action: Authority, Discretion, and Everyday Experiences in Mamluk Egypt* (Oxford: Oxford University Press, 2012); Qādir Muḥammad Ḥasan, "al-Ḥisba khilāl al-ʿahd al-ayyūbī," *BEO* 63 (2015): 191–204. On the *muḥtasib* in the Genizah, see Goitein, *Mediterranean Society*, vol. 6, 77 (index).

109 T-S 16.231, edited in Frenkel, *Alexandria*, doc. 29, partially translated in Goitein, *Mediterranean Society*, vol. 2, 371. About such public shaming, see Christian Lange, "Legal and Cultural Aspects of Ignominious Parading (*Tashhīr*) in Islam," *Islamic Law and Society* 14 (2007): 81–108. We see such punishment carried out by Muslim authorities also in T-S

The everyday relationship between Jewish and Muslim institutions was far from simple and still awaits a thorough study.[110] On the one hand, the Jewish leadership sought to protect Jewish autonomy. On the other hand, at least part of the Jewish court's authority stemmed from their being recognized as part of the state's administration of justice.[111] The Genizah has even preserved a deed of appointment by a Muslim authority of a Jewish judge.[112] On the Islamic side there was also a diversity of opinions among jurists regarding non-Muslim use of Muslim courts.[113] The result was a diverse picture in which the relationship changed according to the personalities involved, the subject matter, the interreligious atmosphere at the time, and so forth. For example, the office of inheritance (*diwān al-mawārith*) was notorious for its eagerness to seize the estates of non-Muslims without heirs and was often unscrupulous in its actions. However, we also find Muslim judges who were reluctant to interfere in internal Jewish matters and turned Jewish litigants that approached them back to Jewish venues.[114]

Accordingly, different venues could be used to complement the process in the local court, such as when the Muslim court would consult a Jewish jurisconsult or when an Islamic institution would use its authority to strengthen the Jewish court.[115] However, litigants could use the plurality, accessibility, and flexibility of the legal arena to challenge, appeal, or even replace the action in the local court. The choice between Muslim venues and

12.1 l.16, edited in Gil, *In the Kingdom of Ishmael,* doc. 812, and perhaps also T-S 13J25.7 l.20, ed. Gil, *Palestine,* doc. 37. Genizah documents occasionally use the fourth form (*ishhār*) to denote public denouncement by a Jewish authority; see ENA 2727.31 ll. 4 and 13, edited in Oded Zinger, "'What Sort of Sermon is This?' Leadership, Resistance, and Gender in a Communal Conflict," in *Jews, Christians and Muslims in Medieval and Early Modern Times: A Festschrift in Honor of Mark R. Cohen,* ed. Arnold Franklin et al. (Leiden: Brill, 2014), 83–98; T-S 10J16.6 l.12, edited in Frenkel, *Alexandria,* doc. 54. See also T-S 13J6.12 l.26 (unpublished).

110 Goitein, *Mediterranean Society,* vol. 2, 395–407 is the best introduction.

111 Ibid., vol. 2, 374; Goitein, "The Interplay of Jewish and Islamic Laws," 61 and 66.

112 T-S NS 320.45, ed. S. D. Goitein, *Palestinian Jewry in Early Islamic and Crusaders Times* (Jerusalem: Yad Ben Zvi, 1980), 77–8 [in Hebrew].

113 Gideon Libson, "Legal Autonomy and the Recourse to Legal Proceedings by Protected Peoples, according to Muslim Sources during the Geonic Period," in *The Intertwined Worlds of Islam: Essays in Memory of Hava Lazarus-Yafeh,* ed. Naḥem Ilan (Jerusalem: Hebrew University, 2002), 334–92 [in Hebrew].

114 See, for example, T-S 13Ja1.1, T-S Ar. 50.197, or Maimonides, *Responsa,* no. 73 and 196, and the discussions in Goitein, *Mediterranean Society,* vol. 2, 402; Ben-Sasson, *Qayrawan,* 311–12.

115 For a remarkable case in which the Muslim judge waits to receive Maimonides's ruling (in his own handwriting!) on a matter of a Jewish couple, see Maimonides, *Responsa,* no. 191.

the movement between them found in the letter of the communal leader from Alexandria can be seen in numerous examples as taking place also between Jewish and Muslim venues.[116] The plurality of venues provided litigants with agency and leverage vis-à-vis Jewish communal institutions, but also tended to prolong disputes and increase the unpredictability of the legal process, as one's opponent could always decide to open a new front in another legal venue.[117]

Outside of legal institutions: The social embeddedness of the legal arena

Beyond these Jewish and Muslim legal venues, litigants had a wide variety of ways to pursue disputes and influence the legal process by extra-legal means. Such means could be used to initiate a legal process, put pressure on the litigants or on the court itself, or avoid the legal process altogether. Only several of such means can be presented here. Whether they meant to influence the legal process or replace it, these extra-legal tactics are important both for helping us connect the legal process to its social surroundings and for thinking about litigants' alternatives beside litigation and therefore understand their choices.[118]

One effective way to protect oneself from losing in court is not to attend in the first place. The court could summon Jews to appear before it, but they could choose to ignore the summons. An amusing testimony in a court

116 I explored three examples in detail in Zinger, "Women, Gender and Law," 221–9.

117 In the mean time, see Zinger, "Women, Gender and Law," 229–33. It seems that the establishment of the Ayyubid dynasty ushered a period of more stringent supervision of communal boundaries, both from the Jewish and the Muslim side. From the Jewish side, the most important development was Maimonides's legislation (Heb. *taqanna*) against the use of Muslim courts and his staunch stance in *Mishne Torah*, Book of Judges, Laws of Sanhedrin, 26:7; see Cohen, *Maimonides and the Merchants*, 135–8. On the connection between the Ayyubids and a more stringent supervision of communal autonomy, see Marina Rustow, "Patronage in the Context of Solidarity and Reciprocity: Two Paradigms of Social Cohesion in the Premodern Mediterranean," in *Patronage, Production and Transmission of Texts in Medieval and Early Modern Jewish Cultures*, ed. Esperanza Alfonso and Jonathan Decter (Turnhout: Brepols, 2014), 33–4; Phillip Ackermann-Lieberman, "Legal Pluralism," 87–9; Zinger, "Jewish Women in Muslim Legal Venues," 168. Goitein, however, held the opposite opinion that "the dangerous practice of turning to the Muslim government . . . became rampant in Ayyubid times," see Goitein, *Mediterranean Society*, vol. 2, 406.

118 This point is made persuasively in Daniel Lord Smail, *The Consumption of Justice: Emotions, Publicity, and Legal Culture in Marseille, 1264–1423* (Ithaca: Cornell University Press, 2003).

notebook reports that on a certain Wednesday a well-known businesswoman came to the synagogue and asked those present why the judge proclaimed a public warning against her. Those present explained that this was done because ʿUlla ha-Levi sued her and she was summoned to court but refrained from coming. Her response was: "What do I owe ʿUlla that he should sue me? All I owe him is five qirāṭs. For five qirāṭs he makes such a fuss."[119] In another case, a representative for orphans who had a claim against an obviously wealthy woman appeared in court when she was present for a different case. The fact that she committed to pay a fine if she should refuse to come when summoned ("whether night or day") suggests that she previously tried to stall and avoid coming to court and that he had to seize the opportunity when she came to court for another matter.[120]

People who had more to lose from litigation could simply flee. This seems to have been an especially common tactic for husbands in marital disputes. In one case, a wife relinquished her *ketubbah* payments and demanded a divorce from her husband according to the ransom (Ar. *iftidā*) procedure.[121] The very same day, the husband fled to the countryside so he would not be forced by the court to divorce her.[122] In another case, a well-known Fusṭāṭ judge reprimanded a husband who ran away after his wife accused him of taking some of her silver items: "You cannot eat and drink while your family goes hungry. Where are you and where is God?"[123] A prescient father set up guards in the city gates and captured his son-in-law as he was trying to leave the city with valuable property after quarreling with his wife.[124]

Running away could be used to avoid the judicial process altogether, but it could also be used to restart the case in a new, more favorable location. In a case of a suspected extra-marital sex, one of the men involved was summoned to appear before the court. However, the local judge reported: "He answered: 'Tomorrow I will come.' When it was morning we sought him, but his wife said he had already left for Fusṭāṭ where he would beseech the cantor for help."[125] A

---

119 CUL Add 3420–19, translated in Goitein, "A Jewish Business Woman," 227 (I have used part of Goitein's translation).

120 See T-S 18J1.23, unpublished. Another example of ignoring the summons of the court can be found in Bodl MS Heb e 94.28, unpublished.

121 On this procedure, see Mordechai Akiva Friedman, "Divorce upon the Wife's Demand as Reflected in Manuscripts from the Cairo Genizah," *Jewish Law Annual* 4 (1981): 101–27.

122 Maimonides, *Responsa*, no. 15.

123 T-S 8J5.8, trans. Goitein, *Mediterranean Society*, vol. 3, 196 (with a slight change).

124 Maimonides, *Responsa*, no. 14.

125 T-S 12.242, this part of the document is unpublished.

couple from al-Maḥalla went to court because the wife could not stand to live in the Egyptian delta but the husband was unwilling or unable to move to Fusṭāṭ. When she realized that she was losing the case in the al-Maḥalla court, she left without her husband's permission for Fusṭāṭ (where she probably had family) and approached a well-known communal official there.[126]

Violence, or the threat of it, could also be an effective tactic. Occasionally a physical confrontation led to litigation or took place alongside it.[127] At other times, violence was used to pressure someone to perform a desired legal act. We see this often in marital disputes, when the husband and his family would beat a wife to pressure her to relinquish the delayed marriage gift she was owed at divorce. For example, in a query to Maimonides we hear of a husband who abused, beat, humiliated and harmed his wife, telling her: "Ransom yourself with your delayed marriage gift (Heb. *me'uḥar*) and I will release you with a *get*."[128] However, we also find men threatened with violence to relinquish a legal claim. Another query to Maimonides tells of how a man was threatened by relatives of the woman he recently betrothed. They claimed that the courtyard included in his bride's dowry was actually theirs. They ordered him to leave the courtyard and added: "If you are wise you would divorce this girl and we will let you leave with the property you brought into the courtyard. If you will not divorce her, we will expel you without anything." In one version of the responsum they also threatened to kill him, and in another they threatened to bring him to Muslim courts.[129]

Violence was also directed at communal officials and members of the court. The administrator of bread distribution in Alexandria fought with a certain *ḥaver* who distributed the charity bread in disregard of the instructions of the local judge. After a stormy court session and after the communal service on Saturday was disrupted, the administrator reported that "On Sunday night, the 10th of Sivan, a man knocked on (the door) at my house. [I/he stood (?)] at the vestibule, and I did not have a light. He said to me: [. . .] if you distribute the charity chest (Heb. *quppa*), I will slaughter you in your bed." People advised the administrator to take him to court, but fearing the consequences, he decided to wait instructions from the *nagid*, Abraham Maimonides.[130]

---

126 CUL Or. 1080 J276, ed. Zinger "Women, Gender and Law," 405–7, doc. 19.

127 See, for example, the very interesting cases found in T-S 24.74 and CUL Or. 1080 J86.

128 Maimonides, *Responsa*, no. 385. See other examples in Zinger, "Women, Gender and Law," 135–6, 157–8.

129 Maimonides, *Responsa*, no. 362.

130 T-S 10J16.6, ed. Frenkel, *Alexandria*, doc. 54.

Because compromise and mediation played a central role in the judicial process, social pressure and public opinion were important aspects of managing a dispute successfully. We therefore hear of litigants turning people in the community against both their opponents and against the court.[131] One way to employ social pressure was disseminating negative information. Spreading "evil rumors" (Ar. *shanāʿa* as a noun or *ashnaʿa* as a verb) was an effective way to hurt an opponent in a society in which one's status depended to a large degree on his or her networks of social relationships.[132] Rumors could bring about a legal investigation by the court.[133] We have examples of slandered parties trying to clear their names by interrupting prayer, refuting the accusations against them and demanding that their slanderers testify before the court about their accusations.[134] Rumors could also be used to pressure parties to give up a legal claim.[135] The usefulness of rumors and social pressures as bargaining chips in the negotiation of settlements can be seen in a case in which a man agreed to a relatively high amount of child support on the condition that his former wife and her family stop slandering and opposing him.[136] The harmful effect of public talk on a person is also reflected in the many Genizah magical fragments meant to silence one's enemies. In several of these fragments the context seems to be a legal dispute (or a dispute that easily could become

131 For turning people against an opponent, see the letter to Maimonides published in Oded Zinger, "'One Hour He Is a Christian and the Next He Is a Muslim!' A Family Dispute from the Cairo Geniza," *al-Masāq* 31 (2019): 20–34. For turning people against the local judge, see T-S 12.242 recto 21, ed. Friedman, *Polygyny*, doc. VI-6. For negative rumors spread against a judge by his enemies, see CUL Add 3341.

132 Spreading negative information about one's opponent was also a common tactic in personal and communal conflicts, see Yagur, "Religious Identity and Communal Boundaries," chapter 3, section 3, and chapter 5, section 3. The way this tactic featured in the legal arena has to be examined as part of this broader trend.

133 See, for example, Bodl MS Heb. d 66.133, T-S 18J2.13; T-S 12.242, recto 4-6; and NLR Yevr.-Arab. I 1701.

134 For two examples, see Per H 160, ed. Gil, *Palestine*, doc. 331.

135 T-S NS J68, translatd in Goitein, *Mediterranean Society*, vol. 5, 201 (a husband giving his wife a bad name so she would ransom herself from the marriage); ENA NS 16.30, recto 3 and 9, ed. Friedman, *Polygyny*, doc. VIII-5 (a husband slandering his wife so he could divorce her without compensation and marry another wife); T-S Ar, 49.166.2, verso 10, ed. Gil, *Palestine*, doc. 388 (a husband claiming that his wife was not a virgin when he married her several years previously); T-S 13Ja1.1, recto 15–16, ed. Gil, *Palestine*, doc. 593 (rumors spread against a man who planned to marry a woman now betrothed to another).

136 ENA 4011.17, ed. Gil, *Palestine*, doc. 537, translated to English in Cohen, *Voice of the Poor*, doc. 49.

a legal one).[137] The effectivness of social pressure, spreading rumors, and perhaps even magical practices on legal disputes shows the integration of the legal arena in the broader social and communal life.

This embeddedness of the legal arena in the social fabric of the community also allowed litigants to use their social relationships to influence the legal procedure in a more focused way. Egyptian Jewish communities were not large and litigants often had social ties with the members of the court, or knew someone who had such ties. Moreover, as Goitein observed: "since the Jewish court was composed of three or more members, litigants themselves frequently had experience of the bench."[138] Such social ties could make a difference in the outcome of disputes. However, they are typically invisible in legal documents that record the official narrative promulgated by the court. However, some investigation can occasionally uncover at least the possibility that such social ties played a role in the proceedings.

To give one example, when the two siblings, Bārra and Ghālib, litigated over their father's inheritance, the court record presents Bārra as deceitful, a forger of documents, and deserving the communal ban. Before the ban was placed, a righteous elder was nominated to mediate a peaceful resolution. The mediator reproached Bārra and tried to convince her to accept only a part of what she claimed her father gave her as a gift before he died, but she refused. While several reasons for the court's antagonistic stance towards Bārra can be proposed (her turning to Muslim courts is an obvious one), the fact that we find Ghālib serving as a member of court in three other cases suggests that he enjoyed a familiarity with the court and the legal process. In fact, in one of these cases, he served alongside the very same righteous elder tasked with mediating between him and his sister.[139]

When we turn to private correspondence, we no longer need to speculate about the possible effect of social connections on the legal process. The Genizah has preserved a sizable corpus of letters showing how litigants harped on commercial, familial and patronage ties to secure a legal advantage. Often

---

137 Gideon Bohak and Ortal-Paz Saar, "Genizah Magical Texts Prepared for or against Named Individuals," *REJ* 174 (2015): 77–110. T-S K1.165 (nos. 12 and 34 in the article) specifically mentions binding the tongue of a Muslim judge. T-S AS 145.24 (no. 58 and 118 in the article) mention finding favor in the eye of a Jewish judge, but here it is possible that the judge was simply the father of the woman the commissioner of the amulet coveted.

138 Goitein, *Mediterranean Society*, vol. 2, 312. Goitein's observation needs to be modified to stress that it was middle- and upper-class Jewish men that frequently had experience of the bench.

139 See a fuller discussion in Zinger, "Seven Documents," doc. 3. A different interpretation is offered in Marina Rustow, *The Lost Archive: Traces of a Caliphate in a Cairo Syngogue* (Princeton, NJ: Princeton University Press, 2020), 364-5.

the correspondence is not between the litigant and the judge, but between a litigant and a middleman who is asked to speak to the judge or obtain a favorable response to a query.[140] A Maghrebi merchant writing from Ashkelon asks a Maghrebi judge in Fusṭāṭ to help him obtain a favorable ruling to a query carried by a Maghrebi companion for "our matter obligates you because your family and our family are one." A grateful father in the town of Malij writes to his benefactor in Fusṭāṭ, a *parnas* who helped him secure a ruling that saved his daughter's marriage: "I pray for you night and day. You are there for me in every calamity. I boast of (knowing) no one but you. To everyone who talks to me, I say: 'my lord, the *parnas*, he shall obtain a ruling for me.'"

Because the Genizah was located in Fusṭāṭ, we usually have letters of litigants writing to the judges or middlemen in the capital. However, on rare occasion we also have the testimony of a judge. A well-known judge from Alexandria wrote a letter to a prominent merchant in Fusṭāṭ informing him how he reconciled the merchant's daughter with her husband who wanted to divorce her. He writes "I am here for you more than any brother and friend. For your favor is upon us and upon anyone who comes to Fusṭāṭ, may God make everlasting this quality of yours."[141] The way social ties are invoked for legal assistance in terms of kinship (real or fictive), "favor" and publicizing the fame of the benefactor reflect how the legal arena was saturated with the Islamicate ethos of group solidarity, patronage and intercession.

Conclusion

The social embeddedness of the legal arena should not be understood as corruption, but as the legal culture of small communities in which justice was not separated from social life. Consisting of multiple accessible venues of overlapping and blurred jurisdictions, the Jewish legal arena in medieval Egypt was dynamic, flexible, and occasionally unpredictable. This constellation gave ordinary Jews substantial power vis-à-vis communal institutions. Indeed, their choices and actions, within, between, and outside legal venues, were the engine that powered the legal system. The entanglement of law with social relationships make

140 A fuller exploration of the role of middlemen will be found in an article I am currently preparing for publication tentatively titled "Toward a Social History of Responsa in Medieval Egypt."

141 The documents for the last three examples are T-S 13Ja1.1, T-S 10J10.13 and T-S Misc. 28.11 + TS NS J120. They are discussed (and the last two are also edited) in Oded Zinger, "Social Embeddedness in the Legal Arena according to Geniza Letters," in *From Qom to Barcelona: Aramaic, South Arabian, Coptic, Arabic and Judeo-Arabic Documents*, ed. Andreas Kaplony and Daniel Potthast (Leiden: Brill, forthcoming).

sense in a legal arena that was geared not only to implementing Jewish law, but also to preserving the social fabric of the community through mediated amicable settlements. The centrality of personal relationships was not a poor replacement for the lack of coercive means, it was integral to the nature of the Jewish legal arena and a central component of its undeniable strength and vitality.[142]

Having surveyed the dynamic legal arena, we can now look back at the local Jewish court with which we started. The complexity of the legal arena is reflected in the different sources of authority upon which the local judge drew, represented schematically in Fig.6. As we have seen, the judge was appointed from above by the *yeshivah* or the head of the Jews. Yet, both as judge and as a communal leader he had to be accepted from below. This meant, among other things, that his flock use his court. Goitein characterized this vertical axis as a "blending of hierocratic and democratic elements."[143] The court personified Jewish law (not only in the content of the law it implemented, but also in the script and legal terminology it used) which was certainly another source of its authority. A different source was the confirmation of the judge's appointment by the Islamic state and the fact that he was considered part of the state administration of justice. A more horizontal element in the court's authority had to do with the way the court's legal acts (whether represented through deeds or acts like excommunication) were respected and upheld by other legal institutions, which I have termed its legal peers.[144] The entanglement of the court in the social fabric of the community, the fact that the members of courts were connected by ties of family, marriage, commerce and patronage to the community, is expressed by the "social peers." The figure is certainly schematic, however, even in its crudeness it reflects the complexity and richness that makes the legal arena such a fascinating topic of study.

---

142 I carry the argument further in the first chapter of the book I am currently writing.

143 Goitein, *Mediterranean Society*, vol. 2, 54–6. For what could happen when the local leader lost the support of his flock, see Cohen, "Geniza Documents Concerning a Conflict," 123–54.

144 The figure is schematic and cannot represent the complexity of legal arena. For example, some legal peers were certainly of higher status than the local judge, introducing a vertical element to what I presented as a horizontal one. Similarly, Muslim judges could be construed as legal peers as well as part of the Islamic state.

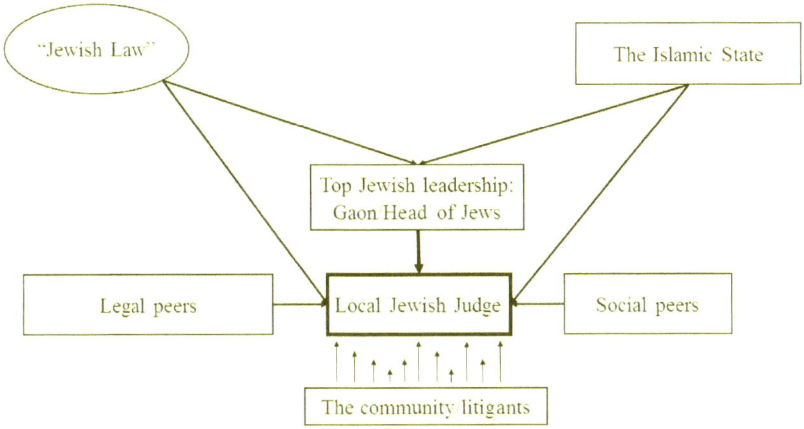

Fig. 6: The different sources of authority of the local Jewish judge.

Genizah letters and legal records offer glimpses into the life stories of Jews in medieval Egypt, with their quarrels, make-ups, righteous drama, behind-the-scenes manipulations, windfalls, and losses. In between the quotidian details and the formulaic expressions was a dynamic legal culture that fused together an ancient legal heritage, Islamic cultural values, political considerations, individual agency, and a deep concern for communal welfare and cohesion. The study of this legal culture is still in its beginnings and the coming years are bound to herald new discoveries and exciting developments.

6

Jewish Economic Life in Medieval Egypt: Images, Theories, and Research

JESSICA GOLDBERG

As it has done with so many aspects of the history of the Jews, the evidence of the documents of the Cairo Genizah has upended much of what was thought to be known about Jewish economic life and commerce in medieval Egypt. Before S. D. Goitein's pioneering research in the 1950s and 1960s, certain theories about Jewish economic activity in medieval Islamicate societies had gained traction in twentieth-century scholarship, and these theories sometimes still form part of a common image of Jews. Scholars posited the prominent or even dominant role of Jews in banking, government administration, or long-distance trade of the medieval Islamic world, with a "court Jew" as the most representative figure of Jewish economic identity. Such an image arose partially from the Islamic sources used: usually the only Jews worth mentioning in the geographies, chronicles, or travelogues upon which these analyses relied were the rare individuals who achieved an unusual prominence in these fields. Islamic evidence of this sort could be used to give a scholarly gloss to theories tracing an unbroken web of Jewish control of banking and long-distance trade from antiquity, through the Islamic Middle Ages, to modernity.[1] The picture of the

1 In addition to the literature built up on the Radhanites (who appear in one paragraph of one ninth-century Islamic geography), Massignon built a theory of Jewish banking in the Islamic world on a few ninth-century loans. Louis Massignon, "L'influence de l'islam au moyen âge sur la fondation et l'essor des banques juives," *Bulletin de l'Institut Français de Damas* (1932): 3-12, followed in this regard by Walter Joseph Fischel, *Jews in the Economic and Political Life*

international Jewish merchant also dovetailed with a master narrative of medieval European and Islamic economic history in which Jews played a critical role as the *only* long-distance traders in early medieval Europe (seventh–eleventh centuries). By virtue of their confessional connections, it was argued that they had acted as cosmopolitan brokers between Europe and Islam, their role taken over only in the twelfth century as Italians gained confidence and power, took over the Mediterranean sea lanes, and helped cause an irreversible economic decline in an Islamicate world dependent on transit trade as its economic lifeblood.[2]

Genizah materials are sources of unparalleled richness for Jewish economic life. We have partnership contracts and quittances involving many economic sectors and a wide range of capital, lawsuits and legal queries from persons across a variety of economic roles, letters of petition asking for forms of aid and explaining the economic circumstances that necessitate it, financial accounts of many types (for example, household holiday shopping lists that manage a few dirhems, shop-keeper's bills, synagogue building accounts, banker's lists dealing in thousands of dinars), commercial letters from long-distance merchants, dowry lists, lists of communal donors and their contributions, lists of recipients of charity and what they were given, family and communal correspondence mentioning economic aspects of life in passing—the majority of materials in the "documentary Genizah," no matter their ostensible subject, have something to say about economic organization and activity.

And though these documents have been recognized for over a half-century for their wealth of information regarding Jewish participation in the economic sphere, perhaps less acknowledged is how richly they document the ambient Islamic economy. Jews moved through markets and neighborhoods in

---

of Mediaeval Islam (London: The Royal Asiatic Society, 1937), and picked up in Gil, *Jews in Islamic Countries in the Middle Ages*, 638–62.

2 See Henri Pirenne, *Mohammed and Charlemagne* (London and New York: Routledge, 2008), 174; and Robert Sabatino Lopez, *The Commercial Revolution of the Middle Ages, 950–1350* (Englewood Cliffs, NJ: Prentice-Hall, 1971), 60–2, who makes the early eleventh-century the high water mark for these men. See also the critiques in B. Blumenkranz, *Juifs et Chrétiens dans le monde occidental 430–1096* (Leuven: Peeters Publishers, 2006); Michael Toch, "Jews and Commerce: Modern Fancies and Medieval Realities," in *Il Ruolo Economico delle Minoranze in Europa. Secc. XIII-XVIII (Atti della XXXI Settimana di Studi, Istituto Francesco Datini, Prato)*, ed. S. Cavaciocchi (Florence: n.p., 2000); idem, "The Economic Activity of German Jews in the 10th-12th Centuries: Between Historiography and History (Hebrew)," in *Facing the Cross: The Persecutions of 1096 in History and Historiography*, ed. Y-T. Assis et al. (Jerusalem: Magness Press, 2000), 32–54.

their daily life, had complex personal, professional, and property relationships with Muslim and Christian neighbors, partners, notables, and officials, used the economic services of individuals across the classes and confessions of Islamic society, and reported in commercial correspondence on general patterns of shipping, port activity and regimes, states of markets, market players, and states of particular industries, revealing bits of general economic life at every turn. A careful sifting through Genizah materials reveals nearly as much about the overall economic organization of the Islamic world as it does about the particular activities of Jewish participants. It is thus unfortunate that both economic historians of the Islamic world and social historians of the Fatimid period have made rather modest use of them.[3] Because indeed, as we will see, Genizah evidence makes it not only impossible to sustain a vision of Jewish exceptionality in the Islamicate world, but equally difficult to sustain the sketch of the Islamicate economy on which such ideas of Jewish participation were premised.

At the same time, both the particular history of the Genizah as the depository of the Fusṭāṭ synagogue of the Rabbanite Jews adhering to the Palestinian *yeshivah* and the still only partially understood patterns of deposit mean the materials provide extremely illuminating but partial and difficult evidence for economic life. Moreover, the history of Genizah scholarship shows that a survey of what the Genizah has to tell us remains necessarily incomplete.

Fusṭāṭ was the administrative capital of Islamic Egypt before the Fatimid conquest of 969 and the establishment of a royal city, Cairo, and it remained the economic capital of Egypt for centuries afterward. But beginning in the ʿAyyubid era, it began to lose position to an expanding Cairo, and much of the population moved away from the area around the synagogue. These facts mean our economic data is sharply tilted toward first Fusṭāṭ, and secondarily Egypt in general, and contains materials from the widest economic variety of people in the period c. 1000–1250. At the same time, during this period, Cairo-Fusṭāṭ was the dominant city of the Islamic Mediterranean (and perhaps the Islamic world) as a whole. Moreover, it was the center of several commercial postal systems in an Islamic world characterized by a fair degree of personal mobility and

3 See Yaacov Lev, *State and Society in Fatimid Egypt* (Leiden: Brill, 1991); Paul Ernest Walker, *Exploring an Islamic Empire: Fatimid History and Its Sources* (London: I.B. Tauris, 2002). There has been some debate on the extent to which these documents reflect the nature of the economy and economic life in the Islamicate world, most especially when considering agency relations among merchants. See especially Ackerman-Lieberman, *The Business of Identity*.

by dense networks connecting individuals around the Mediterranean through ties of family, business, education, and religious community. All these factors meant an astonishing range of people had occasion to write to or visit the city, leaving witness to their connections in paper in the Genizah. Thanks to such travels and deposits, we can learn a great deal not only about Egypt, but about the way Egypt was and was not linked to markets in the Islamic Mediterranean and Indian Ocean, as well as get some glimpses into Islamic Asia in the period c. 1000–1250. There are small but significant finds that reflect on economic patterns in the tenth century, but little prior to it. Though deposits are less rich after 1250, the Genizah continues to give some information about Jewish economic life, but unfortunately, those documents have received relatively little scholarly attention in cataloguing, transcription, or publication.[4]

Perhaps the most important revelation of the past few decades of Genizah research has been the increasing awareness of the idiosyncratic nature of medieval Genizah practices. Depositing worn paper into the Genizah was by no means a universal practice of Jews even in the so-called "classical period," that is, c.1000–1250. What remains to us is thus not a witness of all the everyday writing produced in this community, but a somewhat haphazard sampling dominated by the archives of particular individuals (most often scribes, communal officials, or merchants), who either had a strong sense of the importance of sacred deposits themselves, or whose family members did. Moreover, it is clear that certain kinds of record-keeping documents with legal importance were rarely deposited in the Genizah, but kept in family hands instead. Such considerations mean that many of the kinds of statistical data we might likely draw from these records concerning demography or class structure or sizes of estates cannot be representative. Thus, for instance, though the Genizah attests to greatly varying levels of wealth within the Jewish community, even the most careful analysis of surviving records of distributions to the poor can tell us only about the varied circumstances of poverty, not its relative incidence in the Jewish population.[5]

---

4 Dotan Arad's valuable work on documentary materials in the "late" Genizah is enormously welcome, but still preliminary.

5 See Cohen, *Poverty and Charity*, for an insightful and thorough analysis of the kinds of poverty who the Jewish community understood, and the circumstances that created groups of the poor that were the objects of charity. See also Miriam Frenkel, "On Mark R. Cohen's *Poverty and Charity in the Jewish Community of Medieval Egypt*; idem, *The Voice of the Poor in the Middle Ages: An Anthology of Documents from the Cairo Geniza*," *Zion* 75, no. 2 (2010): 225–32 [in Hebrew], for a contrasting analysis of the use of charity to solidify certain kinds of community relationships among the Jews of medieval Egypt.

Jewish involvement in the Egyptian economy: Embeddedness alongside particularity

Early accounts of Jews in the economy found them only as the courtier or the great international trader. The records of the Genizah document the existence of both these figures, containing documents from or about the few Jewish individuals who also show up in the literary record. Genizah records show, however, that such men were tips of a socio-economic iceberg: Jews could be found in nearly all economic circumstances possible in medieval Islamic society and in most kinds of work. Indeed, the most obvious general thing to say about the Jews in this economy is that there is no evidence they were economically exceptional. That is, it is impossible to find Jews in a profession where we do not also find non-Jews, nor a case of a particular city in which Jews monopolized a particular craft or industry, nor any evidence that Jews were systematically richer or poorer than Muslims or Christians who were their neighbors (for Jews were not physically segregated either, often sharing even the common courtyard houses with non-Jews).

Even the merchant and the courtier, those best-known Jewish players in the economy, had different socio-economic roles compard to what earlier scholars presumed. First and foremost, there is no evidence that Jews occupied these roles disproportionately, that they exercised exceptional power in Islamic society through such positions, or that they occupied such roles because they were more educated or cosmopolitan and thus more able to act as "cross-cultural brokers" than members of other groups.[6] From this point of view, it is perhaps most important to stop and look at the Jewish merchants, for their records form one of the largest coherent document sets in the historical Genizah. For a start, rather than being part of the truly elite, most of the merchants we can document were rather of the "middling sort"—wealthy in comparison to most in the society, but part of the anonymous

6 See especially the discussion of Jewish courtiers in Rustow, *Heresy and the Politics of Community*, 120–3. See Philip D. Curtin, *Cross-Cultural Trade in World History* (Cambridge: Cambridge University Press, 1984), on such brokerage. Cf. Maristella Botticini and Zvi Eckstein, *The Chosen Few: How Education Shaped Jewish History, 70–1492* (Princeton, NJ: Princeton University Press, 2012); idem, "From Farmers to Merchants, Conversions and Diaspora: Human Capital and Jewish History," *Journal of the European Economic Association* 5, no. 5 (2007): 885–926; idem, "Jewish Occupational Selection: Education, Restrictions, or Minorities?," *The Journal of Economic History* 65, no. 4 (2005): 922–48, where such exceptionality is presumed.

mass in comparison to elite fortunes, which outclassed them by least one, and often several orders of magnitude.[7]

Perhaps most importantly for theories of special Jewish cosmopolitanism, none of them, even the wealthiest, had any business connections at all with European or Byzantine Jews, though the Genizah shows that there were indeed some family connections, movement of scholars and scholarship, and pilgrimage across those boundaries.[8] Rather than being "cross-cultural" brokers, merchants of the eleventh century tended to be the opposite: primarily brokers of the production of their home region onto the "international" markets of the Islamic Mediterranean. That is, they were deeply and personally tied to local agricultural and manufacturing production, and they made their money primarily by organizing the movement and sale of regional production in the great cities of the Islamic Mediterranean: Fusṭāṭ-Cairo, Qayrawan-al-Mahdiyya, Palermo, Tripoli, Fez, or Cordoba. Moreover, when they did expand their activities in the twelfth and thirteenth centuries, they did not venture to Europe but into the Indian Ocean, either in Islamicate areas, or areas long ago pioneered by Muslim merchant communities.

As the last sentence should suggest, Jewish merchants were part of a larger Islamic merchant community. Like Jews in many professions, they usually preferred to form partnerships and business associations with fellow Jews. But they were professionally and legally part of a merchant class, the "men of affairs" who sustained the great urban wholesale trading markets, and had plenty of occasions to work and form business relationships with their Muslim counterparts. Like Jews in other professions throughout the Islamic Mediterranean, they were deeply "embedded" in Islamic economic life, as Cohen has suggested was true of Jews under Islam in general social terms.[9]

If the "embeddedness" and "non-exceptionality" of Jews applies as the most general statement about economic activities, still a few key aspects of participation are worth noting. First, the Genizah has some evidence on most sectors of economic activity and work in the Islamic world,[10] and

7 See Jessica Goldberg, *Trade and Institutions in the Medieval Mediterranean: The Geniza Merchants and Their Business World* (Cambridge: Cambridge University Press, 2012), chapter 9, on the relative size of merchant transactions and what it suggests about overall capital.

8 Armand Citarella, "The Relations of Amalfi with the Arab World before the Crusades," *Speculum* 42, no. 2 (1967): 299–312.

9 Cohen, *Under Crescent and Cross*.

10 Mining is an important exception. Though trade in metals documents the existence of a mining sector, we learn nothing about it from the Genizah.

documents at least some participation of Jews in the great majority of them. Of what we might call the main employment areas—agriculture (both arable and husbandry), mining, manufacturing and construction, transportation, trade, services, educated professions, civil service, military, religious professionals—Jews can be documented in all but two: mining and the military. It is not merely the range of economic *sectors* that is worth noting, but the astonishing number of professions attested. The Genizah mentions literally hundreds of professions, especially in the service and manufacturing sectors. The dispersion of what our best estimates suggest were very modest numbers of Jews—both in terms of raw numbers and proportion of society—across professions is remarkable, as is the fact that such professional dispersion was matched geographically: Jews occupied many professional niches within any city in which we find them, and they were widely dispersed among a great many cities and villages across Egypt.[11] Wherever we find Jews, we find occupational diversity—in cities, towns and villages around the Mediterranean. We find concentrations of Jews in some professions in individual cities and a paucity of them in others, an artifact of patterns of urbanism, but there is no evidence of monopolization of any kind of industry or manufacturing by Jews or indeed by any other groups.[12]

While we can find occasional Jews in agriculture and transportation, the Genizah shows employment skewed primarily towards occupations we would consider urban: principally manufacturing and services, with significant participation in civil service, educated professions, and religious professions. To some degree, this is as an artifact of the location of the Genizah and the cultural patterns of Islamic society. The Genizah comes from Fusṭāṭ, and its contents are, in fact, dominated by documents of the urban middling sort—most of whom were substantial artisans or merchants. They shared in the common prejudices of Islamic society, in which the countryside and its residents, whatever their economic significance, lay largely outside the cultural imagination. Yet equally, there is enough secondary evidence from deposits of communal

---

11 Eliyahu Ashtor, "The Number of Jews in Mediaeval Egypt I," *JJS* 18 (1967): 9–42; Norman Golb, *Topography of the Jews of Medieval Egypt: Inductive Studies Based Primarily upon Documents from the Cairo Genizah, Jounal of Near Eastern Studies (JNES)* 24 (1965): 251–70; 33 (1974): 116–49..

12 Cf. Maya Shatzmiller, *Labour in the Medieval Islamic World* (Leiden and New York: Brill, 1994). Such professional clustering is, however, a well-known feature of both the military and pastoral groups in the Islamic economy and society.

materials from places like Ascalon to suggest that even within the former agricultural homeland of the Jews, agricultural participation was modest.

These findings tend to support one great stereotype of the Jewish population: that it was far more urban than other confessional groups. That being said, a closer look at professional diversity and its remuneration, as well as records of letters of petition and charitable disbursement to the poor Jews of the community, provide no evidence that the Jewish community as a whole was either relatively richer or poorer than other urban identity groups, more skilled or more educated.[13] Nor does it seem we should give overmuch attention to literary reports at a given period of the fame of Jews in some industry or another (such as silk working), when documents suggest that against family or city traditions, in particular regarding manufactures, we must place Genizah evidence showing that nearly any professional label we can find attached to Jews can be found attached to non-Jews as well.[14] But finally, there are some important absences: Jews did not participate in some of the most important, and politically sensitive, areas of trading—grain, timber, weapons, slaves, or the transport economy—nor do we find even the poor in certain professions that were considered disreputable: sweepers of streets or cleaners of cesspools.

Thus, Jews were not exceptional, they were embedded. But embedded, as the above sketch suggests, does not mean indistinguishable. To understand the activities of Jews—the extent and nature of their participation in the larger economy, the kinds of economic power they did and did not wield—involves examining three aspects of economic activity in the Genizah period. First, an understanding of the social construction and meaning of work in the Islamic milieu that explains the breadth of Jewish economic participation. Second, the general organization of the economy and economic activity explains the economic position of the Jewish community within the broad economy. Third, Islamic economic and market organization in which forms of affiliation, religious rules, and religious identity were brought to the market in particular ways helps explain patterns of Jewish economic ties within and outside the community.

---

13 Cf. Botticini and Eckstein, *The Chosen Few*; idem, "From Farmers to Merchants"; idem, "Jewish Occupational Selection."

14 Cf. S. D. Goitein, "The Main Industries of the Mediterranean Area as Reflected in the Records of the Cairo Geniza," *JESHO* 4, no. 2 (1961): 168-197. See also idem, *Mediterranean Society*, vol. 1, 75–147., where the same claim is made, but the conflicting prosopographic evidence is noted.

Islamicate attitudes: social, political, and religious meanings of work

Islamic tolerance is usually adduced to explain Jewish economic opportunity in the Islamic world in comparison with the situation of their co-religionists living in later medieval western Christendom. The more defined religious tolerance of Islam, and its special regard for Jews (in comparison to Roman attitudes) as "peoples of the book," certainly played a role, but a more complicated mix of circumstances and attitudes developed in early and middle Islamic societies shaped the nature and limits of economic participation. Perhaps the most important differences between Europe and the Islamicate world are to be found in the general de-coupling of work and religion, and with it changed attitudes about religion, work, and status that came to be shared by the Jewish community.

First, the absence in Islam of a professional clergy controlling both financial resources and doctrinal or theological authority is perhaps the most obvious and powerful change from late antique precedent and contemporary Christian Europe. A lack of a clergy did not mean a complete lack of religious professionals or paid religious work; it meant rather that religious leadership in local communities, both Muslim and Jewish, was largely unremunerated.[15] It was one of the main arenas for the pursuit of social status, and was pursued largely by individuals who also worked in other and varied parts of the economy for their subsistence. Indeed, religious scholarship, leadership, and the social prestige associated with it were most respectably combined with money-making work of various sorts. The example and attitude of Maimonides, who made his living as a court and hospital physician in Cairo while acting as the leader of the Jewish community, and advised a student to earn his bread out of something other than his religious studies, is only a particularly prominent instance of social attitudes and activities.[16] As a great deal of social prestige was funneled into religious knowledge and leadership that was unpaid, so too the ties of social identity to profession weakened, promoting multi-professionalism and professional mobility along many rungs of the social ladder.

---

15 Jewish cantors, for instance, were paid, as were Muslim muezzins.

16 It is echoed in analyses of the professions of the *'ulamā'*, the Muslim religious elite, as documented in the great biographical dictionaries, medieval Islamic equivalents of a scholars' *Who's Who* that often sketch the basic professional facts of scholars' non-scholarly lives. See Hayyim J. Cohen, "The Economic Background and the Secular Occupations of Muslim Jurisprudents and Traditionists in the Classical Period of Islam (until the Middle of the Eleventh Century)," *JESHO* 13, no. 1 (1970): 16-61.

Perhaps the most important result of these attitudes for Jews was the absence of anything that we might call a guild. Though the term "guild" has been applied to various forms of professional affiliation in societies across pre-modern Eurasia, most forms of guild and guild power have serious consequences for minority group labor participation.[17] Whether it is a claim to monopolistic rights over a profession, a close connection of professional groups to political power, the guild having power to control or patrol production in concert with government authority, the conveying of civic status to members of professional groups, limiting the right to practice a profession according to such civic status, or, most importantly, the close association of profession with religious community and religious ritual, guilds tend to create or reinforce segregation of work by social, familial or religious affiliation. Local craft communities could certainly show solidarity, and attempt to band together against outsiders, but such solidarity, without an institutional character, was not a powerful vehicle to create craft segregation or monopoly.[18]

Equally, the example of the prophet Muḥammad in shaping attitudes towards work promoted social approval of the pursuit of profit, rather than simple subsistence, as respectable for every social class and kind of work.[19] Against the famous story of Constantinople, in which the ninth-century Emperor Theophilus had his wife's commercial ship burnt to protect his prestige, we might place the utter respectability of the Zirid Sultan's mother owning commercial ships, an example imitated throughout the political class.[20] Such attitudes helped redefine respectability, at least in part, according to the ways labor was remunerated, rather than designating professions themselves

---

17 See the overview of this issue in a European context in Sheilagh Ogilvie, *Institutions and European Trade: Merchant Guilds, 1000–1800* (Princeton, NJ: Princeton University Press, 2011).

18 Islamic guilds were the subject of academic debate in the twentieth century; see the literature in the bibliography. The combined evidence of the Genizah, chronicles, and market inspector's manuals provide conclusive evidence for their absence in the medieval centuries. The questions of when the preexisting Roman guild system ended, and how the Ottoman one came into existence, remain interesting and vexed.

19 The Qur'ān's insistence that trade and usury not be confused (sura 2:275), admitting the one and condemning the other, suggests both familiarity and critique of Christian condemnations of profit as avarice.

20 See Lopez, *The Commercial Revolution of the Middle Ages, 950–1350*, 65–6, for the Byzantine case; see Michael Brett, *The Rise of the Fatimids: The World of the Mediterranean and the Middle East in the Fourth Century of the Hijra, Tenth Century CE* (Leiden: Brill, 2001); Lev, *State and Society*, on the commercial activities of the Fatimid family.

as more and less respectable. Employment in the Islamic world was often described as slavery, a dependence degrading for a mature man.[21] The wage labor that appears regularly in the legal or documentary records is most often that of unequipped manual laborers, who had only their muscular strength to offer. Most skilled or artisanal work was done on the basis of partnerships in small shops. As everyone in a shop was conceived of as a part owner paid by the profits of the investment, the respectability of profit-making was granted to a larger share of the working classes, no matter how minute their working capital.

Prejudices common in other periods or places—ones that promote leisure as a special sign of status, or against manual labor—cannot be found. Thus, among the Jews, we find a well-to-do merchant doing some tailoring during a low period of trade, or a weaver who became the head of one of the Jewish religious academies in Iraq. Equally, women of the moneyed classes did not live in leisure or manage only the household economy; they could be found weaving not to decorate their own homes, but to sell their production respectably in the marketplace, just as they brokered loans and managed commercial real estate. For women of lower economic status, managing the domestic economy was always central, but as the urban economy could provide a number of common domestic services (such as cooked food and tailored garments), many women had time to work for the marketplace in addition, especially in the textile industry.[22]

The Jews at least tended to see some professions as more respectable than others, in part given the working capital required to do them—potters and oysterers, for example, ranked low in the eyes of the middling sort, while perfumers and goldsmiths usually numbered among them. The records of those who gave and received charity tend to confirm some of these prejudices, but undermine others. The notables of Alexandria despised some of the community as "dyers," for example, but dyers were numbered among the city's wealthiest Jews.

These social attitudes, religious opinions, and institutional frameworks helped promote the kinds of widely dispersed Jewish economic participation we see in the Genizah documents. Both the lack of guilds and the organization of most production into small partnership workshops made it possible

21 See Goitein, *Mediterranean Society*, vol. 1, 87, 161.

22 The burden of domestic work and the gender expectations that made female labor necessary for maintaining a household are made clear in letters that discuss the unwelcome necessity of purchasing a female slave upon a wife's death. See, for example, TS 12.254, in which a merchant finds himself unable to attend to business, or even leave the house, in the absence of female domestic labor.

for members of different identity groups to work in the same industries: sometimes in competition, sometimes developing the solidarity of profession. Since workshops in any industry did not join together as a political or religious group, there was little pressure and indeed few mechanisms to keep industries tied to any community. Lack of special status distinctions among professions also helped make multi-confessional or multi-ethnic participation in varied sectors of the economy largely uncomplicated and uncontested, despite shared values of the social segregation of religious groups embraced equally by Jewish, Muslim, and Christian religious leaders.

Jews and the medieval Egyptian economy

The Egyptian economy, like most pre-modern ones, rested firmly on a base of primary agricultural production. Though scholarship on the Islamic world has often focused on the role of the extra-regional luxuries—particularly gold and spices—that passed through Egypt, such accounts misread the evidence by looking at European interests in Islamic markets. The Egyptian economy *was* much more urban and commercialized than most of Europe throughout the medieval period, but this commercialization had trade in regional agriculture as its base.[23] When we look at the records of even the wealthiest of international merchants, those who dealt in goods from the Islamic Mediterranean and into Islamic Asia and who handled a great variety of luxury exotica, their trade in products like flax, olive oil, and hides—that is, the main agricultural output of their regions—is greater in value by an *order of magnitude* than their dealings in all other kinds of merchandise.[24]

One of the most interesting facts to emerge from the Genizah is how closely tied the countryside was to the great urban economy and international exchange. The very same individuals who sent large commercial loads of flax, olive oil, soap, and hides across the Mediterranean for sale in the great international markets would also travel directly to producers to buy harvest crops and oversee the processing that turned them into bulk commodities.

We must understand Jewish economic activity in light of this agricultural base and its ties to the cities, for Jews were at best marginal participants in either

23 Cf. especially David Abulafia, "Asia, Africa and the Trade of Medieval Europe," in *The Cambridge Economic History of Europe*, vol. 2: *Trade and Industry in the Middle Ages*, ed. M. M. Postan and E. Miller (Cambridge: Cambridge University Press, 1987), 402, but see the longer discussion of the literature in Goldberg, *Trade and Institutions*, chapter 1.

24 See the analyses of these accounts in Goldberg, *Trade and Institutions*, chapter 9.

herding or farming. Jews bought land and invested in commercial agriculture but mostly within rather modest limits. Urban residents bought land near their homes in part for food security—grain shortages could affect even the wealthy, and there is a surprising amount of anxiety over acquisition of staple household flour among the rich. We also find investments in small orchards and bee-keeping aimed at supplying local markets. But mentions of Jewish ownership of estates in the principal commercial crops are very rare, even among the elite; and it is hard not to read this exclusion as related in part to religious identity, especially as the famous Ibn Killīs, who converted from Judaism to Islam in order to become one of the most powerful Fatimid viziers, certainly acquired large estates as a perquisite of office. Nor is this absence merely a question of wealth: though scales of agricultural ownership are not known, there is plenty of Genizah evidence for the existence of small commercial farms that sold directly to wholesalers, in addition to both large private and large government estates.

The high degree of commercialization of agriculture, however, and the direct connections between this production economy and the great commercial capital of Fusṭāṭ, had profound implications for economic organization. It cycled money geographically through arable and pastoral areas, underwrote an enormous amount of artisanal work dispersed across both geographic space and levels of the market, and allowed for a great degree of secondary and tertiary urbanism that allowed "urban" Jews who had little role in agricultural production to be closely tied to the agricultural landscape and economy. In an economy in which major urban wholesale commerce was founded on credit, individual agricultural producers could and did demand ready money for their products, and indeed were able to demand a small amount of earnest money to secure the prospective crop, and sometimes even to demand substantial pre-payment. The Genizah documents of international wholesalers show this was the most substantial movement of specie they made each year: monetary cycles that moved coin from great urban centers back to individual farmers and herders annually, fueling monetary circulation and its attendant commercialization throughout the economy.[25]

25 Much agricultural wealth went back to the cities: some government-owned flax, for instance, was paid for in Fusṭāṭ, with the purchaser issued a receipt for local collection. Even when Genizah merchants gave hundreds of dinars directly to estates in the countryside, many payments were undoubtedly made to estate managers for urban owners, and agricultural buyers from the metropolis sometimes brought market goods in addition to money, ensuring some of the agricultural receipts went back into the merchant's hand.

A surprise of Egyptian Jewish demography is the extent of Jewish residence in smaller cities and villages, and the amount of migration to these small cities and villages we find over the course of the period from individuals originating outside Egypt.[26] Yet most Jewish dwellers in these places, indeed most Jewish migrants in general, tended to be craftspeople. Enough money, and credit in its wake, flowed into the countryside to fund artisanal production, services and marketing of many basic necessities for every social class. Dense webs of transport and connection between the big cities and their regions actually allowed the dispersion of manufacturing in two directions: urban manufacturers could produce for the lower ends of the market, distributing goods into the countryside; while artisans in secondary cities, and even village dwellers, could produce high-end manufactures for the great metropolitan markets.

Manufacturing bases in smaller cities and villages were an important counterpoint to one of the consequences of the urban preference of Islamic society: a tendency for the richest land-owners to maintain a residence and spend their money, in the major cities. This cultural pattern drained resources out of the rural economy, while dispersed manufacturing, alongside the earnings of smaller land-owners and tenant farmers, helped keep goods and money flowing through smaller cities, villages, and countryside. Indeed, metropolitan merchants sustained this system directly, in that they often took long business trips to these manufacturing centers. There, they both sold manufacturing inputs (in Ascalon, for example, a mix of high-grade flax and dyes for its specialty production of linen dresses); and also slowly assembled "lots" of similar manufactures from a collection of independent workshops, bundling them into groups of ten or twenty to be shipped and sold in cities like Fusṭāṭ or al-Mahdiyya, either for wholesale sale and distribution in these lots, or sold retail. Merchants from the metropolis of Fusṭāṭ or the secondary city of Alexandria thus helped knit secondary and tertiary cities, and villages, into the international economy, and sustained a powerful economic base for secondary urbanism.[27]

This organization of economic production also profoundly shaped patterns of Jewish investment and possibilities for economic mobility, in particular the ability to participate in the same industry or even part of a production process with vastly different amounts of capital that appears in a surprising variety of sectors. Capital in this society represented both an opportunity and an anxiety. As discussed above, even wealthy Jews did not buy up agricultural estates,

26 Golb, *Topography*.

27 See Goldberg, *Trade and Institutions*, chapter 8, for a detailed discussion.

the economically obvious place to park capital for most of Egyptian history.[28] Nor were there banks, public debt, or corporations to pay yearly returns—innovations of later ages. An anxiety we see in merchants' correspondence: "Do not let the money sit idle even for a minute," seems to have pervaded economic culture. Indeed, there is a clear preference for trading ventures among those with means and ability. One even finds funds raised for the poor being invested in trade when the fundraising is managed by an aspiring young merchant.[29]

In theory, it was possible for anyone to invest in merchant trade: Islamic and Jewish law both knew of a *qiraḍ* or *muḍāraba* partnership, in which a passive investor received a smaller share of the profits in proportion to his investment than the active trader who managed the purse. But it was not standard business practice, as in later Genoa, for established businessmen to collect investment capital from a large pool of passive investors. [30] Thus, though we find men with means and social connections who were not professional merchants sometimes able to get merchants to trade for them, women of the same class were discouraged from making such investments independently by family and the courts.[31]

Wealthier middle-class women were often endowed by their families with urban real estate, mostly residential but some commercial, as rental properties (indeed, they appear more often than men as owners of real estate in the records). It was a lower risk and lower return investment that we also find being made by synagogues and older merchants.

The majority of our records come from the well-to-do, but those with less to invest had other options acting within the city: it was possible to broker loans or invest as a sleeping partner in a small shop. It is in these areas that we see the most opportunities for artisans to diversify in the economy, and

28 It is not clear whether this lack of investment was particularly Jewish, or how accessible the Egyptian agricultural economy was to the urban middling classes regardless of religious affiliation.

29 See the analysis of such investment in M. Frenkel, "Charity in Jewish Society of the Medieval Mediterranean World," in *Charity and Giving in Monotheistic Religions*, ed. M. Frenkel and Y. Lev (Berlin and New York: Walter de Gruiter, 2009), 343–63.

30 Genoese investment in long-distance trade across social classes has long been the subject of great interest for the development of its commercial economy. See Quentin Van Doosselaere, *Commercial Agreements and Social Dynamics in Medieval Genoa* (Cambridge: Cambridge University Press, 2009), where a full bibliography on the subject can also be found.

31 The existence of cases involving women managing substantial inheritances for their children, and the extensive investment by women who belonged to the large business clans (and thus had a horde of male relatives to look after their interests) demonstrates the appeal of interregional commerce.

accumulate capital beyond workshop production. The successful baker might branch out by brokering a loan to a professional colleague, or investing in a different workshop.[32] In practice, all such investment carried a fair amount of risk (indeed, in accordance with the prescriptions of Jewish and Islamic law), and much of it required fairly active and attentive management. Such investment both sustained the commercialization of the local economy by plowing capital back into local commercial endeavors, and provided an avenue for economic mobility.

If we look at economic mobility, it is clear that one path to wealth was through increasing investment in trade as an outlet of accumulated capital, though this was often mixed with acting as sleeping partner in manufacturing. There is evidence for the success and failure of this route mostly in Muslim biographical dictionaries, but prosopographic evidence from the Jewish communities shows that many wealthy merchants came out of the artisanal sectors.[33] Though names betraying origins in the higher end crafts are most common—those with high capital requirements, like goldsmith, perfumer, silk dealer—a surprising number of names indicating modest artisanal origins also appear. Education could also be the motor of aspirations in both the Jewish community and broader society: some individuals of modest means rose into the scholarly elite through brilliance; physicians could become courtiers; skillful bureaucrats could rise to heads of departments.[34] But education alone was no guarantee of upward social mobility—Genizah records are replete with pleas from educated men of no family looking for some place that would reward their skills; clerking, scribing, and copying, the general resort of such persons, paid less than

32 See Geoffrey Khan, "An Arabic Document of Acknowledgement from the Cairo Genizah," *JNES* 53, no. 2 (1994): 117–24, for an example. On pawn broking, see Miriam Frenkel and Ayala Lester, "Evidence of Material Culture from the Geniza—An Attempt to Correlate Textual and Archaeological Findings," in *Material Evidence and Narrative Sources. Interdisciplinary Studies of the History of the Muslim Middle East*, ed. Daniella Talmon-Heller and Katia Cytryn-Silverman (Leiden: Brill, 2015), 147–87.

33 See Olivia Remie Constable, *Trade and Traders in Muslim Spain: The Commercial Realignment of the Iberian Peninsula, 900–1500* (Cambridge: Cambridge University Press, 1994), for biographical evidence from Andalus.

34 In our period, for instance, we find the Jewish physician of the Zirid Sultan as an important courtier, Abū Isḥāq Ibrāhīm ibn ʿAṭāʾ, mentioned in TS 13 J 36.1 r 25–9. More famous though more than a century earlier is the case of Saʿadya Gaʾon, who, despite his claims to ancient lineage, did not have the traditional family connections to the Academy when appointed Gaʾon of Sura. See *Encylopedia Judaica*, vol. 2, s.v. "Saadiah (ben Joseph) Gaon."

much artisanal work.[35] Indeed, in a world with few places to safely park capital, the yearly pressure of the poll tax to grind at those on the margins, and the limitations women faced in managing their investments or getting the money to which they were legally due, downward mobility is also widely attested in the rolls of recipients of charity and letters of petition.[36]

Jews, the state, and the market

Finally, to understand this commercialization and the nature of economic participation, we should acknowledge how deeply the functions of government were tied to commerce and the market. Government estates produced and sold a great deal of field flax to private investors like the Genizah merchants, for instance, who then made the profits of processing, packaging, and sale on the international market. On the other side, for a long period the Fatimid government purchased large quantities of grain on the commercial market, assuring its own supply and then usually reselling the excess, often not turning a profit on the deal. And while the Fatimids had government officers to handle the acquisition and supply of strategic goods (timber, metals, military equipment), they acquired most of the other imported goods they needed through a simple system of sequestration. That is, they seized potentially needed goods from private merchants when they arrived in the ports, either releasing them or paying the "market price" whenever government need and eventual supply had been fully determined.

Such systems depended upon and took for granted a secure and well-regulated market that would attract goods and trade. Indeed, states took a strong interest in the order of the marketplace—both practically and often rhetorically, as an important indicator of right government. Islamic law and, progressively, Islamic political thinkers also took special interest in the market and its operation. In the case of buying and selling, not only did Islamic law not have a preference for giving custom to members of one's own group, Islamic legists' understanding that profit-seeking was the core aim of economic activity made them explicit in ruling for absolutely equal participation by members of

---

35 See S. D. Goitein, *Jewish Education in Muslim Countries, Based on Records from the Cairo Geniza* (Jerusalem: n.p., 1962) on the dynamics of education, and idem, *Mediterranean Society*, vol. 1, 75–92, 2: 185–90, for wage reports that suggest this comparison.

36 See Cohen, *Poverty and Charity*; idem, *The Voice of the Poor in the Middle Ages*, espeially chapter 5 of the former and chapter 6 of the latter on the particular difficulties of women. On women's challenges in getting paid, see Zinger, "Women, Gender and Law," 48–152, 177–80.

different confessions in the marketplace, which would permit actors maximum freedom to buy the best goods and make the best deals.

Yet interestingly, this legal stance, rather than promoting hugely impersonal markets, had the effect of creating enormous webs of economic sociability. This was because in these markets, purchase was rarely an anonymous spot transaction. Purchase and payment were temporally separate acts, meaning that much market activity floated on a pervasive base of consumer credit.[37] This credit created tiny and innumerable ties of trust and obligation between buyers and sellers in the marketplace. Indeed, Muslim thinkers understood the marketplace as non-anonymous, as a space of personal connections. One's standing, connections, and reputation were part of one's market persona. On a legal plane, transactions were guaranteed by the availability of witnesses, the Muslim class of morally reputable people, turning the market into a kind of religiously guaranteed space. Such notions helped inform an understanding of the state or leader's religious duty to assure reputable behavior across the market, indeed to protect the "reputation" of his market. By the twelfth century, this notion of the ruler's religious responsibility to sustain market order crystallized in the manuals and person of the market inspector, and such manuals proliferated around the Muslim world.[38]

Yet, there was also a crucial distinction here, between the workshop and the commercial buying and selling of the market. In contrast to the interconfessional freedom of sales, Islamic and Jewish legal thinkers expressed explicit worries about interconfessional partnership contracts. Some schools of thought forbade them on the grounds that one could become legally or religiously liable for the actions of a partner who did not follow the religious rules of one's own faith. Jewish partners, for example, might earn illicit profits for work done on the Sabbath by their Muslim co-workers. In other writings and the market inspectors' manuals, one can see that such rules were in part reified by worries about interconfessional sociability, that sociability would naturally grow out of long hours of shared endeavor in the same space. Though both Genizah records and Muslim and Jewish legal opinions show that

37 Though such credit was legally approved as an underpinning for wholesale trade, shopkeeper accounts found in the Genizah suggest how this system had penetrated markets as consumer credit by the eleventh century.

38 ʿAbd al-Rahman ibn Nasr Shayzari, *The Book of the Islamic Market Inspector: Nihayat Al-Rutba Fi Talab Al-Hisba (The Utmost Authority in the Pursuit of Hisba)*, trans. R. P. Buckley (Oxford: Oxford University Press, 1999), provides both a translated example and an overview of the genre's history.

interconfessional workshops and partnerships existed, they show even more clearly they were the exception, and we also find cases of Jewish workers thrown out of Muslim workshops when their (hidden) religious identity was discovered.[39]

Affiliation with the state also provided the greatest opportunities for rapid and radical accumulation of wealth.[40] But equally, it should be noted that the risks and costs of affiliation with rulers may also have had a strong role in limiting economic aspirations even for the upper end of the middling sort. For with great reward came great risk: when a courtier or official lost his place, he could expect to be milked of all his property (just as he could use the revenues of his office personally, the state did not recognize the continued existence of one's private estate once office was taken), and might well lose his life as well.[41] Such dangers weighed all the more heavily in a society where there is little evidence that well-to-do Jews in private life faced dangers of arbitrary property seizure or personal violence from the state.[42]

It is clear in Islamic law that members of religious minorities should not be in positions of power over Muslims, and thus should not be part of government.[43] In the earliest period of Islam, demography made imposition of

39 Goitein, *Mediterranean Society*, vol. 2, 285–6.

40 Provincial officers, for instance, were essentially independent in the day-to-day conduct of their jobs: they were free to hire lesser officers to help them; and to use the revenues that came to their office not only to fulfill its duties, but for personal use and investment. We often find officers running warehouses or fitting out ships, for instance, as commercial enterprises in competition with vessels held by private individuals. See Stern, *Fāṭimid Decrees*; Shayzari, *Market Inspector*, 1–23; Walker, *Exploring*, on diplomas of office and staffing. See A. L. Udovitch, "Merchants and Amirs: Government and Trade in Eleventh-Century Egypt," *Asian and African Studies* 22 (1988): 53–72, on commercial vessels owned by provincial officials; and on general commercial investment by members of government.

41 See the discussion in Lev, *State and Society*, 72–4, on the practice of milking officers at the end of service, and periodically within it. See Aḥmad ibn ʿAlī al-Maqrīzī, *Ittiʿāz al-ḥunafāʾ bi-akhbār al-aʾimma al-fāṭimiyyin al-khulafāʾ*, ed. Jamāl al-Dīn Shayyāl and Muḥammad Ḥilmī Muḥammad Aḥmad (Cairo: al-Majlis al-Aʿlā lil-Shuʾūn al-Islamiyya, 1364–1442 AH), vol. 1, 262; idem, *El-Mawâʿiz Wal-IʿTibâr Fî Dhikr El-Khitat Wal-Âthâr*, ed. Gaston Wiet (Cairo: IFAO, 1911), vol. 3, 11, on the milking of Ibn Killis and then his inheritance. See also ʿIzz al-Dīn Ibn al-Athīr, *al-Kāmil fī al-tārīkh*, ed. Carl Johan Tornberg (Beirut: Dār Sâder, 1965), vol. 7, 17, 63, 110, 42–55, and vol. 10, 337, for extensive lists and details of milking of officers.

42 Inability to pay the poll tax, however, could lead to both, a source of tremendous anxiety for the lower classes.

43 Muslim legal authorities date this restriction to the Pact of ʿUmar, under the rule of the second caliph, ʿUmar ibn al-Khaṭṭāb (r. 634–44), though study suggests it was redacted in the eighth century and perhaps revised later. See *Encyclopedia Judaica*, vol. 2, *s.v.* "Dhimma,"

such rules impossible. Even in the eleventh and twelfth centuries, the religious demography of Egypt still made such a posture difficult to put into practice. At the same time, long tradition now established minority participation in government bureaucracy in many places, bolstered too in some circles of *ʿulamāʾ* by the interpretation that government service was a religiously suspect form of work, since it would make the worker, whatever his day-to-day tasks, complicit in acts of violence or extortion that were naturally part of the running of government.[44]

Such a mix of history and attitudes sustained the participation of religious minorities in government, but episodes of popular outrage and violence against minorities in positions of economic or political power in this period suggest the ethics of this rule against minority power holding were part of popular Muslim sentiment. Such incidents, and documentable Jewish awareness and anxiety about the possibility of anti-Jewish feeling, put certain limits and pressures on Jewish participation in various kinds of government positions, but also in economic arenas that are traditionally of strategic interest to Mediterranean governments: timber, slaves, grain. In the case of grain, for instance, though it was traded on the open market, shortages could cause riots. One government strategy to assuage such feelings was public flogging of grain merchants, and it seems likely that Jews avoided the trade so as not to be subjects to a combustible combination of popular economic and religious sentiment.[45]

Genizah records thus document a small layer of merchants who had the resources and position to join the patronage elite, and shows that most eschewed such ties. But there were ambitious individuals in each generation who did, as well as families we find in courtier circles for generations. Indeed, links of patronage were socially and economically important throughout Islamic society, and the Jewish community as a whole depended upon those with ties to court and provincial officers to soften the blows of official policy, to intervene for individuals, to secure recognition and money for the Jewish

---

and M. R. Cohen, "What Was the Pact of ʿUmar? A Literary-Historical Study," *JSAI* 23 (1999): 100-157; and Luke Yarbrough, "Did ʿUmar b. ʿAbd al-ʿAzīz Issue an Edict concerning Non-Muslim Officials?" in Antoine Borrut and Fred M. Donner, eds., *Christians and Others in the Umayyad State* (Chicago, 2016).

44 See Richard W. Bulliet, *Islam: The View from the Edge* (New York: Columbia University Press, 1994) on the general attitude towards government work; and Luke Yarbrough, "'A Rather Small Genre': Arabic Works against Non-Muslim State Officials,"*Der Islam* 93, 1 (2016), 139–69; and *idem, Friends of the Emir: Non-Muslim State Officials in Premodern Islamic Thought* (Cambridge, 2019) on non-Muslims holding office.

45 Lev, *State and Society*, 162–78.

courts.[46] Some individuals plowed the profits of such patronage back into the Jewish community, marrying their children to great rabbinic families. But equally, those who joined the court circle sometimes converted to Islam to seek greater privilege, or their children did, to more effectively protect the advantages they had accrued.

Finally, one must note the most universal way the state affected the economy of the Jewish population: the imposition of the poll tax. The tax was no trifling symbolic payment, it represented an economic challenge to a substantial part of the Jewish (and of course Christian) population. At a minimum of more than a dinar for each person in a household over nine in a world where a middling artisan's family might live on two dinars a month, this tax placed many a Jewish family of artisans in a more precarious economic position than their Muslim colleagues; it was entirely beyond the means of many of the poor. Though the amount was imposed on each person individually, it also bound Jewish communities together economically. Not only were regions defined by the total amount of poll tax imposed, individuals were forced by the system to register their residence for poll-tax purposes, and a great deal of charity went into poll tax payments. Like much of the charity recorded in the Genizah, collection and disbursement were both organized as communal efforts and as individual acts between particular donors and recipients. In a world where economic respectability was announced by privacy—being *mastūr*, that is, concealed, not having to show one's face—the season of the poll tax traced a yearly line of privilege in the community, reifying a social power of the wealthy that the logic of communal and scholarly status was always working to hide, tying the poor into relations of dependence.[47]

Conclusions

This outline of economic activity and commerce suggests how deeply Jews were embedded as part of an integrated Egyptian economic system; at the same time, certain aspects of their economic participation were distinctive, and religious identity was in general an important part of each person's economic identity in medieval Egyptian society. Members of any religious group could enter the market on equal footing in matters of buying, selling, credit, and

---

46 See Rustow, *Heresy*, 120–3.

47 On the collection and payment of the poll tax, see Goitein, *Mediterranean Society*, 2, vol. 126–38, 380–93. On the idea of being *mastūr*, see Cohen, *Poverty and Charity*, 33–71. On the social dynamics of charity, see Frenkel, "Charity."

contract; they could work in an enormously wide range of occupations; and they become economically "respectable," producing goods and services for many classes of society throughout the cities and villages of Egypt. But religious identity was still brought to market in certain ways.

The poll tax was large enough that it may well have meant the difference between economic security and insecurity for the majority of Jewish and Christian households in comparison with their Muslim neighbors, and have acted as a brake on upward economic mobility. Like the norms of religious leaders that frowned on cross-confessional workshops and partnerships, it created pressures for some kinds of religious economic community—particularly one bound by ties of workplace sociability and necessary charity. Social status did not come directly from wealth, but the centrality of the religious community in providing all forms of economic assistance left enormous scope for turning wealth into status by making the raising of money rather central to participation in communal leadership. Much competition for status, moreover, was contained within the religious community, as the pursuit of even higher status almost invariably entailed engagement with the state, and its attendant dangers to one's future wealth and health. These structural and cultural features of economic life may well have had long-term consequences; and help provide context and explanation for the more constrained non-Muslim participation in the economy in the later medieval and early modern periods.

7

Jewish Family Life in Medieval Egypt[1]

MIRIAM FRENKEL

In the medieval Jewish society of Egypt, as in the whole Genizah society, the notion of a nuclear family consisting of parents and their offspring was as yet indistinct. With no specific term to denote the idea, the Genizah people used a range of overlapping designations. Many of these, such as *bayt, ahl, dār* implied a common dwelling place;[2] others, like *ʿitra* or *ʿashīra,* stood for a lineage group. Some expressions were used more narrowly: the biblical Hebrew word, *mishpaḥa,* for instance, usually denoted a distinguished family, while the Arabic word *ʿāʾila* generally meant a household.[3] But all these terms were also employed in a non-specific way for a variety of social groupings.[4]

For the Genizah people, a Jewish community was conceived as a mosaic of various social and professional groups. This can be seen in the way letters addressed to the community opened with greetings to every social group—scribes, cantors, pupils, young children—with no mention of families, since these were not perceived as a unit in the social structure.

Kinship did play a central role in society, but the family group did not form a social unit. Kinship was rather a social association that was generally

1 This chapter is adapted from Miriam Frenkel, "The Family," in *The Cambridge History of Judaism,* ed. Phillip I. Lieberman, vol. 5: *Jews and Judaism in the Islamic World, Seventh through Fifteenth Centuries* (Cambridge: Cambridge University Press, forthcoming 2021).

2 Joshua Blau, *A Dictionary of Medieval Judaeo-Arabic Texts* (Jerusalem: The Academy of the Hebrew Language and Israel Academy of Sciences and Humanities, 2006), 24, 56, 222–3.

3 Goitein, *Mediterranean Society,* vol. 3, 3; Blau, *Dictionary,* 470.

4 Blau, *Dictionary,* 423; Goitein, *Mediterranean Society,* vol. 3, 2–3.

expected to oblige mutual obligations and loyalties, but these obligations were not bound to any imperative rules or hierarchies. As put by Eve Krakowski: "kinship bonds needed tending to bear social meaning."[5]

Most binding relations within the family were based on individual relationships between relatives, rather than on larger family groups. Indeed, most people mentioned in Genizah letters are identified by their tie to a specific relative: the brother of . . . , the nephew of . . . , and so forth, and only very rarely as members of a particular family group.

The loyalties expected by kinship included mainly social affiliation and financial support. In many cases kinship also implied cohabitation. Nevertheless, in many cases these ties could also be denied or ended. Correspondence between relatives could be interrupted and financial support could be denied, although this was not socially approved.

Egyptian-Jewish families were not organized according to a rigid given structure, but by personal loyalties among individual relatives. Being based on confined individual loyalties, they were also changeable and fluid.[6] Nevertheless, much importance was ascribed to pedigree. Paternal lineage is often mentioned in letters, legal documents, and most conspicuously in genealogical lists preserved in the Genizah. Descent from noble ancestry served political rivals as a legitimate claim for ruling positions just as it served charity petitioners as a proof of them being deserving poor.[7]

Although in social practice maternal kinship ties mattered a great deal, genealogies were mainly patrilineal as is manifested in the many genealogical lists found in the Genizah, most of which feature only the names of male descendants and agnates. Even the bond between husband and wife was considered to be more honourable and worthy when both came from an esteemed paternal lineage. Seeking to reconcile a husband and wife, the head of the Jerusalem yeshiva wrote in 1030, "They are both of an esteemed lineage . . . and the virtue of their forefathers will protect both of them."[8]

5 Krakowski, *Coming of Age*, 58.

6 Ibid., 56–64.

7 Franklin, *This Noble House*, 115–18; Cohen, *Poverty and Charity*, 67–70; Krakowski, *Coming of Age*, 61–2.

8 Gil, *Palestine*, doc. 104.

Family as a functional unit

In spite of what seem to be loose and flexible bonds that tied together most Egyptian-Jewish families, there were several family groups that respond in many ways to the well-known patterns of classic patriarchy. Most of them were families of affluent merchants called after a common ancestor such as the Ibn ʿAwkal family and the Ben Nissim family, or after their places of origin, such as the Tahertis and the Tustaris.[9] These big clans functioned as identity groups. Many political rifts within the Jewish communities ran along those familial lines; as a rule, political rivals were automatically supported by their family members and, by the same token, were judged in terms of their family allegiances. At least several branches of these extended families shared a common domicile or lived in neighbouring dwellings. The most prominent commercial companies, such as the Tahertis or the Ibn ʿAwkal family, were essentially family partnerships.

Similar patterns of family relations were sometimes repeated among less affluent traders and artisans. The degree to which kinship, domestic arrangements, and financial partnership could be intertwined is demonstrated in an agreement concluded in 1181 between two brothers who jointly owned a shop in Fusṭāṭ: the brothers would share a single home and eat at the same table; their meals would be covered by the business and each would receive one dirhem per day. If the younger brother, still a bachelor, declined to partake of his brother's food, he would receive two dirhems per day for living expenses.[10]

Kinship implied financial support. Indigent individuals felt entitled to receive help from affluent relatives even when the actual kinship was rather vague, and their letters invoked every family relation, however remote. On the part of the wealthy, there was an unquestioned commitment to helping needy relatives. In her will, the famed eleventh-century businesswoman known as al-Wuḥsha took the trouble of bequeathing two dinars to an impoverished orphan in Cairo, who, as she knew, was related to her in some way, even though she could not recall the girl's name.[11]

---

9 See Moshe Gil, *The Tustaris, Family and Sect* (Tel Aviv: The Diaspora Research Institute, 1981) [in Hebrew]; Norman Stillman, "The Eleventh-Century Merchant House of Ibn ʿAwkal (a Geniza Study)," *JESHO* 15, no. 1 (1973): 15–88.

10 TS 10 J 4.7, as recorded by Goitein, *Mediterranean Society*, vol. 1, 182.

11 TS Ar.4, f.5, edited and translated in Goitein, "A Jewish Business Woman of the Eleventh Century," 225–47.

Family members used to cover each other's debts, including payment of the poll tax. For the Muslim authorities, too, this was considered the norm: if someone in arrears was absent, the poll tax he owed was automatically levied upon his family members, notably parents and brothers—but also from in-laws. If these relatives failed to pay, they were invariably put in prison. The implications of this could be costly as can be seen in the case of the prominent Tustari family: when Abū Naṣr (Ḥesed) al-Tustarī was killed in 1049, only two years after the assassination of his brother, the vizier Abu Sa῾d (Abraham) al-Tustarī, claims against him were automatically transferred to their surviving brother, Abū Manṣūr, as revealed in a court record issued in 1052. [12]

Likewise, Jewish charitable institutions expected family members to take responsibility for their needy relatives. Alms lists from the Genizah note those instances when a registered pauper had relatives in town, a fact that would disqualify him from communal support.[13]

Nonetheless, in many other cases, obligations implied in kinship relations could be ignored or rejected, even within large solidarity-based families and among the most intimate circle of siblings. This is well demonstrated in a letter written in 1058 by Labraṭ b. Moses b. Sughmār, of the celebrated and influential Banu Sughmar family, to his brother Judah. Referring to another brother, he writes: "I mostly deal with him by keeping away from him completely, and considering him non-existent."[14]

Slaves as kin

In Jewish medieval society, male and female slavery was a widespread urban phenomenon. Slaves in households served as caretakers for children and for their adult owners. Slave women also attended to their mistresses in times of need and when their own kin could not, or would not, come to their aid. They thus functioned as "practical kin," to use Bourdieu's terminology.[15]

---

12 Bodl. Ms Heb. B 3 (2806).1. Cited by Goitein, *Mediterranean Society*, vol. 1, 183. For more on the Tustaris, see Gil, *The Tustaris, Family and Sect*.

13 On these lists, drawn up on the initiative of the Jewish communities, and for samples from them, see Cohen, *The Voice of the Poor*, 107–63.

14 Bodl.MS Heb.b.13.49. Gil, *In the Kingdom of Ishmael*, doc. 615. Cited by Krakowski, *Coming of Age*, 63.

15 Yagur, "Religious Identity and Communal Boundaries," 80–5; Perry, "The Daily Life of Slaves," 69–71; Pierre Bourdieu, *Outline of a Theory of Practice* (Cambridge: Cambridge University Press, 1977), 33–8.

Slaves were deeply embedded in family life. Slave women performed all public labor that was necessary for the medieval household economy—fetching water, going to public bread ovens, and transacting business in the market. As such they enabled the maintenance of free women's social status and honor. On the other hand, slave women often served as concubines and introduced much tension into conjugal life. Sometimes they were lodged in different residences outside their marital homes, with husbands splitting their times between the two places. In other cases, husbands totally abandoned their wives and children and lived with their slave concubines.[16]

Female slaves could sometime join the Jewish community without formal manumission and conversion, mainly through tight connections with their Jewish owners. This generally happened by way of intimate relations between enslaved women and their Jewish male owners, in what can be called "sociological conversion."[17]

Another way in which a householder could sociologically integrate slaves in his family was by apprenticing them to a trade or to management of the household. Male slaves who showed particular promise would often gain the confidence of their masters and be entrusted with major tasks such as buying and selling on the masters' behalf. Indeed, they were a part of the institution of apprenticeship in commerce, which was normally in the hands of biological sons. On the other hand, a slave could be integrated into the master's household not just as an adjoined alien but as legal kin through marriage. There was significant social pressure on masters to free and legally marry slave girls with whom they had had sexual relations or whom they had impregnated.[18]

Once a slave was freed, she had a good chance of marrying into a respectable family even if her former patron did not personally marry her. Her master would not only see to it that she was married but would also make efforts to connect her through this marriage to his own familial network.[19] Many marriage contracts involving former slaves indicate that the erstwhile master provided not only his name and reputation, but also a major part of the wedding dowry, including jewelry, clothing, bedding, and household goods.[20]

Hence, the acquisition of a slave was in many ways equivalent to adoption, and indeed many people were eager to acquire slaves of very tender age. We

16 Perry, "The Daily Life of Slaves," 112–53.

17 Yagur, "Religious Identity and Communal Boundaries," 101–31.

18 Perry, "The Daily Life of Slaves," 107–53.

19 T-S 13 J 3.26 and ENA 2559.13

20 Goitein, *Mediterranean Society*, vol. 1, 145.

repeatedly come across the purchase of slaves between the ages of six months and three years. Similarly, masters went to great lengths and invested a lot of money trying to ransom captive slaves, just as they would do for other family members. These bondage-extenuating mechanisms created a specific sort of kinship, in which other elements substituted for blood ties as the basis of family. These mechanisms incorporated the slave, via the household, into the social networks of Jewish society.[21]

The role of marriage

Matrimony was considered the normal condition for men and women reaching adulthood. Although only men were required by Jewish law to marry, Jewish society expected women to marry as well. Indeed, marriage and childbearing was the sole prospect for a woman. As formulated in the nuptial contracts of this time, marriage was essentially a mutual understanding between the bride who agrees to become a wife, and the groom who undertakes to provide her with food, clothing and the fulfilment of conjugal obligations "as Jewish men faithfully do," and to honour her. Although it was usually left unmentioned, procreation—not merely companionship—was, no doubt, the main raison d'être of marriage, to ensure the physical continuity of Jewish existence as well as its spiritual perpetuation through bringing into the world "sons studying Torah and fulfilling its commandments," to quote the phrasing common in letters of congratulation.

But, as attested by so many Genizah personal letters, marriage was primarily a family affair. Some of the marriages were endogamous, mostly between patrilineal cousins (cousins whose fathers are brothers), but as shown by Eve Krakowski, endogamy was a relatively infrequent practice, not a dominant social norm as was previously assumed.[22] Most marriages among Genizah Jews

---

21 Miriam Frenkel, "Slavery in Jewish Medieval Society under Islam: A Gendered Perspective," in *Male and Female He Created Them—Masculine and Feminine in the Mediterranean Religions and Their Influence on Matrimonial Religious Law*, ed. Matthias Morgenstern (Göttingen: Vandenhoeck&Ruprecht, 2011), 249–59.

22 Goitein claimed that endogamy among Genizah Jews was a prevailing norm. This assertion was followed by other scholars. See, for instance, Ashur, "Engagement and Betrothal Documents"; Joel Kraemer, "Women Speak for Themselves," in *The Cambridge Geniza Collections: Their Contents and Significance*, ed. Stefan Reif (Cambridge: Cambridge University Press, 2002), 178–216; A. L. Motzkin, "The Arabic Correspondence of Judge Elijah and His Family (Papers from the Cairo Geniza)—A Chapter in the Social History of Thirteenth-Century Egypt" (PhD diss., University of Pennsylvania, 1965), 26. Eve Krakowski has lately shown that endogamy was not a dominant social norm and that

were exogamous, that is between previously unrelated families. Both forms of marriage, within the family and outside it, were commended in letters using the same vocabulary of praise and approval. Of special importance was the social bond created by marriage between a man and his wife's male relatives, termed *ittiṣāl* in Genizah writings.

Amidst the widespread immigration of this period, marriage into a powerful local family was an expedient way for a newcomer to integrate. The most celebrated instance of such a strategy was provided by none other than Moses Maimonides. After many years' wandering between Spain, North Africa, and Palestine, Maimonides sealed his decision to settle in Egypt with an immediate marriage. His bride was the daughter of Mishaʾel ben Isaiah ha-Levi al-Shaykh al-Thiqa, a government official and physician whose paternal and maternal lineages included scholars, physicians, and public officials. The marriage thus provided a robust network of relatives to help Maimonides integrate successfully in social and professional life as well as in politics and business. The benefits of such a match were further enhanced when Maimonides's sister married the bride's brother, Abū al-Maʿāli Uziel, a high-ranking government official at the Ayyubid court. It is likely, then, that Maimonides headed a household that included his sister's family together with her brothers-in-law and their families. This new network of dependable relatives proved to be necessary and efficient in securing Maimonides's illustrious career in Egypt.[23]

Marrying into a respected family was regarded as an important goal. Typical of the congratulations offered on such occasions are those sent to Judah ben Moses ibn Sughmār:

> God has granted that you become connected with the most illustrious and finest people, those of whom one can boast in East and West. This is more precious than the Earth and the fullness thereof. Thank and praise God that He has cast your lot with the grandees of Israel [. . . .] May God aid them through you and aid you through them and make you a blessing for one another.[24]

---

marriage between patrilineal cousins was much less common among Genizah Jews than has been supposed. See Krakowski, *Coming of Age*, 213–23.

23 Joel L. Kraemer, *Maimonides, The Life and World of One of Civilization's Greatest Minds* (New York: Doubleday, 2008), 230–2.

24 Bodl. MS. Heb. B. 13.49 as cited by Goitein, *Mediterranean Society*, vol. 3, 56–7.

By the same token, a conspicuous disparity of fortune between two marital partners was regarded as a mismatch: "Why did you let them marry you to an orphan girl who lived in their house and served them? Instead I would have made *them* your in-laws," wrote a frustrated man from Sicily to his relative in Alexandria.[25]

Marriage between two scholarly families offered the desirable prospect of producing "sons studying the Torah." In such cases it was common to praise the fathers for "joining grapes of the vine with grapes of the vine." This well illustrates a genetic perception of family: women were excluded from Torah study, but the bride, being from a learned family, was expected to bring to the union the genes—in modern parlance—of gifted scholars and so give birth to sons who would carry on the tradition of Torah study.

Moreover, since learned families also had wealth and power, marriage between them was one of the most powerful tools in building and preserving a leading elite, which extended across the Islamic world and beyond. [26] However, one's choice of partner was not always based on expediency alone; personal preference could also play a part. In Qayrawan, for example, legal practice in Fusṭāṭ allowed for an engagement to be annulled if the bride and the groom formally announced their mutual dislike.[27] The Genizah contains many documents concerning the dissolution of engagements and betrothal agreements on this ground.

As a family affair, the choice of marital partner minimized the voice of the bride concerning the choice of her future husband. According to classical rabbinic law, a girl of twelve years was considered to have reached legal maturity as a *bogeret,* henceforth entitled to hold her own property, to bear financial responsibility, and to marry herself off without her father's approval. Nevertheless, Genizah writings show that as long as girls remained unmarried, they stayed economically passive and had no autonomy in choosing their husbands. Although the Genizah records some cases in which girls protested against their engagements, the girl's protest usually advanced the interests of her parents, and her reticence was used as a strategy in negotiating the marriage engagement between the two families.[28] Further, contemporary geonic and Egyptian Rabbanite responsa interpret the talmudic dictum concerning

---

25 T-S 20.122. Cited by Goitein, *Mediterranean Society*, vol. 1, 49.

26 Frenkel, "*Compassionate*," 207–35.

27 T-S 13 J 16.5

28 These cases were interpreted by Goitein as a manifestation of the bride's autonomy. Goitein, *Mediterranean Society*, vol. 3, 73. But see Krakowski, *Coming of Age*, 230–9.

the *bogeret* in a way that subverts its original intention. Thus, for example, in a responsa attributed to Hayya Gaʾon:

> It is the custom of all daughters of Israel—even a mature daughter in her father's house, and even a twenty-year-old whose father is still alive, to follow after her father. . . . [She is] not so licentious or impudent as to reveal her will and say, "I want so and so"—rather, she relies on her father.[29]

The age of marriage

According to Rabbinic law, a father may marry off his minor daughter from the age of three. In spite of occasional rabbinic passages that criticized child marriage, medieval Jewish jurists understood this dictum as a legal permission that permits child marriage to be physically consummated. However, child marriage in the Genizah society was very rare. [30] The average age of first marriage is difficult to determine. However, most engagements and betrothals were performed when the bride reached the legal age of maturity at twelve and a half. As actual marriage was normally postponed for several years, the average age of marriage for a girl was likely around fifteen or sixteen. [31] This was probably

29 A. E. Harkavy, *Zikhron kamma geʾonim u-ve-yiḥud Rav Sherira ve-Rav Hay beno ve-ha-Rav R. Yitzhaq al-Fāsī* (Berlin, Itzkawski Press, 1887), no. 194, as cited by Krakowski, *Coming of Age*, 234. See also Gideon Libson, "Betrothal of an Adult Woman by an Agent in Geonic Responsa: Legal Construction Accord with Islamic Law," in *Esoteric and Exoteric Aspects in Judeo Arabic Culture*, ed. B. Hary and H. Ben Shammai (Leiden: Brill, 2006), 175–89.

30 Goitein, *Mediterranean Society*, vol. 3, 76–9; Ashur, "Engagement and Betrothal Documents," 162–72; Friedman, "The Ethics," 83–102; idem, "On Marital Age, Violence and Mutuality as Reflected in the Genizah Documents," in *The Cambridge Genizah Collections: Their Contents and Significance*, ed. S. C. Reif (Cambridge: Cambridge University Press, 2002), 160–77; Avraham Grossman, "Child Marriage in Jewish Society in the Middle Ages until the Thirteenth Century," *Peʿamim* 45 (1990): 108–25 [in Hebrew]. Goitein concluded that child marriage was an insignificant social phenomenon and usually involved poor orphaned girls who were thus provided with the shelter of a home, this being the prime intention. Friedman and Ashur pointed out that in most cases, although the girls were engaged while still minors, the marriage was consummated only when they attained maturity. Krakowski (*Coming of Age*, 113–28) accepts the conclusions at which Goitein, Friedman, and Ashur have arrived, and rejects Grossman's claims that child marriage was a common practice especially from the eleventh century onwards.

31 Ashur, "Engagement and Betrothal Documents," 162–71.

a new medieval social norm, the result of a change in sexual ethics and in the ideology of pedophilia in the Islamicate world.[32]

The legal process of marriage

Marriage was normally accomplished through a three-stage process, although this was often shortened by combining stages two and three. The first stage, engagement (*shiddukhin*), involved signing a contract before witnesses in which the two parties agreed on the conditions of the marriage and the date of the wedding and determined the fines to be paid for failing to honor the contract. The document stipulated the financial conditions of the union: the marital gift, the dowry and any small presents given to the fiancée were to be returned if the engagement were broken. The marital gift was only to become the bride's property on the day of the wedding. The engagement contract also had specific personal injunctions, including clauses that related to the conduct of the couple. In one of these, the groom promised not to marry another wife and not to take a slave girl against the wishes of his future wife. Other clauses dealt with the bride's personal property, the couple's future domicile and restrictions upon their movement and way of life. A detailed list of the bride's trousseau and its value was normally appended to the engagement contract.

The second stage was betrothal (*ʿerusin, qiddushin*), which effect represented a formal marriage and could be terminated only through divorce. The two parties were declared husband and wife, but the marriage could not yet be consummated, the couple did not live together, and the husband did not provide for his wife. It was at this stage before the actual wedding that the union was confirmed and all the financial arrangements finalized, so as to avoid any last-minute misunderstandings. The betrothal had its own ceremony, and a banquet was also customary to mark the occasion.

Finally, the wedding (*dukhūl, kinnus, zifāf*) was the formal culmination of the marriage process, during which the bride was brought to the groom's house in a festive procession. It was at this stage that the marriage contract (*ketubbah*) was written out, with formulaic promises on the part of the groom that were reciprocated by the bride: he undertook to maintain and to honor her, and she agreed to become his wife. Note was made of the nuptial gift (*mohar*), consisting of a legal minimum of twenty-five *dirhems* (equivalent to the talmudic 200 *zuz* to be given a woman at her first marriage), and the groom's "additional

32 Krakowski, *Coming of Age*, 128–41.

marriage gift" (*tosefet ketubbah*) was recorded. This was the principal monetary offering. It was divided into two instalments, one to be paid immediately (*muqdam*) and the other (*me'uḥar*) to be paid in the eventuality that the marriage came to an end, whether through divorce or upon the death of the husband. In the *ketubbah*, the husband mortgaged all his possessions—movables and immovables alike—including his estate after his death, to the debt he owed his wife. Hence, any future sale of his immovables would require the consent of his wife.

The dowry (*nedunyā, jahāz, shuwār*) brought by the bride was also listed in great detail. It was given as an irrevocable gift to the bride by her father and was hence forth considered her exclusive property, providing for her needs in the event of the termination of her marriage. The dowry was entrusted to the future husband, who had to pay it in full when necessary; half was to be returned to the wife's family if she died childless. The dowry included the bride's personal belongings: clothing, jewellery, furniture and domestic items. These possessions were for the most part family heirlooms passed down for generations; money itself played no part. The bride's dowry was on average ten times more valuable than the groom's marital gift. There was inevitably a heavy dependence on the accumulated wealth of the extended family as it was the main economic foundation of a nuclear family.

Appended to these sections of the *ketubbah* was a list of stipulations, some of them standard provisions, others more specifically relating to the circumstances of the couple. Prominent among them was the requirement that the husband trust his wife and declare: "She is trustworthy in her statements concerning everything and no oath of any kind may be imposed on her." This clause probably reflects the anxiety that the wife might remain loyal to her paternal family and put its interests before those of her husband. It might also refer to a husband's suspicions that money earned by the wife might not find its way into the family purse, as was expected, but would be secretly set aside.

It was also often stated that the husband was forbidden to marry a second wife or buy a slave girl without her consent. The prevalence of these two linked clauses attests to the frequency of both polygyny and concubinage with slaves in this society.[33] Other conditions concerned the couple's place of residence and relations with their families. In most cases it was stated that they would live

33 Friedman, *Polygyny*, refutes Goitein's assumption that polygyny was only "a minor social evil." Goitein, *Mediterranean Society*, vol. 3, 150. About concubinage, see Yagur, "Religious Identity and Communal Boundaries," 101–31.

with the husband's relatives. A bride could consent to this and even promise never to demand that her husband move away from his family. She could also make such an arrangement conditional on it not being detrimental to her. In some cases, it was stipulated that the bride would continue to live in her parents' house or in their vicinity, especially when the house was part of her dowry.

Further conditions concerned the freedom of movement of wife and husband. Like their Muslim counterparts, Genizah women could only leave their homes for very specific reasons: to visit their parents, to participate in festivals or assemblies of mourning, or to attend to female friends and relatives. In his code *Mishneh Torah,* Maimonides recommended that married women stay at home seated in the corner.[34] Because the wife's movement was restricted by religious law as well as by social mores, *ketubbot* contain hardly any stipulations restricting the wife's freedom of movement. On the other hand, there are very few instances of marriage contracts that relate to the length of the husband's absence on travels, despite the fact that absenteeism on the part of the husband was perhaps the most conspicuous marital problem of the time. However, there were legal precautions a wife could take to preempt the problem: provision for a conditional divorce that released the wife from the bond of marriage if her husband did not return before a fixed time; the required deposit of the delayed marriage gift from the husband before his departure; or a commitment to leave the wife all she needed to meet her expenses during her husband's absence.

Conditions regulating the interpersonal conduct of spouses exist, but were quite rare. In one instance, for example, a bride was explicitly instructed to respect her father-in-law. In another, a groom promised to avoid the company of frivolous and impious people, and to refrain from beating his wife. [35]

Spousal Relations

(i) Involvement of the extended family

The implications of marriage were far more complex than simply taking a husband or wife; a whole new relationship within the two families involved came into play.[36] When Judah Ibn Sughmār was married, his elder brother, Labraṭ,

34 Maimonides, *Mishneh Torah,* Laws of Marriage, 13:11.

35 About the introduction of marriage agreements in the twelfth century and the political circumstances behind these new diplomatic innovations, their real worth in life, and the ways they could be used by family members, see Krakowski, *Coming of Age,* 241–64.

36 About marriage as a form of reciprocal patronage, creating dyadic links between male in-laws, see Krakowski, *Coming of Age,* 56–64.

wrote to congratulate him and to explain the meaning of his new status: "My boy, you should know how to behave, and God forbid do not contradict your father-in-law. Accept him as a substitute for your own father, may he rest in Eden, and for myself, and accept your mother-in-law as a substitute for your mother, may God have mercy upon her." [37]

Even a marriage between kinsfolk inevitably generated new familial constellations that required certain adjustments. This could present numerous difficulties, especially for the young wife. Given the chaotic reality of urban houses in Fatimid and Ayyubid cities, young couples lived in different, changeable and often fragmented living spaces, which they shared in a variety of ways with relatives or with non-relatives,[38] but in most cases a young wife had to leave her nuclear family and join the household of her husband. She was expected to honor and obey not only her husband but also his parents and sisters, and had to join the other female members of the household in maintaining and keeping the house. No wonder there are so many letters in which she comes across as a "lonely stranger"; there are also numerous references to friction with the couple's relatives. One extreme case comes to light in a complaint addressed to a judge, where it is claimed that a husband beat and cursed his young wife, his sister hit her with a shoe, his father called her names whenever he saw her, and they all spread rumors about her, giving her a bad name.[39] Some families took precautionary steps in the engagement contract, making the marriage conditional on the wife's right to choose the couple's place of residence, or to have her private chamber (*bayt*) in the marital household (*dār*)—in part, at least to avoid the risk of such an outcome.[40]

The extended family was also deeply involved in the couple's economic life. Since the economic foundation of marriage consisted of the dowry given by the wife's family—constituting more than half of the couple's resources—every conjugal misunderstanding took on a wider significance and could bring the families into conflict. Many cases are recorded in which the wife's family did not provide all that was stipulated in the marriage contract. In other instances, the wife's family registered dissatisfaction with her husband's management of the dowry. It should be noted that although the dowry was legally the wife's personal property, it was held by the husband and he could make his own use

37 ENA NS 18.35, recto, lines 35–6. Published by Gil, *Kingdom*, vol. 4, 17, no. 614.

38 Krakowski, *Coming of Age*, 47–56.

39 Mosseri A.16.

40 Krakowski, *Coming of Age*, 266–84.

of it.[41] Indeed, husbands often appropriated the rent that accrued from houses included in the dowry, or used its assets as collateral for their own commercial enterprises; if these failed, the husband could find himself being sued by his wife's family. On the other hand, having a dowry as joint property could also promote strong bonds between the families and between the spouses. In many cases we hear of long-term enterprises jointly managed by the families. Sometimes the wife took an active role in the business, and there are records of wives granting loans and selling, buying or standing security for their husbands, as well as vice versa.

(ii) Treatment of wives

Jewish law written at this time favoured the moderate use of physical force against women. In the eighth century, R. Yehudai Gaʾon, reputed to be the first author of a post-talmudic code of law, stated that "A wife should never raise her voice against her husband, but should remain silent if he beats her—as chaste women do."[42] Maimonides wrote in his own code: "A woman who refuses to do the work to which she is obliged may be forced to do so even with a stick."[43]

That the violence that accompanied married life was widespread is attested in a variety of documents. Engagement contracts sometimes required the husband to refrain from aggressive behavior: "He will not beat her; whenever he will cause her any harm he will pay her ten *dinar*s as a gift; he will not curse her; his mother and sisters will not trouble her." [44] Abused wives submitted petitions such as the following, which was addressed to the head of the Jewish community in Egypt at the beginning of the twelfth century:

> In the name of the All Merciful, may God grant peace to our master and teacher Maṣliaḥ ha-Kohen, the Head of the Yeshiva, may his rule endure for ever. Your maidservant has been married to this man for fifteen years, and has never received a thing from him, not even a piece of silver for going to the bathhouse; he bought me no clothing—not

41 Krakowski compares this legal framework to that prescribed by Islamic law and finds it "considerably more restrictive of female property rights within marriage." See Krakowski, *Coming of Age*, 49. See also Yossef Rapoport, "Matrimonial Gifts in Early Islamic Egypt," *Islamic Law and Society* 7 (2000): 1–36, especially 23–4.

42 Goitein, *Mediterranean Society*, vol. 3, 185, note 123.

43 Maimonides, *Mishneh Torah*, Laws of Marriage, 21:10.

44 Ashur, "Engagement and Betrothal Documents," 97–104.

> even a cap—and I complain about vexation and beating. He keeps saying to me: "Buy your freedom [by renouncing your marital gift]." May God punish him for what he is doing to me. He must pay me my marriage gift; fifteen years I have suffered his bad character and his vexations. Now I throw myself upon God and upon you. I am a captive. Free me.[45]

Evidence of the harsh treatment of women at the hands of their husbands can likewise be seen in written settlements of marital discord, court records and halakhic queries. The marital disputes underpinning these documents were many times the result of poverty. Financial shortage could lead husbands to pressure their wives to relinquish property from the dowry or to mortgage it, and sometimes even to seize it and run away.[46]

Violence against wives was prevalent at all levels of society, from the illiterate poor to the wealthy, educated elite. A typical instance of troubled conjugal life can be seen in the case of the court clerk, cantor, and teacher Solomon ben Elijah and his young wife, Sitt Ghazāl. The correspondence that carries their story deserves close attention on account of the insights it offers.[47] The couple, who were cousins, were married in Sitt Ghazāl's hometown of Alexandria when she was not yet fifteen, and left shortly afterwards for their permanent home in Fusṭāṭ. About a month went by before Solomon realized that his young bride was not the obedient wife he had expected. In a letter to her father, written not long after the wedding, he explained candidly:

> I do not hate her. It is only her character that I hate. I say to her "Don't do this"; she says "All right. I won't." But then she forgets what I said and does it. I do hope God will reform her and her "blessed"[48] character and her "blessed" movements. . . . Oh, my dear cousin, if I were living with you in the same town, I would never leave you, and you would make peace between us.

However, when Sitt Ghazāl herself demanded that they go back to Alexandria, and her family supported the idea, Solomon objected: "In Fusṭāṭ I

45 T-S 8 J 22.27. Translated by Goitein, *Mediterranean Society*, vol. 3, 186, revised by the author.
46 Zinger, "Women, Gender, and Law," 177–80.
47 Most of the correspondence was published by Motzkin. Krakowski has analyzed and dedicated a special chapter to this couple. See Krakowski, *Coming of Age*, 280–93.
48 Euphemism for "cursed."

get to teach children from good families. I am afraid that if I were to give up my teaching here, I would find nothing like it in Alexandria."

Relations between Solomon ben Elijah and Sitt Ghazāl seem to have deteriorated even further after the death of her father. In an attempt to improve matters, her brother wrote to the husband: "All I have with you is the little one. She is a stranger [in Fusṭāṭ], she is an orphan, she is young, and she is your own kin. As for the way you have treated her, no one will think well of you for that." Then he addresses his sister directly:

> My child, you do remember how your mother would attend to her duties. Don't disobey your aunt whenever she assigns you a chore. They only want what is good for you. You know my way. Still, even if there were a year's travel between us I would show you something you haven't been used to [meaning: I will punish you or beat you]. You know that you have no one left except God and these people. There is no one in the family more important than the old man, so serve him so well that I will get a letter from him about how you are doing, and about how you do not need a scolding.

However, the situation only worsened. Sitt Ghazāl fell sick and Solomon became increasingly hostile as one may infer from the letter written to him by Sitt Ghazāl's uncle:

> [Y]our own words testify against what you say and here is the proof: you say she does not even comb her hair. Listen, intelligent one! If she were feeling well, would she go without combing her hair? For were she all right, her body would be perfumed, her hair combed and parted and she would put her eye shadow on. As to what you say that she is shameless and insolent—she is your own, and belongs to you—she is the daughter of your maternal aunt. Does a Jew accuse a child of Israel of shamelessness? My lord evidently does not know that the word "shameless" (Arabic: *waqīḥ*) means *ʿaz panim, mamzer ben nidda* ("insolent, a bastard conceived by a woman during menstruation"). Let my lord beware of using this word.
>
> Coming now to your complaint that she does not do her chores: your mother does not actually know what she does. It is concealed from her. How do you expect any of the housework to be done perfectly by her if you use her as a maid? For you know that she is alone in strange surroundings, an orphan and so young. She has no one to lean upon except God—may He help her in His good ways and console her in her orphanhood. Now, my lord knows that we accepted the fact that she lives with you and that we are separated

> from her. We rely on your generosity, your chivalry, your piety, your learning and your noble lineage. We are all agreed that you are chivalrous, and know that you will not destroy her life by coercing her, for you are so politic and manage things so well.

Later in the letter he offers direct advice concerning Sitt Ghazāl:

> Read her the following words aloud: "Sitt Ghazāl! Remember the training you received from your mother and father. I swear to you by the God who will let me see you have a son, [you should] do and act towards the judge, your great patron, towards your husband and your aunt in the same way you used to act towards your father, grandfather and uncle.[49]

What surfaces from this prolonged correspondence between the leading males of this prominent family concerning a young woman is that using moderate violence towards one considered a disobedient wife was fully accepted as an established norm. Even Sitt Ghazāl's brother, who certainly cared for her, threatened to put her in her place through corporal punishment. It was only when the husband's violence became excessive and the beatings were accompanied by cursing and exploitation that other male members of the family found it necessary to intervene, and even then they adhered to the basic notion that it is the primary duty of a wife to obey her "patron."

The husband could also restrict a woman's liberty and confine her to the house; this was considered to be his privilege, even his duty. As Maimonides states explicitly in his Code:

> It is unseemly for a woman to be constantly going abroad and into streets, and the husband should prevent his wife from going out more than once or twice a month as the need may arise. Rather, it is proper for a woman to sit in the corner of her house, for it is written: The honor of the king's daughter is within [Psalms 45:14].[50]

49 T-S 12.69; T-S 13 J 8.23. Translated in Motzkin, "Arabic Correspondence of Judge Elijah," 61–5.

50 Maimonides, *Mishneh Torah,* Laws of Marriage, 23:2. Translated by Kraemer, *Maimonides,* 341.

However, it was forbidden to prevent a woman from visiting her father's house or her female friends.

Nevertheless, it seems that even these provisions were widely disregarded. Some agreements signed between husband and wife contain clauses in which the wife consents not to leave the house without special permission from her husband and not to complain if he locks her in. Elsewhere the husband agrees not to prevent his wife from going to the synagogue, to the bathhouse, to a party or to a place of mourning, or to sell and buy clothes or visit her sister, all of which suggests that her legal entitlement to these activities was disregarded prior to the agreement.[51]

The ill-treatment of wives also took another form: there are many recorded instances of husbands abandoning their families and disappearing, whether to evade creditors or other foes, or in order to live with another woman. The wife was left with no support and no information as to her husband's fate. Such cases were very common at all levels of society and communal authorities usually intervened in an attempt to find the errant husband and bring him to court, and then either compel him to return to his family or to ensure that they were adequately provided for. In certain cases, he was threatened with excommunication if he refused to free his wife by writing her a bill of repudiation. Meanwhile the family suffered greatly, as can be seen from the following letter written to the head of the Palestinian congregation in Fusṭāṭ by one Ḥaifa daughter of Sulaiman at the end of the eleventh century:

> I am a poor foreigner reporting what I have to endure from my husband, Saʿid ben Muʿammar, the silk weaver. He left me pregnant and departed. Then he came back and stayed a while until I was with child. He left me again. I delivered a boy and took care of him until he was a year old. Whereupon Saʿid came back. Then there was that incident with Ibn al-Zuqilliya, who drove us out of our place. We arrived in Jaffa, where Saʿid abandoned me, leaving me alone in a town where I was a stranger. Thus I was forced to get back to my family. From them, however, I suffered their harsh words, which only God knows. I decided to leave; living on public charity, I finally arrived here, where I learned that Saʿid had come to Malīj, where a

51 T-S 8 J 29.13, S. D. Goitein, "The Sexual Mores of the Common People," in *Society and the Sexes in Medieval Islam*, ed. Giorgio Levi Della Vida and Alaf Lufti al-Sayyid-Marsot (Malibu, CA: Undena Publishing, 1979), 43–61, especially 58; Ashur, "Engagement and Betrothal Documents," 117–23.

> brother of his lives. I went there, but was told that he had returned to the Holy Land. I ask you now to write to someone there who would induce him to have compassion on me and my child; for the boy is now like an orphan; any one looking at him has compassion for him and blames his father. If he responds, fine; otherwise, have him set me free. I do not blame him. I call upon God and Judge, day and night, I am now looking forward to the action to be taken by you and ask God to accept my prayers for you in his mercy.[52]

When the nature of his work obliged the husband to be away for lengthy periods—as was the case of traders as well as craftsmen, physicians, scholars, and cantors obliged to seek livelihoods outside their home town—special arrangements were made to provide for the family during his absence. [53] If this was expected to be especially prolonged, a conditional bill of divorce was given to the wife, according to which the marriage would be annulled if her husband failed to return at the agreed date.

(iii) Personal relations between man and wife

Of all the aspects of family life, the nature of the personal, unmediated relations between husband and wife is the least known. As a rule, husbands did not write directly to their wives, and only in very rare cases did they write about them or even mention them in letters. Women wrote to their husbands (always addressed as "my lord") only under very pressing circumstances and with the aid of a male writer, as they were illiterate. Addressing the wife or referring to her directly went against religious conventions and the code of social conduct. Thus in our attempts to penetrate the dark glass through which we observe this society, certain strategies have to be adopted in reading the relevant documents. For example, it must be kept in mind that a wife was never called by any name equivalent to the English term "wife," but rather in terms that illustrated a wife's role: "the House" (*al-ʾahl*), "the Family" (*al-ʿāʾila*), "the mother of my children," "the one who is with me" (*man ʿindī*), "the small one" (*al-ṣaghīra*), or "the baby" (*al-ṭifla*). Indeed, a wife was expected to be as docile, dependent, and obedient as an infant, as well as an exemplary housewife who did her chores without complaining and stayed inside the house out of public view. She

52 T-S 13 J 8.19 as translated by Goitein, *Mediterranean Society*, vol. 3, 197.

53 Oded Zinger, "Long-Distance Marriage in the Cairo Geniza," *Peʿamim* 121 (2009): 7–66 [in Hebrew].

was expected to produce and raise the next generation, and to be "with" her husband, namely, loyal and helpful. These expectations are exemplified in the words of approval sent to a newly wed husband: "I was happy to learn that your wife is efficient, clean, solid, and doing her chores well."[54]

Although a woman's beauty was no doubt an important factor, it is hardly ever mentioned explicitly in writing. Nevertheless, wives were expected to keep up appearances and to make themselves attractive to their husbands. For his part, a husband was expected to treat his wife with kindness, tenderness, and consideration (*ḥanna, shafaqa, raʿiyya*), as many a pleading father reminded his son-in-law. Husbands felt compelled to bring their wives presents. Weekly and monthly shopping lists drawn up by married men usually included an item labelled "present for the wife." Wives also saw this as their prerogative and did not hesitate to prompt their husbands—though not directly, needless to say, but through a relative.

"Love" in the modern sense of the word barely entered the lexicon of matrimony. Although such affection could be expressed unreservedly by men towards male companions, commercial partners, and other kin, only very rarely was it directed towards a spouse; this was reflected in the love poetry of the time: highly elaborate, it very rarely featured a spouse as the object of love. Religious poetry directed its ardor towards the divine presence, while secular poems often focused on the attributes of a slave girl or boy. Wedding songs were abundant but consisted mostly of conventional images that offer no specific viewpoint.

On the other hand, lengthy periods of separation did occasionally prompt letters that openly articulate emotion and longing. The following letter, written by an India trader away from home, is one of the most passionate declarations penned in this society:

> I do not believe that the heart of anyone travelling away from his wife has remained like mine, all the time and all the years—from the moment of our separation to the very hour of writing this letter—so constantly thinking of you and yearning after you and regretting to be unable to provide you with what I so much desire: your legal rights on every Sabbath and holiday.[55]

---

54 DK XIII, Goitein, *Mediterranean Society*, vol. 3, 166.

55 ENA 2739.16. Translated in Goitein, *Letters of Medieval Jewish Traders*, 223; Goitein, *Mediterranean Society*, vol. 3, 168.

In this last remark, the languishing correspondent was hinting at sexual relations, which were regulated by custom and by law, and stipulated in the marriage contract. The proper time for the fulfilment of a wife's "legal rights" was the night preceding the days of rest—namely Sabbaths and holidays.

Polygyny

The practice of polygyny—being married to more than one woman at the same time—is demonstrated by numerous documents from this period. Indeed, the custom was widespread at all levels of Jewish society throughout the Middle Ages, even though it was generally frowned upon and required the consent of the first wife or else the granting of a divorce. Brides and their families often insisted on prenuptial conditions that prohibited the future husband from taking another wife, and that obliged him, if he did so, to divorce his first wife and repay the marital gift in full. This stipulation was so common that it came to be termed "the well-known clause."[56] The Jewish authorities and Jewish courts also sought to protect the first wife and safeguard her right to divorce if she was opposed to a second wife.[57] In polygynous families, the equal rights of both wives were preserved through a variety of legal stipulations that guaranteed both women all their legal rights (food, clothing, and conjugal relations) in equal measure. In many cases, the court obliged the husband to provide a separate residence for each wife. In his code, Maimonides established this as a binding condition for polygyny.[58]

In many instances the second wife was a freed slave. This was so common that the "well-known clause" in prenuptial agreements had the twofold stipulation that the husband would not take a second wife nor purchase a slave girl without his wife's consent.[59] Freeing and marrying slave girls was especially prevalent among the India traders who spent long years in distant countries.[60]

According to the biblical law for such cases, whenever a man dies childless, it is incumbent upon his brother to marry his widowed sister-in-law (this institution is called levirate marriage, *yibum* in Hebrew), although he is free to refuse the marriage if he performs a special ceremony called

56 A variety of such agreements is to be found in Friedman, *Polygyny*, 55–82.

57 Friedman, *Polygyny*, 241–69.

58 Maimonides, *Mishneh Torah*, Laws of Personal Status (*'Ishūt*), 14:3.

59 Yagur, "Religious Identity and Communal Boundaries," 101–15.

60 Friedman, *Polygyny*, 291–399; Goitein and Friedman, *India Traders*, 55–7, 73–5, 690–2.

ḥalitza.[61] In the Genizah society this law was interpreted literally among the Rabbanite Jews and endorsed by Maimonides, who declared such Levirate marriage to be a religious duty, taking precedence over all other considerations.[62] The widespread nature of this practice largely accounts for the prevalence of polygyny.

Another established custom was sororate, by which a sister took the place of a deceased wife. This had no legal basis in any code of law but was so entrenched in society that a sister would break an engagement contract to marry a bereaved brother-in-law. In many cases this was at the instigation of the late wife's family, in order to regain the family's possessions.

Termination of marriage

According to Jewish law, divorce is the husband's exclusive prerogative and only he can bring about the end of a marriage. It is the man who divorces his wife, even without her consent, as stated in the Mishna: "A woman may be divorced with or without her consent; a man can give divorce only with his full consent."[63]

A wife, on the other hand, could demand her husband divorce her only on very limited and specified grounds. [64] Yet evidence from the Genizah points to a practice of women initiating divorce proceedings against their husbands by relinquishing their delayed marriage gift (*me'uḥar*). The procedure acquired legal status through an established statute, according to which the wife, by declaring herself a "rebellious wife" (moredet) and giving up her marriage gift, could compel her husband to agree to a divorce.[65] This procedure, called "ransom" (*iftidā'*), ostensibly enabled wives who were unhappy with their marriage to initiate divorce even without their husbands' consent. Nevertheless, Genizah documents show that in most cases the husbands were trying to lay a hand on their wives' property. This pressured their wives to "ransom" themselves. This arrangement was normally arrived at not as the result of wives' subjective dislike of their husbands, but in the context of husbands' abuse and neglect.[66]

---

61 Deuteronomy 25:7–9.

62 Maimonides, *Responsa*, vol. 2, 650–5, no. 373.

63 *mYevamot* 14:1 (*bYevamot* 112b).

64 *mKetubbot* 7.

65 Friedman, "Divorce upon the Wife's Demand," 103–26; idem, "The Ransom-Divorce," 287–307.

66 Zinger, "Women, Gender, and Law," 132–80.

In some cases, however, wealthy women from powerful families could obtain a divorce without renouncing their rights and property, and even secure favorable terms from the former husband. This is found in a number of legal documents in which the husband agrees to hand over almost all his property—as one bill of repudiation from 1203 puts it: "all the furniture, clothing, Bible codices, and other books found in the house, and everything belonging to him under the sky." The bill was followed by a declaration on the part of the husband that he had no claims whatsoever against his wife.[67] It seems, then, that the ransom divorce played a different function for privileged women than for weak women: whereas for wealthy women it permitted a legal (albeit expensive) escape from marriage, for abused women it further deteriorated their position vis-a-vis their exploitative husbands.

For the divorce to be valid, the husband had to write a bill of divorce (*geṭ*) and present it to his wife in front of witnesses, who could then testify that the bill "has got into her hand." This symbolic act was invested with great importance. A legal divorce also required a bill of release (*bara'a*), through which husband and wife declared they had no financial claims against each other. In most cases, however, these two basic documents did not suffice, and the process of divorce proved long and exhausting, involving many further judicial procedures that were more intricate and differed from case to case. Generally, Genizah women went to great lengths in order to avoid divorce and to keep their marriages. They preferred to remain married rather than to be alone and were willing to make substantial sacrifices for this goal.[68]

Marriage also came to an end with the demise of one of the spouses. The widower usually remarried shortly afterwards. His economic and social status was not unduly affected since he was the legal heir of his wife's dowry and of her other possessions; moreover, as a widower was exempt from paying the delayed marriage gift, and the necessary domestic duties were taken on by other female relatives. For the widow, however, bereavement was a severe blow. She ceased to be "the mistress of the house," lost her main financial support and in many cases also her home. Thenceforth she was dependent on what remained of her dowry, her personal possessions—if she had any—and the delayed marriage gift. Although a wife was not usually made a beneficiary, in many cases she had been appointed by her husband as executor and administrator, and thus had some control over the family's

---

67 T-S Ar. 54.69, from 1203.

68 Zinger, "Women, Gender, and Law," 164–5.

possessions. Otherwise it was customary for everything in the house to pass into the ownership of the legal heirs. The widow could claim that her rightful due be subtracted from the deceased's estate, but her position was weak and in many cases her claims were simply disregarded. As recorded in many Genizah documents, it took considerable time and effort to acquire these financial assets; in rare instances of success, the sum won did not usually meet her needs.[69] It is hardly surprising, then, that most of the women found enrolled on public charity lists were widows.

Parent-child relations

Procreation was a prime religious injunction and producing sons to sustain the time-honored tradition of Torah study, fulfilling its commandments for future generations of Torah scholars, was of paramount religious and moral importance; in this way God's sacred law would be preserved for eternity. The birth of a son also had the practical advantage of enhancing a family's resources and prestige. It was assumed that he would take up his father's profession or occupation, becoming an assistant or partner in a commercial firm, craft industry or community position. Writings and letters of the time abound in references to sons; they are sent reports, greetings, and blessings. The many endearments they inspire include such expressions as "the shining diamond," "the shy flower," "the blossoming rose."

Daughters were seen in a very different light. The birth of a girl was given only scant, indirect mention, usually in the course of celebrating the mother's well-being after childbirth. The announcement that a girl child had died was always followed by the wish that she would be replaced by a boy. This unfavourable attitude had a twofold cause: first, since women did not study Torah and did not actively participate in religious ceremonies, they were regarded as insignificant for the overall purpose of religious continuity; second, in practical terms, girls imposed a heavy financial burden on the family, as they were not expected to take part in any economic enterprise, and would require an expensive dowry in order to marry.

This did not mean, of course, that girls were not loved and cared for. Expressions of affection found in the Genizah letters include the following, from a young cantor away from home:

69 Goitein, *Mediterranean Socity*, vol. 3, 250–60; Joseph Rivlin, *Inheritance and Wills in Jewish Law* (Ramat-Gan: Bar Ilan University Press, 1999), 76–7, 82 [in Hebrew].

> Thank God, I am perfectly well, but yearn after my "home" (ʾ*ahl*, "my wife") and my daughter. . . . The people here are happy with me, but my mind is troubled. I wish I could fly to you; tell me what I can do. Please, write me how you are, especially my daughter and her mother, for when I am alone, I cry all the time because of my separation from them. . . . While I am writing this, my tears are running down.[70]

The education of children depended upon a family's social and economic standing, but the ideal of the well-reared child was no doubt shared by the entire Jewish community. It is an image reflected in a father's eulogy for his son who died at the age of six: the child is praised for never playing in the streets, for running to the gate of his home to welcome a needy person and share food with him, and for delighting his father with intelligent questions.[71] From this we can infer that the ideal young son ideally spent most of his time at home with his family, was intelligent, eager to learn, generous, and pious. He was also expected to be a loyal member of the extended family, always attentive to his relatives and their needs.

Adolescents

Childhood, according to halakhic precepts, was short: on reaching the age of thirteen, for a boy, and twelve, for a girl, an individual who had attained physical and mental maturity was considered to be fully adult.[72] In reality the transition from childhood to adulthood was much longer and more complicated. Medieval Jewish poets could long for their youth—in al-Ḥarizi's words, "Making love in the villages surrounded by roses and farms and grazing deer while time was still my slave . . ."[73]—but Genizah letters reveal a harsher reality in which mobs of youngsters used to congregate and interfere, sometimes violently, in communal affairs, opposing the traditional leadership, or

70 Bodl. MS Heb.c 28 (Cat.2876), f. 58. Translated by Goitein, *Mediterranean Society*, vol. 3, 229.

71 The eulogy was published by Ezra Fleischer, "Remarks on Medieval Hebrew Poetry," in *Studies in Literature Presented to Simon Halkin*, ed. Ezra Fleischer (Jerusalem: Magness Press, 1973), 183–9 [in Hebrew]. Translation by Goitein, *Mediterranean Society*, vol. 3, 234.

72 Tirza Meacham-Yoreh (ed.) and Miriam Frenkel (trans.), *The Book of Maturity by Rav Samuel ben Hofni Gaʾon and the Book of the Years by Rav Yehudah ha-Kohen Rosh ha-Seder* (Jerusalem: Yad ha-Rav Nissim, 1999([in Hebrew].

73 Judah al-Harizi, *Tahkemoni or The Tales of Heman the Ezrahite*, ed. Joseph Yahalom and Naoya Katsumata (Jerusalem: Ben Zvi Institute, 2010), 235 [in Hebrew].

simply challenging the social order through anarchic lawlessness and drunken brawls. Jewish society developed an efficient system for socializing its adolescents. This was done through the institution of higher learning, the *bet midrash*, whose pupils constituted a very involved segment of the community, usually representing protest and opposition. In this way they were given an opportunity to channel their energies, while taking an independent, active part in community life and rehearsing their future roles in the society.

Another method of socialization was the practice of apprenticeship. As a rule, a merchant's son was sent to a well-known commercial firm or experienced merchant in order to serve as an apprentice and learn the ways of commerce. There usually developed a special relationship, called "education" (*tarbiya*), between apprentice and merchant, the latter being addressed as "my teacher." The period of apprenticeship offered the adolescent boy a transitional period in which he became fully integrated into the adult world while still under the surveillance of his family or of the social and professional milieu in which his family lived. Since the major merchant families had complex networks of marital and business ties, the adolescent was absorbed into a broad, family-like social structure. However, this elaborate mechanism of socialization, which closely supervised a boy's entry into the commercial world, was not always effective. Adolescents who were not absorbed into the socializing frameworks that society prepared for them sometimes created a disturbing presence, which was very pronounced.[74]

Adolescent girls were totally dependent on their relatives. Before her marriage, a girl's life was controlled by her parents or other relatives in her household, who fed and clothed her, controlled her daily life, chose her husband, gave her dowry, and negotiated her marriage contracts, that is, shaped her future married life. When she inherited property or proved capable of working, she was allowed to use her own money only to increase her dowry and prepare herself for marriage. [75] Like mature women, adolescent girls were expected to refrain from visiting public spaces and to seclude themselves at home. This restriction was a marker of social class; lower-class girls could be seen quite frequently in public spaces. Seclusion did not come out of special anxiety for adolescent girls' sexuality; it also applied to married wives, widows, and divorced women. [76]

74 Miriam Frenkel, "Adolescence in Jewish Medieval Society under Islam," *Continuity and Change* 16, no. 2 (2001): 263–81.

75 Krakowski, *Coming of Age*, 142–80.

76 Ibid., 181–206.

Attitude to parents

In all circumstances, however, honoring one's parents was the religious and social norm. Young children, adolescents, and adult children showed respect towards their parents by addressing and referring to them as "my lord" and "my lady," and by kissing their hands and feet. Whenever possible, adult children stayed close by to provide for their parents and to extend any help needed. There were often instances when adults cancelled a planned journey because of a parent's immediate need. Expressions of longing and love exchanged between parents and children are among the most touching texts in the Genizah. Reverence towards parents was also grounded in practical considerations. Girls needed their parents to find a match for them, to protect their interests while married and to support them when their marriage came to an end. Sons relied heavily on their parents' financial assistance in arranging a marriage and, when married, in furnishing the initial needs of a young couple. In many cases, fathers and sons cooperated in a commercial partnership and their economic interests were thoroughly intertwined.

Inevitably, such interdependence did not exist without conflict, which even reached the court in some cases. But in the main, litigation between parents and children was rare and was considered improper. Most quarrels between parents and children were subdued and resolved within the family.

Sibling relations

Brothers were united by strong bonds of love, commitment and cooperation. The firstborn son had a privileged position; he was entrusted as his father's deputy and considered to be the closest to him. The firstborn also felt responsible for his younger siblings and replaced the father when he died.[77]

The most famous expression of love for a younger brother is found in Maimonides's lament for his brother, David:

> The worst disaster that struck me of late, worse than anything I had ever experienced from the time I was born until this day, was the demise of that upright man, may the memory of the upright be a blessing, who drowned in the Indian Ocean. . . . From then until this day, that is, about eight years, I have been in a state of disconsolate mourning. How can I be consoled? For he was my son; he grew up

77 See above, p. XXX.

> upon my knees; he was my brother, my pupil. It was he who did the business in the market place, earning a livelihood, while I dwelled in security. He had a ready grasp of Talmud and a superb mastery of grammar. My only joy was to see him. *The sun has set on all joy* [Isaiah 24:11]. For he has gone to eternal life, leaving me dismayed in a foreign land. Whenever I see his handwriting or one of his books, my heart is churned inside me and my sorrow is rekindled... and were it not for the Torah which is my delight and for scientific matters, which let me forget my sorrow, *I would have perished in my affliction* [Psalms 119:92].[78]

As seen in this letter, it was the custom for brothers to study together. Other evidence shows brothers sending joint halakhic queries, copying manuscripts together, sharing books, writing joint letters and administering fund-raising projects together. Brothers were often financial partners and conducted joint commercial enterprises.

The relationship between brother and sister could also be very close, and expressions of love and devotion were freely articulated in Genizah letters. An elder sister would be treated with great respect and referred to as "my mistress." An elder brother would feel responsible for his sister's well-being and was committed to assisting and protecting her. Younger sisters did not hesitate to turn to their brothers for help when necessary. A brother would represent his sister in the negotiations leading to marriage, sometimes even when the father was still alive; after his death, it was the brother that accompanied his sister through life, providing her with everything needed for the marriage, and admitting her into his household if she was widowed or divorced.

Elder or well-off sisters were also committed to helping their siblings financially. Whether through wealth or force of personality, or other propitious circumstances, sisters were able to gain positions of power within the family. An influential sister could intervene in family disputes and mediate in quarrels between her siblings.

Since the only females with whom a young bachelor could talk freely and intimately were his sisters, it is small wonder that even after marriage he would often find their company more congenial than that of his new wife. This created considerable tension between wife and sister-in-law.

---

78 *Letters and Essays of Maimonides*, ed. and trans. I. Shailat (Maaleh Adummim: Shailat, 1995), 228–30 [in Hebrew]. Translated by Kraemer, *Maimonides*, 255–6.

Conclusions

Family life played a central role in the Jewish-Egyptian society, although the family group itself did not form and was not apprehended as a social unit within this society. Family ties were not imperative and depended on the good will of family members. Never the less, some families, most of them of affluent merchants, like the Ibn ʿAwkal family, the Ben Nissim family the Tahertis, and the Tustaris, formed big clans and functioned as identity groups. Family borders extended sometimes beyond biological ties to include also domestic slaves, who functioned as "practical kin."

Matrimony was considered the normal condition for men and women reaching adulthood. For women it was actually the only prospect in life. Polygyny was legal and common, though generally frowned upon. As can be expected in such a complex institution, Genizah letters attest to a range of relations between family members from deep affection and commitment to alienation and hostility.

8

Situating Egyptian Pietism

ELISHA RUSS-FISHBANE

Judaism and Islam: intertwined destinies

Medieval Egypt was home to a unique chapter in the history of the Jewish-Muslim encounter. Beginning in the latter part of the twelfth century and reaching its zenith in the first half of the thirteenth, Egyptian Jewry gave rise to a mystical movement with conscious roots in both Abrahamic religions. Known to its Jewish members as *ḥasidut* ("piety" or "pietism") and to some modern scholars as Jewish Sufism, the movement constitutes the richest historical engagement of any known Jewish group with the religious heritage of Islam. Its devotees adopted an extensive spiritual regimen, much of which had clear parallels to Sufi rites, under the guidance of trained masters and within committed fellowships. Pietists dedicated themselves to enhanced worship and supererogatory devotions with the aim of cultivating an inner attachment to God, described in its ideal form as prophetic attainment, with the ultimate goal of stimulating a broader religious revival among their coreligionists as the harbinger of messianic redemption. Due to its fortuitous location in medieval Egypt, doubly blessed with a dry climate and the survival of the treasure trove of documents known as the Cairo Genizah, scholars have been able to reconstruct the historical development and literary legacy of this remarkable movement.[1]

Egyptian pietism was not the first instance of Jewish engagement with the Sufi tradition, but it was the first to do so openly and the first to attract a

1 On the Egyptian pietist movement in the thirteenth century, see Elisha Russ-Fishbane, *Judaism, Sufism, and the Pietists of Medieval Egypt* (Oxford: Oxford University Press, 2015).

significant following. The antecedents of Jewish pietism in the Islamic world and what most distinguishes the Egyptian movement from the latter is a matter of some debate to which I shall presently return. What is clear is that Jewish interest in Sufism in thirteenth-century Egypt was not the exclusive domain of an intellectual elite nor the fixation of marginal or eccentric individuals. There is abundant evidence from Genizah documents and manuscripts penned by members of the group that the movement cut across the socio-economic spectrum, from poor devotees on the charity doles to the highest representatives of the communal establishment. Of the latter, the most notable figure, who contributed more than any other to a measure of normalization of the group within Egyptian Jewish society, was the "head of the Jews" (*raʾīs al-yahūd* or *nagid*), Abraham b. Moses Maimonides (1186–1237). By sheer force of his official position and unrivaled prominence as heir to the great Maimonides, Abraham served as the movement's most eloquent spokesman and most powerful defender in the face of communal opposition.

Sufism's impact upon Egyptian Jewry can be traced in more ways than one. The first place to look for Jewish fascination with all things Islamic, included its mystical tradition, is the cache of documents stored for centuries in the Cairo Genizah. The Genizah documents bear silent witness to Jewish interest in a range of classic Sufi authors, including Manṣūr al-Ḥallāj (d. 922), publicly martyred for his ecstatic mystical utterances, and Abū Ḥāmid al-Ghazālī (d. 1111), renowned legal and mystical authority, whose four-part treatise, *Revival of Religious Sciences* (*Iḥyā ʿulūm al-dīn*), likely exerted influence upon Abraham Maimonides, who penned his own magnum opus, *Compendium for the Servants of God* (*Kifāyat al-ʿābidīn*), along a similar four-part structure. Most Sufi works that survived in the Genizah were transcribed from Arabic into Hebrew letters for the convenience of their Jewish readership.

Yet books were only one and likely not even the primary means by which Egyptian Jews were exposed to Sufism. Beginning with state sponsorship of Sufi institutions under Ayyubid rule in the late twelfth century, Sufism became an increasingly fixed part of the cultural landscape throughout the country, especially in the urban centers of Cairo and Alexandria.[2] The first Sufi order established primarily on Egyptian soil, known as al-Shādhiliyya after its founding *shaykh*, Abu ʾl-Ḥasan al-Shādhilī (d. 1258), did not gain traction until the

2 On the rise of Sufism and its institutionalization in medieval Egypt, see Nathan Hofer, *The Popularisation of Sufism in Ayyubid and Mamluk Egypt, 1173–1325* (Edinburgh: Edinburgh University Press, 2015).

late thirteenth and early fourteenth centuries. Yet from at least the late twelfth century, interested Egyptian Jews were readily exposed to a growing network of Sufi institutions and a large number of loosely organized master-disciple circles in their immediate environment. One thirteenth-century Sufi from Fusṭāṭ, Ṣafī al-Dīn ibn Abī l-Manṣūr, authored an account of many informal fellowships across the country, providing first-hand information about key masters and their disciples. Abraham Maimonides occasionally acknowledged to his readers that he had witnessed a given Sufi rite or assumed the latter's familiarity with others. We can only surmise which circles were observed by Jews, yet a review of Ṣafī al-Dīn's Sufi terminology reveals a number of interesting similarities with that of Egyptian Jewish pietism, but also enough differences to suggest that pietist authors were rather eclectic in their absorption of Sufi tradition, drawing upon local and textual sources alike with little discrimination.[3]

If pietist leaders, beginning with the head of the Jews and his prominent associates, openly acknowledged their debt to Islamic mysticism, the result should not be confused with a form of Jewish-Islamic syncretism. The pietists considered their reforms not innovative but restorative. In other words, they understood each of their apparently novel practices to be an authentic part of the original Jewish tradition, whether biblical or rabbinic or both. This assertion came with a double-edged polemic, the one directed outward at Islam, the other inward at their fellow Jews. According to the first, the rites openly admitted to be of immediate Islamic provenance were deemed more authentically Jewish than Islamic. Each of these Jewish rites, according to this view, were adopted over time by the Muslim faithful and integrated into the fabric of their religion to the point of seeming authentically Islamic. By the same token, however, the more severe pietist polemic was directed at the devotees' own coreligionists, who were said to have abandoned these rites or were at least complicit in their present omission. In one telling example of this two-pronged polemic, Abraham Maimonides wrote of the practice of nightly meditation prevalent among the Sufis and practiced in turn by his fellow pietists.

> We witness the Sufis of Islam practicing spiritual discipline in restricting their sleep, which they perhaps derive from the sayings of David, "I will give no sleep to my eyes or slumber to my eyelids" (Ps. 132:4),

3 For an account of the Egyptian Sufi background to Jewish pietism, see Elisha Russ-Fishbane, "Fellowship and Fraternity in Jewish Pietism of Medieval Egypt," in *Ethics and Spirituality in Islam: Sufi adab*, ed. Francesco Chiabotti et al. (Leiden: Brill, 2016), esp. 367–4.

> and "I arise at midnight to give thanks to You" (Ps. 119:62), and others like them. It may also be discerned from the report of the messenger [Moses], of blessed memory, regarding his seclusion in the mountain with the divine presence: "I lay prostrate before the Lord for those forty days and forty nights" (Deut. 9:25).... Take note of these marvelous traditions and grieve at how they were transmitted from us to another religion and have [all but] disappeared from among us! It is in reference to such things that [our sages], of blessed memory, remarked in their interpretation of the verse, "If you do not heed (i.e God's word), my soul shall weep on account of pride" (Jer. 13:17): "What is the meaning of 'on account of pride'? On account of the pride of Israel that has been taken from them and given to the nations of the world."[4]

Abraham's words are a perfect example of the open manner in which he and his fellow pietists both observed and described their Sufi counterparts. He assumed that his readers were sufficiently familiar with the Sufi practice in question and others to which he referred elsewhere, a familiarity derived not merely from books but from some form of first-hand knowledge. At the same time, the present passage provides a window into the double-edged nature of pietist polemic. What was observed among the Sufis was said to be derived from Jewish precedent. Although the author could only speculate as to the precise source of the practice in question, he took for granted that it hailed from an authentic Jewish rite from the days of the ancient prophets of Israel. This serves the double purpose of privileging Jewish antiquity over more recent arrivals, Islam in particular, while making his own adaptation of Sufi prototypes more acceptable in the process. On the other hand, Abraham's most pronounced polemic was directed not at Muslims but at his fellow coreligionists, who were ignorant if not indifferent regarding their lost traditions. It is when discussing this loss, incurred on account of Jewish negligence, that Abraham voiced his most poignant lament. The "pride of Israel," which he identified with those neglected parts of the Jewish heritage, "were transmitted from us to another

---

4 Bodl. MS 1275, 92a, ll. 5–11, 15–20, published by Samuel Rosenblatt, *The High Ways to Perfection of Abraham Maimonides*, vol. 2 (Baltimore: The Johns Hopkins Press, 1938), 322, and cf. Russ-Fishbane, *Judaism, Sufism, and the Pietists of Medieval Egypt*, 221. The rabbinic passage cited at the end is based upon *bḤagigah* 5b.

religion," eagerly assimilated by the latter and all but forgotten by his own people.[5]

Abraham's lament lays the blame for this lost heritage on his people's indifference but not without divine assent. He hinted as much through the accusatory words of Jeremiah ("If you do not heed, my soul shall weep on account of pride"), suggesting that the loss was due to the combination of Jewish heedlessness and providential punishment. This theological dimension, it turns out, was a crucial piece of Abraham's view of sacred history, beginning with the biblical patriarchs and culminating in his own day. In this paradigm, the dynamic relationship between Judaism and Islam began with God's promise to the biblical Abraham that his son, Ishmael, would be blessed to become a great nation: "As for Ishmael, I have heard you: I shall bless him and multiply him and make him very, very numerous" (Gen. 17:20). Unlike Maimonides's reading of this blessing, which limited the promise to the size of Ishmael's nation, the *nagid* understood this as a providential design to elevate the future religion of Ishmael's descendants. Yet, in his view, the elevation of the heirs of Ishmael would only be fulfilled when the descendants of Abraham's chosen son, Isaac, did not live up to their original promise, "during a period of [Israel's] weakness, on account of its sins."[6]

The rise of Islam, according to Abraham Maimonides, was then a part of the providential design by which God favored the descendants of Ishmael over those of Isaac when the latter spurned its own inheritance. But what was true of Israel's exile was equally true of its redemption. When Israel undergoes national repentance and returns to its ancestral tradition, he argued, the Abrahamic promise will be restored to its original heirs.[7] The intertwined destinies of Judaism and Islam are therefore fundamentally inverted. The rise and fall of one, in other words, is intimately and inversely connected with those of the other. In practical terms, this enabled pietist leaders like Abraham Maimonides to justify the adaptation of core features of Islamic tradition by arguing that

---

5 On Abraham's lament on the incorporation of originally Jewish traditions into Islam, see Elisha Russ-Fishbane, "Respectful Rival: Abraham Maimonides on Islam," in *A History of Jewish-Muslim Relations: From the Origins to the Present Day,* ed. A. Meddeb and B. Stora (Princeton, NJ: Princeton University Press, 2013), 858–9.

6 See *Perush Rabbenu Avraham ben ha-Rambam z"l ʿal Bereʾshit u-Shemot,* ed. E. Y. Wiesenberg (London: Rabbi S. D. Sassoon, 1959), 43–5 (Gen. 21:13, wrongly cited by Wiesenberg as 21:17); cf. Russ-Fishbane, "Respectful Rival," 863–4, n. 31.

7 See *Perush,* ed. Wiesenberg, 79 (Gen. 27:29); cf. Abraham Maimonides, *Sefer ha-Maspik le-ʿOvdey Hashem, Kitab Kifayat al-ʿAbidin (Part Two, Volume Two),* ed. Nissim Dana (Ramat-Gan: Bar Ilan University, 1989), 152–3.

they originated in Judaism and were being reintegrated at last into the latter. Much as the neglect of its own heritage was the cause of its own downfall, its restoration was the harbinger of redemption.

According to one formulation, from a surviving paraphrase of a passage in Abraham Maimonides's *Compendium for the Servants of God*, parts of Jewish law that were lost over time were "transferred to the nations" (namely, adopted as part of Islamic tradition). Yet, as part of the providential plan, the latter was to later become the conduit for the restoration of long-lost Jewish practices, such that these laws "become established within Israel from the nations."

> Divine wisdom [has ordained] that it will disappear from among them while they reside [in exile], until they repent and turn in repentance unto God, on account of which they will be delivered. Thus the nations will become the instrument for the rebirth of [Israel] and of the restoration of their dominion.[8]

By means of its devotional reforms, Egyptian Jewish pietism was believed by its devotees to play a key role in the unfolding of the providential design. The mutual relationship between Judaism and Islam, whether the earlier Islamic embrace of Jewish tradition or the Jewish embrace of Islamic rites in medieval Egypt, was conceived as a spiritual encounter of epic proportions stretching back to the divine promise to the patriarchs. For Abraham Maimonides and likeminded pietists, Islam had become the hidden element crucial to solving the riddle of Jewish exile and the key to the promise of Israel's future redemption. This is precisely why Abraham Maimonides frequently attributed the current degraded state of Jewish practice to the exilic condition. In an effort to justify the necessity of his religious reforms, the *nagid* pointed to "the people's general decline over the course of the exile. . . . Many years and multiple generations have passed since they have properly observed those obligatory rites which I have described. . . . 'It is time to act [for] the Lord—they have neglected Your Torah' (Ps. 119:126)."[9]

---

8 See TS Ar. 22.12, ll. 10–16; cf. the full translation and discussion of this passage in Russ-Fishbane, *Judaism, Sufism, and the Pietists of Medieval Egypt*, 241–3.

9 See *Sefer ha-Maspik*, 184; cf. Russ-Fishbane, *Judaism, Sufism, and the Pietists of Medieval Egypt*, 138.

Reforms and Repercussions

If Abraham Maimonides envisioned a pivotal role for the pietist movement in the unfolding providential design and in the historical encounter between these Abrahamic faiths, its impact upon the Egyptian Jewish community was far more concrete. From his double perch as head of the Jews and recognized pietist leader, the *nagid* was in a unique position to reshape Jewish communal practice in his own mold. The reality was far more complex. In areas of communal practice with no connection to pietism, Abraham Maimonides proved himself a determined leader, unafraid to confront established customs he concluded were problematic and to initiate sweeping reforms.[10] He noted several examples of "erroneous" practices that he claimed to have altered or eliminated altogether. We are relatively well informed on the communal reaction to his reforms, and what survives suggests that in some instances his efforts were met with considerable resistance.

The most controversial of the *nagid*'s reforms involved his alteration of the ancient Palestinian (*shāmī*) rite, which had been practiced in Egypt for many years in one of the two main synagogues in Fusṭāṭ.[11] Individual leaders in the Palestinian synagogue resisted Abraham's efforts quite forcefully, issuing a declaration of loyalty to their ancestral rites and even attempting to involve the Muslim authorities in the dispute, hoping to go above the *nagid*'s head altogether. Rather than back down, however, Abraham remained persistent, managing to diffuse the potential repercussions with the Muslim authorities while successfully imposing his targeted changes within the community. In defense of his controversial positions, Abraham invoked the sacred duty to restore public practice to the standards required by the law, even if it becomes necessary to defy communal opposition.

> As for matters required by the law, the elimination or censure [of local practice] does not have regard for custom. . . . It is preferable that these legal objectives be reached without any controversy. But if

10 On Abraham's assertive communal leadership, see Elisha Russ-Fishbane, "The Maimonidean Legacy in the East: A Study of Father and Son," *JQR* 102 (2012): 190–223; Mordechai Akiva Friedman, "Controversy for the Sake of Heaven: Studies on the Liturgical Debate of Abraham Maimonides and His Generation," *Te'udah* 10 (1996): 245–98 [in Hebrew].

11 This was known as the "synagogue of the Palestinians" compared with the "synagogue of the Babylonians," according to the twelfth-century travelogue of Benjamin of Tudela, on which see *The Itinerary of Benjamin of Tudela*, 70–1. See also Russ-Fishbane, "The Maimonidean Legacy in the East," 204–11; Friedman, "Controversy for the Sake of Heaven," passim.

> ignorant and malevolent people [persist] . . . , one ought to do what is required and it will become clear that [their opposition] will not prevail. But the controversy of one who strives after the truth for the sake of heaven will ultimately prevail.[12]

In contrast with his persistence in other areas of synagogue practice, Abraham made no effort to impose his pietist reforms upon the broader community.[13] Not long after he assumed the headship of Egyptian Jewry, Abraham abandoned his honored seat in the Synagogue of the Iraqis and initiated an alternative worship circle in his own residence, in which the pietist reforms were fully implemented.[14] While he never ceased to defend these reforms or advocate for their integration into normative practice, he never insisted that they be adopted over communal opposition, as he did with the other liturgical changes. On one occasion, the *nagid* lamented that his pietist reforms were met with "obstinacy and envy" on the part of those "who oppose the great emendations . . . that I have proposed," yet not once did he overrule his opponents' scruples and push through his emendations in the main synagogues.[15] Why the difference from one set of reforms to the other?

In order to appreciate Abraham's different approaches to religious leadership, we ought to pause in order to review the main pietist reforms one at a time. These reforms, many of which were due to Abraham's personal initiative, were not all of one cloth. They generally fall under two overarching categories, each with a different intended audience: the first the community at large, the second a select (self-selected) subgroup. In his *Compendium for the Servants of God,* Abraham distinguished the two groups in terms of their manner of observance of the law, referring to the first as the "general way" (*sulūk ʿāmm*) and the second as the "particular way" (*sulūk khāṣṣ*).[16] The "general way" constitutes the proper observance of the "exterior commandments" (*al-miṣvot al-ẓāhirah*), or the fulfillment of the minimum requirement under the law.[17] The second, described as the "particular way" (*sulūk khāṣṣ*), consists of contemplating and

12 *Sefer ha-Maspik,* ed. Dana, 178, 180–1.

13 See Russ-Fishbane, *Judaism, Pietism, and the Pietists of Medieval Egypt,* 145–9, in which I provide evidence for this view and discuss the positions of previous scholars.

14 See *Sefer ha-Maspik,* ed. Dana, 98.

15 See ibid., 196.

16 See *High Ways,* ed. Rosenblatt, vol. 1, 132, with a slight departure from Rosenblatt's translation.

17 See ibid.

interiorizing "the purposes and inner meanings of the commandments and that which may be grasped from the aims of the law and from the lives of the prophets and saints and others like them."[18]

The reforms aimed at the "general way" were intended, in principle, for the entire community. They focused on devotional postures and synagogue arrangements believed by the pietists to be part of authentic Jewish practice, yet all of which bear the unmistakable mark of Islamic ritual. For example, rather than line the seats around the synagogue walls, worshipers were instructed to pray in orderly rows. Everyone, including the synagogue leaders, were to face Jerusalem at all times (known, as in Islam, the *qibla*, or "the direction of prayer"). Rather than sit on chairs or cushions, worshipers were directed to sit on their knees. At set times intended for bowing, the latter were no longer to merely bow from the waist but were taught instead to prostrate themselves upon the floor.[19] To any casual observer, the pietist "general" reforms bore the unmistakable mark of prominent features of Islamic worship, a source of deep controversy to which we shall presently return.

The reforms for the "particular way" are in a different category altogether, such that it is doubtful as to whether they may technically be classed as reforms at all. They did not seek to uproot previous rites or to substitute new ones. Their target audience was the relatively tight circle of pietist devotees, although Abraham Maimonides encouraged a broad spectrum of participants from the general community, including the poor and those with meager Jewish knowledge. Those who did join committed themselves to a fellowship of disciples under the direction of a master (*shaykh*). Members of one of the pietist fellowships underwent an initiation ceremony and were expected to heed the direction of the master as well as to support one another in their shared spiritual path.

The training consisted of a disciplined regimen aimed at worldly detachment and inner illumination, known as "the ways of piety" (*darkhe he-ḥasidut*).[20]

---

18 See *High Ways*, ed. Rosenblatt, vol. 1, 132–4. Abraham's two-tiered system, marked by an outer and an inner dimension, bears a striking resemblance to Baḥya ibn Paquda's twin categories of duties of the limbs and duties of the heart. In reality, Abraham's dichotomy went even further than his Andalusi predecessor, in that the particular way emphasized not merely the intention of the heart with each action but the type of intention, privileging those which strengthen the individual's deep connection to the divine and culminating in the attainment of prophecy. On the prophetic dimension of Egyptian pietism, see below.

19 On various forms of bowing in pietist practice, see Russ-Fishbane, *Judaism, Pietism, and the Pietists of Medieval Egypt*, 174–80.

20 See *High Ways*, ed. Rosenblatt, vol. 2, 80, l. 3.

The regimen began with special attire, including a coarse mantle, some made of wool (*ṣūf*), others of cotton or linen. Though variation was granted to each individual, the pietist *habitus* was intended as a spiritual discipline to sever one's attachment to worldly comforts.[21] Pietists were expected to limit their intake of food, often fasting altogether, during the day, while waking in the night or pre-dawn hours for private meditation.[22] Some undertook more rigorous rites of solitary retreat (*khalwa*) in natural settings or at holy sites, such as the revered "synagogue of Moses" in Dammūh, on the west bank of the Nile.[23]

Although these specialized rites were only intended for the spiritual elite, Abraham Maimonides viewed them as part of his overarching project to restore the religion of Israel to its former glory. As he and a number of his colleagues maintained, the ultimate aim of the pietist regimen was the attainment of prophetic inspiration.[24] Unlike biblical paradigms of prophecy, medieval Jewish thought viewed prophecy as the culmination of a process of inner perfection rather than as a vocation initiated by God, sometimes against the will of the prophet.[25] According to Abraham Maimonides' terminology, prophecy was understood to be the "arrival" (*wuṣūl*) of inner illumination at the end of the "path" (*sulūk* or *maslak*) of individual self-discipline. Much as he viewed other aspects of ancient Jewish practice, the *nagid* described the loss of prophecy as a lamentable symptom of the exile. Its restoration would then serve as the harbinger of national restoration, culminating in the messianic redemption. In the double pursuit of personal and national awakening, the pietists cast themselves in the roles of "disciples of the prophets" (*bene ha-nevi'im*), recalling a tradition unknown since biblical times.[26] Yet, even as the *nagid* and his pietist associates looked to revive ancient Jewish tradition, they found a living model for many aspects of their unique path in contemporary Sufism. In the ultimate irony, not lost on the pietists (nor on their detractors), the path to authentic Judaism could not but pass through

---

21 See Russ-Fishbane, *Judaism, Sufism, and the Pietists of Medieval Egypt*, 127–9.

22 See ibid., 102–22.

23 On pilgrimages and solitary retreats to Dammūh, see ibid., 113–14. On this site and its importance to the Egyptian Jewish community, see Golb, "The Topography of the Jews," 255–9.

24 See Elisha Russ-Fishbane, "The Legacy of the Prophets and the Prophetic Path in Medieval Sufism and Egyptian Jewish Pietism," *Pe'amim* 148 (2017): 59–86 [in Hebrew].

25 On the theory and practice of prophecy in Egyptian pietism and its background in medieval Jewish and Islamic thought, see Russ-Fishbane, *Judaism, Sufism, and the Pietists of Medieval Egypt*, 187–218.

26 See ibid., 222–7.

Islam. Although the pietist regimen was not perceived by critics as a threat to the broader Jewish community, its Sufi background was plain to see and was openly acknowledged by pietist leaders.

Objections to Egyptian pietism, whether of the "general" reforms to communal worship or of the "particular" regimen of the pietist elite, were swift in coming. Those aimed at the devotional reforms were extensive, though two stand out in importance. The first maintained that these reforms were fundamentally innovative and, as such, constituted a deviation from normative Judaism.[27] Judging from the numerous occasions in which Abraham penned rebuttals against the accusation of innovation, it was clearly a bone of contention between the opposing camps and would continue to be so after the death of the *nagid*. On one such occasion, in defense of the rite of prostration, Abraham turned the tables on his accusers by claiming that their longstanding neglect of these synagogue rites made them the true opponents of tradition, repeatedly affirming the antiquity and authenticity of his reforms. The *nagid* associated the neglect of tradition, here as on many occasions, with the decline of the people of Israel in its exilic condition.

> Be careful . . . not to confuse a new idea and custom with ancient [ones] that have been neglected to the point of being forgotten and [only] later brought to the attention [of the community], restored, and revitalized. This is the case in the matter . . . of prostration . . . , [which] is an obligation of the law and ancient custom of the people, a fact neglected over many years in exile. And when one has been made aware that it is an obligation and puts it into practice, it appears to the deluded and ignorant as if it is a religious innovation. It is an innovation only in relation to the intermediate time [in which it was defunct], not in relation to the time of the original community.[28]

For a legal authority to say that a set of rites, such as prostration, are original and authentic is equivalent to saying that they are obligatory and binding, as the *nagid* and his disciples maintained. The overarching structure of his *Compendium for the Servants of God* attests to this position as forcefully as any declaration to this effect. The work consisted of four divisions, with the first

27 On the concept of innovation (*bidʿa*), familiar to medieval Islamic culture, see ibid., 80, note 159.

28 See *Sefer ha-Maspik*, ed. Dana, 161.

three devoted to the obligations incumbent upon the entire community as part of the "general way" and the final one addressing the "particular" path of the select few. The chapters in which Abraham addressed his devotional initiatives were included in the second part, in the course of his treatment of the "general" laws of prayer. There is little question that the *nagid* entertained the hope that these reforms would be fully integrated into mainstream Jewish practice. Yet, contrary to his aggressive leadership in other areas of public practice, he and his associates never imposed these devotional reforms upon the community. At one point, he attested that when his fellow pietists attended one of the public synagogues (as opposed to their private worship service), they were careful to conform to mainstream practice. "[They perform these rites] when in their own homes, whether they are praying individually or in groups. But whenever they pray in the synagogues or in big crowds, they do not act differently from [local] practice and do not impose [their own custom] upon them."[29]

Apart from the charge of innovation, perhaps the most severe polemic against the devotional reforms was that of "imitating the gentiles" (*ḥuqqot ha-goyim*), a talmudic prohibition against following the ways of the nations, rooted in the Bible.[30] According to the *nagid*'s own admission, the reforms resembled key rites of Islamic worship and even drew their immediate inspiration from them. In this respect, he seemed to confirm the worst suspicions of his detractors that he was deviating from Jewish tradition. Abraham's chief rebuttal, as we have seen, was to maintain that the reforms were rather restorations of ancient Jewish rites. In order to make his case, he mustered an array of biblical examples and rabbinic laws to suggest that these were in fact the original (and thus intended) worship of Israel. Exempla of patriarchs, prophets, and sages play a disproportionate role in the *nagid*'s elaborate case for the antiquity of his reforms.

In addition to the question of precedent, Abraham offered two principle rebuttals to the charge of imitation. The first sought to limit the scope of the original prohibition of imitation by drawing a distinction between ancient and novel practices. The mere fact that Judaism shares a given practice with another religion need not constitute imitation but coincidence, if not gentile imitation of Judaism. According to this logic, Abraham chided his opponents, many other core Jewish commandments would have to be abandoned for resembling

29 See Abraham Maimonides, *Responsa*, 64, no. 62.

30 For an overview of this prohibition, see Russ-Fishbane, *Judaism, Sufism, and the Pietists of Medieval Egypt*, 76–7.

gentile religions, much as the community had already done in the case of the rites he sought to reinstate.

> Why do you prohibit prostration but not standing during prayer in so far as the gentiles also stand in their prayers? Neither should you face the direction of Jerusalem, whether sitting or standing, in so far as the Christians . . . face [Jerusalem]. . . . Your logic also compels you not to pray or fast or give charity . . . [and] the same would apply to every commandment adopted and integrated by the gentiles, to the point that many of the commandments of the Torah would be abrogated, as the gentiles wish.[31]

Abraham's second rebuttal to the charge of imitation addressed the status of Islam specifically. As we observed at the outset of this essay, Abraham did not shy from the topic of Islam but rather made it a centerpiece of his theological and ideological system. Like his father before him, Abraham did not classify Christianity and Islam in the same category but viewed the former as idolatrous and the latter as unquestionably monotheistic.[32] Unlike most authorities, Abraham interpreted the talmudic ban on imitation as applying exclusively to idolatrous nations or religions. Should anyone adopt genuine Islamic practices with no Jewish precedent, he reasoned, we would prohibit it unconditionally but not on the technical grounds of imitating the gentiles. "I do not apply to this [the category of] *ḥuqqot ha-goyim,* in so far as those who practice such [things], namely the Ishmaelites, are monotheists and prohibit idolatry. All the same," he added for good measure, "there is no need for an imitation of this sort, for what is contained in our law and customs is sufficient."[33]

Like the devotional reforms intended for the broader Jewish community, the spiritual rites and regimen instituted for the pietist fellowship elicited its share of controversy. Tensions over these elite circles of Jewish mystics rose to the surface both in public and private. In one very contentious and public affair,

---

31 *Sefer ha-Maspik,* ed. Dana, 150–1.

32 Much has been written on Maimonides's view of Islam and Christianity. See, for example, Howard Kreisel, "Maimonides on Christianity and Islam," *Jewish Civilization* 3 (1985): 153–62; Eliezer Schlossberg, "Maimonides' Attitude to Islam," *Pe'amim* 42 (1990): 38–60 [in Hebrew]; Daniel Lasker, "Tradition and Innovation in Maimonides' Attitude toward Other Religions," in *Maimonides after 800 Years,* ed. Jay Harris (Cambridge, MA: Harvard University Press, 2007), 167–82.

33 See *Sefer ha-Maspik,* ed. Dana, 157–8.

a number of pietists were accused by some of their coreligionists of heresy and brought before local rabbinic courts to stand trial. Some were charged with blasphemous utterances, not unlike certain Sufi mystics infamous for such utterances when in an ecstatic state.[34] Others were accused of advancing a form of antinomianism, or renunciation of religious law.

Abraham Maimonides, too, bore witness to the fact that some pietists were not only lax in observing the law but perhaps even abandoned it altogether. In his dual capacity as *nagid* and pietist leader, Abraham sought to wrangle this fringe group back into the mainstream. Yet he did not hesitate to come to their defense when these same pietists faced accusations of heresy in the courts. In a strongly worded epistle, Abraham allowed for the possibility that individual pietists may need to be restrained and corrected yet called into question the capacity of ordinary scholars to properly judge the faith of the pietists.

> Judges and adjudicators are not permitted to render judgment on ascetics and devotees without having attained an advanced level in their path. . . . Only those should judge who take into consideration the state of the ascetics and devotees and others among the pietists and render an account of their affairs. Whenever they hear a rumor that one of them has a fault or deficiency in his belief, they should not affirm what they hear . . . , since most people have an aversion to the adherents of these disciplined paths due to its being so different from what they are accustomed to.[35]

Given the serious threat of being branded a heretic or deviant, Egyptian pietists were forced to be circumspect. As members of a mystical brotherhood, fellows were duty bound to support one another in their common goals, including taking care not to expose any member to unsympathetic individuals or authorities. In one letter preserved in the Genizah, a lapsed member of the fellowship was entreated by a former associate to be mindful of his old code of honor and not to expose other members.[36] Others expressed the need for extreme caution even among members of one's own family, should the latter be unsympathetic to the pietist movement. One pietist author counseled his

34 See my discussion in Russ-Fishbane, *Judaism, Sufism, and the Pietists of Medieval Egypt*, 71–6.

35 Bodl. Heb. c 28.45–6, published by S. D. Goitein, "A Treatise in Defence of the Pietists by Abraham Maimonides," *JJS* 16 (1965): 113–14.

36 See TS 10 J 13.8, published by S. D. Goitein, "Abraham Maimonides and His Pietist Circle," *Tarbiz* 33 (1964): 187 [in Hebrew].

readers to keep their pietism a secret from family members who, "when they see one of the practices leading to this noble goal, they declare it to be mere heresy and strictly forbidden. . . . It is therefore essential for anyone who is mindful and astute to be vigilant . . . , to practice without cease while concealing himself to the utmost extent."[37]

The anxiety palpable in these words reflects a paradox at the heart of the Egyptian pietist movement. The main public advocate for the mystical movement consisted of the head of the Jews and his close associates, such as the physician, R. Abraham ibn Abī al-Rabīʿ, and the judge, R. Ḥananel b. Samuel. Yet, even with the vocal support of the *nagid* and his circle, many pietist devotees experienced enough pressure from family members and communal authorities to ensure that their mystical affiliation be kept largely out of public view.

At best, the powerful support at the top proved sufficient to fend off polemicists and opponents during the *nagid*'s lifetime but proved precarious after his death. Almost immediately after the latter's passing, critics of the pietist devotional reforms sent a formal complaint to the Muslim authorities requesting the prohibition of all changes to traditional practice, despite the fact that the pietists restricted their reforms to their own private prayer circles.[38] The answer from the Ayyubid government, which has not been preserved, was apparently non-interventionist, as yet another appeal was made to the newly installed Mamluk regime in 1250, which ruled in favor of the traditionalists. The pietist leadership was forced to close its conventicle and David the Nagid was compelled to attend the main Babylonian synagogue in Fusṭāṭ. Perhaps as a result of this pressure or due to his refusal to comply, David took refuge in Acre and was only reinstalled as Egyptian *nagid* in 1252. Despite support for pietism among the Maimonidean descendants who dominated the Egyptian Nagidate into the fourteenth century, the movement was increasingly reduced to a small circle of dedicated disciples on the margins of the Jewish community.

The encounter between Judaism and Sufism in thirteenth-century Egypt marks a critical transition from a Jewish dialogue with Sufi and Near Eastern models of piety, a dialogue that was indeed centuries in the making, to a concrete pietist movement embedded within the fabric of Jewish communal life. To this end, pietist leaders from Abraham Maimonides on down embraced both an institutional framework and a mechanism of self-perpetuation. In the

37 For this text, a composite of overlapping manuscripts, see Paul Fenton, "A Mystical Treatise on Prayer and the Spiritual Quest from the Pietist Circle," *JSAI* 16 (1993): 145.

38 See TS AS 182.291, published by Khan, *Arabic Legal and Administrative Documents*, 293–4.

first instance, pietism constituted the institutionalization of piety, replete with a recognizable social structure, practical regimen, and designated hierarchy of spiritual direction. In the second, pietism constructed the means by which these human institutions could in principle replicate themselves for successive generations. While Egyptian pietism proved to be short-lived, it was not for lack of a long-term vision of self-perpetuation, most remarkably by means of a reconstituted tradition of prophetic discipleship with messianic pretensions. At the heart of that vision was the fateful intersection between Judaism and Islam, in which the restoration of one religion was said to require a profound engagement with the other. The results of this open engagement were both unprecedented and unrepeated in the *longue durée* of the historical interface between the children of Isaac and the children of Ishmael.

9

Languages and Language Varieties Used by Medieval Egyptian Jews

ESTHER-MIRIAM WAGNER

A multiglossia of languages

The sources extant in the Cairo Genizah allow us unprecedented insights into the linguistic environment of medieval Egyptian Jewry. Not only has the Genizah preserved a wealth of literary texts and documents, which testify to the literacy of its depositors, but from issues discussed in the legal documents and letters we also learn about attitudes towards languages. At the same time, we have to be cautious about inferring too much from quantitative analyses of the Genizah material. The deposition history of the Genizah is patchy, to put it mildly, and we do not know whether, for example, Hebrew-script material was more likely to be deposited than manuscripts written in other scripts.

Arabic was the language spoken by the majority of Jewish Egyptians, and they also wrote it, both in Arabic script and in Hebrew script, with the latter called Judeo-Arabic.[1] But the regular learning and recitation of the

1 We follow the definition of Judaeo-Arabic as suggested by Geoffrey Khan ("Judaeo-Arabic," in *Encyclopedia of Arabic Language and Linguistics*, ed. Kees Versteegh [Leiden: Brill, 2007], vol. 2, 526–36), who based the nomenclature of Judaeo-Arabic on a purely descriptive criterion: the use of Hebrew script. For linguistic reasons, we do not agree with the idea of Judaeo-Arabic as a separate language, as proposed for example in Joshua Blau, *Diqduq ha-ʿaravit-ha-yehudit shel yeme ha-benayim* (Jerusalem: Magness Press, 1980); idem, *The Emergence and Linguistic Background of Judaeo-Arabic* (2nd edition, Oxford: Oxford

religious works of Judaism put them in steady contact with other languages, too. The study of the Bible and works such as the Mishnah familiarized Jewish Egyptians with Hebrew, while the application of religious law, which permeated every aspect of medieval Jewish life, exposed them to Aramaic. The effect was twofold: on the one hand, both Hebrew and Aramaic continued to be used in certain kinds of literature. Divorce deeds and marriage contracts, for example, were written in Aramaic, and liturgical poetry and a large part of communal correspondence in Hebrew. One of the greatest medieval Jewish thinkers, Maimonides, writing in Egypt, composed most of his correspondence, responsa, medical works and philosophical-ethical treatises in Judeo-Arabic, but wrote his Mishnah commentary in Hebrew. On the other hand, the prolonged contact of Hebrew and Aramaic led to the inclusion of Hebrew and Aramaic in the spoken and written Arabic language itself, resulting in language varieties with a substantial Hebrew-Aramaic lexical component.

In the mixing of the three languages, particular registers for different text genres were created. Aramaic and Hebrew would feature heavily in legal treatises, ethical works, or in commentaries on the religious literature. More secular texts, however, would show substantially fewer Hebrew and Aramaic elements.

Other languages were also used by Jewish writers (and probably speakers) in medieval Egypt, as we know from the sources in the Genizah. Documents and literary texts written in a number of languages in Hebrew script have been preserved, such as Judeo-Greek, Judeo-Persian, and Judeo-Armenian, and towards the end of the medieval period also Yiddish and Ladino. Proportionally, however, manuscripts in these languages are vastly outnumbered by sources in Judeo-Arabic and Arabic, Hebrew, and Aramaic.

Literary genres were associated with particular languages. Bible commentaries were in the medieval period written in Judeo-Arabic, legal works employed

---

University Press, 1981; 3rd edition, Oxford: Oxford University Press, 1988), an idea also passionately contested by Ella Shohat in "The Question of Judaeo-Arabic," *Arab Studies Journal* 23, no. 1 (2015): 14–76, and its embedment into a "Jewish languages" framework, as theorized by Paul Wexler, "Jewish Interlinguistics: Facts and Conceptual Framework," *Language* 57, no. 1 (1981): 99–149. For a more differentiated view on Jewish language varieties and Judaeo-Arabic, see Benjamin H. Hary, *Translating Religion: Linguistic Analysis of Judaeo-Arabic Sacred Texts from Egypt* (Leiden: Brill, 2009), 5–49, and for discussion on the topic of Judaeo-Arabic vs. Jewish Arabic in a linguistic and ideological context, including an argument why Judaeo-Arabic should not be used for spoken varieties of Arabic, see Esther-Miriam Wagner, "Judaeo-Arabic Language or Jewish Arabic sociolect? Linguistic Terminology between Linguistics and Ideology," in *Jewish Languages in Historical Perspective*, ed. Lily Khan and Mark Geller (Leiden: Brill, 2018), 189–207.

Hebrew and Aramaic, scientific, medical, and literary sources were composed in Judeo-Arabic and Arabic. The fifteenth century marks a pronounced shift in the literacy of Egypt, with Hebrew firmly establishing itself as the main written language used in literature and documents, replacing Judeo-Arabic.

Documentary sources display great variations in the use of languages over time. The deposition history of the Genizah shows a stronger influence of Hebrew until the early eleventh century and again from the middle of the thirteenth century onwards. During these times, most of the extant correspondence and almost all legal documents are composed in Hebrew. From the early eleventh century throughout the twelfth and into the thirteenth century, however, the preserved documents, in particular letters, are mostly written in Judeo-Arabic. Yet, the fact that most of the extant correspondence from before the eleventh century was composed in Hebrew may be purely coincidental. Much of this early material comprises official communal correspondence, which throughout the medieval period favoured Hebrew. The more mundane documents, such as private and mercantile letters, are not extant from that period, which would perhaps have been written in Judeo-Arabic. The pre-eleventh-century Hebrew material may have been part of a communal archive that was transferred into the Ben Ezra synagogue in the early eleventh century, which would explain why the older material does not touch upon private or secular correspondence. Or it may have been part of another *genizah,* in which only certain materials were stored, or from which only selected sources were transferred over to the new *genizah* in the Ben Ezra synagogue.

For the purpose of an assessment of languages varieties used by medieval Egyptian Jews, it is important to distinguish between written sources, on the one hand, and spoken material, on the other. Written and spoken varieties of languages represent two connected but rather divergent entities, which operate in quite different linguistic environments,[2] and thus have to be discussed separately. A third entity is the reading tradition: reading a text in medieval times meant reading it aloud.[3] The reading tradition presents a special sphere in which a particular connection between spoken and written

2 Esther-Miriam Wagner, *Linguistic Variety of Judaeo-Arabic in Letters from the Cairo Genizah* (Leiden: Brill, 2010), 1–10.

3 Jürg Fleischer, "Paleographic Clues to Prosody?—Accents, Word Separation, and Other Phenomena in Old High German Manuscripts," in *Information Structure and Language Change. New Approaches to Word Order Variation in Germanic,* ed. Roland Hinterhölzl and Svetlana Petrova (Berlin and New York: de Gruyter, 2009), 161–89.

language is forged: written language norms by virtue of being read aloud enter a quasi-spoken realm. In communities with intensive liturgical traditions and parallel translation practices, this means that the language of liturgy may exert a certain influence on the vernacular, from phonetics to syntax.[4]

Education

Maintenance of written language standards, and in the modern period to a degree also spoken ones, is the task of schooling. To understand Jewish Egyptian language varieties, we need to discuss the schooling of individuals, both children and adults, within the communities. In the medieval period, Jewish children were educated in the synagogue, on occasion perhaps together with children of other faiths.[5] The primary focus of infant and adolescent education was to teach children to read Hebrew script, and to a degree to write it, in order to enable them to read the Bible.[6]

Yet, Hebrew was not the only educational target: Arabic calligraphy, too, was part of Jewish schooling for children.[7] However, this must have been the exception rather than the rule, as we find correspondence showing that not all writers of Judeo-Arabic were familiar with Arabic script. In one letter, for example, the author explicitly requests not to receive Arabic-script letters because he cannot read them.[8] There would have been great variations throughout the medieval period. We can perhaps assume greater familiarity of Arabic under the Fatimids, when there was a broad middle class of Egyptian Jews, as opposed to later periods, when economic and political changes brought about substantial social transformations. These changes culminated in the replacement of

4 For the influence of Hebrew verbal syntax, for example, on Yiddish verb positioning, see Henrike Kühnert and Esther-Miriam Wagner, "The Shift in Positioning of the Finite Verb in Older Yiddish," in *Yiddish Language Structures. Empirical Approaches to Language Typology*, ed. Marion Aptroot and Björn Hansen (Berlin: de Gruyter Mouton, 2014), 125–42.

5 Goitein, *Mediterranean Society*, vol. 2, 177, cites a ruling by Hai Ga'on, which states that "non-Jewish children may also study in the synagogue for the sake of good relationship with the neighbours, although it is not desirable."

6 Judith Olszowy Schlanger, "Learning to Read and Write in Medieval Egypt: Children's Exercise Books from the Cairo Genizah," *JSS* 48 (2003): 47–69. Writing and reading were two different aspects of literacy in a medieval context, at least in the European sphere. Moderately learned men may thus have been able to read Hebrew and/or Arabic script but could have been unable to write at all or perhaps only in one alphabet (in the case of Jews, typically Hebrew).

7 Goitein, *Mediterranean Society*, vol. 2, 177.

8 Mosseri IV.45, line 4, written in Judaeo-Arabic: "you should write in Hebrew [script] so that we understand."

civil functionaries and bureaucrats, who had traditionally been representatives of the minority communities, by members of the military aristocracy under the Ayyubids and Mamluks.[9]

A comparison with Christian communities may be enlightening. In the post-medieval Syriac Christian educational context, school children were at first taught how to read Syriac in Syriac script, then moved to reading Arabic in Syriac script (that is, in Garshuni), and only in a third step, Arabic in Arabic script.[10] Goitein remarked that "Christian elementary education in the East was very much like the Jewish,"[11] and thus, this may have been a similar system to that used in medieval Jewish schools. Hence the level of familiarity with Arabic script may have had to do with how long an individual attended school, which also must have varied greatly throughout the medieval period.

Further education depended on the profession in which an individual became engaged. Traders, for example, would learn the art of writing business letters within their mercantile networks.[12] There must have been great variation of writing ability depending on the individual writers and their family background and/or rank within the trade network. Especially the wealthy elite among the traders would presumably have had access to Arabic education, yet the richest traders may have chosen not to write themselves but to use scribes for correspondence. Arabic prescriptive norms shine through in mercantile writing (see below), which presumably was an effect of steady exchange with Muslim and Christian mercantile documents, creating a particular Judeo-Arabic mercantile register. Yet not all traders knew the Arabic alphabet: an eleventh-century Jewish trader would write a note in Hebrew letters to his Muslim business partner and ask a Jewish acquaintance to read it out to him.[13]

---

9 See Martina Müller-Wiener, *Eine Stadtgeschichte Alexandrias von 564/1169 bis in die Mitte des 9./15. Jahrhunderts* (Berlin: Klaus Schwarz Verlag, 1992), in particular 277–86, who describes these developments for Alexandria, where they arrived with some delay as opposed to Cairo (ibid., 123).

10 George Kiraz, in oral conversation at "Allographic traditions" workshop, Institute for Advanced Studies, Princeton, June 9–10, 2016.

11 Goitein, *Mediterranean Society*, vol. 2, 176.

12 For the peculiarities of traders' language, see Esther-Miriam Wagner, "Challenges of Multiglossia: The Emergence of Substandard Judaeo-Arabic Registers," in *Scribes as Agents of Language Change*, ed. Esther-Miriam Wagner, Ben Outhwaite, and Bettina Beinhoff (Berlin: de Gruyter-Mouton, 2013), 259–73; eadem, "The Socio-Linguistics of Judaeo-Arabic Mercantile Writing," in *Merchants of Innovation. The Languages of Traders*, ed. Esther-Miriam Wagner, Bettina Beinhoff, and Ben Outhwaite (Berlin: de Gruyter-Mouton, 2017), 68–86.

13 Goitein, *Mediterranean Society*, vol. 2, 294.

Other professions had, perhaps, other needs. Physicians treated clients from all confessions, they would have needed to read and write Arabic script. Apothecaries, on the other hand, may have been specialists for customers from a particular religious background. This may explain certain documents that have the *basmala* at the top of the page and a final line "may it be useful" in Arabic script.[14] The recipe itself is written in Judeo-Arabic between the two lines of Arabic. An imaginable context is a (Jewish) doctor writing the Arabic script framework, with another scribe filling the recipe in Hebrew script for a Jewish apothecary or for preparation at home.

Of particular interest is the education of those who write for a living: scribes, as they are the ones who set and propagate linguistic standards.[15] Goitein has distinguished three different types of scribes in the Genizah. The first group are government clerks (*kātib*), who worked for the chanceries and were proficient in writing Arabic script. These clerks probably received their training within these government institutions and were very familiar with Muslim prescriptive language norms, which still influenced the way Judeo-Arabic was written until the end of the medieval period. As described above, from the Mamluk period onwards, fewer Jews and Christians were employed in this function. The second group are copyists of books (*nāsiḫ*), who often specialized in one particular script, but were potentially able to copy out books both in the Hebrew and Arabic alphabets. The third group are the community and court scribes (*sofer*) who wrote legal documents and letters for the Jewish community and its legal institutions, mostly in Hebrew script.[16]

These categories were not necessarily exclusive—known court scribes sometimes copied codices as well, as can be seen in the example of the most prolific of Genizah court scribes, Ḥalfon b. Manasse. Ḥalfon, for instance, transcribed at least one Arabic commonplace book by a tenth-century Muslim author into Hebrew characters,[17] and apparently also dabbled in the writing of

14 For instance: T-S Ar. 30.305, published in Efraim Lev and Leigh Chipman, *Medical Prescriptions in the Cambridge Genizah Collections* (Leiden: Brill, 2012), 30–1.

15 For a discussion of the role of scribes in various cultures, see Esther-Miriam Wagner, Ben Outhwaite, and Bettina Beinhoff, "Scribes and Language Change," in *Scribes as Agents of Language Change*, ed. Esther-Miriam Wagner, Ben Outhwaite, and Bettina Beinhoff (Berlin: de Gruyter-Mouton, 2013), 3–18.

16 Goitein, *Mediterranean Society*, vol. 2, 183–5.

17 Ibid., 231.

certain magical texts.[18] Judging by his frequent use of Arabic vocalization signs, he was also very familiar with Arabic-script scribal practise.[19]

The scribes of the third category, the *sofrim*, were trained within the Jewish scriptoria, with emphasis on Hebrew script as all documents for the Jewish court were written in Hebrew, Aramaic, and Judeo-Arabic. When we compare the handwriting of court scribes to those of their successors, we see great similarities. Good examples are Hillel b. ʿEli and his successor Ḥalfon b. Manasse, or any of the more prolific twelfth-century scribes, such as Nathan b. Solomon and Nathan b. Samuel.[20] The Genizah has even preserved examples where students appear to have learned how to write by copying out older documents letter by letter from their teachers in the lines below their teacher's writing.[21] From the handwriting, it is evident that the successors were trained for the jobs by their predecessors and learned all that there was to learn from their teachers. Only occasionally, innovators sneaked in new features, such as Ḥalfon b. Manasse, who seems to be the first to use Arabic vocalization signs in connection with Hebrew script in the context of Genizah legal documents.[22]

Within the different branches of the scribal profession there were thus varying degrees of familiarity with and proficiency in Hebrew and Arabic scripts. A Jewish government clerk would probably have had better training in Arabic than his Jewish court scribe counterpart, who may have had superior Hebrew-script writing skills. Copyists of books may have been trained in both Arabic and Hebrew alphabets but perhaps would have specialized in only one of them.

---

18 See the T-S Genizah Research Unit Cambridge's Fragment of the Month April 2008 by Gideon Bohak and Esther-Miriam Wagner, http://www.lib.cam.ac.uk/Taylor-Schechter/fotm/april-2008/.

19 See Esther-Miriam Wagner, "Script-Switching between Hebrew and Arabic Script in Letters from the Cairo Genizah," in *Allographic Traditions*, special issue of *Intellectual History of the Islamic World*, ed. George Kiraz and Sabine Schmidtke (forthcoming).

20 For a comparison of handwriting and other linguistic features connected to court scribes in the twelfth century, see Esther-Miriam Wagner, "Scribal Practice in the Jewish Community of Medieval Egypt," in *Scribal Practices and the Social Construction of Knowledge in Antiquity, Late Antiquity and Medieval Islam*, ed. Myriam Wissa (Leuven: Peeters, 2017), 91–110; eadem, "Script-Switching between Hebrew and Arabic Script."

21 In the two fragments, Mosseri VII.14 and Mosseri VII 85.4, students copied formulae pertaining to legal texts. The original text was written with wide spaces between the lines, to allow copying word by word. In both these fragments, the similarity between the original letters and their copies is very close.

22 See Wagner, "Script-Switching between Hebrew and Arabic Script."

In the Jewish scriptoria, Jews created their own language standards, partly because the use of the Hebrew alphabet removed them one step from contemporary Muslim standards, which gave them slightly more freedom in their linguistic choices. Yet how much the scribes emulated prescriptive norms followed by their fellow professional writers of other confessions may have depended on exposure to non-Jewish writing. This would have been controlled by the education of individual writers, which made them more or less familiar with non-Jewish norms, and also on their daily interactions with non-Jewish scribes. That explains the great variation in the ability, for example, to emulate contemporary supra-confessional standards, or to use Hebrew and Arabic script in their writing, which we encounter in the Genizah sources.

Although many Arabic materials have been preserved in the Genizah in the form of literary and scientific texts, petitions and other documents, there still appears to be a preference for Hebrew script, at least in the extant Genizah texts and among Rabbanite communities. Yet, this Rabbanite preference for Hebrew script was perhaps not as clear-cut as it is traditionally made out to be. Viewing the corpus of mercantile letters published by Gil,[23] which contains over a thousand letters, we may get the impression that Judeo-Arabic was the *only* form of communication among eleventh-century Genizah merchants. Yet from actual Genizah correspondence between Jewish merchants we learn that they wrote to each other in Arabic script, too, as we find the request that future correspondence "should only be in Hebrew script . . . because I cannot read the Arabic (script)" (לא יכון אלא בכט עבראני . . . לאני מא אקרא אלערבי) from those less linguistically versatile (T-S NS 323.13).[24] That we do not have an equivalent mercantile corpus in Arabic script in the Genizah may be due to a medieval understanding that the deposition of Hebrew-script materials into a Genizah was more imperative than that of Arabic-script documents.

Sectarianism may also have played a role. The Karaites, for example, appear to have had a penchant for using Arabic script in the eleventh-thirteenth centuries.[25] This has sometimes been described as a zealous endeavor to avoid using the holy Hebrew script for the purposes of writing mundane Arabic, or, perhaps somewhat to the contrary, as demonstrating the grounding of Karaite writers in Arabic scribal culture. For the classical

---

23 Gil, *In the Kingdom of Ishmael.*

24 See also Goitein, *Mediterranean Society*, vol. 2, 179.

25 Geoffrey Khan, "On the Question of Script in Medieval Karaite Manuscripts: New Evidence from the Genizah," *Bulletin of the John Rylands University Library of Manchester* 75 (1993): 133–41.

Genizah period, however, Khan has pointed out that the use of Arabic script may have been substantially motivated by sectarian opposition to the Rabbanites who used Hebrew script in their communal correspondence and legal documents, rather than by greater absorption into Islamic culture. Later on, however, the Karaites also change to using Hebrew script.

Written, spoken, and read Judaeo-Arabic

Judaizing and Arabicizing: Code-switching and script-switching

Jewish varieties of languages typically contain a large number of loanwords from, and code-switches into, Hebrew and Aramaic. These borrowings often feature prominently in descriptions of Jewish sociolects, both in historical accounts dealing with Jewish language varieties, such as the pre-Islamic *al-Yahūdiyya*,[26] and in modern descriptions, who used this and other features to postulate distinct Jewish languages with a direct language chain back to Palestinian Hebrew.[27]

This inclusion of Hebrew and Aramaic marks the language varieties as the sociolect of a distinct confessional group and provides its users with a Jewish identity. No satisfying models to describe the code-switching between Arabic and Hebrew have been developed yet. Pioneering scholarship on code-switching by authorities such as Carol Myers-Scotton and Penelope Gardner-Chloros has focused on modern spoken languages, but those speakers who code-switch are usually bilingual in two spoken languages. Medieval Hebrew, however, was not a spoken language in the same sense as these modern varieties. The mechanisms of transferal of Hebrew words and grammatical structures was perhaps more subtle and rooted in the reading tradition of the Bible and other religious works. How influential the reading of texts aloud is for language contact can be seen in studies on Yiddish, where for example syntactical calques from Hebrew to the spoken language of Jews could be transferred through word-by-word translations in daily Bible study.[28]

---

26 For a discussion of *al-Yahūdiyya*, see Gordon D. Newby, "Observations about an Early Judaeo-Arabic," *JQR* 61 (1971): 212–21.

27 Hary, *Translating Religion*, 21–2, or in Wexler, "Jewish Interlinguistics."

28 See, for example, for this process in Yiddish: Erika Timm, *Historische jiddische Semantik. Die Bibelübersetzungssprache als Faktor der Auseinanderentwicklung des jiddischen und des deutschen Wortschatzes* (Tübingen: Niemeyer, 2005); Kühnert and Wagner, "The Shift in Positioning of the Finite Verb in Older Yiddish."

Over the last years, code-switching in written, mainly historical texts has been gaining attention from scholars.[29] Judeo-Arabic sources contain valuable examples demonstrating differences and similarities between written code-switching and spoken code-switching. In writing, just as in the neuro-linguistics of spoken texts where hesitation times before code-switches are measured, we have the opportunity to observe hesitation or deliberation.

For example: in the fifteenth-century letter Bodl. MS Heb.c.72.23/17: in the phrase פי אל דונייא עולם, the author first wrote the word "world" in the Arabic language, then crossed it out, and replaced it with the Hebrew word for "world." Although both terms should designate the same thing, the concept of the Hebrew word was obviously better fitting, to the degree that the Arabic word was crossed out and replaced by the preferred alternative.

Other interesting features concern code-switched Hebrew adverbs in legal texts, which clearly operate as structural markers in texts, such as ʿakhshav, "now." This function of code-switching is particular for written code-switching, and still awaits exploration within Judeo-Arabic texts.

Also in the written medium, another phenomenon related to code-switching is script-switching, where the writers switch between Hebrew and Arabic script. Writers may switch from one script to another for various purposes. In the Genizah, we have examples where writers switch scripts when they change language. In a letter, dated to 1065 CE, the author Judah b. Abraham writes the standard opening blessings and other epistolary niceties in Hebrew, in the Hebrew alphabet. When he code-switches to the Arabic language for the main part of his letter, he also changes into Arabic script.[30] In his writings, certain languages are thus locked in with their respective standard scripts.

Other writers, such as the eleventh-century dignitary Daniel b. ʿAzaryah, use script-switching on a more idiosyncratic basis.[31] In the latter's Judeo-Arabic letters, the phrases most commonly switched into Arabic script are polite blessings and formulae, which can be switched in any place within the line. Switches

29 See Mark Sebba, Shahrzad Mahootian, and Carla Johnsson (eds.), *Language Mixing and Code-Switching in Writing: Approaches to Mixed-Language Written Discourse* (London: Routledge, 2011); Paivi Pahta, "Code-Switching in English of the Middle Ages," in *The Oxford Handbook of the History of English*, ed. Terttu Nevalainen and E.C. Traugott (Oxford: Oxford University Press, 2012), 1–12; Penelope Gardner-Chloros and Daniel Weston, "Codeswitching and Multilingualism in Literature," *Language and Literature* 24, no. 3 (2015): 182–93.

30 T-S 13J13.2.

31 For a more detailed study of the script-switching found in the writing of Daniel b. ʿAzaryah and Ḥalfon b. Manasse, see Wagner, "Script-Switching between Hebrew and Arabic Script."

into Arabic script of other phrases and words appear to be acceptable only at the end of lines, where the switch helps to save space and the fitting of words into the same line. The main purpose of switching into Arabic script thus appears to be the speeding up of the writing process, in particular with blessings and polite wishes, which are an essential part of letter writing but do not contribute vital information. Yet, there is also an element of Daniel showing off his own skill and superior literacy in Arabic and Hebrew script. Interestingly, Daniel appears to avoid script-switching in correspondence with more comprehensive religious content, which shows that Arabic script may not be appropriate in every context.

Other Genizah writers, like Ḥalfon b. Manasse, use Arabic vocalization signs in their Hebrew script texts, showing their close familiarity with Arabic script in addition to Hebrew script.

As idiosyncratic as features such as script-switching and the use of Arabic vocalization signs may have been in the individual writers, they demonstrate that Arabic script was seen as appropriate to be used in the context of Hebrew-script Judeo-Arabic texts, and exemplify the Arabic/Judeo-Arabic/Hebrew linguistic continuum that was a feature of medieval Egypt.

Judaeo-Arabic writing by medieval Egyptian Jews

For the use or mixing of particular languages, text genres play an important role. Within written Judeo-Arabic, as within every language, there are various distinct registers, which are created by the degree or amount of language mixing and the use of specific code-switched languages. The more Jewish-marked a Judeo-Arabic text is, the larger the Hebrew and Aramaic component usually is. Halakhic discussions of Jewish laws, commentaries on the body of religious literature, and discussions on the morals and proper conduct of Jewish Egyptians contain long passages in Hebrew and Aramaic. Aramaic is usually only used in legal texts, which incorporate Aramaic in addition to Hebrew, because, as has been mentioned above, it is *the* legal language of the ancient Middle East, in which much of Jewish law had been codified. Scribes appear to have been very much aware of the difference between Hebrew and Aramaic—the same person would use Aramaic in legal documents, but not in correspondence. Ethical treatises may switch in Hebrew words and phrases from the Bible and religious literature punctuating discussions of Jewish moral themes. *Belles-lettres*, scientific and philosophical literature mostly copied from Arabic *Vorlagen*, however, usually do not show any Hebrew at all. Magical texts may use a particularly angular script to show similarity to Aramaic script, but only use gibberish and made-up words, in the case of recipes and curses augmented by passages in Judeo-Arabic. There are distinctions of more religious and more secular matters in legal documents: deeds concerning marriages and divorces are written in Hebrew and Aramaic, whereas agreements for business partnerships or inheritance matters and the like are discussed in Judeo-Arabic.

In correspondence, code-switching between Judeo-Arabic and Hebrew occurs commonly, but there is great variation in the amount of code-switching occurring in different genres of letter. Individual medieval writers would vary the Hebrew content of their letters according to the type of correspondence. Code-switching to Hebrew was most commonly used in correspondence pertaining to religious and communal matters but was avoided in mercantile correspondence.[32] This can be seen even in letters on various topics by the same writer. While an author may use forty percent Hebrew in a letter pertaining to communal affairs, he may shy away from using Hebrew in business correspondence. Analyses of letters composed by traders reveal that, despite writing in Hebrew script and addressing their correspondence to fellow Jewish businessmen, they would use hardly any Hebrew words, and that the amount of Hebrew code-switching in mercantile letters would range between zero and two percent. In the medieval Egyptian economic system, where Jews, Muslims and Christian formed business partnerships with one another in large trade networks spanning the Mediterranean, avoiding phraseology marked as "Jewish" thus seems to have been beneficial in the mercantile sphere.[33]

From a linguistic point of view, this is not surprising. Letters pertaining to trade generally inhabit a special place within correspondence.[34] Merchants possess a particular kind of literacy, termed "pragmatic literacy" by Parkes,[35]

---

32 Esther-Miriam Wagner and Magdalen Connolly, "Code-Switching in Judeo-Arabic Documents from the Cairo Geniza," *Multilingua* 37, no. 1 (2018): 1–23.

33 This phenomenon in medieval Judeo-Arabic letters stands in stark contrast to early modern traders' letters in Yiddish, written in an entirely different economic system, which contain a large component of Hebrew. See Esther-Miriam Wagner and Henrike Kühnert, "Codeswitching in Yiddish and Judaeo-Arabic," in *Dat ih dir in nu in huldi gibu*, ed. Sergio Neri, Roland Schuhmann, and Susanne Zeilfelder (Wiesbaden: Reichert, 2016), 495–504.

34 For a comprehensive overview, see Esther-Miriam Wagner and Bettina Beinhoff, "Merchants of Innovation: the Language of Traders," in *Merchants of Innovation. The Languages of Traders*, ed. Esther-Miriam Wagner, Bettina Beinhoff, and Ben Outhwaite (Berlin: de Gruyter Mouton, 2017), 3–16, and the edited volume above generally.

35 Malcolm Parkes, "The Literacy of the Laity," in *The Mediaeval World*, ed. David Daiches and Anthony Thorlby (London: Aldus Books), 555–577, 555.

which is owed to the circumstances of their education, the extent of their correspondence, and their particular acts of writing. The Genizah sources reveal that medieval business letters were often sent out in four or five different copies in different ships to ensure their safe arrival.[36] The businessmen had to write very expressively and precisely to make themselves understood. Other writers express anger and frustration over failed transactions or mismanagement. Emotion is often a trigger for inclusion of colloquial words and expressions, which the mercantile writers also used deliberately to connect to their business partners readers in a more intimate fashion, important in an economy built on interpersonal trust. Business letters are thus often a most useful source for the spoken vernacular of the time, which enables us to make some conclusions about the spoken language.

Spoken languages and dialects

In absence of recordings of medieval speech, we can only speculate about the way Jewish Egyptians talked, but the language preserved in documents, in particular in traders' and private letters, help us to understand certain features of the spoken language. In addition, we can infer parallels from comparative modern examples and from sociolinguistic theory.

Sociolinguists such as William Labov and Jim and Lesley Milroy[37] established theories suggesting that social groups, such as religious communities, develop specific phenomena in speech that distinguish them from other social groups, provided that there is a sufficient level of segregation between the speakers of the factions. The segregation ensures that speakers of a particular group for the most part communicate only among themselves, leading to a closed network of speakers where linguistic forms particular to the group emerge. This leads to distinct sociolects which in speech differentiate speakers of one group from another, providing the speaker with a social identity and enforcing ties within the social network despite the potential disadvantages associated with low-prestige language varieties.

36 These copying practices are described in great detail in the letter T-S 13J17.3 (published in Hebrew by Gil, *In the Kingdom of Ishmael*, vol. 2, 528–32). The writer mentions how he sent four copies of the same letter in four different ships, five copies of the same letter to his uncle in Qayrawan, and how he copied the recipients' letters to be forwarded on to others. Writers had to copy their own letters a number of times.

37 Lesley Milroy and James Milroy, "Social Network and Social Class: Toward an Integrated Sociolinguistic Model," *Language in Society* 21, no. 1 (1992): 1–26.

In the modern Egyptian context, there is conflicting information about distinct sociolects between the different religious groups. Holes, for example, advises caution regarding the belief that religious groups and sects are always, or even usually, associated with language difference. He states that "the Copts of Egypt, whether they live in Cairo or southern Egypt, do not have a 'communal' Arabic dialect different from that of their Muslim neighbours, and there is no evidence that they ever did."[38] This raises complex questions. Can we compare the modern situation of the linguistics of Egyptian Muslim-Christian relations to the medieval period? Potentially, the lack of distinct features could be a relatively new phenomenon induced by the sociolinguistic levelling associated with Egyptian nationalism. Indeed, contrasting developments, that is, Arab Christians speaking differently from their Muslim neighbors, have been posited by Enam al-Wer, who suggests the existence of a Christian sociolect in the West Bank.[39]

The most famous description of a separation between Christian, Jewish, and Muslim varieties within a town is that of early twentieth-century Baghdad, as described by Blanc,[40] where Jews and Christian used urban speech forms, the so-called *qeltu*-dialects, whereas the majority of the Muslim population spoke a bedouinized dialect, the so-called *gilit*-dialects. We also find such particular Jewish features in the case of Jewish Egyptian sociolects corroborated by Rosenbaum, who describes a range of peculiarities particular to spoken Jewish language varieties such as a preference in Modern Jewish Egyptian Arabic of *u* over Standard dialect *i*.[41] According to Hary,[42] in the case of particular verbal forms the Jewish dialect preserves older urban Cairene dialectal forms, which had been lost in Christian and Muslim dialects. In this feature, Cairene Jewish Arabic thus may show an intriguing parallel to Baghdadi Jewish Arabic, which also retains features of older urban speech.

38 Clive Holes, "Confessional Varieties," in *Handbook of Arabic Sociolinguistics*, ed. Enam al-Wer and Uri Horesh (London: Routledge, 2019), 72.

39 This was in oral communication in the discussion rounds at the *Arabic in the Ottoman Empire* conference, organised by me at the Faculty of Asian and Middle Eastern Studies, University of Cambridge on April 21 and 22, 2016. For her work on Arabic socio-linguistics, see Enam al-Wer, "Sociolinguistics," in *Handbook of Arabic Linguistics*, ed. Jonathan Owens (Oxford: Oxford University Press, 2013), 241–63.

40 Haim Blanc, *Communal Dialects in Baghdad* (Cambridge, MA: Harvard University Press, 1964).

41 Gabriel Rosenbaum, "The Arabic Dialect of Jews in Modern Egypt," *Bulletin of the Israeli Academic Center in Cairo* 25 (2002): 37.

42 Hary, *Translating Religion*, 23.

At the same time, we also have to be critically aware of how such linguistic differences, in particular regarding Jewish forms of language, may have come about and be assessed, and of how ideological agenda may create difference. As Gal and Irvine have argued, "speakers and observers notice, justify and rationalize linguistic difference, placing them within larger ideological frames . . . sometimes exaggerating or even creating linguistic differentiation."[43] The diverse Baghdadi dialects are not so much a product of internal segregation, but more influentially of migration. Muslim Bedouins came to settle in Baghdad, and because of the cultural prestige associated with Bedouin speech forms, their way of talking spread among the Muslim population, but was not adopted by Jews and Christians. This particular phenomenon is also restricted to Baghdad. In other Iraqi towns, in contrast, Muslims, Jews and Christians all spoke the urban *qeltu*-dialects.

Similarly, we find traces of language forms used by medieval Jewish Moroccans in Egyptian written Judeo-Arabic, and we can presume that Moroccans also imported linguistic features into Egyptian Jewish speech forms. This has led Joshua Blau to stress the importance of Maghrebi features as part of typical Egyptian Judeo-Arabic throughout his writing career. For Blau, there was even proof that "in the twelfth century, at least, the speech of the Egyptian Jews belonged (presumably unlike that of their Muslim neighbours) to the Maghrebine dialect group."[44] When we look at the specific details of some of these Maghrebi features, a more complex picture develops.[45] Hary thus remarks that "these forms, which are frequently found in the West Delta as well as in Cairene Judaeo-Arabic . . . may well have developed parallel to

43 Susan Gal and Judith T. Irvine, "The Boundaries of Languages and Disciplines: How Ideologies Construct Difference," *Social Research* 62, no. 4 (1995): 992–1023; cf. Wagner, "Judaeo-Arabic Language or Jewish Arabic Sociolect?"

44 Blau, *The Emergence and Linguistic Background of Judaeo-Arabic*, 2nd edition, 55; and idem, *Studies in Middle Arabic* (Jerusalem: Magnes Press, 1988), 113.

45 An often-cited example is the paradigmatically levelled verbal inflection of the first person singular and plural, *niktib/niktibu*. Yet, these forms cannot serve as particularly convincing example for the Maghrebization of Jewish Egyptian Arabic, as the dichotomy *niktib/niktibu* is not an exclusively Western Arabic phenomena but part of the indigenous Egyptian dialectal repertoire too. See Peter Behnstedt, "Zur Dialektgeographie des Nildeltas," *Zeitschrift für arabische Linguistik* 1 (1978): 64–92; Abdelghany Khalafallah, *A Descriptive Grammar of Saei:di: Egyptian Colloquial* (The Hague: Mouton, 1969).

the Maghrebi forms."[46] This goes along with other examples of Jewish Arabic retaining older phenomena.[47]

Following the case study from Baghdad, such phenomena must have varied throughout Egypt, too. In the cosmopolitan port town of Alexandria, the linguistic situation was probably very different from more conservative Fusṭāṭ or Cairo. In the villages in the Delta with a reasonable Jewish presence, local Jews may have completely adopted the local dialects in order to fit in, or perhaps at times increased the usage of marked Jewish forms to stand out. Chronology would have played an important role, too, with form varying markedly over time.

Nonetheless, the influx of Maghrebi traders—who were an important part of the Jewish trade networks—in Egyptian towns may have constituted an important factor in shaping distinct vernaculars of Egyptian minority groups, just as Bedouin immigration did in the case of Baghdadi Arabic. Probably, already existing Egyptian forms received additional prestige through the Maghrebi connections.

From a modern context we know that the linguistic repertoire of minority group speakers can be extremely variable. Sharma, for example, describes how British Asian speakers of English vary the inclusion of sociolinguistic features depending on the ethnicity, gender, level of education and personal relationship of their interlocutors. Her work demonstrates how important the setting of any conversation is. Sharma's speakers use typical phonological "Indian" features[48] mostly within a familiar setting. Fewer of these "Indian" features, or even none, may be found in conversations with friends of the same ethnic and religious background. A conversation between an upper middle-class lawyer and a male working-class speaker from the same British Asian background

46 Benjamin Hary, *Multiglossia in Judaeo-Arabic* (Leiden: Brill, 1992), 278.

47 Other examples: the retention of the urban Cairene demonstrative *de* or the abovementioned verbal pattern *fuʿul*. Blau and Hopkins also interpreted the occurrence of *shewa* in T-S Ar.18(1).113 as elision or reduction of short vowels in unstressed syllables and as a sign of oxytone stress, characteristic of Maghrebi phonology (Joshua Blau and Simon Hopkins, "A Vocalized JA Letter from the Cairo Genizah," *JSAI* 6 [1985]: 417–76). Khan, however, has shown that this *shewa* most likely represented short vowels, mainly *a* but also *i* and *u*, rendering the theories of Maghrebi syllable structure and stress patterns somewhat doubtful (Geoffrey Khan, "The Function of the *Shewa* Sign in Vocalized Judaeo-Arabic Texts from the Genizah," in *Genizah Research after Ninety Years: The Case of Judaeo-Arabic*, ed. Joshua Blau and Stefan C. Reif [Cambridge: Cambridge University Press, 1992], 107–11).

48 Devyani Sharma, "Style Repertoire and Social Change in British Asian English," *Journal for Sociolinguistics* 15, no. 4 (2011): 464–92; such as retroflexion of [t], monophthongalization of [e] and [o], and light pronunciation of [l].

could result in the working-class speaker suppressing typical Indian forms that he normally uses. We could thus imagine medieval highly educated Jewish protagonists, such as scribes or scholars, talking to other highly educated members of the community in a much different linguistic register than that they used at home. Within the context of the *intelligentsia*, in close contact with educated elite Muslim or Christian Egyptians, we may assume an intercommunal high register of speech, explicitly shunning language forms marked as Jewish. The same may apply to traders in particular business circumstances, who would try to use a supra-confessional koine to communicate. In other circumstances, however, it may be beneficial to use particular Jewish language forms as a secret language, such as among goldsmiths.[49]

In the realm of spoken Jewish medieval form of Arabic, we may thus presume a diversity of different registers, bound to particular circumstances, such as familiar conversation, between business partners or in intellectual circles, with varying amounts of loanwords and code-switches from Hebrew.

The reading tradition of Judaeo-Arabic

The actual pronunciation, or more properly, the reading tradition, of the letters differed greatly from both Standard Arabic and colloquial vocalization, and there was a substantial gap between orthography and actual pronunciation within the Judeo-Arabic reading.[50] For example, while a form with the spelling מעה ("with him") may indicate Classical Arabic morphology, the vocalisation מְעֻה shows that the pronunciation was closer to the vernacular, that is, something like *maʿu(h)*. Or, the demonstrative pronouns אלדי and אלתי occur in forms reminiscent of Classical Arabic *allaḏī* and *allatī*. When we look at the vocalization, however, it becomes clear that these are pseudo-classical forms. They follow the spelling as in Classical Arabic, transferred into Hebrew script, but the vocalization reveals how they are read. These are artificial forms created for the reading traditions of these texts, as neither *aldī* nor *əldi* are part of the

49 See Geoffrey Khan on vocalized Judaeo-Arabic texts, such as T-S Ar.18(1).113 and T-S 8.3: "Vocalized Judaeo-Arabic Manuscripts in the Cairo Genizah," in *"From a Sacred Source": Genizah Studies in Honour of Professor Stefan C. Reif*, ed. Ben Outhwaite and Siam Bhayro (Leiden: Brill, 2010), 201–18. For modern phenomena, see idem, "A Note on the Trade Argot of the Karaite Goldsmiths of Cairo," *Mediterranean Language Review* 9 (1995–7): 74–6; also idem, "Hebrew as a Secret Language in Yemenite Judeo-Arabic," in *Encyclopedia of Hebrew Language and Linguistics*, ed. Geoffrey Khan (Leiden: Brill, 2013), vol. 3, 518–20.

50 Blau and Hopkins, "A Vocalized JA Letter from the Cairo Genizah"; Khan, "Vocalized Judaeo-Arabic Manuscripts in the Cairo Genizah."

vernacular. Yet the texts avoid vernacular demonstrative pronouns, while also not reading the ostensibly Classical Arabic words in their Classical forms.

The reading tradition also appears to feed back into the spoken language, which may for example explain the existence of the negation particle *lam* as an "living asystemic" form.[51]

Such examples demonstrate that in addition to spoken and written forms of Egyptian Jewish Arabic, the performative action of reading texts produced yet another linguistic layer, which has to be factored in when Judeo-Arabic materials are being analyzed.

Summary

While Arabic was the spoken language and also used as a written one, religious education and documentary scribal practice exposed Egyptian Jews to Hebrew and Aramaic on a daily basis. This steady language contact led to the inclusion of Hebrew and Aramaic into the spoken and written Arabic language, resulting in language varieties with a substantial Hebrew-Aramaic lexical component. The mixing of the languages created particular registers, with the Aramaic and Hebrew content varying decidedly between more religious and more secular genres. Features such as script-switching and the use of Arabic vocalization signs added additional layers, exemplifying the Arabic/Judeo-Arabic/Hebrew linguistic continuum that was a feature of medieval Egypt.

In spoken medieval Jewish Arabic, we can assume a diversity of different registers, all bound to particular circumstances, such as conversation between family members, between business partners or in intellectual circles. All these spoken registers would have substantially varied in the amounts of loanwords and code-switches taken from Hebrew, with the reading tradition of texts another separate entity within the linguistic spectrum.

51 Humphrey T. Davies, "Seventeenth-Century Egyptian Arabic: A Profile of the Colloquial Material in Yūsuf al-Širbīnī's *Hazz al-Quḥūf fī šarḥ Qaṣīd Abī Šādūf*" (PhD diss., University of California at Berkeley, 1981), 302–3. See the discussion on *lam* in Wagner, *Linguistic Variety*, 141–50; and idem, "Challenges of Multiglossia."

10

Hebrew Poetry in Medieval Egypt

JOSEPH YAHALOM

Many poetic pieces have reached us among the documents from the *genizot* that were discovered in Egypt in the nineteenth century—the Rabbanite Ben-ʿEzra *genizah*, and the Karaite Dar-Simḥah *genizah*. Most of these come from the tenth through thirteenth centuries. Nonetheless, we do not have complete acquaintance with the texts composed in Egypt during that era. Even great poets, whose works were collected in *dīwān*s, are known to us only partially, because the fragments of their *dīwān*s, which were buried in the *genizah*, have been scattered around the entire world, and reconstructing them takes long, focused work. The work of putting them together and assembling them has taken place over the entire twentieth century, and even now, in the twenty-first, it is not complete. Therefore, our knowledge remains partial.[1]

The great quantity of poetry that has been uncovered in various *genizot*, written at various levels of refinement and sophistication, definitely indicates the central place that Hebrew poetry had in the spiritual and social life of Egyptian Jewry of this period. Cairo, with its prosperous economy and powerful political center, attracted scholarly, creative, and ambitious individuals. In such an intellectual environment, the great aesthetic innovation of writing Hebrew poetry, on the model of Arabic poetry with all its refinements, penetrated

1 Ḥayyim Schirmann's book *New Poems from the Genizah* (Jerusalem: Israel Academy of Sciences and Humanities, 1966) [in Hebrew] gives us a taste, in the various sections of the book, of dozens of Hebrew compositions by medieval Egyptian poets, with no attempt at completeness.

local awareness already at an early stage of its history. According to the great grammarian Yonah ibn Janāḥ, it was specifically in Egypt that they knew the correct version of a certain secular panegyric written by the Spanish poet Isaac ibn Mar Shaʾul of Lucena, in a quantitative meter, following the model of Arabic poetry. Thus, in Egypt they were acquainted with this poem as early as the late tenth century. Writing a secular panegyric, on the model of Arabic poetry, was a great novelty in this period, even for the courtier society in progressive al-Andalus; but it seems that the Jewish community in Egypt showed interest in this new genre, which distinguished between long and short vowels, already quite early in its existence.

Writing poetry was one of the central media through which the leadership, and those attached to it, expressed themselves. Our goal here is to provide an overview of their poetic works.

Samuel b. Hoshaʿna (d. after 1012)

Samuel son of Hoshaʿna, a member and emissary of the Palestinian *yeshivah*, was also a famous, beloved poet. His work is found in many copies; roughly 800 fragments are known from the Cairo Genizah. He signs his work in acrostics, comprised of specific letters that appear at the beginnings of lines, such as: *Shemuʾel yizkeh*—"Samuel, may he be meritorious"—or, in a later period in his life: *Shemuʾel he-Ḥaver,* "Samuel the member," that is, member of the Palestinian *yeshivah.*

Liturgical poems—the yotzerot

Liturgical poems, known as *yotzerot,* are special compositions for the weekly Torah readings. Samuel was the author of about 500 of the most elaborate, erudite cycles of such poems. He wrote complex sequences of *yotzerot* for every Sabbath, in accordance with the annual cycle of the weekly reading of the Torah. Each sequence of such *yotzerot* is made up of seven components of various lengths. In some of the poems, the poet reaches creative heights that can compete with the greatest achievements of the Golden Age of al-Andalus. Of special notice is the *ʿofan,* in which the poet gives a masterful presentation of the song of the angels.

The *geʾulla* [salvation] poems, which come at the conclusion, the climax, of the *yotzer* sequence, are unique: their poetics are more sublime than those of any of the earlier components. In one of the components of this section (starting with the words *adonai malkenu,* "Lord our king"), the poet has room to present contemporary matters and prayers for the future, though always maintaining the connection to the biblical passages read that day, and the liturgical position of the poem. Making the connection between contemporary issues and the content of the weekly Torah-portion presents a challenge to the poet, which he overcomes impressively.

Thus, for example, he mentions the crickets (locusts), which are fighting against the Jews, destroying the produce of their fields:

> The effusion of blessings, which the blameless one reserved for his tribes—
> Since the day we were dispersed, we have been lacking them, and the finery of our crown has been stripped,
> And the crickets have eliminated and finished off all our sweet delights.
> Where is the blessing of the inhabitant, the unique one, and the one who peeled streaks (i.e. Jacob in Haran, cf. Gen. 30:37)?
> Pour out Thy blessing upon their descendants, and may they blossom like a crocus.[2]

In Samuel's poetry locusts symbolize Israel's enemies, as manifested in the following poem, in which he compares the Four Monarchies (Daniel 7:7), which have ruled over the world and over the Jews, to four types of locusts (based on *midrashim* on Joel 1). Like locusts, they do violence to the farmers' produce, and eventually force them to leave their land:

> And locust, weevil, sauterelle, and grasshopper have ascended upon my Land, They have consumed my grapevine and fig-tree, and my farmers have wilted [in despair] and been removed.[3]
> My vinedressers and plowmen have yielded no profit in any work that they have done.

2 In the *adonai malkenu* poem for the Torah-portion *Vayeḥi* (Gen. 47:28–50:26).

3 The Hebrew root here is R-ʿ-L, which usually means "poison"; but here, in accordance with Syriac, it seems to mean "removed, shaken." Cf. the poet's *zulath* for *Vayyiggash*: "And I will make a firm covenant, forever, so that they will no longer be removed." (*Zulath* is a poem leading from the beginning of the blessing to the verse *mi khamokha* ["Who is like unto Thee?," Exodus 15:11]. It is a permanent part of the *yotzer*.)

In another place he refers to the burden of the taxes, which caused many Jews to flee Palestine, so its population decreased:

> Brethren dwelling together is so good, so pleasant,
> But we have been pushed[4] to the opposite—brother from brother, we have been separated, wandering, and straying,
> And banished from our inherited holdings, and kept away from our beloved estates!
> Our land brings forth produce for strangers, not for workers,
> They have melted us with taxes, and we are humiliated under their hands.

From the poet's description, it is clear that even the individuals that remained on their land did not have true ownership of it. The land did, indeed, continue to produce fruit, but this was enough only to pay the taxes that the Jewish sharecropper needed to pay. The expression "not workers" (*lo tzenuʿim*, whose usual sense would be "not humble") seems to refer here to the rulers, who were rustic and ignorant, similar to the Arabic use of the word *jāhil*, "foolish";[5] these are the people who take the major part of the land's fruits.

Introductions to letters

Samuel's poetic ability found its expression also in introductory passages to letters. In an autograph letter, he asked for recommendations for Nathan ben Abraham, one of the younger members of the Palestinian *yeshivah*. Samuel adorned the letter with an eloquent introductory passage, praising the addressee, Shemariah ben Elḥanan, head of the Babylonian (Iraqi) Jewish community in Fusṭāṭ,[6] whom he calls "light of the east and lamp of the west," and heaps words of praise on his important position. The introductory passage is written in extremely eloquent rhyming prose, and takes up more than half of the length of the letter—as is appropriate for an official address to the high institution that this *gaʾon* represented.[7] Among other things, Samuel

4 Hebrew *muṭmaṭnu*, a four-letter root created from the hollow root *muṭ*, "to totter."

5 Ze'ev Ben-Ḥayyim, "Tzanuaʿ," *Leshonenu* 57 (1953): 51–4.

6 See Gerson D. Cohen (ed.), *A Critical Edition with a Translation and Notes of the Book of Tradition (Sefer ha-qabbalah) by Abraham Ibn Daud* (Philadelphia: Jewish Publication Society, 1967), 46–7 (Hebrew section), 63–4 (English section).

7 The Islamic intelligentsia and rulers were raised on such elaborate style in their letters. On epistolary culture in Arabic society, see Albert Arazi and Ḥaggai Ben-Shammai, "Risāla," in

demonstrates his poetic abilities, and uses a great number of rhetorical devices and plays on sounds. To describe the addressee's position, he uses a Latin-derived word *esqivtar* as the equivalent of the Arabic title *kātib*, which literally means "scribe, amanuensis," but in this context refers to a position of actual authority:

> His head is like cypress, the *esqivtar*,
> And he is glorious [*yiqar*] in wisdom.[8]

The mixing of different registers of the Hebrew language, combining the Biblical imperfect form *yiqar* ("he is glorious") in the second line, indicating a quality, and the foreign word *esqivtar* in the first line, from the Latin *scriptor*, is one of the features of the new style of the school of Saʿadia Gaʾon, which Samuel adopted in his writing.[9]

Historical Poems

Samuel follows the great political events of his day in his poetry. In a poem he wrote at the beginning of the last quarter of the tenth century, signed *Shemuʾel he-Ḥaver*, he mentions three kings, who are fighting over the Land of Israel. In 972 the Byzantine emperor John Tzimiskes (d. 976) went on a great expedition of conquest in the east. In a letter he wrote to Ashot, King of the Armenians, he boasted about the emissaries from Ramle and Jerusalem who had asked him to appoint a governor over them, and they even took on the obligation to raise taxes for him. These were representatives of the Arab tribes allied with the Damascene ruler Alp Takīn, who, along with these allies, joined Tzimiskes in his war against the Fatimids, who had conquered portions of the Land of Israel, and on May 24, 970, had already conquered Ramle. The Byzantines, with John Tzimiskes at their head, and Alp Takīn's troops, with Arab tribes, were about to face the Fatimid caliph, al-Muʿizz (d. 975).

In Samuel's poem, one king has come from the west (the Maghreb—the Fatimid caliph al-Muʿizz), one from the east (Damascus—Alp Takīn), and

---

Encyclopedia of Islam, ed. Clifford E. Bosworth et al., vol. 8, 532–45 (Leiden: Brill, 1995); see also Tova Beʾeri, "Early Epistolary Poems from the Genizah," *Qovetz ʿal Yad* N.S. 18/28 (2005): 43–79 [in Hebrew].

8 See Joseph Yahalom and Naoya Katsumata (eds.), *The Yotzerot of R. Samuel the Third* (Jerusalem: Yad Ben-Zvi, 2014), 1004 [in Hebrew].

9 Menahem Zulay, *The Liturgical Poetry of Saʿadya Gaon and his School* (Jerusalem: Schocken, 1962), 147 [in Hebrew].

the third is a Man of Seʿir (that is, Esau/Edom, an epithet for Christians—Tzimiskes).The Christian sent messengers to the rulers of Jerusalem, and asked them to expel the Jews from the city:

> Three kings come, roused up by God,
> One from the west, bringing young and old;
> One from the east, to rouse up war;
> And besides them, there is the hairy man,
> Who has sent messengers from Seʿir, to deceive them,
> To get them to expel from the City the multitudes of my [Jews] in his land.[10]

In 1001, Samuel included in a letter a unique historical poem in which he recounted a miracle: "the two enemies have been subdued—one in Egypt, and one among us." The poem has two parts: An Egyptian part, most of which is lost, seems to have spoken of a Turkish ("Agagite") enemy; whereas the Palestinian part speaks of a Christian enemy ("uncircumcized Edomites"). In the Palestinian part, he mentions the coastal cities Acre, Tyre, Ashkelon, and Caesarea, as well as other communities whose names have not survived, which suffered from the violence of the local Christian ruler. According to the poem, the enemies "flayed my skin, / and darkened my light and my appearance." Further on, in a section whose continuation is cut off, he mentions the coastal cities that were not spared by the events: "He despoiled the homes of Ashkelon, and destroyed the residents of Gaza, and made the community of Ḥatzerim [Caesarea] go wander"; and moreover: "He plunders the inhabitants of Acre, and exiled the people of Tyre." A writ of relief from the caliph finally arrived "on a Wednesday, at the end of the month of Marḥeshvan." This Wednesday, the last day of Marḥeshvan, was November 19, 1001.

The letter, along with the poem, was sent to a place far from either the Land of Israel or Egypt, to an individual named Abraham.[11] In the prose words

10 See Yahalom and Katsumata, *Samuel the Third*, 999. It may be that we should read lines 5–6 as: "Who has sent messengers from Seïr: Expel my multitudes from the city," that is, the messengers' announcement was to expel. Gil, *Palestine*, vol. 1, 278 ff.

11 Benjamin Z. Kedar, "Notes on the History of the Jews of Palestine in the Middle Ages," *Tarbiz* 42 (1973): 401–4 [in Hebrew]; Joseph Yahalom, "The Temple and the City in Hebrew Liturgical Poetry," in *The History of Jerusalem: The Early Islamic Period (638–1099)*, ed. Joshua Prawer (Jerusalem: Yad Ben-Zvi, 1987), 223–4 [in Hebrew]. For some reason, Gil, *Palestine*, 367 ff., is of the opinion that the addressee was a resident of Fusṭāṭ.

at the head of the poetic letter, Samuel emphasizes that he has written the text in verse so that it can be remembered and spread. Therefore, he instructs the addressee: "Send for R. Hillel, and teach it to him, with explanation, very well, so that he will recite it . . . in front of the prince, may God protect him; and if he recites it in front of the prince Rabbi Moses, he should add that this letter is."[12] There the text is cut off, but even what survives is enough to reflect the importance of using verse for the expressive presentation of the events, and, perhaps most importantly, the role of the poet as the mouthpiece of the Palestinian community in Fusṭāṭ, and the representative of its leadership.

In summer 1011, there was an outbreak of terrible plague in Egypt, which claimed many victims, including Shemariah ben Elḥanan, the leader of the Babylonian community in Fusṭāṭ. In the aftermath of the great rabbi's death, bitter strife broke out between two potential heirs, his son, Elḥanan ben Shemariah, and Abraham (Barhun) ben Sahlān, a scion of a famous family, and one of the most talented leaders of the Babylonian community in Egypt. Consequently, the Jewish community`s relations with the Fatimid authorities deteriorated as well, and needed to be restored. Samuel was summoned for this task.[13]

He wrote a short poem, demonstrating his support of Elḥanan, and another, long poem written on the model of liturgical poems and appended to the first one. The second poem described the sorry state of the nation and its suffering under the Fatimid regime, and stated that despite the growing outside pressure, the Jewish community continues to walk in straight paths and follow the old ways of replacing leaders, which have been preserved punctiliously since ancient times. This meant, of course, that Abraham (Barhun) ben Sahlān should not be allowed to steal the leadership.

> If this is so, then my master should adjure, and implore
> That Barhūn not be allowed to teach anything and govern,
> So that no revenue be given to him, at the time of planting or harvest,
> For he has put-up-a-shield to receive [such revenue], and acted impatiently,
> And acted haughtily, pleading [for favors] from his master.[14]

12 Yahalom and Katsumata, *Samuel the Third*, 1001–2.

13 Gil, *Palestine*, vol. 2, document 19. Therefore, we should not associate the exact date of Shemariah ben Elḥanan's death and that of the cantor, Paltiel, at the end of 1011, too closely, as Gil does in *A History of Palestine*, 377.

14 Yahalom and Katsumata, *Samuel the Third*, 1031.

Samuel's involvement in the incident was effective; Elḥanan ben Shemariah was indeed appointed as the unquestioned leader of the Babylonian community in Fusṭāṭ.

Commemoration of the events of 1010

During al-Ḥākim's reign (996–1021), acts of hostility and persecution against the religious minorities in Egypt reached their heights. In 1010 the agitated local Muslim population rioted against the Jews all over Egypt.

Samuel himself spent a terrifying night in prison, where he had been thrown by marauders who had attacked a funeral procession for a local cantor, in which Samuel had been involved. In response to this experience, he wrote two sequences of liturgical poems for the *ʿamidah* prayer, known as *qerovot*. Among other things, the community thanks God that He has kept the poet-cantor alive, so that there would be someone who could mark the day, and tell the story of the events to future generations, and thus keep the story alive: "He freed His servant, and redeemed him, to mark their deliverance."[15]

In his liturgical poems, Samuel refers to contemporary threats to his community, and knows how to breathe hope back into the hearts of his concerned listeners. He has the skill of directing the themes of the weekly Torah-portion into edifying messages about current events, and questions that were of utter importance at the time. The inclusion of personal aspects within a public liturgical poem was an innovation in the context of the liturgical poetry of the time. Indeed, using liturgical poetry for personal expression is one of the hallmark innovations of the period.

Samuel also wrote a poetical description of these events, known nowadays as "The Egyptian Scroll" (*Megillat Mitzraim*). He wrote it in the manner of the Biblical books, divided into verses and equipped with cantillation signs. He follows the Biblical Book of Esther in praising al-Ḥākim bi-amr Allāh, the ruler who had shown favor to him. Samuel's poetical work served as a kind of official document, in which he expressed great respect for the ruler, who was otherwise known for his persecutions of the religious minorities in Egypt.[16] Samuel depicted him as a sort of Ahasuerus of his day. He also managed to mention himself at the height of the plot:

> [The attackers] gathered twenty-three men [from the Jews], and brought them to be imprisoned in two cells. Their pain was great,

15 Ibid., 1019.

16 Ibid., *Samuel the Third*, 1008. Al-Ḥākim bi-amr Allāh is called there by a Hebrew calque of his name: "our master *ha-Dan be-Omer El*," "Who Rules at God's Command."

> as they spent the night hungry and thirsty. [The attackers] took some of their clothes as an oppressive tax. And among them was a member of the Sanhedrin, an old, gray-haired man, poor, broken-spirited, and God-fearing; he was third in position in the leadership, and his name was Samuel ben Hoshaʿna.[17]

The same events were also commemorated by Samuel in a liturgical poem: "Egyptians oppressed / adversarial enemies / brought about pangs / like the pangs of woman in labor."[18]

Samuel wrote it in a style that had been reserved for narrative poems in which the repeating rhyme interweaves matters.[19] Typical of such tetrameter lines is the shortness of their members; they are limited to two to three words. Eventually, it became obligatory to have exactly five syllables in each member—on the model of Arabic quantitative poetry.

In his attempt to express the traumatic experience that he had suffered, the poet-leader used an unusually varied pallette of methods. First, in traditional liturgy, in the style of *piyyut,* in which he unexpectedly alludes to his own status and function in representing the communal experience. Second, in a historical poetical work divided into verses and equipped with Scripture-like cantillation signs, in which he likewise managed to mention himself, and last, in a monorhymed secular poem, on the model of the Arabic *qaṣida,* the most modern genre of the time. It seems that the monorhymed poem was the method that most suited the poet's personal expression; sadly, what is preserved of that poem does not reach that point. In any event, the events of 1010 were immortalized in three different ways, which reflect the most central layers in the history of Hebrew literary expression. Samuel unhesitatingly made use of all of them.

Abraham ha-Kohen

Beyond what we have seen in the use of liturgical forms for public expression, we also find, in this period, use of defined liturgical forms of *piyyut* for very

---

17 Yahalom and Katsumata, *Samuel the Third,* 1009.

18 Ibid., 1028.

19 It is relevant that narrative *seder ʿavodah* poems for Yom Kippur were written in non-rhyming long lines of four members (tetrameters); moreover, Arabic *qaṣīda* poems are written in long tetrameter lines. Each of these surely influenced the adoption of rhyming tetrameters for Hebrew narrative poems.

personal expression. A tragic event in Abraham ha-Kohen's life was expressed in a long *qerovah,* which goes through all the eighteen blessings of the *ʿamidah* (a "*qerovah* of eighteen"). From this *qerovah,* which Abraham seems to have written while in prison, we are presented with his personal story. The author was thrown into prison in Egypt on Kislev 15, 4783 AM/November 12, 1022 CE, since he was unable to pay a debt of 150 dinars. On Purim of that year, he was unable to hear the reading of the Book of Esther. Otherwise, he suffered from cold and from lice; and he prayed for the downfall of his enemy, the creditor. From the formulations used for the closing doxologies, we can see that Abraham ha-Kohen belonged to the Palestinian community in Egypt, which used the Palestinian prayer rite.

Yeshuʿah b. Nathan the Dayyan, of Gaza

We see a more developed private use of liturgical forms in the work of Yeshuʿah b. Nathan the Dayyan, of Gaza. He wrote a composition made up of a sequence of eight parts, designated for an *ʿamidah* prayer, which contains the *qedushah* (Isaiah 6:3—"Holy, holy, holy"—and other verses about God's holiness), known as a *qedushta.* The work is anchored in the death of Josiah, the poet's only son, at the age of six. Various refrains, throughout the *qedushta,* rhyme with the name "Yoshiyyahu" (Josiah), emphasizing the same sounds, and the fourth poem is signed with the acrostic *yoshiyyahu shemo,* "Josiah is his name."

The bereaved father describes the son's qualities:

> He would arise in the morning, [to be] with his teacher,
> To read [Scripture] all day; he did not lose spirit. . . .
> And he would say: "Father, what does this verse mean?" . . .
> And at night, he would begin, as I would sit on the bed, embracing him,
> He would say the passage about fringes [Numbers 15:38–40, the third paragraph of the Shemaʿ], on his tongue. . . .
> How can I be consoled for someone, of whose praise this is a part?
> How can I be quiet or silent, and how can I forget him—
> Until consolation comes from the lofty, awesome, and holy One![20]

The closing words "the lofty, awesome, and holy One" (*ḥayy ve-qayyam nora u-marom ve-qadosh*), and the rhetorical formulation beginning with the

20 Fleischer, "Remarks on Medieval Hebrew Poetry," 186–7.

word "until" fit the normal method of concluding the fourth poem in a *qedushta*. However, the pain expressed in a standard *qedushta* is that of the Jewish people, not the personal pain of a father, who writes out the poem in his own hand. Yeshuʿah found the classical format of the *qedushta* to be a fitting genre in which to express his personal grief. But he incorporated a specific structure of eulogy in the sixth poem of his *qedushta*.

Eulogies for the death of young children stereotypically would console the parents by citing historical examples of fathers that had lost their children. In the pre-Arab period, the language of these eulogies was Aramaic, the spoken language, which everyone understood.[21] Yeshuʿah dedicates the sixth poem in his *qedushta* to this form of eulogy; he gives it the heading *sidra*, "order." Here he mentions, in order, the patriarchs who were bereaved of their children: Adam lost Abel, Teraḥ lost Haran, Judah lost Er and Onan, and so forth. At the end, he asks stereotypically: "Are you better than all these, who were the foundations of the world?"[22]

In the seventh poem, Yeshuʿah brings the work to one of its highest points. Here, Yeshuʿah tells us the questions that his son Josiah asked on the last Sabbath of his life, and he had no idea how timely these questions would be, so soon. The son asked his father: Will there be a tragic day when all humanity will be destroyed? Who will bury the last to die? The macabre dialogue between father and son is presented nearly verbatim. This is the text of the dialogue:

> For he asked me a difficult question, / which has no answer <. . .> /
> "On the day of reckoning, will all people die?"
> When I heard the question that he had asked, / I said: "Yes, [God] will conceal all." / He said: "The ones that die last—who will bury them?" / I said: "They will be cast out on the surface of the field, like dung."
> He responded with speech, with sweet utterance: "Will they come back to life, and be as before?" / I said to him: "Yes, they will again stand."
> He asked : "Who will revive them?" / I said: "The One dwelling on high."
> He said: "Who will remove the dirt from them?" / I said: "The creator

21 Cf. Joseph Yahalom and Michael Sokoloff (eds.), *Jewish Palestinian Aramaic Poetry from Late Antiquity (Shirat Bené Maʿarava)* (Jerusalem: Israel Academy of Sciences and Humanities, 1999), 309 [in Hebrew].

22 Menahem Zulay, "Liturgical Poems on Various Historical Events," *Studies of the Research Institute for Hebrew Poetry* 3 (1936): 180–3 [in Hebrew].

> of heaven, who stretched it out, / will say to the wind: Hover, and reveal them."
> He asked : "What will then be of them?" I said: "It will blow breath into them." He said: "In what place?" I said: "In the nose." . . .
> I embraced him, and kissed his lips, uttering truth, / and I did not realize that his utterance was concerning himself.[23]

The *qedushta* is designated, by virtue of its very liturgical nature, for public prayer, to express the heart's feelings based on the content specific to the day on the liturgical calendar. Yeshuʿah of Gaza chose one of the most complex, dignified liturgical programs, the *qedushta,* and brazenly poured his most personal feelings into it. It is unclear, whether there in fact was a synagogue in Gaza that allowed the author to perform his personal composition in their presence, or whether he wrote it merely to keep in a drawer.

ʿEli b. ʿAmram

ʿEli ben ʿAmram was a member of the Palestinian community in Fusṭāṭ. He is known mainly for his panegyric poems. In his youth, he already composed a secular panegyric, with a fixed number of syllables in each stanza, in honor of Elḥanan ben Shemariah (d. 1026), the leader of the Palestinian community in Fusṭāṭ. The poem is written in tetrameter lines, but, unlike in earlier periods, these tetrameters contain precise numbers of syllables. Each member of the line contains five syllables, and thus the full stanza, with four members, contains twenty syllables. The poet has adopted a syllabic version of the Arabic *ṭawīl* meter, which is used in many poems by Dunash ben Labrāṭ and his followers.[24]

---

23 Shulamit Elizur, "A New Fragment of the *Qedushta* of R. Yeshuʿah Beribbi Nathan of Gaza in Memory of his Son Josiah," in *The Cairo Geniza Collection in Geneva: Texts and Studies,* ed. David Rosenthal (Jerusalem: Magness Press, 2010), 197–8 [in Hebrew].

24 Fleischer sees this meter as a sort of "translation" of Dunash's *arokh* (Arabic: *ṭawīl*) meter into a syllabic system (Ezra Fleischer, *Hebrew Poetry in Spain and Communities Under its Influence,* ed. Shulamit Elizur and Tova Beʾeri [Jerusalem: Ben-Zvi Institute, 2010], 85, supplementary comment to note 36 [in Hebrew]). He views poems that have 6+6 syllables in a line as a syllabic "translation" of the Andalusi *marnin* meter, which the poet has imitated from Andalusi models (ibid., 1411, note 32, in an article from 2006). In this article, he speaks also of "a naïve attempt to imitate the rhythm of the Arabic *rajaz* meter [Hebrew: *marnin*]" (ibid., 83, note 22). In fact, one should view the syllabic meters that are constructed on the model of quantitative meters as independent attempts to adopt the Arabic meters, which are

For other panegyric poems, with a recurring rhyme at the end of each line (*ḥaruz mavriaḥ*), ʿEli ben ʿAmram used precise quantitative meters, which distinguish between short and long vowels. It is possible that this transition between ʿEli ben ʿAmram's two kinds of meter reflects a general change in the manner of writing secular panegyrics. It might be also that in grappling with Arabic poetry, ʿEli ben ʿAmram made a prosodic distinction in his Hebrew poetry, between the poems that he addressed to the intellectual elite, the scholars and heads of *yeshivot,* on the one hand, and the poems that he addressed to political and governmental leaders, on the other hand. In the poems that he addressed to the scholars, he was less strict in his adoption of the norms of Arabic prosody, and was content to count only the number of syllables, not the specific lengths of the vowels.[25] This seems to have been one of the traditional ways of adopting Arabic prosody in Hebrew, and it made his writing necessarily more fluent and relaxed. On the other hand, when he wrote for patrons and political leaders, he did so in stricter meters. Here, he was precise not only regarding the number of vowels, but also regarding their lengths. In the poems he wrote for the Jewish viziers, we can see his effort to adopt the modern, precise and quantitative, system of meter.

Writing in the modern style, with precise quantitative meter, and lines broken into two equal parts, was not easy for ʿEli ben ʿAmram. In the last line of a poem in this style, which he wrote for Abraham ha-Kohen b. Isaac ben Furāt, one of the nobles of the Egyptian community, our poet wrote, with apologetic humbleness: "And judge my lines favorably, with your great kindness, / in accordance with my practice, and the difficulty of the work."[26]

Indeed, he is right. The use of quantitative meter took special effort, and it was associated also with adopting a creative style that included, among other things, innovating new words and forms.

Following the custom of liturgical poetry, ʿEli ben ʿAmram uses a signature in the acrostic of the lines, where he signs the names of his addressees. On the other hand, the themes of Arabic panegyric poems are missing, and he does

---

not necessarily dependent on Andalusian models. (Joseph Yahalom, "The Origin of Precise Scanning in Hebrew Poetry—Syllabic Metre," *Leshonenu* 47 (1983): 25–61 [in Hebrew].)

25 Of the nine secular poems that Judah ha-Levi wrote in syllabic meters, six of them are addressed to the rabbinic leader [*nagid*] of the Jews of Egypt, Samuel ben Ḥananiah. See Ḥayyim Brody (ed.), *Dīwān of Abu-l-Hasan Yehudah ha-Levi* (Berlin: Mekize Nirdamim, 1894–1930), vol. 1, poems 57, 61, 76, 77, 90, 102 [in Hebrew]. Poem 67 is addressed to Aaron ibn al-ʿAmmānī, and poem 95 to the successor of R. Isaac Alfasi in Andalus; cf. also poem 129.

26 Jacob Mann, *The Jews in Egypt*, vol. 2, 85.

not know how to adopt the rhetorical means and developed ornamental style that are typical of the genre in Arabic. Similarly, his panegyrics (*qaṣīdas*) are lacking the hedonistic prelude, the *nasīb*, that is typical of this Arabic genre; they lack descriptions of feasts in the garden, the delights of wine, music, beautiful plants, and the like.

It may be assumed that Egyptian Jewish society did not develop the hedonistic courtly aspect of poetry in the way familiar from the Andalusi cultural sphere. In the courtly culture of al-Andalus, poets would sit together, in the company of the patron, the host of the party, whom the former would praise. While presenting their panegyrics, the poets would enjoy the pleasures of the party. They enjoyed the view of the cultivated garden, the beautiful fountains, and the girls dancing behind a curtain. Their sense of smell took pleasure in the fragrant trees, whose aroma wafted through the air, and their sense of taste had the satisfaction of drinks, which were generously provided. In Egypt, perhaps it was less common to spend time in poetry and comradery that included reading panegyrics in the context of a feast in the middle of beautiful nature. Instead, panegyrics became part of epistolary correspondence. The poet would send his poems to financiers and administrators who worked in the service of the caliphate, in positions of authority. The Hebrew poet was able, thus, to make social connections not only with Jewish patrons, but also with Muslim ones.

Many of the poems, towards the end, include a small reminder that the poet expects compensation for his creative effort—an especially prosaic matter. The only possible compensation that a poet could expect for a poem that was sent to a faraway recipient was some kind of gift. We see this in a poem that ʿEli ben ʿAmram wrote for Yehosef, son of Samuel ha-Nagid. ʿEli ben ʿAmram seems to have written to Yehosef during the decade (1056–66) when he served as *nagid* in Granada, retaining his father's rank; he writes that he expects gifts from him: "Open up your hand, O master of all leaders / with gifts and fine clothing."[27]

Solomon ha-Kohen b. Joseph

Solomon ha-Kohen, a member of the Palestinian *yeshivah*, wrote a poem in syllabic, non-quantitative, meter, in 149 stanzas, celebrating the successful action by the Fatimid general and ruler Badr al-Jamālī, removing the threat of a

27 MS Oxford 2873/43; see Beʾeri, "ʿEli he-Ḥaver," 283, note 22. Cf. also ibid., 300, stanza 20; ibid., 318, stanza 40; and passim.

Turkman invasion of Fusṭāṭ.[28] In this poem, Solomon ha-Kohen was influenced by the two great war poems of Samuel ha-Nagid, "Praise" and "Psalm," which are likewise written each in 149 lines, corresponding to the number of psalms in the Book of Psalms (the first two Psalms were considered a single chapter at the time). Samuel ha-Nagid's two poems, which were written a year apart from each other, were surely known in the Near East, for Samuel ha-Nagid himself designated them to be read on a special festive day, a "second Purim," in Jewish communities around the world. As he concludes his first poem: "And make it heard in Afriqé and in Tzoʿan, / and make it known, O children of the Chosen Temple."[29] "Tzoʿan," a biblical name for a city in Egypt, is known as an epithet of Fusṭāṭ in the Middle Ages.

Despite using a similar structure, Solomon ha-Kohen demonstrates great independence in his meter. Unlike Samuel ha-Nagid's poems, which are written in precise quantitative meter, Solomon ha-Kohen's poem is written in a simple syllabic meter: six syllables in the first half of the line, and six in the second half, with a fixed caesura after every three syllables.[30] In the last three lines, the poet indicates his name, along with the exact date of writing:

> On Monday, when four [days] remained / in the month of Shevat;
> and in years,
> Year 4837 since Creation, / and since the destruction—1009.[31]
> He is Solomon ha-Kohen, / son of Yehosef, descendant of *geʾonim*.

Thus, this poem, written on the occasion of the defeat of Atsiz ibn Uwaq the Turkman before the gates of Cairo, was concluded on Monday, Shevat 26, 4837 *anno mundi* (January 23, 1077/Jumāda II 24, 469). The poet includes a description of the destruction and plunder in Jerusalem, confident that Atsiz's defeat at the gates of Cairo befell him as punishment for what he did to the Jews of Jerusalem.

---

28 Yahalom, "Temple and City," 227–35.

29 Dov Jarden (ed.), *Dīwān of Shmuel ha-Nagid: Ben Tehillim* (Jerusalem: Hebrew Union College Press,1965-1991), 14, 16 [in Hebrew].

30 An identical system of prosody was used already in panegyrics by a poet named ʿAlvan ben Abraham, who was active in Syria around the year 1000; his poems are written in lines of two members, imitating the Arabic lines of *delet* and *soger*. Only the second member of each line has a rhyme, and this rhyme runs through the entire poem. The unit of three syllables effectively reflects the Arabic *hazaj* meter.

31 The poet writes the number in *gematriya*, using the word *mastimim* (literally "enemies," fitting the context, for the Temple was destroyed by the enemies, the Romans). The final *mem* represents 600, following the system in which final letters have given values.

In the last years of Fatimid rule in Palestine, there was already a faction of the Palestinian *yeshivah* in Egypt, which included Solomon ha-Kohen b. Joseph. It may be that by this time, it was already unthinkable in Egypt to write such a poem in a meter that was not careful about the precise number of syllables. It is nonetheless important to note that Solomon ha-Kohen b. Joseph did not consider himself obligated to follow Samuel ha-Nagid in writing in quantitative meter, which would have meant being concerned also about the lengths of vowels; thus, he was content with a simple syllabic meter. Outside of Egypt, life flowed in a different rhythm.

Joseph ibn Abitur

Joseph ibn Abitur, surnamed "Ben Shatnash," came to Egypt from al-Andalus in the late 1080s, and he cannot have been an especially young man at the time.[32] In al-Andalus, he was involved in a bitter conflict over leadership of the *yeshivah* in Cordova, the capital. There they banned him, because he had attempted to take this leadership position himself; but the dwindling Palestinian community in Fusṭāṭ warmly clasped him to their bosom. He came not only with great poetic skills, but apparently also with notes and sketches of poems that he had written back in al-Andalus. He even knew many of them by heart. Approximately fifty fragments of autographs of his poems were found in the Cairo Genizah.[33] Amazingly, his poems for Yom Kippur are typically written in clean, orderly writing, which suggests that the author was not working hard on a first draft in his new home. And indeed, Judah al-Ḥarīzī, in the early thirteenth century, tells us that Ibn Abitur was the first in al-Andalus to write a full *maʿamad* (service for the entire day) for Yom Kippur:

> The poems of the *gaʾon*, R. Joseph b. Shatnash, are pleasing and good; they are hewed out from a good quarry. He was the first of the authors in Andalus to write a *maʿamad* for Yom Kippur.[34]

Such a *maʿamad* includes *yotzerot* (liturgical poems inserted into the blessings surrounding the morning recitation of the Shemaʿ), and *qerovot* for each of the *ʿamidah* prayers of Yom Kippur. Each such *qerovah*

32 Fleischer, *Spain and Communities under Its Influence*, 412.

33 Joseph Yahalom, "Qedushat Zachor by Yaʿaqov: a Palestinian pronunciation as reflected in unique Babylonian and Tiberian pointing systems," *Ginzei Qedem* 12 (2016): 96–7 [in Hebrew].

34 Joseph Yahalom and Naoya Katsumata (eds.), *Taḥkemoni, or the Tales of Heman the Ezraḥite* (Jerusalem: The Ben-Zvi Institute, 2010), 111 [in Hebrew].

includes a full series of poems. The *qerovah* for Mussaf includes a major *seder ʿavodah*, describing the Temple service of Yom Kippur, in which Ibn Abitur follows the steps of his great predecessor, Saʿadia Gaʾon. His *seder ʿavodah* was imitated by the great Andalusi poets Solomon ibn Gabirol, Isaac ibn Ghiyyāt, and Moses ibn ʿEzra. Ibn Abitur's great poetic output includes about six hundred poems, and he must have composed some of them in Egypt.

Ibn Abitur wrote a *baqqashah* (supplicatory prayer), in a meter that would later be typical for Ibn Gabirol's *reʾshut* poems (poems introducing a liturgical unit). His *baqqashah* starts: "My God, I declare Thy beauty, / I thirst and yearn; // I kneel, with an ailing heart; / I bow and prostrate myself."

As is customary in poems of the *baqqashah* genre, these opening words recur at the conclusion: "The cup of time flows over, / my heart is very ailing. // My God, I declare Thy beauty, // I thirst and I yearn."[35]

The poem is written lyrically, presenting the feelings of a sinner, who recognizes his shameful status, and begs mercy for his life. In one of the stanzas, the poem's speaker confesses having had vile thoughts: "My sin, my shame, / my thoughts are reproachful, // and constantly facing me. / Remove my embarrassment!" Therefore, the speaker pleads, saying: "Not as I deserve, / shouldst Thou judge me, according to my actions. . . . // O merciful one, give me understanding, / please do not judge me.

We must consider Ibn Abitur the first influence on important trends in the development of Andalusi liturgical poetry.[36] In other instances, it seems that although Ibn Abitur had abandoned al-Andalus in his youth, his ways of writing were still connected to the early trends that were typical of the writing of poets of the second generation in al-Andalus, after Menaḥem and Dunash.

---

35 Fleischer, *Spain and Communities under its Influence*, 478–81. See Fleischer's note there, at the end of the poem: "In the printed text, there is an additional stanza, apparently not original: 'The cup of time flows over, / my heart is very ailing. // My God, I declare Thy beauty, // I thirst and I yearn.'" But in fact, it seems that the printed text preserves the version that the editor Ibn Mar Shaʾul had in front of him. Alternatively, it is possible that Ibn Mar Shaʾul was the first to declare that a metered *baqqashah* should have a structure that repeats the opening words at the end; for in the Genizah fragments of Ibn Abitur's *baqqashah*, this final stanza is not found.

36 Later imitations did not make use of internal rhyme at all. Thus, *Elohai al terivenu ke-fishʿi* ("My God, do not fight against me, in accordance with my iniquity"), and *Elohai al ke-maʿasai tigmeleni* ("My God, do not compensate me in accordance with my deeds"); see Tova Beʾeri (ed.), *Le-David Mizmor: The Poems of David ha-Nasi* (Jerusalem: Mekiẓe Nirdamim, 2009), 148–9 [in Hebrew]; Joseph Yahalom and Joshua Blau, "Poetic Flowers and Beautiful Stories: Early Versions of Passages of Alharizi's Tahkemoni," *Peʿamim* 96 (2003): 8–9 [in Hebrew].

Ibn Abitur's great innovation is the introduction of the sensitive personal strain into Hebrew liturgical poetry, as we see in his metrical *seliḥah* poems. He also began to poeticize sensitive points in the liturgy, which had previously not received the attention of poets[37]—for example, the introductory prayer *Nishmat Kol Ḥai,* which opens up the worshippers' hearts, and serves to begin the Sabbath morning prayer . The structure that Ibn Abitur established for the *Nishmat* poems was accepted in Andalusi liturgical poetry of all generations. In the second stanza of the poem *Nishmat Yeshurun . . . Teyaḥadakh,* the poet speaks in the name of "the remnants of Sepharad":

> The soul / and spirit of the precious remnants of Sepharad / Designates Thee,
> O Dependable One, who wearest light as an official garment,
> Thou hast pulled down the heavens and descended.[38]

One can read the expression "remnants of Sepharad" as referring to the Jews in their diaspora in al-Andalus, which was known as "Sepharad" in medieval Hebrew; but it might also be the poet's own personal prayer, in his exile *from* al-Andalus, in Egypt.

Personal expression echoes also in an *ahavah* poem, which Joseph ibn Abitur wrote for the Sabbath when the Torah-portion *Vayyeshev* (Genesis 37:1–40:23) is read. The touching story of the Biblical Joseph, as told in the Torah-portion, attracted the special attention of Joseph the poet. Here he mentions Joseph's love for God, to whom he remained faithful and for whom he retained his love, despite all his sufferings and all that had been decreed upon him from Heaven, by divine judgment, even as he was sold as a slave (Psalms 105:18). Joseph the poet feels that he needs God's help so that he can love Him as God requests in the Torah: "to love the Lord thy God" (Deuteronomy 30:20 et passim). We must note that the "love" that our poet discusses in this *ahavah* is not God's love for His people, as typical in *ahavah* poems, but, extraordinarily, human love for God—the Biblical Joseph's love for his creator, and Joseph ibn Abitur's love, in which he prays for help to be able to fulfill the commandment to love God:

> On this day, I recall the righteousness of the righteous [Joseph], and his love for God, his creator,

---

37 Fleischer, *Spain and Communities under Its Influence*, 419–20.

38 Jonah Fraenkel (ed.), *Maḥzor for Shavu'ot According to the Customs of All Branches of the Ashkenazic Rite* (Jerusalem: Koren, 2000), 91–2 [in Hebrew]. The last line of the stanza is a biblical citation, from II Sam. 22:10.

> Even when he suffered the ruling of His judgment, even when they afflicted his leg with a chain.
> And I ask for [God]'s help to love Him and fear Him, as He commanded when He said: To love the Lord thy God, to listen to His voice.
> As it is written: To love the Lord thy God, to listen to His voice [Deut. 30:20].[39]

Joseph ibn Abitur lived in Egypt for about fifty years (before 976–after 1024), and certainly wrote some of his work there, even though we suppose that he was already renowned as a great poet in al-Andalus. His assumption that he would serve as head of the *yeshivah* in Cordova, as the successor to his teacher Moses ben Ḥanokh, even to the extent of being chosen over his teacher's own son, surely derived not only from his greatness in Torah scholarship, but also from his fame as a beloved poet. Even though he was banned in al-Andalus and forced to leave, nonetheless his poems were accepted there, and left a deep influence on the poetry of his generation and subsequent ones.

Judah ha-Levi and Aharon ibn al-ʿAmmānī

Judah ha-Levi, who is known primarily as an Andalusi poet, spent less than a year in Egypt. He was on his way to the Land of Israel, and surely wrote some of his famous odes to Zion there. One of them is a poem in which he needs to apologize to his hosts that he is leaving "Egypt" (Fusṭāṭ). In this poem, *Le-mitzrayim ʿalé kol ʿir tehilla* ("To Egypt, praise beyond all cities"), he acknowledges that the Egyptian region is where great miracles occurred for the Israelites, and that Moses received revelation in the wilderness of Egypt—but nonetheless, he notes, there is one place that is superior to Fusṭāṭ and Egypt in general, namely Jerusalem, where he is headed.[40]

Judah ha-Levi disembarked upon Egyptian soil after a difficult journey by sea, on Elul 24, 4900 AM/September 8, 1140 CE. He was supposed to continue from Alexandria to the Land of Israel, but winter storms prevented him from continuing his maritime journey. Thus, he spent the autumn holidays in the company of a local physician and *dayyan* (judge in a religious court), Aharon ibn al-ʿAmmānī, who had been born in Jerusalem to a family whose origins were in Amman, in Transjordan. It seems that Judah ha-Levi's attraction to people with connections to the Land of Israel was what led him to his Jerusalemite host.

---

39 Ezra Fleischer, *The Yotzerot* (Jerusalem: Magness Press, 1984), 279 [in Hebrew].

40 Brody, *Dīwān*, vol. 2, 180.

Ultimately, one of the latter's relatives was able to boast that "although many Alexandrians had invited Judah ha-Levi to come eat in their houses, he had not come to them, but to us he came all the time, and composed panegyric poems for our sake."[41] According to the author of the letter that tells this story, the event caused an uproar in the local community. The community was especially enraged by the method in which the host published the poems: he collected the literary exchange between himself and the poet in a *dīwān* with headings in Arabic, explaining the circumstances in which they had been composed.

Fragments of two copies of Ibn al-ʿAmmānī's *dīwān* made their way to the Ben ʿEzra *genizah* in Cairo.[42] In one of the poems,Ibn al-ʿAmmānī recounts how he was forced to leave Jerusalem, due to the pressure of the Christians ("the Edomites"), and had to move to Egypt (the land of the "ʿAnamites"). There, Judah ha-Levi ("the lion's whelp") came to him and lavished praises on him. The communal leadership was in the hands of wealthy Iraqi Jews, so Ibn al-ʿAmmānī's native Palestinian prayer rite, from Jerusalem, was largely rejected. Judah ha-Levi, however, expressed interest in Palestinian customs. Ibn al-ʿAmmānī writes in his poem, which has been wrongly attributed to Judah ha-Levi:

> And from my sanctum, when my trappers had my Temple, / the Edomite pushed me to the ʿAnamites. . . .
> Until the lion's whelp came to fence off my vineyard, / and the fox fled, which had been destroying my vineyards.

Judah, the "lion's whelp" (see Genesis 49:9, which gives this epithet to the Biblical Judah), who chased away the foxes that had been destroying the

41 Moshe Gil and Ezra Fleischer, *Yehudah ha-Levi and his Circle* (Jerusalem: Magness Press, 2001), document 48 [in Hebrew]. The document has survived, even though the sender asks Judah ha-Levi to burn it when he is finished reading it. We are fortunate that he did not do as instructed. The document was first published by Shelomo D. Goitein, "Letters about R. Yehudah ha-Levi's Stay in Alexandria and the Collection of his Poems," *Tarbiz* 28 (1959): 352–4, document 1 (Hebrew translation on 356–8) [in Hebrew]. More recently, it was published again by Frenkel, *"Compassionate,"* 99, document 76 [in Hebrew]. In Frenkel's opinion, the letter was not written to Judah ha-Levi. In fact, most of the verso of the letter deals with complaints about Ibn al-ʿAmmānī the judge, and his faction, including complaints about the poem mentioned therein, which is by Ibn al-ʿAmmānī, not by Judah ha-Levi. See below.

42 Ḥayyim Schirmann, "Poets Contemporary with Mose [sic] ibn Ezra and Yehudah ha-Levi (III)," *Studies of the Research Institute for Hebrew Poetry in Jerusalem* 6 (1946): 267 [in Hebrew]; idem, *New Poems*, 237–8. See also Sara Cohen, *The Poems of R. Aaron al-ʿAmmānī* (Jerusalem: Mekize Nirdamim, 2008), 309–10 [in Hebrew].

field (Song of Songs 2:15), responded to him in a poem with the same meter and rhyme, *Se'u harim* ("Give [my regards], O mountains"). In this poem, he encourages al-ʿAmmānī, and says:

> The Jerusalemite has holiness as his inheritance; / he inherited it from his early ancestors.
> Holy people come from the place of the Temple; / and their birthplace is in the mountains of spices.[43]

Ultimately, the complete *dīwān* of Judah ha-Levi included many poems that he had written to Ibn al-ʿAmmānī, including a group of twelve consecutive such poems (§§67–78 in the *dīwān*). It is important to note that Judah ha-Levi's *dīwān* does not include a single poem written by Aharon ibn al-ʿAmmānī to Judah ha-Levi, although it includes such poems by Moses ibn ʿEzra, Judah ibn Ghiyyāt, and others.[44] Perhaps we should see this as a sign of a negative attitude towards al-ʿAmmānī's Egyptian *dīwān* on the part of the local editor of Judah ha-Levi's complete *dīwān*, Ḥiyya the Maghrebī (d. after 1160), who seems to have been the son of another Andalusi-Maghrebī who had settled in Egypt, Isaac ben Samuel al-Kanzī ha-Sefaradi (d. after 1127).[45]

A developed *qaṣīda* that Judah ha-Levi wrote in honor of his host, which he opens with a hedonistic description of the pool and the water fountains in Ibn al-ʿAmmānī's courtyard, is criticized quite explicitly in the letter that was sent to the poet. The author of the letter says that critics have examined this hedonistic poem, and asked, rhetorically: Should a man who is about to go on pilgrimage to the Holy Land speak such words of folly? The letter cites the last line of a poem that Ibn al-ʿAmmānī wrote to Judah ha-Levi during Hanukkah, after Judah had left Alexandria: "And discern between the lions and the lambs, / and between the lilies and the cut thorns."[46] It is not clear who the "cut thorns"

43 Brody, *Dīwān*, vol. 2, 258; see also Cohen, *al-ʿAmmānī*, 19, 26. Ḥayyim Schirmann, *Studies in the History of Hebrew Poetry and Drama* (Jerusalem: Mossad Bialik, 1979), vol. 1, 304 [in Hebrew], raises the possibility that Ibn al-ʿAmmānī fled Palestine after the Crusader conquest in 1099.

44 This is in spite of the fact that at least one such poem, *Se'ippai ba-ḥanukkah* ("My thoughts on Hanukkah") was known to the editors of the *dīwān*. In only one heading, to the poem *Re'é ki 'anené gishmi* ("See the clouds of rain," poem 71), does it mention that it was written in response to a poem by the host in Alexandria. For the remnants of this *dīwān*, see Cohen, *al-ʿAmmānī*, 309; and Schirmann, *New Poems*, 237–8.

45 Fleischer, *Spain and Communities under Its Influence*, 840.

46 Brody, *Dīwān*, vol. 1, 116; Gil and Fleischer, *Yehudah ha-Levi and His Circle*, 466.

are, to whom Aharon ibn al-ʿAmmānī is alluding in his poem, but it is clear that he did not like them. The author of the letter, who was offended, cites these words as part of his complaint against Ibn al-ʿAmmānī.[47]

While in Fusṭāṭ, Judah ha-Levi had to serve as an advocate for Ibn al-ʿAmmānī, in the presence of the *nagid* of the Jews of Egypt, Samuel ben Hananiah. In a letter that Judah ha-Levi sent to Ibn al-ʿAmmānī from Fusṭāṭ, he calmed him down, and wrote to him that the *nagid* has great appreciation for him, and that the words of calumny against him have not found receptive ears. And thus he wrote:

> He considers you to be of high value, and your soul is dear in his eyes, and raises holiness, rather than lowering it, whereas the words of calumny, in his eyes, neither raise nor lower anything. . . . He deserves kingship, and you deserve to be his second in command and the general of his army. . . . You are praised through his position, and he is praised through your poetry.[48]

Judah ha-Levi certainly was of the opinion that his praise of Ibn al-ʿAmmānī's talents as a poet would make the latter happy.[49] It must be remembered that

47 Yeshuʿah erroneously includes this poem as Judah ha-Levi's, in his edition of the poet's *dīwān*, based on the heading that he found in David ben Maimon's *dīwān* (MS Firkovich 209.1, in the appendix): "R. Aaron he-Ḥaver responded (*jāba*) to him during the days of Hanukkah, and wrote to him." Yeshuʿah read the word *jāba* ("responded") as *ghāba* ("was missing"), for both are spelled with the letter *gimmel* in Judeo-Arabic, and thus understood the sentence as: "R. Aaron he-Ḥaver was missing from him during the days of Hanukkah, and he [Judah ha-Levi] wrote to him." In fact, the poem is in response to one that Judah ha-Levi had written to Ibn al-ʿAmmānī, in the same meter and rhyme, as was the custom of poets that responded to each other's poems: "Slow separation from friends and brothers . . . / Can hearts contain the separation from Aaron? / The hearts are crying and moaning" (Brody, *Dīwān*, vol. 2, 260). The poem appears in the fragments of Ibn al-ʿAmmānī's *dīwān*, alongside the poem *Seʿippai ba-Ḥanukkah* ("My thoughts on Hanukkah are not cheery" [Schirmann, *New Poems*, 237]). Based on Yeshuʿah's *dīwān* (MS Oxford 1971), Samuel David Luzzatto published the poem in *Betulat Bat Yehudah* (Prague: n.p., 1840), 82, with the heading: "In Alexandria, to the same addressee [Ibn al-ʿAmmānī], when he [Judah ha-Levi] left there." Based on this, Brody, too, included it (*Brody, Dīwān*, vol. 1, 116), with the heading "In Alexandria, to R. Aaron ben Zion ben al-ʿAmmānī, when he left there [Egypt]." I would like to thank Joshua Blau for his help in deciphering the Arabic heading.

48 Brody, *Dīwān*, vol. 1, 209 ff.

49 The published edition of Ibn al-ʿAmmānī's poems contains mainly *seliḥot* and *qinot* (Cohen, *al-ʿAmmānī*, §§1–51), but he wrote metrical secular poems, some of which were even erroneously attributed to Judah ha-Levi.

monorhymed metrical secular poems that he wrote to Judah ha-Levi were misidentified as being by Judah ha-Levi himself; even Yeshuʿah ha-Levi, who assembled Judah ha-Levi's *dīwān*, was unable to distinguish between them.

Ibn al-ʿAmmānī is known mainly from his syllabic liturgical poems, where the rhyme changes from one stanza to the next. His stanzas are constructed as typical of poems with refrains, namely, the stanzas are split into two: a long part, with a rhyme unique to the stanza, and a shorter part, with a rhyme that runs through the poem. The rhyme of the shorter part introduces the refrain, which has the identical rhyme. In many instances, Ibn al-ʿAmmānī chooses to construct this rhyme out of a repeating key word, which he derives from a fragment of a biblical verse. He also made use of a girdle poem of Judah ha-Levi, written in precise quantitative meter, which Ibn al-ʿAmmānī decided to imitate, in the way that the Andalusi poets wrote in this specific genre.

Ibn al-ʿAmmānī's *seliḥah* is signed not only in the initial letters of its five stanzas, *Aharon ḥazaq* ("Aharon, be strong!"), but also, simply with the name "Aharon," in the opening line. Aharon signs his name here not only in the initials of the words of the opening line, but also a second time, in the initials of the stanzas. Moreover, the fixed rhyming word "Zion," which recurs at the ends of the lines of the short sections of the stanzas, is one of the characteristics of Ibn al-ʿAmmānī's liturgical poetry. Ibn al-ʿAmmānī maintains a connection to the poem of Judah ha-Levi that served as his model, by inserting a human object of praise into his poem—this time, none other than the Messiah: "Set him as a prince, / may his throne be like the sun before Thee, and a head."

Ibn al-ʿAmmānī's songs enjoyed great circulation, and are known from over a hundred fragments in the Genizah. In time, the members of his family, too, became known as cantors and poets: his sons Yeshuʿah and Zadok, and his grandson Jacob.[50] From the correspondence between Meir ben Yakhin, in Fusṭāṭ, and Judah ha-Melammed, one of the grandsons of Aharon ibn al-ʿAmmānī in Alexandria, it is clear how much the Jewish communities in Egypt admired poems from this Alexandrian school.[51]

Eleazar ha-Kohen ben Khalfūn

Eleazar ha-Kohen ben Khalfūn was a well-regarded poet, whose poems were gathered in a *dīwān*. He wrote a panegyric in honor of Samuel ben Hananiah,

50 Shraga Abramson, "Liturgical Poems of Rabbi Yaʿaqov bar Yehudah he-Ḥaver Amani," *Studies of the Research Institute for Hebrew Poetry* 7 (1958): 165 [in Hebrew].

51 Frenkel, *"Compassionate,"* 144–5.

the *nagid* of the Jews of Egypt (d. 1159), and also in honor of Maimonides, who arrived in Egypt around the year 1165.[52] He mostly wrote liturgical poetry for the synagogue, but was very careful to write them in quantitative meter. Unlike Ibn al-ʿAmmānī, he imitated girdle poems with great precision; he was as meticulous about their structure as the greatest Andalusi poets were when, for their enjoyment, they imitated girdle poems of their predecessors. In these poems, the short sections have the rhyme that recurs through all the stanzas, and there is no refrain.

Eleazar ha-Kohen wrote the girdle poem *Eikh evḥar dod zulatakh* ("How can I choose any beloved but Thee?")[53] as an imitation of the poem *Rav lakhem moḥikhai be-riv* ("It is too much that you contentiously rebuke me"), which has been erroneously attributed to Judah ha-Levi.[54] The secular poem ends with the desperate cry of the lovesick girl, whose beloved has abandoned her. The motif of intentional parting recurs in this poem. The parting is intended to test the bond between the lovers, and is supposed to strengthen it. Eleazar's imitation is written for liturgical use as an *ahavah* poem, to be recited in the blessing "who chooses His people Israel with love" in the morning prayer. In this *ahavah,* he makes sophisticated use of the secular motive of parting, with an interesting rhetorical reversal of his own:

> I have seen all the lovers, / they do not love as I do.
> They distance themselves from their beloved, / but my thoughts, O beloved, cling to Thee.

That is: unlike lovers in general, who go far away from each other in order to increase their desire, the thoughts of the one who loves God constantly cling to Him, without letting go.

In his liturgical poetry, Eleazar ha-Kohen is extremely careful about using precise quantitative meter. He views himself as obligated to ultimate perfection there, unlike in a conventional eulogy that he wrote for one of the scholars

52 Schirmann, *New Poems,* 109; Alexander Scheiber, "New Poems from the Kauffmann Collection," in *Ḥayyim (Jefim) Schirmann Jubilee Volume,* ed. Shraga Abramson and Aaron Mirsky (Jerusalem: Schocken, 1970), 393–4 [in Hebrew].

53 Fleischer, *Spain and Communities under Its Influence,* 1340 ff. The poem's heading indicates that it is to be sung to the tune of a poem by a poet named Dunash, of unknown era, who was already writing a liturgical poem that imitated the secular. See ibid., 1333, note 28.

54 Brody, *Dīwān,* vol. 2, 321–2; Yonah David (ed.), *The Poems of Joseph ibn Tzaddiq* (New York: American Academy for Jewish Studies, 1982), 33–5 [in Hebrew].

of the time, in which he used tetrameter lines where only the final members rhymed with a fixed rhyme throughout the poem. In this eulogy, he settled for a syllabic meter, as was customary in this type of long-winded monorhymed poems.[55] From this point of view, it seems that we can consider Eleazar ben Khalfūn a poet who follows the traditional Near Eastern track, but on the other hand, we see from his liturgical poetry, which is written in stanzas of variable rhyme, that he is an innovator, on the Andalusi model.

Moses Darʿī

Judah ha-Levi's poems left a great impression on a Karaite poet who came to Egypt from the Maghreb, named Moses Darʿī. Members of his community had established a neighborhood in Jerusalem, where many of the Karaite scholars and Biblical commentators lived. Jerusalem was the destination for many Karaites, and their spiritual center, and Moses Darʿī expressed this in his liturgical poetry. In the poems that he wrote for Friday evenings, he placed Jerusalem at the summit of his desires. He constructed these poems around a refrain, based on a verse, or part of a verse, from the weekly Torah-portion. He split the verse symmetrically, down the middle; the resulting two halves determined the rhyme and syllabic meter of the opening stanza.

Thus, for example, for the Sabbath of the Torah-portion *Naso* (Num. 4:21–7:89), he has chosen the verse "May the Lord lift up His countenance upon thee, and give thee peace" (Num. 6:26). This verse has sixteen syllables in Hebrew, and thus fits the number of syllables in Judah ha-Levi's *seliḥah, Yerushalayim heʾanḥi* ("Moan, O Jerusalem"), which Darʿī uses as the model for his own poem.[56] In Judah ha-Levi's poem, the lines are split in the middle, with a fixed caesura, leaving seven syllables in each half. However, Darʿī was more elaborate than his source: he splits the lines of his poem by means of an internal rhyme; he even splits the refrain, the biblical verse, on this rhyme, even though this means splitting in the middle of a word. Divisions of units down the middle of words is characteristic of Darʿī poems.

55 Alexander Scheiber, "A Fragment from the Dīwān of Eleazar ha-Kohen," *Sinai* 35 (1954): 184 [in Hebrew].

56 Dov Jarden (ed.0, *Liturgical Poetry of Judah ha-Levi* (Jerusalem:Dov Jarden 1977-1985), vol. 2, 612. The poem serves as the model also for fifteen other poems by Moses Darʿī. See Joachim Yeshaya, *Poetry and Memory in Karaite Prayer: The Liturgical Poetry of the Karaite Poet Moses ben Abraham Darʿī* (Leiden: Brill, 2014), 53.

Darʿi's *dīwān* includes over five hundred Hebrew poems, more than half of which belong to a cycle of poems for lifecycle events, including wedding songs and funeral eulogies.[57] Darʿi's secular poems are written in accordance with the best of the Andalusi tradition, in all the standard genres; but he also wrote some Arabic panegyrics, apparently in accordance with the preferences of the addressees.[58] In one of his debate poems, he shows that he is a faithful Karaite: he blames the wicked Rabbanite Jews for inventing things in their commentaries on the Torah that have no basis in the text. He rejects the claim that the details of the commandments were revealed to Moses at Sinai in an oral Torah. The poem is written in a syllabic meter, of eight syllables per line, containing no *sheva*s at all:

> Far be it from me to associate with
> a wicked people, to walk on their path;
> Or to pay attention to their deceptions,
> Their lies or mockeries;
> Or to be inclined to their nonsense,
> The falsehood, or the vanity of their books;
> Or to study the commandments of their Mishnā,
> Learned by rote from each other;
> I deny their saying that it is an oral tradition and a secret
> commanded by the Rock to this congregation on Mount Sinai;
> In the written Law I confide,
> given by God to the people of His portion;
> One Torah, to which I add nothing—
> one Law, which I shall not revise.[59]

Moses Darʿī was one of the greatest poets in the wealthy, established Karaite community in Egypt. This is evident in his secular social poetry. Alongside this, he did not neglect liturgical poetry, even though it was not rooted in the same

57 Leon J. Weinberger, *Jewish Poet in Fatimid Egypt: Moses Darʿi's Hebrew Collection* (Tuscaloosa: University of Alabama Press, 1988) [in Hebrew].

58 Uri Melammed, of the Academy of the Hebrew Language, is working on an edition. See Arie Schippers, "Some Remarks on Judaeo-Arabic Poetical Works: An Arabic Poem by Moses Darʿī," in *Studies in Medieval Jewish Poetry*, ed. Alessandro Guetta and Masha Itzhaki (Leiden: Brill, 2009), 141–56.

59 Joachim Yeshaya, *Medieval Hebrew Poetry in Muslim Egypt: The Secular Poetry of the Karaite Poet Moses ben Abraham Darʿī* (Brill: Leiden, 2011), 77 ff. English translation by Yeshaya, ibid.; reprinted here with his permission.

Rabbanite statutory liturgy that is reflected in Judah ha-Levi's poems, which he was imitating.

Moses Maimonides

In the generation after Judah ha-Levi's visit to Egypt, R. Moses b. Maimon arrived there. Maimonides is known as a philosopher, a halakhist, and a communal leader of Egypt; he received an excellent Andalusi education, which included the ability to express himself in poetry. His poetic abilities find their expression mainly in his Hebrew opening poems to his works, which, among other functions, serve as a kind of declaration of his belonging to the Arab-Jewish cultural world. The Hebrew poems serve also as an introduction, a heading, to the Judeo-Arabic text in prose, in which he describes, in brief, the nature and importance of the work.

In the opening poem to his commentary on the Mishnah, he modestly describes his work as the writing of "one lowly in might, young in years." At the same time, the poem opens with these words: "The book written about Moses's law, / the explanation of its ways, and its righteous ruling," and continues by presenting the author's name as "Moses, the son of Maimon," who seeks his portion "on the mountain of understanding." The third time that he mentions the name "Moses" is in the conclusion, where the point of the poem is expressed, where he expresses his hope and prayer: "Then may he see God's goodness, and then / may Moses rejoice in the sweetness of his gift, his portion."[60]

This time, Maimonides incorporates language from the Sabbath morning prayer, which speaks of the Biblical Moses, who brought down the Torah from the Mountain of Understanding; but Moses Maimonides is surely using these words to refer to himself. With this sophisticated incorporation of language from the sacred liturgical text, Maimonides demonstrates his high abilities in the Hebrew culture of the time.

In the introductory poems to his other books, too, Maimonides is known for his use of Biblical verses to make his concluding point; he harnesses them in a subtle way to one of the ideas from his poem.[61] A number of poets have

60 This is in the *mahir* meter. Cf. Yosef Qafiḥ, ed., *Mishnah with Commentary of Maimonides* (Jerusalem: Mossad ha-Rav Kook. 1963), vol. 1: *Order Zera'im*, before p. 1 [in Hebrew]. See also Alexander Marks, "Texts by and about Maimonides," *JQR* 25 (1934/5): 389.

61 Cf. Michael Schwartz (trans. and ed.), *Maimonides: The Guide of the Perplexed, Hebrew Translation from the Arabic, Annotations, Appendices, and Indices* (Tel Aviv: Tel Aviv

made sophisticated use of the words said by Joseph, when describing his dream to his brothers: "my sheaf arose, and also stood upright" (Gen. 37:7). They also bring with them a whiff of boasting, which fits the conclusion of a poem of this genre, which was widespread among the Andalusi poets. One can use the phrase abstractly, to describe a spiritual accomplishment, but one can also use it in other ways. Thus, Maimonides uses it in his introductory poem to the *Mishneh Torah*, which would come to describe his accomplishment in writing this great anthology:

> In the field of contemplation, the reapers have reaped / wisdom, which is sweet to everyone of generous heart.
> After them, the gleaners have gleaned, / and my soul joins them, comes close [to them].
> Many sheaved have been harvested by them, but / my sheaf arose, and also stood upright.[62]

Anatoli b. Joseph

Arabic-Jewish learned culture, on the Andalusi model, spread also to Jewish centers that were far from the hotbed of the Andalusi center. This can be seen in the personality and literary activity of Anatoli b. Joseph, who was born in Marseille, and was active mainly in Lunel, and, later on, in Sicily.[63] He ultimately ended up in Alexandria, where he was appointed *dayyan* at the time of Maimonides. Maimonides greatly respected Anatoli b. Joseph, and wrote a letter to him in elegant literary Hebrew, unlike his usual practice of writing letters in Judeo-Arabic.[64] When Anatoli died (in 1221), and, in fact, even

University, 2002), 767–79 [in Hebrew]. See also Maud Kozodoy, "Prefatory Verse and the Reception of the Guide of the Perplexed," *JQR* 106 (2016): 257–82.

62 Cf. Baruch Toledano (ed.), *Sefer al-Murshad al-Kāfī by R. Tanḥum ben Joseph the Jerusalemite* (Tel Aviv: Aḥdut, 1961), 23–4 [in Hebrew]. For an imitation of the poem, see Yahalom and Katsumata, *Taḥkemoni*, 280. For humoristic uses of this Biblical quotation, cf. Dov Jarden (ed.), *Maḥberot Immanuel ha-Romi* (Jerusalem: Mossad ha-Rav Kook, 1957), 135 [in Hebrew]; and David Yellin (ed.), *Gan ha-Meshalim veha-Ḥidot: Dīwān of Don Todros Son of Yehudah Abu-l- ʿĀfiah* (Jerusalem: Ha-Sefer, 1931–5), vol. 2, part 1, 131, §725: "And when she sat next to me, my sheaf arose, and also stood upright" [in Hebrew].

63 Frenkel, *"Compassionate,"* 128–33; Mordecai Akiva Friedman, "Maimonides Appoints R. Anatoly *Muqaddam* of Alexandria," *Tarbiz* 83 (2015), 144 ff. [in Hebrew].

64 Yitzhak Shailat (ed.), *The Letters and Essays of Moses Maimonides* (Maʿale Adummim: Shailat, 1995), vol. 2, 470: "Your letters and questions—your fragrant oil—I have smelled, /

before, people began to voice their opposition to the appointment of learned people from France, or from Europe in general, to the position of *dayyan*. The opponents based themselves on an old ordinance, which stated that *dayyanim* are invalid if they do not have full command of the local language, and are unable to listen to testimony without the help of a translator.[65]

The surviving poems of Anatoli's *dīwān* show that he was an excellent Hebrew intellectual, who exchanged poems with poets in Sicily, in the most sophisticated Andalusi style, monorhymed *qaṣīdas,* in precise quantitative meter, including ornamental use of rhetorical devices, in the fashion of Arabic poetry. Among other things, he uses images from Bedouin life in the desert, and weeps over the ruins of tents, in the manner of a great lover, though he wrote no actual love songs.[66] His corpus also contains sophisticated girdle poems, typical of Andalusi society. He wrote one such poem in honor of the wedding of Abraham, son of Maimonides. This poem is written in the standard manner, with stanzas divided into two parts, the longer part in a rhyme that changes from stanza to stanza, and the shorter one in a rhyme that recurs throughout the poem.[67]

Anatoli ben Joseph's poetry leaves it difficult for us to suspect him of not being fluent in Arabic or of not being well-versed in Arabic poetry. Yet, on the other hand, we see various signs of influence of the cultural environment from whence he hailed. Various factors of integration, which are specific to Provençal poetry, can first be seen in Hebrew in Anatoli's poetry. Thus, he opens and closes long *qaṣīda*s with an identical line; and, moreover, he sometimes adds a short dedicatory poem to the end of a long *qaṣīda,* where he mentions the

---

and they are like flowerpots of spices before me. / Therefore, I have said to all my faithful: / see, the aroma of the field that the Lord has blessed. / And they all rejoiced about your arrival in our land, / and you peered through our lattices, / and gazed through our windows. / May God guide you through our palaces."

65 Alexandra Cuffel, "Call and Response: European Jewish Emigration to Egypt and Palestine in the Middle Ages," *JQR* 90 (1999): 73–4.

66 Samuel Miklos Stern, "A Twelfth-Century Circle of Hebrew Poets in Sicily," *JJS* 5 (1954): 60–79, 110–13: "When I pass by the foundations that have been destroyed, / and the habitations, the dwellings of people that love, which have been devastated" (66). In a friendship poem to one of his friends, he describes a scene of kissing: "And I shall descend to the couch of love; / between his lips is honey, and I kiss him while drowsing, / and he gives me of the wine of his lips to drink, in a golden cup, / which my friend supports with his saliva." (Elisheva Hacohen, *The Poems of R. Anatoli ben Joseph* [MA thesis, The Hebrew University of Jerusalem, 1996], 158 [in Hebrew].)

67 Ḥayyim Schirmann, *The History of Hebrew Poetry in Christian Spain and Southern France,* ed. and ann. Ezra Fleischer (Jerusalem: Ben-Zvi Institute, 1997), 448–50 [in Hebrew].

name of the addressee, and takes pride in the poem that he has written in honor of this person. All these are features of Provençal poetry.[68] Thus, Anatoli's personality is more complex than we would have thought.

Joseph ha-Maʿaravi

Joseph ha-Maʿaravi was a student of Maimonides, and the primary addressee of his *Guide for the Perplexed*. He was born in Ceuta, Morocco, but as a result of the attempts of the zealous Almohad tribes to convert the Jews, he seems to have ended up in Christian Spain, and then in Egypt. The romances and love stories sung by wandering troubadours left an impression on his young soul. In an allegorical love story that he sent from Alexandria to Maimonides in Cairo, he cleverly incorporated the two narrative genres that he knew: Arabic *maqāma* and romance.

The story is about the love of Maskil and Yemimah, who meet on the banks of the Nile.[69] They are instantly attracted to each other, as if by a magic wand, and they exchange heartfelt love poems. When Maskil wants to finally approach his beloved, she first mentions the name of her guardian, Prince Moses, from whom Maskil will need to receive permission for their marriage. She says that Prince Moses is the one that rescued her from her persecutors, and brought her from lowly to lofty status. After Maskil demonstrates his abilities in Jewish Andalusi culture, by composing a long *qaṣīda*, Prince Moses gives his blessing to their wedding, which is performed in front of many people. Joseph ha-Maʿaravi wanted to use this story to convince Maimonides to accept him as a student. He wanted to study all the rational fine points, and allegorical interpretations, which Maimonides used to defend the passages in the Torah that had been the object of harsh criticism by people faithful to the Arabic rationalist *kalām*. From this point of view, Yemimah represents the Torah, which had been humiliated, but whose glory Maimonides had augmented. In this reading, Maskil, who wants her hand in marriage, represents Joseph ha-Maʿaravi's own yearning to receive Torah from Moses.

---

68 Ibid., 446 ff. We see this feature already in the lament poem *Zot ha-telaʿa* ("This is the travail") by Judah ha-Levi, mourning the death of Solomon ibn Feruziel (Brody, *Dīwān*, vol. 2, 93–100).

69 Joseph Yahalom (ed.), *Libbavtini: Love Stories from the Middle Ages* (Jerusalem: Carmel, 2009), 73–95 [in Hebrew]; see also Joseph Yahalom, "A Romance Maqāma: The Place of the 'Speech of Tuvia ben Tzedeqiah' in the History of Hebrew Maqāma," *Hispania Judaica* 14 (2010), Hebrew section, 113–28.

If this work were to follow the standard frame-story of the *maqāma* genre, the fictional narrator with the patronymic name Toviyyah ben Tzidqiyyah would need to meet the hero at the beginning of the *maqāma,* and to be impressed with him and his stories. At the end of the *maqāma,* he would have to depart from the hero merely in order to enable another meeting at the beginning of the next *maqāma.* However, this work is more complex than that. Alongside the fictional narrator, there is also another character, namely, the true narrator, who was an eyewitness to the events described in the main story—in this case, Maskil's father. At the end of the story, the fictional narrator departs not from the hero, as the *maqāma* genre would require, but from the true narrator. This ruins the fixed format of the *mqāma,* which opens every chapter with a new meeting between the narrator and the hero—which is possible only if the fictional narrator and the hero have parted ways at the end of the previous chapter.

A standard *maqāma* also would have no place for the hero's allegorical name, Maskil. Finally, especially the ways that Maskil is described as a young man, experienced in adventures, who has been rescued from a great storm at sea, after much wandering, are typical of a romance story. The author, himself a young, wandering intellectual, wanted to join the great teacher and study Torah from him. And indeed, he got his wish, due to his successful demonstration of multifaceted erudition in his *maqāma,* against the background of Andalusi culture, in which he was so steeped. From Alexandria, Joseph ha-Maʿaravi went to Fusṭāṭ, where he met Maimonides, and had discussions with him, which ultimately became the kernel of the *Guide to the Perplexed.*[70]

Aside from this famous *maqāma,* which Joseph ha-Maʿaravi wrote in Alexandria, we do not know of any other belletristic compositions by him; but nonetheless, this composition left a great impression on his contemporaries. In many ways, it represented the first entrance of components of the romance into Hebrew literature. It is mentioned not only by Judah al-Ḥarīzī, but also in 1225, by a certain Ḥayyim ben Samḥūn as the model imitated by the important Spanish writer Judah ibn Shabbetai (1168–after 1225), for his work *The Offering of Judah the Hater of Women* (*Minḥat Yehudah soné ha-nashim*).[71]

70 Schwartz, *The Guide of the Perplexed,* 5–8 ("Epistle to the Student").

71 Schirmann and Fleischer, *Christian Spain and Southern France,* 69.

Joseph b. Tanḥum the Jerusalemite

In the second half of the thirteenth century a faithful perpetuator of the Andalusi tradition of Hebrew poetry lived in Egypt, Joseph ben Tanḥum the Jerusalemite (1262–after 1330). He was distinguished in his broad Hebrew and Arabic erudition; indeed, he wrote in both languages. From his Hebrew writing 860 poems survive in manuscripts.[72] His main patron was the *nagid* of the Jews of Egypt, David ben Abraham ben Moses Maimonides (c. 1222–1300). When Joseph was only sixteen years old, he presented to David Maimuni a collection of poems based on homonyms (*shire tzimmudim*), in which each stanza concludes with a word that sounds the same, but has a different meaning. In this collection, he is following the famous homonym poems of Moses ibn ʿEzra in his work *Sefer ha-ʿAnaq*; it has the same number of chapters, ten, in accordance with the poems' contents.[73] Joseph wrote a second collection of homonym poems, *Maqāmat al-Tanjīs*, at a later point in his life, in which he included also a commentary, in Arabic, on his uses of homonyms and rare words. His rich *dīwān*, which remains unpublished, is divided into seven sections: liturgical poems, *maqāma*s, epistles, panegyrics, songs of love and wine, eulogies and laments, and, finally, riddles in Arabic and Hebrew.

Joseph the Jerusalemite, like many other Egyptian poets, was not born in Egypt, but in the Land of Israel. All his life he wanted to return to Jerusalem and to Hebron, although he lived in Fusṭāṭ from 1276 onward. The *nagid*, David Maimuni, who had been forced to leave Islamic Fusṭāṭ for five years and flee to Crusader Acre, was able to return to his office of *nagid* in Egypt in 1289, at which point our poet gave him a warm welcome in a letter studded with panegyric poems.[74]

Especially famous is the lament that Joseph ben Tanḥum wrote for the slaughtered Jews of Acre, including his father, the famous grammarian Tanḥum the Jerusalemite. In 1291, the Egyptian sultan al-Sharāf destroyed Acre, the last fortress of the Crusader kingdom in Palestine. Along with the Christians,

---

72 Hayim Vitaly Yehudah Sheynin, *An Introduction to the Poetry of Joseph Ben Tanhum Ha-Yerushalmi and to the History of Its Research: A Study Based Primarily upon Manuscripts from the Cairo Genizah* (PhD diss., University of Pennsylvania, 1988). This dissertation is based, to a great extent, on fragments of *dīwān*s in the Firkovitch collection, which originate in the Dar Simḥah *genizah*. Since this dissertation, not much further work has been done on Joseph ben Tanḥum.

73 Judith Dishon (ed.), *The Book of the Perfumed Flower Beds by Joseph ben Tanḥum ha-Yerushalmi* (Beer Sheva: Ben Gurion University of the Negev, 2015) [in Hebrew].

74 Ḥayyim Brody, "Hidden Treasures," *Qovetz ʿal Yad* 9 (1893): 2–19 [in Hebrew].

only a few of whom escaped, the Jewish community—men, women, and children—was massacred by the conquerors. In his long lament, Joseph expresses his sorrow for the murder of the Jews of Acre:

> Woe, for the sages, whose mouths had much wisdom, sweet like honey to the jaws. . . .
> The society of nobles, slaughtered for their love of God, to whom they spread out their hands. . . .
> Dignified women, [from whom the babes] suckled the breasts of the Holy Language, before they suckled [actual] breasts.
> And they lost the sons, for whom they toiled in vain, and for naught they sat upon the birthing-stool.
> Woe, for the children, who knew not good or evil, at whom the enemies gnashed teeth,
> And they destroyed the palace of the living God, along with the children, who had never used their hands to sin.[75]

In the intellectual society where the poet had been born and raised, in Jerusalem, the mothers were very learned, and they would teach the boys Hebrew before they were entrusted to the men. He himself was already able to write a large book of homonym poems at the age of fifteen. Joseph the Jerusalemite mourns these children, for whom their mothers toiled in vain, for they were massacred in the Acre synagogue at an age when they had not yet even tasted sin.

Al-Ḥarīzī on Egyptian Poetry: instead of a conclusion

The great critic of Egyptian Hebrew poetry, Judah al-Ḥarīzī (1165–1225) came to Egypt from the extreme west of the time. However, he came not as a curious young man, yearning for knowledge, like his contemporary Joseph ha-Maʿaravi and many others, but as an already-renowned poet (in 1216). His criticism of the local poets may have been connected to questions of differing mentality and poetic and social practices of an unfamiliar type. He lavished praises on Joseph ha-Maʿaravi's *maqāma*, whose author resembled him in origin and education, but he was not so pleased with the local poets, who were accustomed to write also in Arabic. The local Jewish courtly culture was not comprehensive

75 Ḥayyim Schirmann, "Laments for the Persecutions in Palestine, Africa, Spain, Germany, and France," *Qovetz ʿal Yad* 3/13 (1940): 62–4 [in Hebrew].

enough to be the sole venue for a Jewish poet in Egypt, so he, too, needed to write poetry also in Arabic. Ultimately, al-Ḥarīzī fit himself to this local practice; over a hundred Arabic poems survive from his pen, which he wrote in the East; and he surely wrote others, which have not survived.[76] All this occurred during his journeys through the East, which began in Egypt; we have not even a single Arabic poem from his career in the West.

While in Egypt, al-Ḥarīzī was extremely critical of local compositions. In order to insult the local poets, al-Ḥarīzī constructed a scheme of seven criteria for successful poetry. At the very bottom of the schema, he placed his contemporary poets in the East, especially those in Egypt. He referred to them with the following re-interpretation of a Biblical verse: "moreover I have seen the oppression wherewith the Egyptians oppress them" (Ex. 3:8), where he reads the word "oppression" (*laḥatz*) as "force," that is, he views the poetry in Egypt as very forced. His chapter on the evaluation of poetry concludes thus:

> And when I went through the lands of the East, I saw communities, / very great and praiseworthy, / with all sorts of qualities.
> But the poems that they write—I listened, and heard that they do not speak properly.
> For all their poetry is like broken pottery, like straw without wheat. . . .
> And I felt greatly sorry for the poems whose beauty the Egyptians ruined, / and they crushingly oppressed them, and afflicted them, and I saw the force wherewith the Egyptians force them.[77]

Al-Harīzī was wrong. Hebrew poetry in Spain indeed reached heights that the Egyptian poets could only attempt to imitate. It was not for nothing that Joseph ben Tanḥum the Jerusalemite began his career by writing a book of homonym poems in which he attempted to out-do Moses ibn ʿEzra's famous book in this genre. On the other hand, *genizah* fragments preserve examples of poetry that indicate the unique path of Egyptian poets, who continued the old Eastern tradition of poetry. In the circles around the *yeshivot,* they continued to write monorhymed poems also in syllabic meters, which in Spain were reserved exclusively for liturgical poetry. Perhaps this was one of the reasons that aroused al-Harīzī's critique against the local poets. Unlike them, he felt

76 Joshua Blau, Joseph Yahalom, and Paul Fenton (eds.), *Kitāb al-Durār* (Jerusalem: Yad Izhak Ben-Zvi, 2009).

77 Yahalom and Katsumata, *Taḥkemoni*, 22.

free to present Arabic panegyrics, too, to local benefactors. On contrast, the local poets felt beholden to the Hebrew liturgy of the synagogue where they got paid, and continued therefore to use Hebrew as their general poetic language. As a total stranger, al-Harīzī was free to express himself simultaneously not only in Hebrew, but also in Arabic. He was also free to circulate his Arabic poems among Jews as well as among gentiles. His superiority over the local poets was thus conspicuous.[78]

78 Joseph Yahalom, "Arabic and Hebrew as Poetic Languages within Muslim and Jewish Society: Judah Alḥarizi, between East and West," *Leshonenu* 74 (2012): 305–21.

11

The Jews in Medieval Egypt under the Mamluks (1250–1517)

AMIR MAZOR

When Obadiah of Bertinoro, the famous commentator on the Mishnah, visited Cairo in February 1488, he mentioned that "the custom of the Jews is always to represent themselves as poor in the country of the Arabs; they go about as beggars, humbling themselves before the Arabs; they are not charitable towards one another."[1] This and other gloomy observations by travelers who visited Egypt and the Holy Land at that time are usually quoted by modern historians in order to illustrate the severe deterioration in the situation of the Jews in Egypt towards the end of the Mamluk period.

Indeed, it is widely accepted among scholars that the Mamluk period witnessed a significant decline in the circumstances of the Jews in Egypt and Syria, and in Mamluk Islamicate society in general.[2] Recently, a few studies have tried to challenge this thesis.[3] However, as all historical sources indicate, the Mamluk period does mark deterioration in almost in every aspect

---

1 E. N. Adler, ed., *Jewish Travelers: A Treasury of Travelogues from Nine Centuries* (New York: Hermon Press, 1966), 227–8.

2 See, for instance, Eliyahu Ashtor and Reuven Amitai, "Mamluks," *Enyclopedia Judaica*, 2nd edition, vol. 13, 438–41; Norman A. Stillman, *The Jews of Arab Lands: A History and Source Book* (Philadelphia: Jewish Publication Society of America, 1979), 67–75.

3 Nathan Hofer, "The Ideology of Decline and the Jews of Ayyubid and Mamluk Syria," in *Muslim-Jewish Relations in the Middle Islamic Period: Jews in the Ayyubid and Mamluk Sultanates (1171–1517)*, ed. Stephan Conermann (Göttingen: V & R Unipress, 2017), 95–120, and see the references at 97, note 8.

of Jewish life. Nevertheless, depicting the situation of Egyptian Jewry during this whole long period as a nadir, as it is sometimes described by modern historians, is somewhat superficial. Reality, as always, was more complicated and complex.

The Mamluk sultanate

The mamluks were slave soldiers, often of Turkish and Central Asian origin, sold and brought from the north-eastern boundaries of the Islamic world. The system had deep roots, and mamluk military slavery formed the backbone of the Islamic armies as early as the start of the ninth century. In 1250, however, the Mamluk officers in Cairo took the throne and became, for the first time in Islamic history, *de facto* and *de jure* Muslim rulers. Through the next decade, and after defeating the Mongol forces in the battle of ʿAyn Jālūt in Palestine (1260), the Mamluks would succeed in expanding their dominion, ruling now over Greater Syria (al-Shām) in addition to Egypt. Cairo, the residence of the sultan and the viceroy, remained the center of Mamluk rule, whereas Syria was divided into several districts, each headed by a governor, a mamluk *amir* (officer) who was appointed from Cairo. The biggest and most important district was Damascus, and the others were Aleppo, Hama, Homs, Kerak (Transjordan), Safad, Tripoli and Gaza.

The Mamluk sultanate was based on the constant importation of manpower into Egypt and Syria. Usually, the slave-soldiers were brought to the sultanate as young boys, converted to Islam, and received religious and military training, after which they were manumitted and began a military career in which they could advance to the ranks of officers (*amirs*). The Mamluk period is generally divided into two halves, the Turkish period (1250–1382) and the Circassian period (1382–1517), sometimes mistakenly also known as "the Baḥrī" or "the Burjī" periods respectively.[4] Whereas during the first period

4 The term "Baḥrī" refers to the Baḥriyya, a regiment that was built up by the last important Ayyubid sultan, Najm al-Dīn al-Ṣāliḥ Ayyūb (r. 1240–9). The regiment was thus named, because its mamluks were garrisoned in the Rawḍa Island in the Nile River (*baḥr al-nīl*), outside Cairo. The term Burjī also refers to a place where a regiment dwelt. The mamluks of the Burjiyya were stationed by sultan Qalāwūn (r. 1279–90) in the towers (*burj*, pl. *abrāj*) of the Cairo citadel. However, contemporary historians do not use these terms regarding the two periods. Moreover, only two sultans of the Turkish period were in fact members of the Baḥriyya (Baybars I and Qalāwūn), whereas Barqūq (r. 1382–9 and 1390–9), the first sultan of the Circassian period, had no relation to the Burjiyya regiment. See David Ayalon,

most mamluks and sultans were of Turkish or Turco-Mongol origin, in the second one they were largely Circassians.

Precisely because the mamluks were born as non-Muslims, they tended to demonstrate zeal for Sunni Islam. In order to prove their loyalty to their new religion and in gratitude to the culture that raised them from slavery to high military and political positions, the mamluks continued all the more forcefully the fostering of Sunni Islam, a process that was initiated by Saladin after the removal of the Shiʿī Fatimid Caliphate in 1171. Mamluk sultans and amirs established many dozens of Islamic institutions, such as Islamic law colleges (*madrasas*) and sufi convents (*khānqāhs*, *ribāṭs*, or *zāwiyyas*). In addition, they appointed four chief judges, one for each Sunni rite, instead of the single Shāfiʿī judge appointed by Saladin.

The mamluks' identification with the Islamic cause definitely contributed to their military success against their enemies. In fact, the Mamluk sultanate had to deal with several significant external threats, especially during the first decades of its existence. The most important ones were the Crusaders and the Mongols. The Mamluks conducted a fierce war against the remnants of the Frankish principalities in Syria, until they brought about the final expulsion of the Crusaders from Palestine in 1291. A more serious threat to the sultanate came from the Mongol Ilkhanate in Iran, Iraq, and Azerbaijan, with whom extensive conflicts were ongoing for more than a half century. During these wars Syria was even occupied by the Mongols for few months in 1300. A peace treaty was signed between the two states only in 1323.[5] Afterwards, the sultanate generally had no serious external enemies, except the Turco-Mongol conqueror Timur Leng, who succeeded in conquering Syria for a short period in 1400, and the Ottomans who threatened the sultanate toward the end of the Mamluk period. The latter brought about the end of the Mamluk sultanate in Egypt and Syria, in 1516–17.

"Baḥrī Mamluks, Burjī Mamluks—Inadequate Names for the Two Reigns of the Mamluk Sultanate," *Tārīḫ* 1 (1990): 22–4, 39.

5 On the Mamluk-Ilkhanid struggle and confrontations in 1260–81, see Reuven Amitai-Preiss, *Mongols and Mamluks: The Mamluk-Ilkhanid War, 1260–1281* (Cambridge: Cambridge University Press, 1995). For a later period: Amir Mazor, *The Rise and Fall of a Muslim Regiment: The Manṣūriyya in the First Mamluk Sultanate, 678/1279–741/1341* (Göttingen: V & R Unipress, 2015), vol. 10 of *Mamluk Studies*, 113–28.

Economic and demographic trends

During the Mamluk period, Egypt suffered an ongoing severe economic crisis. The crisis was the consequence of several circumstances. The most important one was the outbreak of plagues and epidemics in Egypt. The Black Death in 1348–49 caused the loss of a third of the population of Egypt and Syria. During the fifteenth century and until the end of the Mamluk period there were no less than another twelve epidemics. The continuous outbreaks of this pandemic brought about significant depopulation of both cities and rural areas; villages were abandoned. The revenues from lands, which supported the ruling and military establishment, steadily diminished; the quantity and quality of manufactured goods substantially declined. The implications of the plague, as well as global developments, brought about a clear decline also in international trade from the late fourteenth to the mid-fifteenth centuries. Furthermore, Mongol invasions of Syria during the first seven decades of the Mamluk sultanate and at the beginning of the fifteenth century, increased the devastation of the country and the decline of crafts. In order to replenish the depleted treasury, the sultans adopted abusive policies that included imposing heavy taxes on the populations, cruel confiscations, monopolies of certain commodities and suppression of *laissez-faire* trade, together with outrageous corruption and exploitation of peasants.[6]

All these harsh circumstances badly affected the whole Egyptian economy, but were particularly destructive for the Jews, since there were certain levies and contributions which were imposed only on *dhimmīs*, such as the taxes on production and consumption of wine, and on communal events such as burials and weddings, and higher rates of customs on goods. More *ad hoc* fines were

6 P. M. Holt, *The Age of the Crusades: The Near East from the Eleventh Century to 1517* (London: Longman, 1986), 194–5; R. Stephen Humphreys, "Egypt in the World System of the Later Middle Ages," in *The Cambridge History of Egypt*, vol. 1: *Islamic Egypt, 640–1517*, ed. Carl F. Petry (Cambridge: Cambridge University Press, 1998), 457–60; Sato Tsugitaka, *State and Rural Society in Medieval Islam: Sultans, Muqta's and Fallahun* (Leiden: Brill, 1997), 236–9; Ira M. Lapidus, *Muslim Cities in the Later Middle Ages* (Cambridge, MA: Harvard University Press, 1967), 25–38; E. Ashtor (Strauss), *Toledot ha-yehudim be-Mitzrayim ve-Suryah taḥat shilton ha-mamlukim* [*The History of the Jews in Egypt and Syria under Mamluk Rule*] (Jerusalem: Mossad ha-Rav Kook, 1944–51), vol. 2, 157–8, 162–3 [in Hebrew]; Georg Christ, *Trading Conflicts: Venetian Merchants and Mamluk Officials in Late Medieval Alexandria* (Leiden: Brill, 2012), 32–4.

imposed on the Jewish community at random, and it seems that these fines were imposed on the Jews in Egypt more than on Syrian Jewry.[7]

The continuous economic decline brought about a substantial diminution of the Jewish Egyptian middle class, which flourished during the Fatimid and Ayyubid periods. The number of Jewish artisans and industrialists, as well as the number of great merchants, drastically decreased.[8]

This demographic decline was significant especially if we bear in mind that since the last quarter of the tenth century, with the establishment of the new city of Cairo as the capital of the Fatimid caliphate, Egypt came to be a prominent center for Jews. Nevertheless, the decline in Egyptian Jewish population started already in the Ayyubid period, due to disastrous famine and epidemics in the years 1217 and 1235–36. These natural disasters continued even more forcefully during the Mamluk period, and brought about serious diminution of the Jewish, as well as of the general, population.[9]

One of the implications of the economic and demographic decline was the dwindling of cities and towns. Several dozens of Egyptian cities and villages with Jewish population are mentioned in Genizah documents from the pre-Mamluk period.[10] At the end of the Fatimid period, there were about forty-two communities in Egypt. The well-known Jewish traveler, R. Benjamin of Tudela, who visited Cairo around 1168, mentions fifteen communities, to which twenty-seven may be added. The biggest congregations were in the cities of Cairo and Alexandria, which included several thousands of Jews.[11]

7 Ashtor, *History*, vol. 2, 310–16. According to Ashtor's calculations, the authorities did not exploit the *dhimmīs* by imposing special heavy poll taxes on them, see in depth: ibid., 263ff. esp. 269–70, 291. On the high rate of taxes imposed on Jews in certain posts on the caravan route between Egypt and Syria, see the testimony of Meshullam of Volterra: Adler, *Jewish Travelers*, 176. The law regarding heavy rates of customs for non-Muslims was not applied in the Fatimid period but revived by Saladin for a certain time, see Goitein, *Mediterranean Society*, vol. 2, 289; and vol. 1, 345.

8 Ashtor, *History*, vol. 2, 155–7, 163. On the professions of Jews in this period see: ibid., vol. 1, 176ff, 2:158ff.

9 Goitein, *Mediterranean Society*, vol. 2, 139–42; Michael Dols, *The Black Death in the Middle East* (Princeton, NJ: Princeton University Press, 1977), 33–4; Holt, *The Age of the Crusades*, 194.

10 Golb, "The Topography of the Jews," 266–70; idem, "The Topography of the Jews of Medieval Egypt. VI. Places of Settlement of the Jews of Medieval Egypt."

11 Ashtor, "The Number of Jews in Medieval Egypt I," 13.

In the Mamluk period, however, we have indications for only around twenty-five communities in all Egypt.[12]

It would be very speculative to give exact numbers of Jews during these periods. The estimations, however, clearly indicate a decrease in the general population from the Fatimid period to the late fifteenth century. Estimations of the population size of pre-Mamluk Cairo-Fusṭāṭ, of both Rabbanites and Karaites until the plague and famine of 1201–2, range from 1500,[13] through more than 4000,[14] to 7000.[15] However, at the end of the fifteenth century, when the vast majority of Egyptian Jewry lived in Cairo, there were, according to the Jewish travelers Meshullam of Volterra (1481) and Obadiah of Bertinoro (1488), about 700–800 families of Jews. According to Obadiah, there were 500 families of Rabbanite Jews, 150 Karaite families, and fifty Samaritans.[16] In Alexandria the diminishing of the community is more discernable: from the 3000 mentioned by Benjamin of Tudela, or 700–800 if we accept Ashtor's estimate—to 25–60 families or even less. The Karaite community in the city vanished totally.[17]

---

12 For recent survey of Jewish communities in Mamluk Egypt, see Dotan Arad, "The Mustaʿrib Jews in Syria, Palestine and Egypt 1330–1700" (PhD diss., The Hebrew University, 2013), 26–36 [in Hebrew]; see also Abraham David, "The Jewish Settlements from the Sixteenth Century to the Eighteenth Century," in *Toledot yehudey Mitzrayim ba-tequfah ha-Ottomanit 1517–1914* [*The Jews in Ottoman Egypt 1517–1914*], ed. J. M. Landau (Jerusalem: Misgav Yerushalayim, 1988), 13–26 [in Hebrew]. Arad mentions evidence for the following communities (besides Cairo-Fusṭāṭ): al-Khanqāh, Banhā al-ʿAsal, Minyat Ghamr, Bilbays, Fāqūs, Minyat Ziftā, Sunbāṭ, Maḥalla al-Kubrā, Jawjar, Damīra, Fāraskūr, Dimyāṭ, Malīj, Alexandria, Dammūh, Fayūm, al-Ṭūr in Sinai, and another three communities in places whose locations in Egypt are unknown: Naqqāṣ, Fīsha, and Fāw. Other communities might have existed in Qalyūb, Baḥṭīṭ, Samanūd, Manzalā, Fūwa, and Qaṭyā. Ashtor discussed some of these communities and raised the possibility of Jewish communities also in Qūṣ, Rashīd (Rosetta), and al-Ṣāliḥiyya (Ashtor, *History*, vol. 1, 246–51; vol. 2, 112–13, 423).

13 See E. Ashtor, "Prolegomena to the Medieval History of Oriental Jewry," *JQR* 50 (1959–60): 56–8; idem, "The Number of Jews I," 20; idem, "The Number of Jews in Medieval Egypt II," *JJS* 19 (1968): 12.

14 Goitein, *Mediterranean Society*, vol. 2, 139–40; Norman Stillman, "The Non-Muslim Communities: The Jewish Community," in *The Cambridge History of Egypt*, vol. 1: *Islamic Egypt 640-1517*, ed. Carl F. Petry (Cambridge: Cambridge University Press, 1998), 202, note 7.

15 If we accept one version of the problematic manuscript of Benjamin's travelogue. The number in the manuscript could also be read as 2000 only, see Ashtor, *History*, vol. 1, 32, note 4.

16 Adler, *Jewish Travelers*, 171, 225.

17 Ashtor, "The number of Jews I," 13; idem, "The number of Jews II," 12. Jacob Mann presumed that there were 300 families in Alexandria in 1028, see Mann, *The Jews in Egypt*, vol. 1, 88, cf. Ashtor, "Prolegomena," 58–60. According to Meshullam there were in 1481 about sixty families, all Rabinnites. Meshullam notes that some Jews in the city remember that

The dwindling Jewish communities in Egypt moved mainly to the capital. During the Mamluk period, most of the Jews of Fusṭāṭ gradually moved to the adjacent new city of Cairo. In the first half of the fourteenth century there were still about 200 Jewish families in Fusṭāṭ.[18] The Jews in Fusṭāṭ used to live mainly around the ancient neighborhood of Qaṣr al-Shamaʿ, and the nearby Maṣṣāṣa (or Mamṣūṣa) quarter and the adjacent lane known as *zuqāq al-Yahūd* ("the lane of the Jews"). The two ancient synagogues—the Babylonian and the Palestinian—remained and were maintained also when Jews did not live in the city anymore, in the sixteenth century. There was another Karaite synagogue in this quarter. In Cairo, from the eleventh century Jews mainly lived in the Zuwayla neighborhood, known until modern time as the neighborhood of the Jews. According to both Muslim and Jewish sources, in the fifteenth century there were five or six synagogues in Cairo.[19]

The integration of Jews into Mamluk society

The extent of Jewish integration in Islamicate social, cultural and intellectual life was definitely limited in Mamluk times, compared to former periods. Still, by no means were the Jews in Mamluk Egypt an isolated community. In this aspect, a comparison with Latin Europe in the late Middle Ages is instructive. Jews never lived in total "ghetto-like" isolation as in Europe. There were mosques, Sufi convents, and other Islamic institutions in the Jewish districts of Cairo, as well as in other Muslim cities.[20] Jews participated in official public and religious events and ceremonies such as royal processions and coronations. These events took place, for instance, following an appointment of a sultan or a caliph in Cairo, or as part of a welcome reception for a new governor of a city, or

once there were 4000 house owners (Adler, *Jewish Travelers*, 161). Obadiah mentions that there are only about twenty-five families in the city (ibid., 222).

18 S. D. Goitein, "Dimdumey ʿerev shel beyt ha-Rambam" [The Twilight of the House of Maimonides], *Tarbiz* 54 (1984): 100 [in Hebrew].

19 Stillman, "The Jewish community," 202; Adler, *Jewish Travelers*, 167, 171–2; Taqī al-Dīn Aḥmad ibn ʿAlī al-Maqrīzī, *al-Mawāʿiẓ wa-l-iʿtibār bi-dhikr al-khiṭaṭ wa-l-āthār fī Miṣr wa-l-Qāhira* (Cairo: Bulaq, 1854), vol. 2, 471–2; Ashtor, *History*, vol. 1, 237ff, 243–4; vol. 2, 317, 421.

20 Lapidus, *Muslim Cities*, 85–6, 271; S. D. Goitein, "*Cairo: An Islamic City in the Light of the Geniza Documents*," in *Middle Eastern Cities*, ed. Ira M. Lapidus (Berkeley and Los Angeles: University of California Press, 1969), 80–1; Paul B. Fenton, "Sufis and Jews in Mamluk Egypt," in *Muslim-Jewish Relations in the Middle Islamic Period: Jews in the Ayyubid and Mamluk Sultanates (1171–1517)*, ed. Stephan Conermann (Göttingen: V & R Unipress, 2017), 45–6; Ashtor, *History*, vol. 1, 242–3; al-Maqrīzī, *Khiṭaṭ*, vol. 2, 368.

following news about Muslim victory in the battlefield. Jews also participated in public ceremonial events such as royal celebrations in the sultan's court or funerals of distinguished statesmen or scholars. On the other hand, they also took part in the public humiliation of hated officials who were removed from their high position. Jews, together with Christians and Muslims, used to worship at the same sacred sites and to take part in prayers for rain, for the inundation of the Nile or for the end of epidemics.[21] In this respect it is instructive that during the Black Death, in the mid-fourteenth century, European Jews were victims of massive pogroms and were believed to have poisoned wells "in attempt to destroy Christian civilization." On the other hand, nowhere in the Mamluk sultanate at that time were Jews blamed for this epidemic, which was perceived as a natural disaster. Moreover, in Damascus, Muslims, Christians and Jews prayed together, pleading to the one God for salvation and the removal of evil destiny.[22]

In addition to official and public events, Jews maintained daily and more intimate conviviality with Muslims through encounters in public places. Jews and other *dhimmīs* were usually not prevented from visiting public baths [*ḥammāms*], together with Muslims, in contrast to Latin Europe at that time, where Jews were forbidden from visiting public baths on the same days as Christians. In the Mamluk period, however, Jews and Christians had to distinguish themselves from Muslims when they visited the baths (see below). Social encounters between Jews and Muslims took place also in the public houses in the Jewish neighborhoods, where they drank and spent hours together.[23]

Jews were not excluded from intellectual life either, especially until the mid-fourteenth century. They took part not only in theological disputations

---

21 Ashtor, *History*, vol. 1, 328–34; vol. 2, 105; Muḥammad ibn Aḥmad ibn Iyās, *Badāʾiʿ al-zuhūr fī waqāʾiʿ al-dhuhūr*, ed. Muḥammad Muṣṭafā (Cairo and Wiesbaden: Franz Steiner Verlag, 1392/1972), vol. 2, 282; Daniel Boušek, "'. . . And the Ishmaelites Honour the Site': Images of Encounters between Jews and Muslims at Jewish Sacred Places in Medieval Hebrew Travelogues," *Archív Orientální* 86, no. 1 (2018): 26; Fenton, "Sufis and Jews," 43–4; see also Mark R. Cohen, "Sociability and the Concept of Galut in Jewish-Muslim relations in the Middle Ages," in *Judaism and Islam: Boundaries, Communication and Interaction. Essays in Honor of William M. Brinner*, ed. Benjamin H. Hary et al. (Leiden: Brill, 2000), 37–51. For Mamluk Syria, see Hofer, "The Ideology," 102–3, 114.

22 Cohen, *Under Crescent and Cross*, 169; Ismāʿīl ibn ʿUmar Ibn Kathīr, *al-Bidāya wa-l-nihāya* (Beirut: Dār al-Iḥyāʾ al-Turāth al-ʿArabī, 1413/1993), vol. 14, 261. This episode was also witnessed by the famous traveler Ibn Baṭṭūṭa, see: *Voyages d'Ibn Batoutah*, ed. and trans. C. Defrémery and B. R. Sanguinetti (Paris: n.p., 1853), vol. 1, 227–9. A similar event in Egypt is mentioned regarding the plague of 1419, see: Ibn Iyās, *Badāʾiʿ al-zuhūr*, vol. 2, 46.

23 Ashtor, *History*, vol. 1, 334–5; Cohen, "*Galut*," 39.

[*munāẓarāt*] with prominent Muslim religious scholars [*ʿulamāʾ*]—a phenomenon that Muslim sources occasionally mention, but also in secular scientific discussions. Prominent Jewish physicians in Mamluk Egypt had distinguished Muslim teachers and close associates.[24]

Jews especially became entranced by the appeal of Islamic spiritual and intellectual Sufism, including the writings of great Muslim Sufis, such as the famous Abū Ḥāmid al-Ghazālī (d. 1111). One of the prominent leaders of the Judaeo-Sufi circle in Egypt, known as *ḥasidim*, was Maimonides's son, Abraham (1186–1237). In his writings, Abraham Maimonides laid the foundations for a Jewish Sufism. He presented Islamic Sufism as a restoration of forgotten ancient Jewish customs rooted in the biblical and the rabbinical traditions. This new pietistic tendency would continue to be fostered in the Mamluk sultanate by members of this *ḥasidim* circle and especially by members of the Maimonidean dynasty.[25] Instructive evidence of the strong appeal of Sufism among Egyptian Jews is a case, known from a Genizah document from the fourteenth century, in which a Cairene Jew entered a Sufi convent on Muqaṭṭam hill near Cairo, abandoning his wife and three children.[26]

Muslim-Jewish intellectual influences did not go only in one direction, from Islam to Judaism. There are some references to Muslim intellectuals who were acquainted with Jewish philosophical and medical writings, studied them and cited them in their treatises. This is especially true for the learning of Maimonides's *Guide for the Perplexed* and *Mishneh Torah* among the Muslims.[27]

---

24 Ashtor, *History*, vol. 1, 350–1; Fenton, "Sufis and Jews," 47–8; Joel Kraemer, "The Andalusian Mystic Ibn Hūd and the Conversion of the Jews," *IOS* 12 (1992): 65; Amir Mazor, "Jewish Court Physicians in the Mamluk Sultanate during the First Half of the 8th/14th Century," *Medieval Encounters* 20 (2014): 48–49, 50–52.

25 On several aspects of Sufi spiritual, intellectual and social influences on Jews in Mamluk Egypt, see Fenton, "Sufis and Jews," 41–62; Kraemer, "Andalusian Mystic," 60ff, esp. 65–6. On Abraham Maimonides and his descendants, see also Russ-Fishbane, *Judaism, Sufism and the Pietists of Medieval Egypt*, esp. the bibliography at 6, note 15.

26 S. D. Goitein, "A Jewish Addict to Sufism in the Time of the Nagid David II Maimonides," *JQR* 44 (1953–4): 37–49.

27 See about the learning and teaching of the Maimonides's *Guide for the Perplexed* among Muslims: Kraemer, "Andalusian Mystic," 71–2; Fenton, "Sufis and Jews," 49; Ashtor, *History*, vol. 1, 352–6; Moritz Steinschneider, *Die Hebraeischen Übersetzungen des Mittelalters und die Juden als Dolmetscher* (Berlin: Kommissionsverlag des Bibliographischen Bureaus, 1893), 361–3; Gregor Schwarb, "ʿAlī ibn Ṭaybughā's Commentary on Maimonides' Mishneh Torah, Sefer ha-Maddaʿ, Hilkhot Yesodei ha-Torah I–IV: A Philosophical 'Encyclopaedia' of the 14th Century" (forthcoming. I thank Prof. Schwarb for sharing with me a draft of his article). For quotations of famous Jewish doctors in a Muslim medical work, see Ṣalāḥ al-Dīn ibn Yūsuf al-Kaḥḥāl al-Ḥamawī, *Nūr al-ʿuyūn wa-jāmiʿ al-funūn*, ed. Muḥammad

It should be noted, however, that most of the evidence for all the cases of Muslim-Jewish intellectual symbiosis mentioned above are from the first century of the Mamluk sultanate.

Self-Government: The Nagidate

At the head of the Jewish communities in Mamluk Egypt stood the *nagid*. The origin of the office of the *nagid* is a controversial issue among scholars.[28] However, it is clear that by the Mamluk period, the office of the Jewish *nagid* was already strongly established in Egypt, with officially defined responsibilities, as detailed in contemporary Muslim sources. The *nagid* was responsible for the consolidation of the Jewish community, its administration according to the religious laws, ensuring compliance with the Pact of ʿUmar, supervision of religion and social services and maintenance of law and order by the community. He was the sole representative of the Jewish community, including the Karaites and Samaritans, before the Muslim authorities. He also had deputies, at least in the fifteenth century, in Jerusalem and Damascus. Thus, in the Mamluk period, the Jewish *nagid* was the supreme and most powerful Jewish authority, responsible for every aspect of Jewish communal life.[29]

The descendants of Moses Maimonides (1138–1204) served as *nagid*s during most of the Turkish and the beginning of the Circassian periods. After the tenure of the last Maimonidean *nagid,* R. David b. Joshua (around 1400), an unclear period in the Nagidate lasted until the 1450s. During this period, at least four *nagid*s held this post. It was only in the second half of the fifteenth century that the Nagidate became strong again, until the office was demolished in 1517 with the Ottoman conquest. The four last *nagid*s reigned for long periods. Being closely connected to the Muslim authorities, they enjoyed considerable political power. They were also highly esteemed by the Jews of Egypt and by world Jewry.

The first two of these *nagid*s were R. Joseph b. Khalīfa and his son, Solomon. The Jewish traveler Meshullam of Volterra testified that R. Joseph served as a physician of the sultan. This is a significant remark, for since the

Ẓāfir al-Wafāʾī (Riyadh: Markaz al-Malik Fayṣal li-l-Buḥūth wa-l-Dirāsāt al-Islāmiyya, 1987), 112–13, 143, 149, 502 (Maimonides). Other Jewish physicians are quoted on 175, 287, 292, 520, 544.

28 For the different views see, for instance: Elinoar Bareket, "Nagid," in Encyclopedia Judaica, 2nd edition, vol. 14, 731; Stillman, "The Jewish Community," 204.

29 Stillman, "The Jewish community," 205; Bareket, "Nagid"; Goitein, *Mediterranean Society*, vol. 2, 33–40.

reign of Abraham b. Moses Maimonides in the Ayyubid period, there was no clear evidence of *nagids* who served as court physicians.[30] Joseph's son, Solomon, whom Meshullam met in 1481, is described by the later as "a Jewish lord, rich and learned and much honored."[31] We learn from Meshullam's observations that Solomon had strong authority over his people, high prestige, and good relations with the sultan and with the Mamluk elite. The last two *nagids* were Nathan (Jonathan) ha-Kohen Sholel (r. 1484–1502) and his nephew, Isaac (r. 1502–17, d. 1524). They were even more powerful and vigorous as scholars and as political leaders. They contributed much to the spiritual revival of Egyptian Jewry. R. Isaac Sholel, the last *nagid*, encouraged cultural religious activity in Cairo and in Jerusalem. During his tenure he took care of a *yeshivah* in Cairo, which included great and famous scholars. He also supported the students of the *yeshivahs* in Palestine financially and exempted them from paying taxes. He assisted the Sephardi exiles who arrived in Egypt and appointed the great scholars among them, who were intellectually superior to the local *musta ʿrib* Jews (see below), as *dayyans* and as yeshiva members. His efforts to establish Egypt as spiritual center for Jews succeeded, as we learn from responsa sent to the sages of Egypt from remote communities.[32]

30 Adler, *Jewish Travelers*, 172. One of the judges (*dayyans*) in the court of the *nagid* Solomon was also a physician of the sultan (ibid., 173); A physician *nagid* was appointed in 1285, and Ashtor (*History*, vol. 1,130) suggests that he might be a physician of the sultan, see: al-Maqrīzī, *Sulūk*, vol. 1, 728; Muḥammad ibn ʿAbd al-Raḥīm Ibn al-Furāt, *Taʾrīkh Ibn al-Furāt* [=*Taʾrīkh al-Duwal wa-l-Mulūk*], ed. Q. Zurayq (Beirut: al-Maṭbaʿa al-Amrīkānīyya, 1936), vol. 8, 18.

31 Adler, *Jewish Travelers*, 172.

32 See on the *nagids* of the fifteenth century, Dotan Arad and Esther-Miriam Wagner, *Wisdom and Greatness in One Place: The Alexandrian Trader Moses Ben Judah and his Circle* (Leiden: Brill, forthcoming), introduction. On Isaac Sholel and his activity: Abraham David, *Ḥevra yehudit Yam Tikhonit be-shalḥey yemei ha-beynayim le-or mismakhey genizat Kahir* [*A Jewish Mediterranean Society in the Late Middle Ages as Reflected in Cairo Genizah Documents*] (New York and Jerusalem: The Jewish Theological Seminary of America, 2016), 235–41 [in Hebrew]. On Isaac Sholel and his reforms see: Ashtor, *History*, vol. 2, 505ff. It is questionable, however, how strong the authority of the *nagids* over the provincial communities outside Egypt was during the fourteenth and especially the fifteenth century, see: Elhanan Reiner, "Hanhagat ha-kehila be-Yerushalayim be-shalḥey ha-tequfa ha-Mamlukit: Teʿudot u-verurim be-shuley parashat ha-zekenim" [Jewish Community Leadership in late Mamluke Jerusalem], *Shalem* 6 (1992): 23–81, esp. 33–7 [in Hebrew].

State policy towards the Jews and their legal status

The Mamluk period is characterized by a stricter enforcement of the Pact of ʿUmar.[33] This attitude of the Mamluk sultans toward Jews and Christians stood in a strict contrast to the policies of the preceding heterodox Ismāʿīlī Fatimid caliphs (969–1171). Except for a short period during the reign of the caliph al-Ḥākim bi-Amr Allāh (1007–21), in which *dhimmīs* were persecuted, the long Fatimid period was characterized by a tolerant attitude towards Jews and Christians. Genizah documents indicate that the requirements for *dhimmīs* to wear distinguishing clothing were not normally enforced and that Jews were employed as high court administrators and physicians.[34] This situation worsened during the Ayyubid sultanate. In order to justify his image as a holy warrior (*mujāhid*) against the infidel crusaders, Saladin strengthened Sunnism in Egypt and implemented some of the laws included in the Pact of ʿUmar. Thus, for example, in the middle of the thirteenth century, Jews in Cairo wore distinctive yellow marks on their turbans, whereas Christians wore their distinctive belt, *zunnār*.[35]

The pressure on the non-Muslims became much stronger during the Mamluk period. This was due to several circumstances:

1. The offensive policy against the crusades, conducted by the early Mamluk sultans, generated an anti-*dhimmī* atmosphere, which was directed against Christians and Jews alike.
2. The Mongol invasions, accompanied by severe epidemics and droughts, brought about economic crises, which increased the people's frustration resulting in religious persecution.
3. As mentioned above, the Mamluk rulers, who were originally non-Muslim military slaves, were anxious to prove their loyalty to their new religion and to gain the support of the ʿ*ulamā*ʾ in order to legitimize and strengthen their rule. Hence, they tended to accept the demands of the ʿ*ulamā*ʾ and the people, and to increase the burden on the *dhimmīs*.

---

33 On the Pact of ʿUmar, see, for instance, Cohen, *Under Crescent and Cross*, 54–64.

34 Goitein, *Mediterranean Society*, vol. 2, 285–9, 374–80. Stillman, "The Jewish community," 201.

35 Al-Maqrīzī, *Khiṭaṭ*, vol. 1, 367, l. 29; Goitein, *Mediterranean Society*, vol. 2, 288; Stillman, *The Jews of Arab Lands*, 68; idem, "The Jewish Community," 207–8.

In what follows we offer a chronological review of the persecutions suffered by Jews during the Mamluk era.

During the Turkish period (1250–1382)

At this time, anti-*dhimmī* persecutions were particularly intense. The opening shot was an event in 1265, when *dhimmī*s in Cairo were accused of setting the city on fire. Sultan Baybars (r. 1260–77) gathered a large group of Christians and Jews in the citadel of Cairo, and ordered them to be burned alive. The group of *dhimmīs* was finally released in return for a huge amount of money,[36] but this was the beginning of a long series of persecutions. During the 1280s, Sultan Qalāwūn (r. 1279–90) issued decrees that prohibited Jews and Christians from working in governmental offices or in the service of Mamluk officers (amirs), unless they converted to Islam.[37] The harsh conditions of Jews under Qalāwūn, which were described by a contemporary Muslim historian as a state of "extreme humiliation and degradation," continued deep into the 1290s, when the Jews in Cairo became the target of mob harassment and were prohibited from riding horses or mules.[38]

During the fourteenth century, two major waves of anti-*dhimmī* persecutions took place. The first occurred in 1301 when the discriminatory laws of the Pact of ʿUmar were renewed, accompanied by riots against the *dhimmīs* in several towns of Egypt. *Dhimmī* houses of worship were closed by the authorities or destroyed by the mob. While churches were usually the main target for destruction, synagogues were closed and sealed in 1301 for several years, and in 1321 a Karaite synagogue in Damascus was destroyed.[39] Private Jewish residences in Alexandria which were taller than those belonging to Muslims were ruined by the mob. Laws regarding discriminatory clothes were imposed with greater specification: Jews were obliged to wear yellow turbans, Christians, blue, and Samaritans, red ones. As we have already seen, Jews in Egypt wore yellow signs on their turbans already toward the end of the Ayyubid period,

---

36 Ashtor, *History*, vol. 1, 63–7; al-Maqrīzī, *Sulūk*, vol. 1, 535; Ashtor and Amitai, "Mamluks," 439.

37 Al-Maqrīzī, *Sulūk*, vol. 1, 753; al-Maqrīzī, *Khiṭaṭ*, vol. 2, 498, ll. 2–5.

38 Al-Maqrīzī, *Khiṭaṭ*, vol. 2, 497ff; Ibn Kathīr, *al-Bidāya wa-l-nihāya*, vol. 13, 413.

39 Al-Maqrīzī, *Sulūk*, vol. 2, 157, 215; Tamer el-Leithy, "Sufis, Copts and the Politics of Piety: Moral Regulation in Fourteenth-Century Upper Egypt," in *The Development of Sufism in Mamluk Egypt*, ed. Richard McGregor and Adam Sabra (Cairo: Institut français d'archéologie orientale, 2006), 80, note, 22; Joel L. Kraemer, "A Jewish Cult of the Saints in Fāṭimid Egypt," in *L'Egypte Fatimide: son art et son histoire*, ed. Marianne Barrucand (Paris: Presses de l'Université de Paris-Sorbonne, 1999), 598.

but it was only during the Mamluk period that Jews were to be identified exclusively and distinctively with the yellow color, whereas other religions were to be identified by different colors. These persecutions resulted in a substantive wave of conversion to Islam.[40]

The second wave of persecutions broke out in 1354. As many times before, the pretext was "the arrogant behavior" of high-level Copt bureaucrats. The Mamluk elite gave in to the demands of the *ʿulamāʾ*. The Head of the Jews [*nagid*], together with the Coptic patriarch and other representative of the *dhimmīs* were gathered and were obliged to promise to maintain all the discriminatory laws of the Pact of ʿUmar that was ceremonially read in front of them. This time, however, the laws were even more restrictive and some new innovations were introduced: Non-Muslim men were to distinguish themselves even in the public baths by wearing a distinctive metal neck ring, Jewish and Christian women were prohibited from bathing with Muslim women, and *dhimmīs* were prohibited from building even houses that were at the same height of those belonging to Muslims. In addition, *dhimmī* bureaucrats were prohibited from government service even after they converted; *dhimmīs* had to limit the size of their turban to no more than ten cubits; *dhimmīs* were prohibited from purchasing Muslim slaves or slave girls as well as slaves who were owned by Muslims, and from converting slaves to Judaism or Christianity.[41] Of substantial economic implication was the law placing all inheritance matters under the jurisdiction of government authority. *Dhimmīs* could now receive their share in an inheritance only if they could prove that

40 See a summary of the main Arabic sources on this wave of persecutions in Ashtor, *History*, vol. 1, 84–103; Donald P. Little, "Coptic Conversion to Islam under the Bahri Mamluks, 692–755/1293–1354," *BSOAS* 39, no. 3 (1976): 554–8; Stillman, *The Jews of Arab Lands*, 69. For the most detailed list of restrictions that was imposed on the *dhimmīs*, see Shihāb al-Dīn Aḥmad al-Nuwayrī, *Nihāyat al-Arab fi Funūn al-Adab* (Cairo: al-Hayʾa al- Miṣriyya al-ʿAmma lil-Kitāb, 1992–8), vol. 31, 416ff. On the closure of synagogues, as mentioned by Muslim and Jewish sources, see al-Maqrīzī, *Sulūk*, vol. 2, 157; Ashtor, *History*, vol. 1, 101–2; Dotan Arad, "Being a Jew under the Mamluks: Some Coping Strategies," in *Muslim-Jewish Relations in the Middle Islamic Period: Jews in the Ayyubid and Mamluk Sultanates (1171–1517)*, ed. Stephan Conermann (Göttingen: V & R Unipress, 2017), 22. For the clothing regulations, see also Leo A. Mayer, *Mamluk Costume: A Survey* (Genève: Albert Kundig, 1952), 65–6.

41 Stillman, *The Jews of Arab Lands*, 69–70; idem, "The Jewish Community," 209; Mayer, *Mamluk Costume*, 66; Ashtor, *History*, vol. 1, 303–8. See the text of the decree as mentioned by al-Qalqashandī: Shihāb al-Dīn Aḥmad ibn ʿAlī al-Qalqashandī, *Ṣubḥ al-Aʿshā fī Ṣināʿat al-Inshāʾ*, ed. Muḥammad Ḥusayn Shams al-Dīn (Beirut: Dār al-Kutub al-ʿIlmiyya, 1987), vol. 13, 378ff, and partial translation: Stillman, *The Jews of Arab Lands*, 273–4. As for the slave law, see Ashtor, *History*, vol. 2, 235; al-Qalqashandī, vol. 13, 383.

they were eligible to inherit in accordance with Muslim law. The most extreme law was perhaps the one which obliged all the family members of a convert, to convert as well.[42] This state policy was accompanied by mob riots. In Cairo people attacked and destroyed *dhimmī* buildings higher than those belonging to Muslims,[43] Christians and Jews were attacked in the streets by the mob and forced to pronounce the *shahāda* (the Islamic creed), that is, to convert to Islam.[44]

The rise of Islamic zeal during the Turkish period was demonstrated also by the abundance of anti-*dhimmī* polemical literature and responsa (*fatwas*). These works were written by important *ʿulamāʾ* such as Ghāzī Ibn al-Wāsiṭī (d. 1312), Ibn al-Rifāʿa (d. 1310), the famous Taqī al-Dīn Ibn Taymiyya (d. 1328), his student Ibn Qayyim al-Jawziyya (d. 1350), and others. These treatises called for increasing the pressure on the *dhimmīs*, humiliating them and keeping them away from Muslim society.[45]

During the Circassian period of the Mamluk Sultanate (1382–1517)

Persecutions of *dhimmīs* in Egypt lessened to a certain extent at this time and were less acute than the Turkish period. Christians were no longer accused of conspiring with the enemies of Islam, since the Crusade state had been vanquished almost a century before. In addition, in the fifteenth century, the numbers of *dhimmi*—and especially Christian—bureaucrats and high officials were significantly reduced, and subsequently the hatred of the people and *ʿulamāʾ* for the *dhimmīs* subsided to a large extent. It was also especially during this time that the Mamluk elite severely tyrannized and abused all sectors of Egyptian

42 Stillman, *The Jews of Arab Lands*, 274; Tamer el-Leithy, "Coptic Culture and Conversion in Medieval Cairo, 1293–1524 A.D." (unpublished PhD diss., Princeton University, 2005), 96–97.

43 Ashtor, *History*, vol. 2, 219–20.

44 Little, "Coptic conversion," 567; el-Leithy, "Sufis," 81; al-Maqrīzī, *Khiṭaṭ*, vol. 2, 499, l. 35.

45 For the important anti-*dhimmī* literature that emerged and flourished during the first half of the fourteenth century, targeted mostly against Christian Copts, see: el-Leithy, "Sufis," 76, note 6. For selected articles on this literature, see: Cohen, *Under Crescent and Cross*, 229, note 101. For more recent studies, see Luke B. Yarbrough, *Friends of the Emir. Non-Muslim State Officials in Premodern Islamic Thought* (Cambridge: Cambridge University Press, 2019), esp. 219–260; Paulina B. Lewicka, "Did Ibn al-Ḥājj Copy from Cato? Reconsidering Aspects of Inter-Communal Antagonism of the Mamluk Period," in *Ubi sumus? Quo vademus? Mamluk Studies—State of the Art*, ed. Stephan Conermann (Göttingen: V & R Unipress, 2013), 231–61; Daniel Boušek, "Campaign against 'The Protected People' in the Mamluk Period: Ghāzī Ibn al-Wāsitī and his 'Response to the Protected People'," in *The Mediterranean in History. Tribute to prof. Eduard Gombár's 60th Birthday*, ed. Joseph Zenka (Prague: Karolinum, 2012), 205–30, esp. 208–12 [in Czech]. See also n. 86 below.

society. However, it would be mistaken to describe the Circassian period as a better time for Jews than the previous one. The prolonged economic crisis left its marks especially during this period and increased the frustration of the people. The sultans reacted by enforcing the sumptuary laws against the *dhimmīs* more frequently and by imposing heavy contributions and taxes upon them.[46]

Several sultans adopted strict anti-*dhimmī* policies in order to gain the support of influential circles of the *ʿulamāʾ* and to strengthen their rule. Sultan al-Muʾayyad Shaykh (1412–21) increased the poll taxes on the *dhimmīs*, harassed them for drinking wine, imposed discriminatory laws regarding their clothing, and prohibited them from riding even on donkeys. Non-Muslims were dismissed from positions in the state bureaucracy all over Egypt.[47] Barsbāy (1422–38) declared immediately after his coronation that non-Muslims were prohibited from serving in government posts or working in the service of amirs. In 1426, he ordered *dhimmīs* to reduce the size of their turbans and to put iron rings around their necks in public baths. He also harassed *dhimmīs* in Cairo who possessed stocks of wine and sold it.[48] During Jaqmaq's reign (1431–53), a Rabbanite synagogue in Fusṭāṭ was partly destroyed by the authorities in 1442 after anti-Islamic blasphemy was discovered in its dais. Following this incident, other *dhimmī* houses of worship were closed or converted to mosques by the authorities, and churches were destroyed by the people.[49] In 1448, Jaqmaq issued a decree that for the first time prohibited non-Muslim physicians from treating Muslims. In 1450, another decree obliged *dhimmīs* to decrease the size of their turbans even more than had been required for the first time in the discriminatory decrees of 1354.[50] Sultan Khushqadam (1461–67) intensively enforced the laws of the Pact of ʿUmar, among them the sumptuary laws and the occupation regulations, except for the regulations that forbade Jews from practicing medicine and money changing, two typically Jewish occupations that were too necessary to be denied to them.[51]

A certain relief for the *dhimmīs* occurred mainly during the reigns of the last Mamluk sultans, Q̱āitbāy (1468–96) and Q̱ānṣūh al-Ghūrī (1501–16).

---

46 Ashtor, *History*, vol. 2, 62; Ashtor and Amitai, "Mamluks," 440.

47 Ashtor, *History*, vol. 2, 67–9; Stillman, *The Jews of Arab Lands*, 70–1; Ashtor and Amitai, "Mamluks," 440.

48 Ashtor, *History*, vol. 2, 70–2; Ashtor and Amitai, "Mamluks," 440.

49 Mark R. Cohen, "Jews in the Mamlūk Environment: The Crisis of 1442 (a Geniza Study, T-S. AS 150.3)," *BSOAS* 47 (1984): 425–48.

50 Ashtor, *History*, vol. 2, 72–5; Ashtor and Amitai, "Mamluks," 440. For dress regulations of the Circassian period, see also Mayer, *Mamluk Costume*, 67.

51 Ashtor, *History*, vol. 2, 75–6; Ashtor and Amitai, "Mamluks," 440.

However, like other sectors of the population, Jews in Egypt suffered from especially heavy taxes.[52] It should be noted also that during this late period, in 1498, a relatively rare act of the destruction of a synagogue in Dammūh, Egypt, was undertaken by sultan al-Nāṣir Muḥammad, Qāitbāy's son (r. 1496–98). In his reign, there were also riots by the mamluk novices in the Jewish neighborhood of Zuwayla.[53]

The deteriorating status of Jews can be also examined through the medical prism. The medical occupation in the Muslim world had always been non-sectarian, characterized by a universal spirit. Jewish, Christian and Muslim physicians formed a spiritual brotherhood that transcended the barriers of religion, language, and countries.[54] But, during the Mamluk period, orthodox Muslim circles forcefully opposed the treatment of Muslim patients by Jewish and Christian physicians, Muslim scholars warned against hiring non-Muslim physicians as well as against buying medicines from them, Muslim physicians refused to teach non-Muslims,[55] and Jews could no longer serve as "Head of the Physicians" in Cairo, nor, as it seems, in other public hospitals.[56] The decree of 1448, prohibiting Jews and Christians from practicing medicine among Muslims, despite not being enforced for long, marks a momentous reversal of the longstanding non-confessional nature of the medical profession in the

52 Ashtor, *History*, vol. 2, 414–15, 504; Ibn Iyās, *Badā'i' al-zuhūr*, vol. 3, 248, 320.

53 Ibn Iyās, *Badā'i' al-zuhūr*, vol. 3, 375, 385–6; Ashtor, *History*, vol. 2, 502–3; Kraemer, "A Jewish Cult," 598.

54 Stillman, "The Jewish Community," 209; idem, *The Jews of Arab Lands*, 71–2; Goitein, *Mediterranean Society*, vol. 2, 241.

55 Moshe Perlmann, "Notes on the Position of Jewish Physicians in Medieval Muslim Countries," *IOS* 2 (1972): 316–19; Salo W. Baron, *A Social and Religious History of the Jews* (New York: Columbia University Press, 1980), vol. 17, 175, 378, note 61; Ashtor, "Prolegomena," 154–5; Ashtor, *History*, vol. 1, 107–8, 341–3; Stillman, *The Jews of Arab Lands*, 72; Doris Behrens-Abouseif, *Fatḥ Allāh and Abū Zakariyya: Physicians Under the Mamluks*, vol. 10 of *Suppléments aux Annales Islamologiques* (Cairo: Institut français d'archéologie orientale, 1987), 14; Paulina B. Lewicka, "Healer, Scholar, Conspirator. The Jewish Physician in the Arabic-Islamic Discourse of the Mamluk Period," in *Muslim-Jewish Relations in the Middle Islamic Period: Jews in the Ayyubid and Mamluk Sultanates (1171–1517)*, ed. Stephan Conermann (Göttingen: V & R Unipress, 2017), 121–44.

56 Mazor, "Jewish Court Physicians," 64–5, note 92. As for the office of the "Head of Physicians," it was occupied in the Ayyubid period by the Jewish Ibn Jumayʿ and not by Moses Maimonides as usually (mistakenly) said, see Muḥammad ibn Aḥmad al-Dhahabī, *Ta'rīkh al-islām wa-wafayāt al-mashāhīr wa-l-a'lām*, ed. ʿAbd al-Salām Tadmurī (Beirut: Dār al-Kitāb al-ʿArabī, 1996), vol. 48, 299. Recently, however, evidence for a Jewish physician in a public hospital in Cairo was found, see: Doris Behrens-Abouseif, *The Book in Mamluk Egypt and Syria (1250-1517)—Scribes, Libraries and Market* (Leiden: Brill, 2018), 148.

Islamic world. Indeed, dynasties of distinguished Jewish court physicians, who flourished during the Fatimid and Ayyubid periods, disappeared and became converts.[57]

Testimonies by Christian European travelers, confirmed by Muslim and Jewish sources, indicate unequivocally that at least some of these regulations were indeed enforced in practice. Thus, for example, the Jews of Egypt at this time, especially in Cairo and Alexandria, used to wear yellow turbans, whereas Christians and Samaritans wore blue and red ones respectively.[58] Similarly, we have sufficient evidence to conclude that Jews and Christians indeed did not ride mules. They rode donkeys inside the cities, and in the fifteenth century—only outside them.[59] Nevertheless, one should bear in mind that Muslim citizens, who were not part of the Mamluk elite, were also prohibited from riding horses, and sometimes even mules.

Thus far, we have seen that Egyptian Jewry by no means lived in a tolerant atmosphere during the Mamluk period. Some of the most discriminatory and humiliating anti-*dhimmī* laws were promulgated during this time and strictly enforced to an extent unprecedented in Egypt. Nevertheless, some caveats should be taken into consideration regarding this gloomy description:

First, most of the discriminatory and humiliating regulations against *dhimmīs* were *enforced for limited periods or never enforced at all.* This is admitted by contemporary Muslim historians and this is the reason for the need to promulgate these laws again and again. This is especially true regarding the dismissal

57 Amir Mazor, "Jewish Court Physicians," 61–2; Amir Mazor and Efraim Lev, "The Phenomenon of Dynasties of Jewish Doctors in the Mamluk Period," *EJJS* 15 (2021), 1-29.

58 See, for instance, the reports of the following travelers: a German traveler in 1350: *Ein Niederrheinischer Bericht über den Orient*, ed. Reinhold Röhricht and Heinrich Meisner (Berlin: n.p., 1887), 24ff; John Maundeville (first half of the fourteenth century): Thomas Wright (ed.), *Early Travelers in Palestine* (New York: Ktav Publishing House, 1968), 183; Simone Sigoli for Alexandria in 1384: Lionardo Frescobaldi, Giorgio Gucci, and Simone Sigoli, *Visit to the Holy Places of Egypt, Sinai, Palestine, and Syria in 1384*, trans. Theophilus Bellorini and Eugene Hoade (Jerusalem: Franciscan Press, 1948), 162. The same report for Alexandria, ten years later: L. Le Grande, "Relation du Pélerinage a Jerusalem de Nicolas de Martoni, notaire Italien (1394–5)," *Revue de l'orient latin* 3 (1895): 587–8; a Belgian traveler to Alexandria: Adorne Anselme, *Sire de Corthuy Pélerin de Terre-Sainte sa famille, sa vie, ses voyages et son temps* (Brussels: n.p., 1855), 153. For Cairo at the end of the fifteenth century: *Die Pilgerfahrt des Ritters Arnold von Harff* (Cologne: n.p., 1860), 95. For Jewish reports, see Meshullam in 1481: Adler, *Jewish Travelers*, 163. For more reports, including Muslim sources and discussion, see Ashtor, *History*, vol. 2, 210–14.

59 Frescobaldi, Gucci, and Sigoli, *Visit*, 164; Adler, *Jewish Travelers*, 163; Ashtor, *History*, vol. 2, 214–16.

of *dhimmī* bureaucrats, who were indispensable to the Mamluk sultanate.[60] Jewish bureaucrats continued to serve during the Turkish period in state offices and in the households of Mamluk amirs, though their number and status in Egypt was much lower than in Syria.[61] The number of Jewish state bureaucrats in Egypt grew during the Circassian period, when Jews served mainly in financial offices, such as customs officials, state officials, and money changers.[62] Other decrees were also not always implemented, such as the slave law and the law that prohibited *dhimmīs* from buying lands, both issued in 1354.[63] Other laws were rather symbolic and were not enforced. For instance, the prohibition of using Arabic honorific bynames (*kunya*), or the requirement to make way for Muslims on the streets.[64] In addition, the recurring declarations of the anti-*dhimmī* measures were sometimes related more to internal conflicts within the Mamluk military elite, and less to the *dhimmīs*. In several cases, the promulgations of these laws corresponded very closely with ascensions of senior amirs to the sultanate or to other positions of power. Hence, the anti-*dhimmi* measures were announced as no more than a "flexing of muscles" in a political rivalry and subsequently were enforced for a limited period, as a result of mere expression of power, and not as a permanent state policy.[65]

Second, *dhimmīs* received the *protection* of the secular or even of the religious authorities against intolerant actions by Muslim figures and of the mob. This was true in periods of anti-*dhimmī* persecution, and even more so in less unsettled periods, such as during the reigns of the first two Circassian sultans, Barqūq and his son Faraj (r. 1382–1412), and the last sultans Qāitbāy and Qānṣūh al-Ghūrī.[66] Muslim chronicles mention several episodes in this

---

60 Al-Maqrīzī, *Sulūk*, vol. 2, 924; Little, "Coptic Conversion," 54.

61 Ashtor, *History*, vol. 1, 204–5, 347. It also seems that in the Syrian provinces, the enforcement of the discriminatory laws was looser, see Hofer, "The Ideology," 110–11.

62 Ashtor, *History*, vol. 2, 170, 176–7. Most of the Jews mentioned in contemporary Muslim sources were money changers [*ṣayrafīs*]. See, for instance, in Egypt: Behrens-Abouseif, *Fatḥ Allāh*, 23; Ashtor, *History*, vol. 2, 29, note 9, 91–3, 177. In Syria: al-Maqrīzī, *Kitāb al-Muqaffā al-Kabīr*, ed. Muḥammad al-Ya'lāwī (Beirut: n.p., 1991), vol. 2, 256; al-Maqrīzī, *Sulūk*, vol. 4, 442–3; Ashtor, *History*, vol. 1, 205. As mentioned above (note 51), the prominent position of *dhimmīs*—mainly Jews—as money changers was so significant, that they were excluded from Khushqadam's decree of 1463.

63 Ashtor, *History*, vol. 2, 221, 235–6.

64 Ashtor, *History*, vol. 2, 218.

65 Hofer, "The Ideology," 109–10. In this context, Ashtor mentions a case in Cairo, 1401, in which a law ordering the *dhimmīs* to obey the clothing restrictions was canceled due to a conflict between two senior amirs, see Ashtor, *History*, vol. 2, 31–2.

66 Ashtor, *History*, vol. 2, 6–7, 31–2, 504.

regard. For instance, in 1315, when a Muslim citizen rode along the streets of Cairo, striking Jews and Christians who passed by with his sword, he was captured and beheaded.[67] In 1354, during the violent rampages against the *dhimmīs*, the government prohibited any *dhimmi* being harmed.[68] In similar cases Jews gained the protection of the police for their lives, or of the chief judges for their synagogues.[69] Documents from the archives of the Jewish communities in Cairo indicate that Jews were permitted to renovate their synagogues in Cairo several times, especially during the fifteenth century, when the case was found legal by Islamic law.[70]

Third, Jews, as well as Copts, managed to develop several ploys and *stratagems* in order to deal with their depressed situation. One of the most ingenious was the *single-generation conversion,* when an individual converted, while his family, including his children, remained in their original religion. This practice enabled the social advancement of an individual, and on the other hand, prevented a drastic demographic decline of the community. Of more significance, it brought economic benefits to the community of the converted *dhimmī,* who managed to enable the reversion of property within his family and original community.[71] However, the new inheritance laws of 1354, discussed above, aimed to end the ploys of *dhimmīs* using this type of conversion. It is hard to say for how long and to what extent these laws were enforced. Nevertheless, the Jewish response to the 1354 laws was the adoption of the Islamic *waqf.*[72] In contrast to former periods in which endowments were made according to the Jewish halakha,

---

67 Al-Maqrīzī, *Sulūk*, vol. 2, 139–40.

68 Al-Maqrīzī, *Khiṭaṭ*, vol. 2, 499, l. 36.

69 Ibn al-Furāt, *Ta'rīkh Ibn al-Furāt*, vol. 9, 90; Cohen, "The Crisis of 1442," 446; Ashtor, *History*, vol. 1, 93, vol. 2, 99–100.

70 Donald S. Richards, "Dhimmi Problems in Fifteenth-Century Cairo: Reconsideration of a Court Document," in *Studies in Muslim-Jewish Relations*, vol. 1, ed. Ronald L. Nettler (Chur: Harwood Academic Publishers, in cooperation with the Oxford Centre for Postgraduate Hebrew Studies, 1993), 127-163; Arad, "Being a Jew," 26–27; Christians as well were allowed to renovate their houses of prayer, if the case was found legal, see: Ashtor, *History*, vol. 2, 208–209.

71 El-Leithy, "Coptic Culture and Conversion," 67–100, esp. 95–6. Cases of this practice among Jews are known from mid-twelfth-century Baghdad (Goitein, *Mediterranean Society*, vol. 2, 303), early fifteenth-century Mamluk Syria (el-Leithy, "Coptic Culture and Conversion," 73–8), and pre-Mamluk Egypt (ibid., 95). There is little doubt, hence, that this practice was not adopted also by Jews in Mamluk Egypt.

72 On Islamic *waqf*, see "Waḳf," in *Encyclopedia of Islam*, ed. Peri. J. Bearman et al. (Leiden: Brill, 2002), vol. 11, 59ff; and *Encyclopedia of Islam*, ed. Peri. J. Bearman et al. (Leiden: Brill 2004), vol. 12, 823–8.

during the Mamluk period Jewish consecrations were made according to the Islamic *waqf* laws. By using this strategy, Jews managed to retain their property within the community and it was also considered legally valid by the Muslim state law.[73]

Jews also managed to manipulate the Mamluk juridical system by taking advantage of the latitude in the Islamic legal field. Following the reform of Sultan Baybars I (1260–77), four chief judges were appointed, one from each Sunni school of law [*madhhab*].[74] This remarkable innovation allowed litigants to 'shop' for the most advantageous ruling among four recognized legal schools.[75] Thus, for instance, in case of single-generation conversion, Jewish women preferred to appeal to Mālikī judges since this *madhhab* is the only one that rules that a child does not follow his mother's (new) religion, but only that of his father, who remained Jewish.[76] In other cases, such as the permission to renovate synagogues, Jews tended to appeal to Ḥanafī judges, since this rite is more liberal regarding *dhimmī* laws.[77] It seems that Jews learned to preserve legal documents and to manipulate court cases with them, and that this was one of the main means for the community as well as for individuals within it to secure their interests when appealing to Muslim courts and *muftis*.[78]

Jews also found several "tricks" to deal with the danger of demolishing or closing of synagogues. In order to conceal newly built synagogues, they kept their external appearance neglected.[79] Jews also turned private houses into synagogues, and made efforts to camouflage them.[80] Interestingly, Jews protected their synagogues also by relating the places on which the synagogues were built to pre-Islamic biblical or old rabbinic figures, and by dating their erection to before the Muslim period. This is because according to the Pact of ʿUmar, non-Muslims are not allowed to build new houses of worship. Hence,

73 Arad, "Being a Jew," 35–8.

74 On the four legal schools in Islam, see, for instance: Joseph Schacht, "Fiḳh," in *Encyclopedia of Islam*, ed. Clifford E. Bosworth et al. (Leiden: Brill, 1995), vol. 2, 887–90; Christopher Melchert, *The Formation of the Sunni Schools of Law, 9th–10th Centuries C.E.* (Leiden: Brill, 1997).

75 El-Leithy, "Coptic Culture and Conversion," 86.

76 Ibid., 73–9, and esp. 84.

77 Ashtor, *History*, vol. 2, 103, 194, 209–10; Rustow, "At the Limits," 155–6.

78 See recent studies on this topic: Tamer el-Leithy, "Living Documents, Dying Archives: Towards a Historical Anthropology of Medieval Arabic Archives," *al-Qantara* 32 (2011): 389–434, esp. 395–6; Hofer, "The Ideology," 115–9; Rustow, "At the Limits," 146–51. See also n. 70 above.

79 Arad, "Being a Jew," 24–5.

80 Ashtor, *History*, vol. 2, 209.

for instance, the place on which the synagogue of Dammūh was built, was believed to be the spot on which Moses prayed. Al-Maqrīzī mentions that the Jews claim that the building itself was built forty years after the destruction of the Second Temple by Titus, "which would be more than 500 years before the appearance of Islam."[81] Similarly, in the well-known Ben-Ezra Synagogue, i.e. the synagogue of the Palestinians in Fusṭāṭ, a wooden inscription over its gate states that the building was erected in 336 of the era of Alexander, which is around 450 years before the destruction of the Second Temple by Titus, and around 600 years before Islam. Likewise, the Karaite synagogue in Fusṭāṭ was believed by Jews to be the abode of the prophet Elijah and was built as a synagogue in 315 of the era of Alexander.[82]

Fourth, the rulings against Jews in Mamluk Egypt should be placed in the correct cultural context. It should be remembered that, in stark contrast to medieval and modern Europe, where Jews were a tiny isolated minority within a Christian society, in the Islamicate society of the Mamluk sultanate they constituted one segment among the several ethnic and class groups of which the Mamluk sultanate was composed. That is why, for example, the practice of discriminating clothing was not considered an act of outstanding humiliation for Jews in the Mamluk society in which each group adopted external features of its own, which were considered to be a mark of identity and a sign of self-definition. Moreover, yellow clothes drew far less attention than the blue clothes of the Christians.[83] Indeed, Christians used to borrow yellow clothes from Jews in order to escape the rage of the mob.[84] In addition, we have indication that in certain circumstances, Jews could dress like Muslims in order not to be identified.[85]

Indeed, it was the dominant community of the Christian Copts that was the trigger for the occasional declarations of the discriminatory laws, and they were also the main target of most of the mob riots and coercive conversion. This was mainly due to the fact that they occupied the highest

---

81 al-Maqrīzī, *Khiṭaṭ*, vol. 2, 464–5. English translation in Richard Gottheil, "An Eleventh-Century Document concerning a Cairo Synagogue," *JQR* 19, no. 3 (1907): 502–3; Kraemer, "A Jewish Cult," 581, 598; Simḥa Assaf, *Meqorot u-Meḥqarim be-Toledot Israel* [*Sources and Studies in Jewish History*] (Jerusalem: Mossad ha-Rav Kook, 1946), 155–6 [in Hebrew].

82 al-Maqrīzī, *Khiṭaṭ*, vol. 2, 471; Arad, "Being a Jew," 25–6.

83 Arad, "Being a Jew," 28; Cohen, *Under Crescent and Cross*, 110–11, 116–20.

84 Little, "Coptic Conversion," 564; Arthur. S. Tritton, *The Caliphs and Their Non-Muslim Subjects: A Critical Study of the Covenant of 'Umar* (London: H. Milford and Oxford University Press, 1930), 75; al-Maqrīzī, *Khiṭaṭ*, vol. 2, 516, ll. 26–7; Ashtor, *History*, vol. 1, 338–9.

85 Arad, "Being a Jew," 28–30.

positions in state bureaucracy. Jews, who were also considered *dhimmīs*, were, of course, affected as well, yet they were only secondary victims of anti-*dhimmī* decrees and riots. It was almost exclusively churches and monasteries that were ruined and it was only Christians who were occasionally accused of arson in Cairo or Damascus. Consequently, Christian Copts were the main target for conversion. Though during the Mamluk period conversion became a common phenomenon among Jews, the number of Jewish converts was much lower than that of convert Copts.

In the same way, anti-*dhimmī* polemical works were not written particularly against Jews, but against *dhimmīs* in general, and actually against the Christians, who formed the majority among the infidels. Moreover, these treatises were written precisely because reality stood, to a large extent, in contradiction to the ideal of their writers.[86] Hence, despite the general increasing pressure on Jews by the state and the people, state policy and the position of the Jews should be examined in the social, legal and economical contexts of the Islamicate society of the Mamluk sultanate.

The last phase

During the second half of the fifteenth and the beginning of the sixteenth centuries the situation of the Jews of Egypt improved significantly. The relatively tolerant policy of the sultans Qāitbāy and Qānṣūh al-Ghūrī caused Jews once again to fill important offices in government and court, such as physicians and financial officials. Several Jews were appointed as directors of the Egyptian mint in Cairo, among them was the last *nagid*, Isaac Sholel.[87] A Czech traveler who visited Egypt at the end of the fifteenth century reported that many Jews worked as scribes in the service of the government.[88]

---

86 See el-Leithy, "Sufis," esp. 76–7; Joseph Sadan, "What does *Manhaj al-Ṣawāb* Want from the Jews?," in *Adaptations and Innovations: Studies on the Interaction between Jewish and Islamic Thought and Literature from the Early Middle Ages to the Late Twentieth Century, dedicated to Professor Joel L. Kraemer*, ed. Y. Tzvi Langermann and J. Stern (Paris: Peeters, 2007), 315–30. It is these very same parameters that were different in Christian Europe at that time: polemic literature was written only against the single large "infidel" majority—the Jews; anti-Jewish works were not only an ideal, but in many cases—obligatiory state laws. Ashtor, *History*, vol. 1, 104ff; 209–10; Cohen, *Under Crescent and Cross*, 52.

87 Abraham David, *A Jewish Mediterranean Society*, 273–7; Ashtor, *History*, vol. 2, 178–9, 521–4.

88 Martin Kabatnik, *Cesta do Jerusalema a Kaira* (Prague: n.p., 1894), 32. I thank Blanka Gorecka and Vera Linhatova for assistance in translation.

The revival was also discerned in trade. The severe decline in handcraft and industry during the second half of the fifteenth century caused many Jews become traders. Obadiah of Bertinoro indeed mentioned that "among the Jews in Cairo there are money changers and merchants, for the country is large (...). For trade there is no better place in the world than Cairo. It is easy to grow rich."[89] The two Italian Jewish travelers, Meshullam of Volterra and Obadiah of Bertinoro, also mention several wealthy men among the Jews of Cairo. Similarly, a German traveler who visited Cairo towards the end of this century testified that there are rich and distinguished people among the Jews, especially among the Samaritans and Karaites, but also among the Rabbanites.[90] It also seems that there was prosperity in terms of foodstuffs. Meshullam and Obadiah note that in Alexandria and Cairo there is a variety of cheap food available for Jews, including fruits, vegetables, meat, cheese, bread, fish, and fowl.[91]

The highly cultured Sephardic exiles who arrived in Egypt toward the end of the fifteenth century, after the expulsion from Spain, improved not only the demographic situation, but also the economic and spiritual life of Egyptian Jewry. The Sephardim were intellectually superior to the local Jews of native Arabic-speaking origin (referred as the *musta'ribs*), and soon after their arrival in Egypt they became the chief rabbis of communities and established important *yeshivot.*[92]

Interestingly enough, the intellectual and cultural supremacy of the Sephardim brought about the dominance of their tradition also among the *musta'ribs,* who appointed Sephardi rabbis and judges [*dayyanim*]. It was only few generations until a complete integration between the two congregations was achieved.[93] The social, cultural, economic and demographic conditions of Egyptian Jewry continued to improve during the sixteenth century, with the prosperity that followed the Ottoman conquest of Egypt in 1517.

Conclusions

It would not be wrong to describe the situation of the Jews under the Mamluks as a general decline almost in every aspect of Jewish life: legal, economical,

89 Adler, *Jewish Travelers,* 228. A similar report is mentioned by the Czech traveler of 1490, see: Kabatnik, *Cesta do Jerusalema a Kaira,* 32.

90 Adler, *Jewish Travelers,* 172–3, 227–8; Ashtor, *History,* vol. 2, 419, 523, 525.

91 Adler, *Jewish Travelers,* 160, 228.

92 Ashtor, *History,* vol. 2, 458ff.

93 Ibid., 496–99.

demographic, intellectual, and security. The deterioration in some of these aspects started already in the Ayyubid period, continued during the first century of Mamluk rule, escalated even more from the mid-fourteenth century and only in the second half of the fifteenth century started to recover. It would not be wrong also to conclude that the worsening condition of Egyptian Jewry derived—to a significant extent—from the strengthening of anti-*dhimmī* Islamic zeal among the populace, as well as among the military, political and religious elite. However, this deterioration was also in large extent a result of a long period of duress, from which the Egyptian populace at large suffered, due to the recurring epidemics, the Mongol invasions, the decline in international trade and the exploitative policy of the sultans. In order to evaluate the situation of the Jews during the long Mamluk period more precisely, however, a multi-aspect analysis of the whole Mamluk period on a diachronic axis is required, based on a diversity of sources.

Within the limits of the current general survey, the best way to evaluate the general situation of Egyptian Jewry under the Mamluks would perhaps be comparative. Compared to the situation of Fatimid Egypt, the Jews in the Mamluk period were humiliated and suffered a significant decline. However, compared to their brothers in Christian lands, their situation was considerably better. In contrast to their European co-religionists, even during the oppressive period of Mamluk rule, Jews usually received protection from the authorities for their life and property and for any kind of injustice; they were much more integrated in general social, economic, and even intellectual life; above all, they were not exposed to the abysmal hatred which lead to pogroms and expulsions of their brethren in Christian Europe.

Bibliography

Abramson, Shraga. "Liturgical Poems of Rabbi Ya'aqov bar Yehudah he-Ḥaver Amani." *Studies of the Research Institute for Hebrew Poetry* 7 (1958): 163–81. [In Hebrew.]

________. *In the Centers and the Diaspora in the Gaonic Period.* Jerusalem: Mosad ha-Rav Kook, 1965. [In Hebrew.]

Abulafia, David. "Asia, Africa and the Trade of Medieval Europe." In *The Cambridge Economic History of Europe*, vol. 2, *Trade and Industry in the Middle Ages*, edited by M. M. Postan and E. Miller. Cambridge: Cambridge University Press, 1987.

Adler, E. N. (ed.). *Jewish Travelers: A Treasury of Travelogues from Nine Centuries.* New York: Hermon Press, 1966.

Ackerman-Lieberman, Philipp. "Legal Writing in Medieval Cairo: 'Copy' or 'Likeness' in Jewish Documentary Formulae." In *"From a Sacred Source": Genizah Studies in Honour of Professor Stefan C. Reif*, edited by Ben Outhwaite and Siam Bhayro, 1–24. Leiden: Brill, 2011.

________. "Commercial Forms and Legal Norms in the Jewish Community of Medieval Egypt." *Law and History Review* 30 (2012): 1007–52.

________. *The Business of Identity: Jews, Muslims, and Economic Life in Medieval Egypt.* Stanford: Stanford University Press, 2014.

________. "Legal Pluralism among the Court Records of Medieval Egypt." *BEO* 63 (2014): 79–112.

Al-'Asqalani ibn Ḥajar Shihāb al-Dīn Ahmad ibn 'Ali al-Shafi'i. *Raf' al-iṣr 'an quḍat miṣr.* Cairo: Maktabat al-Khanji, 1418/1998.

Al-Balādhurī, Abū al-'Abbās Aḥmad ibn Yaḥya ibn Jābir. *Futūḥ al-buldān.* Edited by M. De Goeje. Leiden: Brill, 1866.

Al-Balawī, 'Abd Allāh ibn Muḥammad al-Madīnī. *Sirat Aḥmad ibn Ṭūlūn.* Edited by M. K. 'Ali. Damascus: al-Maktaba al-'Arabiyya, 1939.

Al-Dhahabī, Muḥammad ibn Aḥmad, *Ta'rīkh al-Islām wa-wafayāt al-mashāhīr wa-l-a'lam.* Edited by 'Abd al-Salām Tadmurī. Beirut: Dār al-Kitāb al-'Arabī, 1996.

Al-Dimashqī, Abū Muḥammad 'Abd al-'Azīz al-Kattānī. *Dhayl tahrikh mawlid al-ulama.* Riyad: Dar al-'Asima, 1988.

Al-Khālidī Maḥmad ibn Hishām. *Al-Tuḥaf wa-l-hidāya.* Edited by Sāmī al-Dahān. Cairo, 1956.

Al-Kindi, Abu 'Umar Muḥammad ibn Yūsuf ibn Ya'qūb. *Wulah misr.* Edited by Rhuvon Guest. London: Luzac, 1912.

________. *Wulah misr.* Edited by Ali Umar. Cairo: Maktabat al-thaqāfa al-diniyya, 1428/2008.

Al-Maqrīzī, Taqī al-Dīn Aḥmad ibn ʿAlī. *Kitāb al-muqaffā al-Kabīr.* Edited by Muḥammad al-Yaʿlāwī. Beirut: n.p., 1991.

________. *Ittiʿāz al-ḥunafāʾ bi-akhbār al-aʾimma al-fāṭimiyyin al-khulafāʾ.* Edited by Jamāl al-Dīn Shayyāl and Muḥammad Ḥilmī Muḥammad Aḥmad. Cairo: al-Majlis al-Aʿlā lil-Shuʾūn al-Islamiyya, 1364–1442 AH/1944–2020.

________. *El-Mawâʿiz wal-Iʿtibâr fî dhikr el-khitat wal-âthâr.* Edited by Gaston Wiet. Cairo: IFAO, 1911.

Al-Nuwayrī, Shihāb al-Dīn Aḥmad. *Nihāyat al-Arab fī Funūn al-Adab.* Edited by al-Bāz al-ʿArīnī. Cairo: al-Hayʾa al-Miṣriyya al-ʿAmma lil-Kitāb, 1992.

Al-Qaddūmī, Ghāda (trans.). *Book of Gifts and Rarities [Kitab al-hadāyā wa al-tuḥaf]: Selections Compiled in the Fifteenth Century from an Eleventh-Century Manuscript on Gifts and Treasures.* Cambridge, MA: Harvard University Press, 1996.

Al-Ṣadafī, Abū Saʿīd ʿAbd al-Raḥmān ibn Aḥmad ibn Yūnus, al-Miṣrī . *Taʾrīkh Ibn Yūnus al-Ṣadafī.* Edited by A. F. ʿAbd al-Fattāḥ. Beirut: Dār al-Kutub al-ʿIlmīyah, 2000.

Al-Wer, Enam. "Sociolinguistics." In *Handbook of Arabic Linguistics,* edited by Jonathan Owens, 241–63. Oxford: Oxford University Press, 2013.

Albeck, Shalom, and Menachem Elon. "Acquisition." In *Encyclopedia Judaica,* 1:359–63.

Alharizi, Judah, *Tahkemoni or The Tales of Heman the Ezrahite,* ed. Joseph Yahalom and Naoya Katsumata (Jerusalem: The Ben Zvi Institute, 2010) [in Hebrew].

Alharizi Judah, Kitab al-Durar; A Book in Praise of God and the Israelite Communities, Assembled and Edited by Joshua Blau, Paul Fenton, and Josepf Yahalom. Jerusalem: The Ben Zvi Institute, 2009. [In Hebrew.]

Allony, Nehemya. "Reflections of the Rebellion against *ʿArabiyya* in our Literature from the Middle Ages." In *Studies in the Bible and the Hebrew Language Offered to Meir Wallenstein,* edited by Chaim Rabin et al., 80–136. Jerusalem: Qiryat Sefer, 1979. [In Hebrew.]

Amitai-Preiss, Reuven. *Mongols and Mamluks: The Mamluk-Ilkhanid War, 1260–1281.* Cambridge: Cambridge University Press, 1995.

Amram, David Werner. "An Injunction of a Jewish-Egyptian Court of the Thirteenth Century." *The Green Bag* 13 (1901): 339–43.

Anselme, Adorne. *Sire de Corthuy Pélerin de Terre-Sainte; sa famille, sa vie, ses voyages et son temps.* Brussels: n.p., 1855.

Aptowitzer, V. "Formularies of Decrees and Documents from a Gaonic Court." *JQR* 4 (1913): 23–51.

Arad, Dotan, and Esther-Miriam Wagner. *Wisdom and Greatness in One Place: The Alexandrian Trader Moses Ben Judah and his Circle.* Leiden: Brill, forthcoming.

Arad, Dotan. "Being a Jew under the Mamluks: Some Coping Strategies." In *Muslim-Jewish Relations in the Middle Islamic Period: Jews in the Ayyubid and Mamluk Sultanates (1171–1517),* edited by Stephan Conermann, 21–39. Göttingen: V & R Unipress, 2017.

________. "The Mustaʿrib Jews in Syria, Palestine and Egypt 1330–1700." PhD diss., The Hebrew University, 2013. [In Hebrew.]

Arad, Mordekhai. *Sabbath Desecrator with* Parresia: *A Talmudic Legal Term and its Historic Context*. New York and Jerusalem: The Jewish Theological Seminary of America, 2009.

Arzi, Albert, and Ḥaggai Ben-Shammai. "Risāla." In *Encyclopedia of Islam*, edited by Clifford E. Bosworth et al., 8:532–45. Leiden: Brill, 1995.

Ashtor (Strauss), Eliyahu. *Toledot ha-yehudim be-Mitzrayim ve-Suryah taḥat shilton ha-mamlukim* [*The History of the Jews in Egypt and Syria under Mamluk Rule*]. Jerusalem: Mossad ha-Rav Kook, 1944–51. [In Hebrew.]

________. "Prolegomena to the Medieval History of Oriental Jewry." *JQR* 50 (1959–60): 55–68, 147–166.

________. "The Number of Jews in Medieval Egypt I." *JJS* 18 (1967): 9–42.

________. "The Number of Jews in Medieval Egypt II." *JJS* 19 (1968): 1-22.

________. "Un mouvement migratoire au haut Moyen Age: Migrations de l'Irak vers les pays méditerranéens." *Annales: Histoire, Sciences Sociales* 27/1 (1972): 185–214.

________. "The Venetian Supremacy in Levantine Trade: Monopoly or Pre-Colonialism?" *Journal of European Economic History* 3 (1974): 5–53.

——— "The Economic Decline of the Middle East during the Later Middle Ages—An Outline." *Asian and African Studies* 15 (Haifa, 1981): 253–286. Reprinted in his *Technology, Industry and Trade: The Levant versus Europe 1250–1500*, edited by B. Z. Kedar, art. II. London: Variorum Reprints, 1992.

Ashtor, Eliyahu, and Reuven Amitai, "Mamluks," *Enyclopedia Judaica*, 2nd edition, vol. 13, 438–41.

Ashur, Amir. "Engagement and Betrothal Documents from the Cairo Genizah Engagement and Betrothal." PhD diss., Tel Aviv University, 2006. [In Hebrew.]

________. "On the Identification and Biography of the 'Poet for all Seasons' and his Contact with Maimonides: T-S 10K8.3, T-S 8K13.8, T-S NS 264.98." *Fragment of the Month* (November 2016). Accessed June 27, 2017. https://www.repository.cam.ac.uk/handle/1810/262866.

Assaf, Simḥa. *The Book of Sheṭarot (Formulary) of R. Hai Ga'on*, supplement to *Tarbiz* 1, no. 3 (1930). [In Hebrew.]

________. "Old Genizah Documents from Palestine, Egypt and North Africa." *Tarbiz* 9 (1937–8): 11–34 and 196–218. [In Hebrew.]

________. *Meqorot u-Meḥqarim be-Toledot Israel* [*Sources and Studies in Jewish History*]. Jerusalem: Mossad ha-Rav Kook, 1946. [In Hebrew.]

________. "From the Palestinian Liturgy." In *Sefer Dinaburg*, edited by Yitzhak Baer, 116–130. Jerusalem: Qiryat Sefer, 1949. [In Hebrew.]

Ayalon, David. "Baḥrī Mamluks, Burjī Mamluks—Inadequate Names for the Two Reigns of the Mamluk Sultanate." *Tārīḫ* 1 (1990): 22–24, 3–53.

Balamoshev, C. "The Jews of Oxyrhynchos Address the *Strategos* of the Nome: An Early Fourth Century Document." *Journal of Juristic Papyrology* 47 (2017): 27–43.

Baneth, D. Z. "Genizah Documents on Jewish Communal Affairs in Egypt." In *Alexander Marx Jubilee Volume*, Hebrew section, 75*–93*. New York: Jewish Theological Seminary of America, 1950. [In Hebrew.]

Bareket, Elinoar. *The Jewish Leadership in Fusṭāṭ in the First Half of the Eleventh Century.* Tel Aviv: The Diaspora Research Institute, 1995. [In Hebrew.]

________. *Shafrir Mitzrayim.* Tel Aviv: Tel Aviv University, 1995. [In Hebrew.]

________. "Books of Records of the Jerusalemite Court from the Cairo Genizah in the First Half of the Eleventh Century." *HUCA* 69 (1998): 12–15. [In Hebrew.]

________. "The Head of the Jews in Egypt under Fatimid Rule (Hebrew)." *Zmanim* 64 (1998): 34–43. [In Hebrew.]

________. *Fustat on the Nile: The Jewish Elite in Medieval Egypt.* Leiden: Brill, 1999.

Baron, Salo Wittmayer. *A Social and Religious History of the Jews.* New York: Columbia University Press, 1980.

Barth, Fredrik. "Introduction." In *Ethnic Groups and Boundaries,* edited by F. Barth, 9–38. Bergen: Universitatsforlaget, 1969.

Be'eri, Tova (ed.). *Le-David Mizmor: The Poems of David ha-Nasi.* Jerusalem: Mekize Nirdamim, 2009. [In Hebrew.]

________. "'Eli he-Ḥaver ben ʿAmram: A Hebrew Poet in Eleventh Century Egypt." *Sefunot* N. S. 8/23 (2003): 279–345. [In Hebrew.]

________. "Early Epistolary Poems from the Geniza." *Qovetz ʿal Yad* N. S. 18/28 (2005): 43–79. [In Hebrew.]

Behnstedt, Peter. "Zur Dialektgeographie des Nildeltas." *Zeitschrift für arabische Linguistik* 1 (1978): 64–92.

Behrens-Abouseif, Doris. *Fatḥ Allāh and Abū Zakariyya: Physicians Under the Mamluks,* vol. 10 of *Suppléments aux Annales Islamologiques.* Cairo: Institut français d'archéologie orientale, 1987.

________. *Islamic Architecture in Cairo: An Introduction.* Leiden: Brill, 1989.

________. *The Book in Mamluk Egypt and Syria (1250-1517)—Scribes, Libraries and Market.* Leiden: Brill, 2018.

Ben-Ḥayyim, Ze'ev. "Tzanuaʿ." *Leshonenu* 57 (1953): 51–54.

Ben-Sasson, Menahem. "Fragments from Saʿadya's Sefer ha-ʿEdut ve-ha-Shetarot." *Shenaton ha-Mishpat ha-ʿIvri* 11–12 (1984–86): 135–278. [In Hebrew.]

________. "The Gaonate of R. Samuel b. Joseph ha-Cohen, which Was 'like a Bath of Boiling Water.'" *Zion* 51 (1985): 379–409. [In Hebrew.]

________. "Appeal to the Congregation in Islamic Countries in the Early Middle Ages." In *Knesset Ezra: Literature and Life in the Synagogue Presented to Ezra Fleischer,* edited by S. Elizur et al., 327–50. Jerusalem: Ben Zvi, 1994. [In Hebrew.]

________. *Emergence of the Local Jewish Community in the Muslim World: Qayrawan, 800–1057.* Jerusalem: Magness Press, 1997. [In Hebrew.]

Ben-Sasson, Menahem, and Robert Brody (eds. and trans.). *Sefer ha-ʿEduyot ve-ha-Sheṭarot le-Rav Saʿadya Ga'on.* Jerusalem: The Israel Academy for Sciences and Humanities, in press.

Ben-Shammai, Haggai. "New Sources for the History of the Karaites in Sixteenth-Century Egypt (Preliminary Description)." *Ginzei Qedem: Genizah Research Annual* 2 (2006): 11–22. [In Hebrew.]

Benoit, P., J. T. Milik, and R. de Vaux, *Les Grottes de Murabba'at*, vol. 2 of *DJD*. Oxford: Clarendon, 1961.

Berkovitz, Jay R. *Protocols of Justice: The Pinkas of the Metz Rabbinic Court 1771–1789*. Leiden: Brill, 2014.

Bernstein, Simon. "*Ma'amad* Poems by R. Joseph ibn Abitur." *Sinai* 31 (1952): 284–309. [In Hebrew.]

Bianquis, Thierry. "Ibn al-Nabulusi, un martyr sunnite au IVe siecle de l'Hegire." *Ann. Islam* 12 (1974): 45–66.

Blanc, Haim. *Communal Dialects in Baghdad*. Cambridge: Harvard University Press, 1964.

Blau, Joshua. *Diqduq ha-'aravit-ha-yehudit shel yeme ha-benayim*. Jerusalem: Magnes Press, 1980.

________. *The Emergence and Linguistic Background of Judaeo-Arabic*. 2nd edition, Oxford: Oxford University Press, 1981. 3rd edition, Oxford: Oxford University Press, 1988.

________. *Studies in Middle Arabic*. Jerusalem: Magnes Press, 1988.

________. *A Dictionary of Medieval Judaeo-Arabic Texts*. Jerusalem: The Academy of the Hebrew Language and Israel Academy of Sciences and Humanities, 2006.

Blau, Joshua, Paul Fenton, and Joseph Yahalom (eds.). *Kitāb al-Durār*. Jerusalem: Yad Ben-Zvi, 2009.

Blau, Joshua, and Simon Hopkins. "A Vocalized JA Letter from the Cairo Genizah." *Jerusalem Studies in Arabic and Islam* 6 (1985): 417–76.

Blau, Joshua, and Joseph Yahalom. "Poetic Flowers and Beautiful Stories: Early Versions of Passages of Alharizi's Tahkemoni." *Pe'amim* 96 (2003): 5–19. [In Hebrew.]

Blidstein, Gerald J. "Who is not a Jew?—The Medieval Discussion." *Israel Law Review* 11 (1976): 369–90.

________. "The License to Teach and its Social Implications in Maimonides." *Tarbiz* 51 (1982): 577–87. [In Hebrew.]

________. "On the Freedom of Instruction and the Authority to Rule: A Study of Two Maimonidean Responsa." In *Study and Knowledge in Jewish Thought*, edited by Howard Kreisel, 147–55. Beer Sheva: Ben Gurion University Press, 2006.

Blumenkranz, Bernhard. *Juifs et Chrétiens dans le monde occidental 430–1096*. Leuven: Peeters Publishers, 2006.

Bohak, Gideon, and Ortal-Paz Saar. "Genizah Magical Texts Prepared for or against Named Individuals." *REJ* 174 (2015): 77–110.

Bonfil, Robert. *History and Folklore in a Medieval Chronicle: The Family Chronicle of Aḥima'az ben Paltiel*. Leiden: Brill, 2009.

________. "The Right to Cry Aloud: A Note on the Medieval Custom of 'Interrupting the Prayer'." In *From Sages to Savants: Studies Presented to Avraham Grossman*, edited by Joseph R. Hacker et al., 145–56. Jerusalem: Zalman Shazar, 2010. [In Hebrew.]

Bonadeo, Cecilia Martini, *'Abd al-Laṭīf al-Baġdādī's Philosophical Journey from Aristotle's Metaphysics to the "Metaphysical Science"* (Leiden: Brill, 2013)

Bosworth, Clifford Edmund. "The Tahirids and Arabic Culture." *Journal of Semitic Studies* 14/1 (1969): 45–79.

Botticini, Maristella, and Zvi Eckstein. *The Chosen Few How Education Shaped Jewish History, 70–1492.* Princeton, NJ: Princeton University Press, 2012.

________. "From Farmers to Merchants, Conversions and Diaspora: Human Capital and Jewish History." *Journal of the European Economic Association* 5, no. 5 (2007): 885–926.

________. "Jewish Occupational Selection: Education, Restrictions, or Minorities?" *The Journal of Economic History* 65, no. 4 (2005): 922–48.

Bourdieu, Pierre. *Outline of a Theory of Practice.* Cambridge: Cambridge University Press, 1977.

________. "The Force of Law: Toward a Sociology of the Juridical Field." *The Hastings Law Journal* 38 (1987): 805–53.

Boušek, Daniel. "Campaign against 'The Protected People' in the Mamluk Period: Ghāzī Ibn al-Wāsitī and his 'Response to the Protected People.'" In *The Mediterranean in History. Tribute to Prof. Eduard Gombár's 60th Birthday,* edited by Joseph Zenka. Prague: Karolinum, 2012. [In Czech.]

________. "'. . . And the Ishmaelites Honour the Site': Images of Encounters between Jews and Muslims at Jewish Sacred Places in Medieval Hebrew Travelogues." *Archív Orientální* 86, no. 1 (2018).

Brett, Michael. *The Rise of the Fatimids: The World of the Mediterranean and the Middle East in the Fourth Century of the Hijra, Tenth Century CE.* Leiden: Brill, 2001.

Brody, Ḥayyim (ed.). "Hidden Treasures." *Qovetz ʿal Yad* 9 (1893): 2–19. [In Hebrew.]

________. *Dīwān of Abu-l-Hasan Yehudah ha-Levi.* Berlin: Mekize Nirdamim, 1894/1930. [In Hebrew.]

Brody, R., and E. J. Weisenberg. *A Hand-List of Rabbinic Manuscripts in the Cambridge Genizah.* Cambridge: Cambridge University Press, 1998.

de Boer, P. A. H. "Notes on an Oxyrhynchus Papyrus in Hebrew: Brit. Mus. Or. 9180 A." *Vetus Testamentum* (1951): 49–57.

Brooten, Bernadette J. "Iael Prostates in the Jewish Donative Inscription from Aphrodisias." In *The Future of Early Christianity: Essays in Honor of Helmut Koester,* edited by A. T. Kraabel, G. W. E. Nickelsburg, N. R. Peterson, 153–54. Minneapolis: Fortress Press, 1991.

Bulliet, Richard W. *Islam: The View from the Edge.* New York: Columbia University Press, 1994.

Calder, Norman. "The Social Function of Fatwas." In *Islamic Jurisprudence in the Classical Era,* edited by Colin Imber, 167–74. Cambridge: Cambridge University Press, 2010.

Christ, Georg. *Trading Conflicts: Venetian Merchants and Mamluk Officials in Late Medieval Alexandria.* Leiden: Brill, 2012.

Citarella, Armand. "The Relations of Amalfi with the Arab World before the Crusades." *Speculum* 42, no. 2 (1967): 299–312.

Cohen, Gerson D. (ed.). *A Critical Edition with a Translation and Notes of the Book of Tradition (Sefer ha-qabbalah) by Abraham Ibn Daud.* Philadelphia: Jewish Publication Society, 1967.

Cohen, Hayyim J. "The Economic Background and the Secular Occupations of Muslim Jurisprudents and Traditionists in the Classical Period of Islam (until the Middle of the Eleventh Century)." *JESHO* 13, no. 1 (1970): 16–61.

Cohen, Mark R. "New Light on the Conflict over the Palestinian Gaonate, 1038–1042, and on Daniel b. ʿAzarya: A Pair of Letters to the Nagid of Qayrawan." *AJS (Association for Jewish Studies) Review* 1 (1976): 1–40.

________. *Jewish Self-Government in Medieval Egypt: The Origins of the Office of Head of the Jews, ca. 1065–1126*. Princeton, NJ: Princeton University Press, 1980.

________. "Geniza Documents Concerning a Conflict in a Provincial Egyptian Jewish Community during the Nagidate of Mevorakh b. Saadya." In *Studies in Judaism and Islam Presented to Shelomo Dov Goitein on the Occasion of his Eightieth Birthday*, edited by S. Morag et al., 123–54. Jerusalem: Magness Press, 1981.

________. "Administrative Relations between Palestinian and Egyptian Jewry during the Fatimid Period." In *Egypt and Palestine: A Millennium of Association (868–1948)*, edited by Amnon Cohen and Gabriel Baer, 113–35. Jerusalem and New York: Ben Zvi Institute and St. Martin's Press, 1984.

________. "Jews in the Mamlūk Environment: The Crisis of 1442 (a Geniza Study, T-S. AS 150.3)." *BSOAS* 47 (1984): 425–48.

________. "Correspondence and Social Control in the Jewish Communities of the Islamic World: A Letter of the Nagid Joshua Maimonides." *Jewish History* 1 (1986): 39–48.

________. *Under Crescent and Cross: The Jews in the Middle Ages*. Princeton, NJ: Princeton University Press, 1994.

________. "Jewish Communal Organization in Medieval Egypt: Research, Results, Prospects." In *Studies in Muslim-Jewish Relations* 3: *Proceedings of the Founding Conference of the Society for Judaeo-Arabic Studies* (1997): 73–86.

________. "What Was the Pact of ʿUmar? A Literary-Historical Study." *JSAI* 23 (1999): 100-57.

________. "Four Judaeo-Arabic Petitions of the Poor from the Cairo Geniza." *JSAI* 24 (2000): 446–71.

________. "*Sociability and the* Concept *of Galut* in Jewish-Muslim relations in the Middle Ages." In *Judaism and Islam: Boundaries, Communication and Interaction. Essays in Honor of William M. Brinner*, edited by Benjamin H. Hary et al., 37–51. Leiden: Brill, 2000.

________. *Poverty and Charity in the Jewish Community of Medieval Egypt*. Princeton, NJ: Princeton University Press, 2005.

________. *The Voice of the Poor in the Middle Ages: An Anthology of Documents from the Cairo Geniza*. Princeton, NJ: Princeton University Press, 2005.

________. *Under Crescent and Cross: The Jews in the Middle Ages*. 2nd edition. Princeton, NJ: Princeton University Press, 2008.

________. *Maimonides and the Merchants: Jewish Law and Society in the Islamic Middle Ages*. Philadelphia: University of Pennsylvania Press, 2017.

Cohen, Sara. *The Poems of R. Aaron al-ʿAmmānī*. Jerusalem: Mekize Nirdamim, 2008. [In Hebrew.]

Cohn, Haim Hermann, and Menachem Elon. "Oath." In *Encyclopedia Judaica*, 15:360–64.

Constable, Olivia Remie. *Trade and Traders in Muslim Spain: The Commercial Realignment of the Iberian Peninsula, 900–1500.* Cambridge: Cambridge University Press, 1994.

Cook, David. "Apostasy from Islam: A Historical Perspective." *JSAI* 31 (2006): 248–88.

Cotton, H. M., and A. Yardeni. *Aramaic, Hebrew and Greek Documentary Texts from Nahal Hever and Other Sites*, vol. 27 of *DJD*. Oxford: Clarendon, 1997.

Cowley, A. E. "Hebrew and Aramaic Papyri." *JQR* 16 (1904): 1–8.

________. "Notes on Hebrew Papyrus Fragments from Oxyrhynchus." *Journal of Egypt Archaeology* 2 (1915): 209–13.

Crone, Patricia. *Roman, Provincial and Islamic Law.* Cambridge: Cambridge University Press, 1987.

Cuffel, Alexandra. "Call and Response: European Jewish Emigration to Egypt and Palestine in the Middle Ages." *Jewish Quarterly Review* 90 (1999): 61–102.

Curtin, Philip D. *Cross-Cultural Trade in World History.* Cambridge: Cambridge University Press, 1984.

David, Abraham. "The Jewish Settlements from the Sixteenth Century to the Eighteenth Century." In *Toledot yehudey Mitzrayim ba-tequfah ha-Ottomanit 1517–1914* [*The Jews in Ottoman Egypt 1517–1914*], edited by J. M. Landau, 13–26. Jerusalem: Misgav Yerushalayim, 1988. [In Hebrew.]

________. *Ḥevra yehudit Yam Tikhonit be-shalḥey yemei ha-beynayim le-or mismakhey genizat Kahir* [*A Jewish Mediterranean Society in the Late Middle Ages as Reflected by Cairo Genizah Documents*] New York and Jerusalem: The Jewish Theological Seminary of America, 2016. [In Hebrew.]

David, Yeḥezkel. "Divorce among the Jews according to Cairo Genizah Documents and Other Sources." PhD diss., Tel Aviv University, 2000. [In Hebrew.]

David, Yonah (ed.). *The Poems of Joseph ibn Tzaddiq*. New York: American Academy for Jewish Studies, 1982. [In Hebrew.]

Davies, Humphrey Taman. "Seventeenth-Century Egyptian Arabic: A Profile of the Colloquial Material in Yūsuf al-Širbīnī's *Hazz al-Quḥūf fī šarḥ Qaṣīd Abī Šādūf.*" PhD thesis, University of California at Berkeley, 1981.

Davies, M. C., and B. Outhwaite. *Hebrew Bible Manuscripts in the Cambridge Genizah Collections.* Cambridge: Cambridge University Press, 1978–2003.

Davis, Stephen J., Bilal Orfali, and Samuel Noble (eds. and trans.). *A Disputation over a Fragment of the Cross: A Medieval Arabic text from the History of Christian-Jewish-Muslim relations in Egypt.* Beirut: Dar al-Machreq, 2012.

Dishon, Judith (ed.). *The Book of the Perfumed Flower Beds by Joseph ben Tanḥum ha-Yerushalmi.* Beer Sheva: Ben Gurion University of the Negev, 2015. [In Hebrew.]

Dols, Michael. *The Black Death in the Middle East.* Princeton, NJ: Princeton University Press, 1977.

Drory, Rina. *Models and Contacts: Arabic Literature and its Impact on Medieval Jewish Culture.* Leiden: Brill, 2000.

Ebstein, Michael. "Ḏū l-Nūn al-Miṣrī and Early Islamic Mysticism." *Arabica* 61 (2014): 559–612.

Edelby, Néophyte. "The Legislative Autonomy of Christians in the Islamic World." In *Muslims and Others in Early Islamic Society*, edited by Robert Hoyland. Aldershot: Aldgate, 2004.

el-Leithy, Tamer. "Coptic Culture and Conversion in Medieval Cairo, 1293–1524 A.D." Unpublished PhD diss., Princeton University, 2005.

________. "Sufis, Copts and the Politics of Piety: Moral Regulation in Fourteenth-Century Upper Egypt." In *The Development of Sufism in Mamluk Egypt*, edited by Richard McGregor and Adam Sabra, 75–119. Cairo: Institut français d'archéologie orientale, 2006.

________. "*Living* Documents, Dying Archives: Towards a Historical Anthropology of Medieval Arabic Archives." *al-Qantara* 32 (2011): 389–434.

Elizur, Shulamit (ed.). *Poet at a Turning Point: Rabbi Yehoshua bar Khalfa and his Poetry*. Jerusalem: Yad Ben-Zvi, 1994. [In Hebrew.]

Elizur, Shulamit. "A New Fragment of the *Qedushta* of R. Yeshu'ah Beribbi Nathan of Gaza in Memory of his Son Josiah." In *The Cairo Geniza Collection in Geneva: Texts and Studies*, edited by David Rosenthal, 195–99. Jerusalem: Magnes Press, 2010. [In Hebrew.]

Elon, Menachem. *Jewish Law: History, Source, Principles*. Translated by Bernard Auerbach and Melvin J. Sykes. Philadelphia: Jewish Publication Society, 1994.

________. "Compromise." In *Encyclopedia Judaica*, 5:124–29.

Encyclopedia of Islam, vol. 11. Edited by P. J. Bearman et al. Leiden: Brill, 2002.

________, vol. 12. Edited by P. J. Bearman et al. Leiden: Brill, 2004.

Engel, E., and M. Mishor. "An Ancient Scroll of the Book of Exodus: The Reunion of Two Separate Fragments." *Israel Museum Studies in Archaeology* 7 (2015): 24–61.

Ergene, Bogaç. *Local Court, Provincial Society and Justice in the Ottoman Empire*. Leiden: Brill, 2003.

Evetts, B. T. A (ed. and trans.). *Churches and Monasteries of Egypt and Some Neighbouring Countries, Attributed to Abu Salih, the Armenian*. Oxford: Clarendon Press, 1895.

Fadel, Mohammad. "al-Qaḍi." In *The Oxford Handbook of Islamic Law*, edited by Anver M. Emon and Rumee Ahmed. http://www.oxfordhandbooks.com/view/10.1093/oxfordhb/9780199679010.001.0001/oxfordhb-9780199679010-e-7.

Fattal, Antoine. *Le Statut Légal des Non-Musulmans en Pays d'Islam*. Beirut: Dar el-Machreq, 1995.

Fedorov, Michael. "On the Portraits of the Sogdian Kings (Ikhshīds) of Samarqand." *Iran* 45 (2007): 153–60.

Fenton, Paul B. "A Mystical Treatise on Prayer and the Spiritual Quest from the Pietist Circle." *JSAI* 16 (1993): 145.

________. "Sufis and Jews in Mamluk Egypt." In *Muslim-Jewish Relations in the Middle Islamic Period: Jews in the Ayyubid and Mamluk Sultanates (1171–1517)*, edited by Stephan Conermann, 41–62. Göttingen: V & R Unipress, 2017.

Finkelstein, Menachem. *Conversion: Halakhah and Practice*. Ramat-Gan: Bar-Ilan University Press, 2006.

Fischel, Walter Joseph. *Jews in the Economic and Political Life of Mediaeval Islam.* London: The Royal Asiatic Society, 1937.

Fleischer, Jürg. "Paleographic Clues to Prosody?—Accents, Word Separation, and Other Phenomena in Old High German Manuscripts." In *Information Structure and Language Change. New Approaches to Word Order Variation in Germanic*, edited by Roland Hinterhölzl and Svetlana Petrova, 161–89. Berlin and New York: de Gruyter, 2009.

Fleischer, Ezra. "Remarks on Medieval Hebrew Poetry." In *Studies in Literature Presented to Simon Halkin*, edited by Ezra Fleischer, 183–204. Jerusalem: Magnes Press, 1973. [In Hebrew.]

________. *The Yotzerot.* Jerusalem: Magnes Press, 1984. [In Hebrew.]

________. *Hebrew Poetry in Spain and Communities under Its Influence.* Edited by Shulamit Elizur and Tova Be'eri. Jerusalem: The Ben-Zvi Institute, 2010. [In Hebrew.]

Fraenkel, Jonah (ed.). *Maḥzor for Shavu'ot According to the Customs of All Branches of the Ashkenazic Rite.* Jerusalem: Koren, 2000. [In Hebrew.]

Franklin, Arnold E. *This Noble House: Jewish Descendants of King David in the Medieval Islamic East.* Philadelphia: University of Pennsylvania Press, 2013.

Frenkel, Miriam. "Adolescence in Jewish Medieval Society under Islam." *Continuity and Change* 16, no. 2 (2001): 263–81.

________. *"The Compassionate and the Benevolent": The Leading Elite in the Jewish Community of Alexandria in the Middle Ages.* Jerusalem: Ben Zvi Institute, 2006. [In Hebrew.]

________. "Charity in Jewish Society of the Medieval Mediterranean World." In *Charity and Giving in Monotheistic Religions*, edited by M. Frenkel and Y. Lev, 343–63. Berlin and New York: Walter de Gruiter, 2009.

________. "On Mark R. Cohen's *Poverty and Charity in the Jewish Community of Medieval Egypt*; idem, *The Voice of the Poor in the Middle Ages: An Anthology of Documents from the Cairo Geniza.*" *Zion* 75, no. 2 (2010): 225–32. [In Hebrew.]

________. "Genizah Documents as Literary Products." In *"From a Sacred Source": Genizah Studies in Honour of Professor Stefan C. Reif*, edited by Ben Outhwaite and Siam Bhayro, 140–6. Leiden and Boston: Brill, 2011.

________. "Slavery in Jewish Medieval Society under Islam: A Gendered Perspective." In *Male and Female He Created Them—Masculine and Feminine in the Mediterranean Religions and Their Influence on Matrimonial Religious Law*, edited by Matthias Morgenstern, 249–59. Göttingen: Vandenhoeck&Ruprecht, 2011.

________. "The Family." In *The Cambridge History of Judaism*, vol. 5, *Jews and Judaism in the Islamic World, Seventh through Fifteenth Centuries*, edited by Phillip I. Lieberman. Cambridge: Cambridge University Press, forthcoming 2021.

Frenkel, Miriam, and Ayala Lester, "Evidence of Material Culture from the Geniza—An Attempt to Correlate Textual and Archaeological Findings." In *Material Evidence and Narrative Sources. Interdisciplinary Studies of the History of the Muslim Middle East*, edited by Daniella Talmon-Heller and Katia Cytryn-Silverman, 147–87. Leiden: Brill, 2015.

Frenkel, Y. "The Impact of the Crusades on the Rural Society and Religious Endowments: The Case of Medieval Syria." In *War and Society in the Eastern Mediterranean, 7–15th Centuries,* edited by Y. Lev, 237–48. Leiden: Brill, 1997.

Frescobaldi, Lionardo, Giorgio Gucci, and Simone Sigoli. *Visit to the Holy Places of Egypt, Sinai, Palestine, and Syria in 1384.* Translated by Theophilus Bellorini and Eugene Hoade. Jerusalem: Franciscan Press, 1948.

Friedman, Mordechai Akiva. "The Ethics of Medieval Marriages." In *Religion in a Religious Age,* edited by S. D. Goitein, 93–94. Cambridge: Association for Jewish Studies, 1974.

________. "The Ransom-Divorce: Divorce Proceedings Initiated by the Wife in Mediaeval Jewish Practice." *IOS* 6 (1976): 289–93.

________. *Jewish Marriage in Palestine: A Cairo Geniza Study.* Tel Aviv: Tel Aviv University Press, 1980.

________. "Divorce upon the Wife's Demand as Reflected in Manuscripts from the Cairo Genizah." *Jewish Law Annual* 4 (1981): 101–27.

________. "New Fragments from the Responsa of Maimonides." In *Studies in Geniza and Sephardic Heritage Presented to Shelomo Dov Goitein on the Occasion of his Eightieth Birthday,* edited by S. Morag et al., 115–20. Jerusalem: Magness Press, 1981. [In Hebrew.]

________. "Responsa of Hai Gaʾon—New Fragments from the Genizah." *Teʿuda* 3 (1983): 71–82. [In Hebrew.]

________. *Jewish Polygyny in the Middle Ages.* Jerusalem: Bialik Institute, 1986. [In Hebrew.]

________. "Responsa of Abraham Maimonides on a Debtor's Travails." In *Genizah Research after Ninety Years: The Case of Judaeo-Arabic,* edited by J. Blau and S. C. Reif, 82–92. Cambridge: Cambridge University Press, 1992.

________. "Controversy for the Sake of Heaven: Studies on the Liturgical Debate of Abraham Maimonides and His Generation." *Teʿudah* 10 (1996): 245–98. [In Hebrew.]

________. *Maimonides, The Yemenite Messiah and Apostasy.* Jerusalem: Ben-Zvi Institute, 2002. [In Hebrew.]

________. "On Marital Age, Violence and Mutuality as Reflected in the Genizah Documents." In *The Cambridge Genizah Collections: Their Contents and Significance,* edited by S. C. Reif, 160–77. Cambridge: Cambridge University Press, 2002.

________. "Maimonides, Zuta, and the *Muqaddams*: A Story of Three Excommunication Bans." *Zion* 70 (2005), 473–528. [In Hebrew.]

________. "Contracts: Rabbinic Literature and Ancient Jewish Documents." In *The Literature of the Sages, Second Part: Midrash and Targum; Liturgy, Poetry, Mysticism, Contracts, Inscriptions, Ancient Science; and the Languages of Rabbinic Literature,* edited by S Safrai et al. Aspen: Fortress Press, 2007.

________. "Abraham Maimonides on his Leadership, Reforms and Spiritual Imperfection." *JQR* 104 (2014): 504–5.

________. "Maimonides Appoints R. Anatoly *Muqaddam* of Alexandria." *Tarbiz* 83 (2015), 135–61. [In Hebrew.]

Friedman, Yohanan. *Tolerance and Coercion in Islam: Interfaith Relations in the Muslim Tradition.* New York: Cambridge University Press, 2003.

Fyzee, Asaf A. A. (trans.), Ismail K. H. Poonawala (rev.). *The Pillars of Islam, Daʿaim al-Islam of al-Qadi al-Nuʿman.* Oxford: Oxford University Press, 2002–4.

Gabra, Gawdat. *The A to Z of the Coptic Church.* Lanham: Scarecrow Press, 2009.

Gal, Susan, and Judith T. Irvine. "The Boundaries of Languages and Disciplines: How Ideologies Construct Difference." *Social Research* 62, no. 4 (1995): 967–1023.

Gallego, Maria Angeles, "The Calamities that Followed the Death of Joseph Ibn Migash: Jewish Views on the Almohad Conquest." In *Judaeo-Arabic Culture in al-Andalus: 13th Conference of the Society for Judaeo-Arabic Studies, Cordoba 2007*, edited by Amir Ashur, 79–98. Cordoba: Cordoba Near Eastern Research Unit, 2013.

Garcin, Jean-Claude. "The Mamluk Military System and the Blocking of Medieval Moslem Society." In *Europe and the Rise of Capitalism*, edited by J. Baechler, J. A. Hall, and M. Mann, 113–30. Oxford: Blackwell, 1988.

Gardner-Chloros, Penelope, and Daniel Weston. "Codeswitching and Multilingualism in Literature." *Language and Literature* 24, no. 3 (2015): 182–93.

Ghāda al-Qaddūmī (trans.). *Book of Gifts and Rarities [Kitab al-hadāyā wa al-tuḥaf]: Selections Compiled in the Fifteenth Century from an Eleventh-Century Manuscript on Gifts and Treasures.* Cambridge, MA: Harvard University Press, 1996.

Geller, M. J. "An Aramaic Incantation from Oxyrhynchos." *ZPE* 58 (1985): 96–8.

Gil, Moshe. *Documents of the Jewish Pious Foundations from the Cairo Geniza.* Leiden: Brill, 1976.

________. *Palestine during the First Muslim Period (634–1099).* 3 vols.Tel Aviv: Tel Aviv University and the Ministry of Defense, 1983. [In Hebrew.]

________. "Palestine during the First Muslim Period (634–1099): Additions, Notes, Corrigenda." *Teʿuda* 7 (1991): 281–351. [In Hebrew.]

________. *A History of Palestine, 634–1099.* Translated by Ethel Broido. Cambridge: Cambridge University Press, 1992.

________. *In the Kingdom of Ishmael.* 4 vols. Jerusalem and Tel Aviv: Bialik Institute and Tel Aviv University Press, 1997. [In Hebrew.]

________. *Jews in Islamic Countries in the Middle Ages.* Leiden and Boston: Brill, 2004.

________. *The Tustaris, Family and Sect.* Tel Aviv: The Diaspora Research Institute, 1981. [In Hebrew].

Gil, Moshe, and Ezra Fleischer. *Yehudah ha-Levi and his Circle.* Jerusalem: Magnes Press, 2001. [In Hebrew.]

Goitein, Shelomo Dov. "A Jewish Addict to Sufism in the Time of the Nagid David II Maimonides." *JQR* 44 (1953–4(: 37–49.

________. "Letters about R. Yehudah ha-Levi's Stay in Alexandria and the Collection of his Poems." *Tarbiz* 28 (1959): 343–61. [In Hebrew.]

________. "The Main Industries of the Mediterranean Area as Reflected in the Records of the Cairo Geniza." *JESHO* 4, no. 2 (1961): 168–197.

________. *Jewish Education in Muslim Countries, Based on Records from the Cairo Geniza.* Jerusalem:The ben Zvi Institute, 1962. [In Hebrew.]

________. "Abraham Maimonides and His Pietist Circle." *Tarbiz* 33 (1964): 187. [In Hebrew.]

________. "The Synagogue Building and its Furnishings According to the Records of the Cairo Genizah." *Eretz-Israel: Archeological, Historical and Geographical Studies* 7 (1964): 93–4. [In Hebrew.]

________. "Court Records from the Cairo Genizah in JNUL." *Kiryat Sefer* 41 (1965–66): 263–76. [In Hebrew.]

________. "A Treatise in Defence of the Pietists by Abraham Maimonides." *JJS* 16 (1965): 113–14.

________. *Studies in Islamic History and Institutions*. Leiden: Brill, 1966.

________. "A Jewish Business Woman of the Eleventh Century." *JQR* 50 (1967): 225–42.

________. *A Mediterranean Society: The Jewish Communities of the Arab World as Portrayed in the Documents of the Cairo Geniza*. 5 volumes plus index volume by Paula Sanders. Berkeley, Los Angeles, London: University of California Press, 1967–93.

________. "Cairo: An Islamic City in the Light of the Geniza Documents." In *Middle Eastern Cities*, edited by Ira M. Lapidus, 80–96. Berkeley and Los Angeles: University of California Press, 1969.

________. "The Struggle between the Synagogue and the Community." In *Hayyim (Jefim) Schirmann: Jubilee Volume*, edited by Shraga Abramson and Aaron Mirsky, 70. Jerusalem: Schocken Institute, 1970. [In Hebrew.]

________. "The Head of the Palestinian Academy as Head of the Jews in the Fatimid Empire: Arabic Documents on the Palestinian Gaonate." *Eretz-Israel* 10 (1971): 64–75. [In Hebrew.]

________. *Letters of Medieval Jewish Traders*. Princeton, NJ: Princeton University Press, 1973.

________. "Elhanan b. Shemarya as a Communal Leader." In *Joshua Finkel Festschrift*, edited by Sidney B. Hoenig and Leon D. Stitskin, Hebrew section, 117–37. New York: Yeshiva University Press, 1974. [In Hebrew.]

________. "The Public Activity of Rabbi Elḥanan ben Shemarya '*Rosh ha-Seder* of all Israel'." In *Joshua Finkel Festschrift: In honor of Joshua Finkel*, edited by Sidney B. Hoenig and Leon D. Stitskin, 117–37. New York: Yeshiva University Press, 1974. [In Hebrew.]

________. "New Sources on the Palestinian Gaonate." In *Salo Wittmayer Baron Jubilee Volume*, edited by Saul Lieberman in association with Arthur Hyman, English section, 523–25. Jerusalem: American Academy for Jewish Research, 1974.

________. "Parents and Children: A Geniza Study on the Medieval Jewish Family." *Gratz College Annual of Jewish Studies* 4 (1975): 47–68.

________. "The Sexual Mores of the Common People." In *Society and the Sexes in Medieval Islam*, edited by Giorgio Levi Della Vida and Alaf Lufti al-Sayyid-Marsot, 43–61. Malibu, CA: Undena Publishing, 1979.

________. "The Interplay of Jewish and Islamic Laws." In *Jewish Law in Legal History and the Modern World*, edited by Bernard S. Jackson, 61–77. Leiden: Brill, 1980.

________. *Palestinian Jewry in Early Islamic and Crusaders Times*. Jerusalem: Yad Ben Zvi, 1980. [In Hebrew.]

________. "Dimdumey ʿerev shel beyt ha-Rambam" [The Twilight of the House of Maimonides]. *Tarbiz* 54 (1984): 67–104. [In Hebrew.]

Goitein, S. D., and Mordechai A. Friedman. *India Traders of the Middle Ages: Documents from the Cairo Geniza ("India Book")*. Leiden: Brill, 2008.

________. *Joseph Lebdī: Prominent India Trader: Cairo Genizah Documents*, vol. 1 of *India Book*. Jerusalem: Ben Zvi Institute, 2009. [In Hebrew.]

________. *Ḥalfon the Traveling Merchant Scholar: Cairo Genizah Documents*, vol. 4, pt. A of *India Book*. Jerusalem: Ben Zvi Institute, 2013. [In Hebrew.]

________.*Judah ha-Levi: A Poet Laureate: Cairo Genizah Documents*, vol. 4, pt. B of *India Book*. Jerusalem: Ben Zvi Institute, 2013. [In Hebrew.]

Golb, Norman. "Legal Documents from the Cairo Genizah." *JSocS* 20 (1958): 17–46.

________. "The Topography of the Jews in Medieval Egypt: Inductive Studies Based Primarily upon Documents from the Cairo Genizah." *Jounal of Near Eastern Studies (JNES)* 24 (1965): 251–70; 33 (1974): 116–49.

________. "Jewish Proselytism—a Phenomenon in the Religious History of Early Medieval Europe." The Tenth Annual Rabbi Louis Feinberg Memorial Lecture, Judaic Studies Program, University of Cincinnati, March 3, 1987. Accessed June 27, 2017. https://oi.uchicago.edu/sites/oi.uchicago.edu/files/uploads/shared/docs/jewish_proselytism.pdf.

________. "The Autograph Memoirs of Obadiah the Proselyte of Oppido Lucano and the Epistle of Barukh b. Isaac of Aleppo." Prepared for the Convegno Internazionale di Studi Giovanni-Obadiah da Oppido: Proselito, viaggiatore e musicista dell'età normanna. Accessed June 27, 2017. https://oi.uchicago.edu/sites/oi.uchicago.edu/files/uploads/shared/docs/autograph_memoirs_obadiah.pdf.

Goldberg, Jessica. *Trade and Institutions in the Medieval Mediterranean: The Geniza Merchants and Their Business World*. Cambridge: Cambridge University Press, 2012.

Golden, Peter B., et al. (eds. and trans.). *The King's Dictionary—The Rasûlid Hexaglot: Fourteenth-Century Vocabularies in Arabic, Persian, Turkic, Greek, Armenian, and Mongol*. Leiden: Brill, 2000.

Gottheil, Richard. "An Eleventh-Century Document concerning a Cairo Synagogue." *JQR* 19, no. 3 (1907): 467–539.

Grossman, Avraham. "The Origins and Essence of the Custom of 'Stopping-the-Service.'" *Milet* 1 (1983): 199–220. [In Hebrew.]

________. "Child Marriage in Jewish Society in the Middle Ages until the Thirteenth Century." *Pe'amim* 45 (1990): 108–25. [In Hebrew.]

Guest, R. "Cairene Topography: El-Qarafa According to Ibn Ez-Zaiyat." *Journal of the Royal Asiatic Society* 1 (1926): 57–61.

Guillaume, A. "Further Documents on the Ben Meir Controversy." *JQR* N.S 5 (1914–15): 543–47.

Gulak, Asher. *'Otzar ha-Sheṭarot ha-Nehugim be-Yisra'el* [*A Treasury of Jewish Deeds*]. Jerusalem: Po'alim Press, 1926.

N. Hacham and T. Ilan, Corpus *Papyrorum Judaicarum* vol. IV (Jerusalem and Berlin: De Magnes and De Gruyter, 2020); vol. V, in press, vol. VI, in preparation.

Hacohen, Elisheva. *The Poems of R. Anatoli ben Joseph*. MA thesis, Hebrew University, 1996. [In Hebrew.]

Halakhot Gedolot. Edited by Azriel Hildesheimer. Jerusalem: Mekize Nirdamim, 1972.

Halberstam, S. J. *Sepher Haschetaroth: Dokumentenbuch von R. Jehuda ben Barsilai aus Barcelona*. Berlin: Itzkowski, 1898. [In Hebrew.]

Halkin, Abraham S. (ed.). *Moshe ben Yaʿaqov ibn Ezra: Kitab al-Muḥāḍara wal-Mudhākara*. Jerusalem: n.p., 1975.

Hallaq, Wael. "The Qāḍī's Dīwān (sijill) before the Ottomans." *BSOAS* 61 (1998): 415–36.

Harkavy, Abraham E. *Zikhron kamma geʾonim u-ve-yiḥud Rav Sherira ve-Rav beno ve-Rav ha-Rav R. Yitzhaq al-Fāsī*. Berlin, Itzkawski Press, 1887.

________. *Zikkaron la-Rishonim*, vol. 5. St. Petersburg: Mekize Nirdamim, 1891.

Hary, Benjamin H. *Translating Religion: Linguistic Analysis of Judaeo-Arabic Sacred Texts from Egypt*. Leiden: Brill, 2009.

________. *Multiglossia in Judaeo-Arabic*. Leiden: Brill, 1992.

________. *Translating Religion: Linguistic Analysis of Judaeo-Arabic Sacred Texts from Egypt*. Leiden: Brill, 2009.

Ḥasan, Qādir Muḥammad. "al-Ḥisba khilāl al-ʿahd al-ayyūbī." *BEO* 63 (2015): 191–204.

Hirschfeld, Hartwig. "Some Judeo Arabic Legal Documents." *JQR* 16 (1925): 279–86.

Hofer, Nathan. "The Ideology of Decline and the Jews of Ayyubid and Mamluk Syria." In *Muslim-Jewish Relations in the Middle Islamic Period: Jews in the Ayyubid and Mamluk Sultanates (1171–1517)*, edited by Stephan Conermann, 95–120. Göttingen: V & R Unipress, 2017.

________. *The Popularisation of Sufism in Ayyubid and Mamluk Egypt, 1173–1325*. Edinburgh: Edinburgh University Press, 2015.

Hoffman, Adina, and Peter Cole. *Sacred Trash; The Lost and Found World of the Cairo Geniza* New York: Next Book-Schocken, 2011.

Holes, Clive. "Confessional Varieties." In *Handbook of Arabic Sociolinguistics*, edited by Enam al-Wer and Uri Horesh, 63–80. London: Routledge. 2017.

Holt, Peter Malcolm. "An Early Source on Shaykh Khadir al-Mihrani." *BSOAS* 46 (1983): 33–39.

________. *The Age of the Crusades: The Near East from the Eleventh Century to 1517*. London: Longman, 1986.

Howard, Deborah. "Venice and Islam in the Middle Ages: Some Observations on the Question of Architectural Influence." *Architectural History* 34 (1991): 59–74.

Hoyland, Robert G. *Seeing Islam as Others Saw It: A Survey and Evaluation of Christian, Jewish and Zoroastrian Writing on Early Islam*. Princeton, NJ: Princeton University Press, 1997.

Humphreys, Stephen R. "The Expressive Intent of the Mamluk Architecture of Cairo: a Preliminary Essay." *Studia Islamica* 35 (1972): 69–119.

________. "Egypt in the World System of the Later Middle Ages." In *The Cambridge History of Egypt*, vol. 1, *Islamic Egypt, 640–1517*, edited by Carl F. Petry, 445–61. Cambridge: Cambridge University Press, 1998.

Ibn ʿAbd al-Ḥakām Abū al-Qāsim ʿAbd al-Raḥman. *Futūḥ Miṣr wa-akhbāruhā* [*The History of the Conquest of Egypt, North Africa and Spain*]. Edited by Ch. Torrey. New Haven: Yale University Press, 1921.

Ibn ʿAsākir, abū al-Qāsim ʿAli. *Ta'rikh madinat Dimashq*. Edited by M. al-ʿAmrawi. Damascus: Dar al-Fikr, 1415/1995.

Ibn al-Athīr. ʿIzz al-Dīn, *al-Kāmil fī al-tārīkh*, ed. Carl Johan Tornberg (Beirut: Dār Sāder, 1965).

Ibn Jamāʿa. *Taḥrir al-aḥkām fi tadbīr ahl al-islam*. Edited by F. A. Ahmad. Qatr: Dar al-Thaqafa, 1988.

Ibn Kathīr, Ismāʿīl ibn ʿUmar. *al-Bidāya wa-l-nihāya*. Beirut: Dār al-Iḥyā' al-Turāth al-ʿArabī, 1413/1993.

Ibn Khaldūn, Walī al-Dīn ʿAbd al-Raḥman al-Mālikī. *al-Taʿrīf bi-ibn khaldūn wa-riḥlatih^{i} gharb^{an} washarq^{an}*. Beirut: Dār al-Kutub al-Lubnānī, 1979.

Ibn al-Zayyāt, Shams al-Dīn Muḥammad. *Kitāb al-Kawākib al-sayyāra fī tartīb al-ziyāra fī al-qarāfatayn al-kubrā wa-al-ṣughraā*. Baghdād: Maktabat al-Muthanná, 1968.

Ibn al-Zubayr, Rashīd. *al-Dhakhā'ir wal-tuḥaf*. Edited by M. Hamid Allah. Kuwait: Da'irat al-matbuʿat, 1959.

Ilan, Tal. "The Jewish Community in Egypt before and after 117 CE in Light of Old and New Papyri." In *Jewish and Christian Communal Identities in the Roman World*, edited by Y. Furstenberg, 201–24. Leiden: Brill, 2016.

________. "Another Ketubbah on a Papyrus from Byzantine Egypt?" *Eretz Israel: Ada Yardeni Memorial Volume* (forthcoming). [In Hebrew.]

________. "Julia Crispina of the Babatha Archive Revisited: A Woman between the Judean Desert and the Fayum in Egypt, between the Diaspora Revolt and the Bar Kokhba War." In *Gender and Social Norms in Ancient Israel, Early Judaism and Early Christianity: Texts and Material Culture*, edited by Michaela Bauks, Katharina Galor, and Judith Hartenstein, 269–76. Göttingen: Vandenhoeck and Ruprecht, 2019.

________. "An Addendum to Bagnall and Cribiore, *Women's Letters from Ancient Egypt*: Two Aramaic Letters from Jewish Women." In *Israel in Egypt: The Land of Egypt as Concept and Reality for Jews in Antiquity and the Early Medieval Period*, edited by Alison Salvesen, Sarah Pearce, and Miriam Frenkel, 397-416. Leiden: Brill, 2020.

Irwin, Robert. "Under Western Eyes: A History of Mamluk Studies." *MSR* 4 (2000): 27–51.

The Itinerary of Benjamin of Tudela. Edited and translated by Marcus Nathan Adler. London: Henry Frowde, 1907.

ʿIzz al-Dīn Ibn al-Athīr. *al-Kāmil fī al-tārīkh*. Edited by Carl Johan Tornberg. Beirut: Dār Sāder, 1965.

Jarden, Dov (ed.). *Dīwān of Shmuel ha-Nagid: Ben Tehillim*. Jerusalem: Hebrew Union College Press, 1965–1991. [In Hebrew.]

________. *Liturgical Poetry of Judah ha-Levi*. Jerusalem: Dov Jarden, 1977–1985. [In Hebrew.]

________. *Maḥberot Immanuel ha-Romi*. Jerusalem: Mossad ha-Rav Kook, 1957. [In Hebrew.]

Judah al-Harizi. *Tahkemoni or The Tales of Heman the Ezrahite.* Edited by Joseph Yahalom and Naoya Katsumata. Jerusalem: Ben Zvi Institute, 2010. [In Hebrew.]

Kabatnik, Martin. *Cesta do Jerusalema a Kaira.* Prague: n.p., 1894.

Kanarfogel, Ephraim. "Returning to the Jewish Community in Medieval Ashkenaz: History and Halakhah." In *Turim I: Studies in Jewish History and Literature Presented to Dr. Bernard Lander,* edited by Michael A. Schmidman, 69–97. New York: Touro College Press, 2007–8.

________. "Changing Attitudes towards Apostates in Tosafists Literature, Late Twelfth–Early Thirteenth Centuries." In *New Perspectives on Jewish-Christian Relations,* edited by Elisheva Carlebach and Jacob J. Schacter, 297–327. Leiden and Boston: Brill, 2012.

Kedar, Benjamin Z. "Notes on the History of the Jews of Palestine in the Middle Ages." *Tarbiz* 42 (1973): 401–18. [In Hebrew.]

Kelleher, Marie A. *The Measure of Woman: Law and Female Identity in the Crown of Aragon.* Philadelphia: University of Pennsylvania Press, 2010.

Kennedy, Hugh. "Egypt as a Province in the Islamic Caliphate, 641–868." In *The Cambridge History of Egypt,* vol. 1: *Islamic Egypt 640-1517,* edited by Carl F. Petry, 62–85. Cambridge: Cambridge University Press, 1998.

Khalafallah, Abdelghany. *A Descriptive Grammar of Saei:di: Egyptian Colloquial.* The Hague: Mouton, 1969.

Khan, Geoffrey. "The Historical Development of the Structure of Medieval Arabic Petitions." *BSOAS* 53 (1990): 8–30.

________. "The Function of the *Shewa* Sign in Vocalized Judaeo-Arabic Texts from the Genizah." In *Genizah Research after Ninety Years: The Case of Judaeo-Arabic,* edited by Joshua Blau and Stefan C. Reif, 107–11. Cambridge: Cambridge University Press, 1992.

________. *Arabic Legal and Administrative Documents in the Cambridge Genizah Collections.* Cambridge: Cambridge University Press, 1993.

________. "On the Question of Script in Medieval Karaite Manuscripts: New Evidence from the Genizah." *Bulletin of the John Rylands University Library of Manchester* 75 (1993): 133–41.

________. "An Arabic Document of Acknowledgement from the Cairo Genizah." *JNES* 53, no. 2 (1994): 117–24.

________. "A note on the Trade Argot of the Karaite Goldsmiths of Cairo." *Mediterranean Language Review* 9 (1995–7): 74–76.

________. "Judaeo-Arabic." In *Encyclopedia of Arabic Language and Linguistics,* vol. 3, edited by Kees Versteegh, 526–36. Leiden: Brill, 2007.

________. "Vocalized Judaeo-Arabic Manuscripts in the Cairo Genizah." In *"From a Sacred Source": Genizah Studies in Honour of Professor Stefan C. Reif,* edited by Ben Outhwaite and Siam Bhayro, 201–18. Leiden: Brill, 2010.

________. "Hebrew as a Secret Language in Yemenite Judeo-Arabic." In *Encyclopedia of Hebrew Language and Linguistics,* vol. 3, edited by Geoffrey Khan, 518–20. Leiden: Brill, 2013.

Khoury, Raif Georges. "Al-Layth Ibn Sa'd (94–175/713–791), grand maitre et mécène de l'Egypte, vu à travers quelques documents islamiques anciens." *Journal of Near Eastern Studies* 40/3 (1981): 189–202.

Klar, Benjamin (ed.). *Megillat Aḥima'atz*. 2nd edition. Jerusalem: Tarshish, 1974.

Klein–Franke, F. "Eine aramäische tabella devotionis (T. Colon. inv. nr. 6)." *ZPE* 7 (1971): 47–52.

________. "A Hebrew Lamentation from Roman Egypt." *ZPE* 51 (1983): 80–4.

Kleinman, Ron S. *Methods of Acquisition and Commercial Customs in Jewish Law: Theory, Practice and History.* Jerusalem: Bar Ilan University Press, 2013. [In Hebrew.]

Kotansky, R. *Greek Magical Amulets. The Inscribed Gold, Silver, Copper, and Bronze Lamellae,* part 1: *Published Texts of Known Provenance. Text and Commentary.* Opladen: Westdeutscher Verlag, 1994.

Kotansky, R., J. Naveh, and S. Shaked. "A Greek-Aramaic Silver Amulet from Egypt in the Ashmolean Museum." *Le Muséon* 105 (1992): 5–25.

Kozodoy, Maud. "Prefatory Verse and the Reception of the Guide of the Perplexed." *Jewish Quarterly Review* 106 (2016): 257–82.

Kraemer, Joel L. "The Andalusian Mystic Ibn Hūd and the Conversion of the Jews." *IOS* 12 (1992): 59–73.

________. "A Jewish Cult of the Saints in Fāṭimid Egypt." In *L'Egypte Fatimide: son art et son histoire,* edited by Marianne Barrucand: 579–601, Paris: Presses de l'Université de Paris-Sorbonne, 1999.

________. "Women Speak for Themselves." In *The Cambridge Geniza Collections: Their Contents and Significance,* edited by Stefan Reif, 178–216. Cambridge: Cambridge University Press, 2002.

________. *Maimonides, The Life and World of One of Civilization's Greatest Minds.* New York: Doubleday, 2008.

Kraft, R. A. "The 'Textual Mechanics' of Early Jewish LXX/OG Papyri and Fragments." In *The Bible as Book: The Transmission of the Greek Text,* edited by S. McKendrick and O. A. O'Sullivan, 51–68. London: British Library and Oak Knoll Press, 2003.

Krakowski, Eve. *Coming of Age in Medieval Egypt: Female Adolescence, Jewish Law, and Ordinary Culture.* Princeton, NJ: Princeton University Press, 2017.

Krakowski, Eve, and Marina Rustow. "Formula as Content: Medieval Jewish Institutions, the Cairo Geniza, and the New Diplomatics." *JSS* 20 (2014): 111–46.

Kreisel, Howard. "Maimonides on Christianity and Islam." *Jewish Civilization* 3 (1985): 153–62.

Kühnert, Henrike, and Esther-Miriam Wagner. "The Shift in Positioning of the Finite Verb in Older Yiddish." In *Yiddish Language Structures. Empirical Approaches to Language Typology,* edited by Marion Aptroot and Björn Hansen, 125–42. Berlin: de Gruyter Mouton, 2014.

Lange, Christian. "Legal and Cultural Aspects of Ignominious Parading (*Tashhīr*) in Islam." *Islamic Law and Society* 14 (2007): 81–108.

Lapidus, Ira M. *Muslim Cities in the Later Middle Ages.* Cambridge, MA: Harvard University Press, 1967.

Lasker, Daniel. "Tradition and Innovation in Maimonides' Attitude toward Other Religions." In *Maimonides after 800 Years*, edited by Jay Harris, 167–82. Cambridge, MA: Harvard University Press, 2007.

Lavee, Moshe. "'Proselytes Are as Hard to Israel as a Scab is to the Skin': A Babylonian Talmudic Concept," *JJS* 53 (2012): 22–48.

Le Grande, L. "Relation du Pélerinage a Jerusalem de Nicolas de Martoni, notaire Italien (1394–5)." *Revue de l'orient latin* 3 (1895): 587–8.

Letters and Essays of Maimonides. Edited and translated by I. Shilat. Maaleh Adummim: Shilat, 1995. [In Hebrew.]

Lev, Efraim, and Leigh Chipman. *Medical Prescriptions in the Cambridge Genizah Collections.* Leiden: Brill, 2012.

Lev, Yaacov. *State and Society in Fatimid Egypt.* Leiden: Brill, 1991.

________. *The Administration of Justice in Medieval Egypt from the Seventh to the Twelfth Century.* Edinburgh: Edinburgh University Press, 2020.

Levine, L. I. *The Ancient Synagogue: The First Thousand Years.* New Haven: Yale University Press, 2000.

Lewicka, Paulina B. "Healer, Scholar, Conspirator. The Jewish Physician in the Arabic-Islamic Discourse of the Mamluk Period." In *Muslim-Jewish Relations in the Middle Islamic Period: Jews in the Ayyubid and Mamluk Sultanates (1171–1517)*, edited by Stephan Conermann, 121–44. Göttingen: V & R Unipress, 2017.

________. "Did Ibn al-Ḥājj Copy from Cato? Reconsidering Aspects of Inter-Communal Antagonism of the Mamluk Period." In *Ubi sumus? Quo vademus? Mamluk Studies—State of the Art*, ed. Stephan Conermann, 231–61. Göttingen: V & R Unipress, 2013.

Lewis, Bernard. *Race and Slavery in the Middle East.* New York: Oxford University Press, 1990.

Lewis, N. (with Y. Yadin). *The Documents from the Bar-Kokhba Period in the Cave of Letters: Greek Papyri.* Jerusalem: Israel Exploration Society, 1989.

Libson, Gideon. "The Origin and Development of the Anonymous Ban (*Ḥerem Setam*) during the Geonic Period." *Shenaton ha-Mishpat ha-ʿIvri* 22 (2001–2004): 107–232. [In Hebrew.]

________. "Legal Autonomy and the Recourse to Legal Proceedings by Protected Peoples, according to Muslim Sources during the Geonic Period." In *The Intertwined Worlds of Islam: Essays in Memory of Hava Lazarus-Yafeh*, edited by Naḥem Ilan, 334–92. Jerusalem: Hebrew University, 2002. [In Hebrew.]

________. *Jewish and Islamic Law: A Comparative Study of Custom during the Geonic Period.* Cambridge: Harvard University Press, 2003.

________. "Betrothal of an Adult Woman by an Agent in Geonic Responsa: Legal Construction Accord with Islamic Law." In *Esoteric and Exoteric Aspects in Judeo Arabic Culture*, edited by B. Hary and H. Ben Shammai, 175–89. Leiden: Brill, 2006.

________. "The 'Court Memorandum' (*Maḥḍar*) in Saadiah's Writings and the Genizah and the Muslim *Maḥḍar*." *Ginzei Qedem* 5 (2009): 99–163. [In Hebrew.]

Lifshitz, Berachyahu. "The Legal Status of the Responsa Literature." In *Authority, Process and Method: Studies in Jewish Law*, edited by Hanina Ben Menahem and Neil S. Hecht, 59–100. Amsterdam: Harwood Academic Publishers, 1998.

Liphschits, Itay E. "The Procedural Limits of Compromise (*Pesharah*)." *Shenaton ha-Mishpat ha-ʿIvri* 24 (2007): 63–122. [In Hebrew.]

Little, Donald P. "Coptic Conversion to Islam under the Bahri Mamluks, 692–755/1293–1354." *BSOAS* 39, no. 3 (1976): 552–69.

Loewe, H. "The Petrie-Hirschfeld Papyri." *Journal of Theological Studies* 24 (1923): 126–41.

Lopez, Robert S. "Trade in Medieval Europe: the South." In *The Cambridge Economic History of Europe*, vol. 2, *Trade and Industry in the Middle Ages*, edited by M. M. Postan and Edward Miller, assisted by Cynthia Postan. 2nd edition. Cambridge: Cambridge University Press, 1987.

________. *The Commercial Revolution of the Middle Ages, 950–1350*. Englewood Cliffs, NJ: Prentice-Hall, 1971.

Maimonides, Abraham. *Responsa*. Edited and translated by A. H. Freimann and S. D. Goitein. Jerusalem: Mekize Nirdamim, 1937.

________. *Sefer ha-Maspik le-ʿOvdey Hashem, Kitab Kifayat al-ʿAbidin (Part Two, Volume Two)*. Edited by Nissim Dana. Ramat-Gan: Bar Ilan University, 1989.

Maimonides, Moses. *Responsa*. Edited and translated by Joshua Blau. Jerusalem: Mekize Nirdamim, 1986.

________. *Responsa*. Edited and translated by Joshua Blau. 2nd edition. Jerusalem: Rubin Mass-Makhon Moshe, 2014. [In Hebrew.]

Maimonides, Moses. *Mishneh Torah*. Edited by Y. Kafih. Jerusalem: Makhon Mishnat ha-Rambam, 1984–1996.

Mallat, Chibli. *Introduction to Middle Eastern Law*. Oxford: Oxford University Press, 2007.

Mann, Jacob. "Piyyutim from Prison." *Ha-Tzofeh le-Ḥokhmat Yisraʾel* 6 (1922): 1–15.

________. *The Jews in Egypt and in Palestine under the Fatimid Caliphs: A Contribution to Their Political and Communal History*. With a Preface and Reader's Guide by Shelomo D. Goitein. 2 vols. New York: Ktav, 1970.

________. *Texts and Studies in Jewish History and Literature*. With Introduction by Gershon D. Cohen. 2 vols. New York: Ktav, 1972.

Marassini, P. "I frammenti aramaici." *Studi Classici ed Orientali* 29: *Nuovi papiri magici in Copto, Greco e Aramaico*, edited by E. Bresciani, S. Pernigotti, F. Maltomini, and P. Marrassini (1979): 125–30.

Margoliouth, David S. "A Jewish-Persian Law Report." *JQR* 11 (1899): 671–5.

________. *Mohammed and the Rise of Islam*. New York and London: Putnam, 1905.

Marks, Alexander. "Texts by and about Maimonides." *Jewish Quarterly Review* 25 (1934/5): 371–428.

Marmon, Shaun E. "Domestic Slavery in the Mamluk Empire: A Preliminary Sketch." In *Slavery in the Islamic Middle East*, edited by S. E. Marmon, 1–23. Princeton, NJ: Markus Wiener, 1999.

Marwick, E. Lawrence. "The Order of the Books in Yefet's Bible Codex." *Jewish Quarterly Review* 33 (1942–3): 445–60.

Massignon, Louis. "L'influence de l'islam au moyen âge sur la fondation et l'essor des banques juives." *Bulletin de l'Institut Français de Damas* (1932): 3–12.

Masud, Muhammad Khalid, Brinkley Messick, and David Powers (eds.). *Islamic Legal Interpretation: Muftis and Their Fatwas.* Oxford: Oxford University Press, 1996.

Mayer Leo Ary. *Mamluk Costume: A Survey.* Genève: Albert Kundig, 1952.

Mazor, Amir. "Jewish Court Physicians in the Mamluk Sultanate during the First Half of the $8^{th}/14^{th}$ Century." *Medieval Encounters* 20 (2014): 38-65.

________. *The Rise and Fall of a Muslim Regiment: The Manṣūriyya in the First Mamluk Sultanate, 678/1279–741/1341.* Göttingen: V & R Unipress, 2015

Mazor, Amir, and Efraim Lev. "The Phenomenon of Dynasties of Jewish Doctors in the Mamluk Period." *EJJS* 15 (2021), 1-29.

MacCoull, Leslie S. B. *Coptic Legal Documents: Law as Vernacular Text and Experience in Late Antique Egypt.* Tempe: ACMRS and Brepols, 2009.

Meacham-Yoreh, Tirza (ed.), and Miriam Frenkel (trans.). *The Book of Maturity by Rav Samuel ben Hofni Ga'on and the Book of the Years by Rav Yehudah ha-Kohen Rosh ha-Seder.* Jerusalem: Yad ha-Rav Nissim, 1999(. [In Hebrew.]

Melchert, Christopher. *The Formation of the Sunni Schools of Law, 9th–10th Centuries C.E.* Leiden: Brill, 1997.

Mendels, D., and A. Edrei. *Zweierlei Diaspora: Zur Spaltung der antiken jüdischen Welt.* Göttingen: Vandenhoeck & Ruprecht, 2010.

Miller, Peter N. "Two Men in a Boat: The Braudel-Goitein 'Correspondence' and the Beginning of Thalassography." In *The Sea: Thalassography and Historiography*, edited by Peter N. Miller, 31–33. Ann Arbor: University of Michigan Press, 2013.

Milroy, Lesley, and James Milroy. "Social Network and Social Class: Toward an Integrated Sociolinguistic Model." *Language in Society* 21, no. 1 (1992): 1–26.

Mirsky, Aaron (ed.) *Itzhak ibn Khalfun: Poems.* Jerusalem: Mossad Bialik, 1961. [In Hebrew.]

Mirsky, Aaron. *Yosse ben Yosse: Poems Edited with an Introduction, Commentary and Notes.* Jerusalem: Mossad Bialik, 1991.

Mishor, M. "A Hebrew Letter from Oxford." *Leshonenu* 54 (1989): 215–64. [In Hebrew.]

________. "Papyrus Fragments of Hebrew Letters." *Leshonenu* 55 (1991): 281–88. [In Hebrew.]

________. "Oxford Bodleian Library Ms Heb e. 120." *Leshonenu* 63 (2001): 53–59.

Mitter, Ulrike. "Origin and Development of the Islamic Patronate." In *Patronate and Patronage in Early and Classical Islam*, edited by M. Bernards and J. Nawas, 70–133. Leiden and Boston: Brill, 2005.

Motzkin, Aryeh (Leo), "The Arabic Correspondence of Judge Elijah and His Family (Papers from the Cairo Geniza)—A Chapter in the Social History of Thirteenth-Century Egypt." PhD diss., University of Pennsylvania, 1965.

Muḥammad ibn ʿAbd al-Raḥīm Ibn al-Furāt. *Taʾrīkh Ibn al-Furāt* [*=Taʾrīkh al-Duwal wa-l-Mulūk*]. Edited by Q. Zurayq. Beirut: al-Maṭbaʿa al-Amrīkānīyya, 1936.

Muḥammad ibn Aḥmad ibn Iyās. *Badāʾiʿ al-zuhūr fī waqāʾiʿ al-dhuhūr.* Edited by Muḥammad Muṣṭafā. Cairo and *Wiesbaden*: Franz Steiner Verlag, 1392/1972.

Müller, Christian. "Settling Litigation without Judgment: The Importance of the *Ḥukm* in Qāḍī Cases from Mamlūk Jerusalem." In *Dispensing Justice in Islam: Qadis and Their Judgments*, edited by Khalid Masud, Rudolph Peters, and David S. Powers, 47–70. Leiden: Brill, 2006.

Müller, D. H., and D. Kaufmann. "Über die hebräischen Papyri." In *Mittheilungen aus der Sammlung der Papyrus Erzherzog Rainer*, vol. 1, edited by J. Karabaček, 38–44. Vienna: Verlag der k.k. Hof- und Staatsdruckerei, 1886.

Müller-Wiener, Martina. *Eine Stadtgeschichte Alexandrias von 564/1169 bis in die Mitte des 9./15. Jahrhunderts*. Berlin: Klaus Schwarz Verlag, 1992.

Newby, Gordon Darnell. "Observations about an Early Judaeo-Arabic." *Jewish Quarterly Review* 61 (1971): 212–21.

O'Sullivan, Shaun. "Coptic Conversion and the Islamization of Egypt." *Mamluk Studies Review* 10 (2006): 71–4.

Ogilvie, Sheilagh. *Institutions and European Trade: Merchant Guilds, 1000–1800*. Princeton, NJ: Princeton University Press, 2011.

Olszowy-Schlanger, Judith. *Karaite Marriage Documents from the Cairo Geniza: Legal Tradition and Community Life in Mediaeval Egypt and Palestine*. Leiden: Brill, 1998.

________. "Karaite Legal Documents." In *Karaite Judaism: A Guide to Its History and Literary Sources*, edited by Meira Polliack, 255–73. Leiden: Brill, 2003.

________. "Learning to Read and Write in Medieval Egypt: Children's Exercise Books from the Cairo Genizah." *Journal of Semitic Studies* 48 (2003): 47–69.

________. "Les archives médiévales dans la genizah du Caire: registres des tribunaux rabbiniques et pratiques d'archivage reconstituées." *Afriques: Débats, méthodes et terrains d'histoire* 7 (2016): 4.

Pahta, Paivi. "Code-Switching in English of the Middle Ages." In *The Oxford Handbook of the History of English*, edited by Terttu Nevalainen and E.C. Traugott, 1–12. Oxford: Oxford University Press, 2012.

Parkes, Malcolm, "The Literacy of the Laity." In *The Mediaeval World*, edited by David Daiches and Anthony Thorlby, 555–77. London: Aldus Books, 1973.

Peirce, Leslie. *Morality Tales: Law and Gender in the Ottoman Court of Aintab*. Berkeley: University of California Press, 2003.

Perlmann, Moshe. "Notes on the Position of Jewish Physicians in Medieval Muslim Countries." *IOS* 2 (1972): 315–19.

Perry, Craig. "The Daily Life of Slaves and the Global Reach of Slavery in Medieval Egypt, 969–1250 CE." PhD diss., Emory University, 2014.

Perry, Micha. "Communal Scribes and the Rise of a Uniform Hebrew Style around the Mediterranean in the Eleventh Century." *Zion* 82 (2017): 267–308. [In Hebrew.]

Perush Rabbenu Avraham ben ha-Rambam z"l ʿal Bereʾshit u-Shemot. Edited by E. Y. Wiesenberg. London: Rabbi S. D. Sassoon, 1959.

Die Pilgerfahrt des Ritters Arnold von Harff. Cologne: n.p., 1860.

Pirenne, Henri. *Mohammed and Charlemagne*. London and New York: Routledge, 2008.

Poonawala, I. K. "Al-Qāḍī al-Nuʿmān and Ismaʿili Jurisprudence." In *Medieval Ismaʿili History and Thought*, edited by F. Daftary. Cambridge: Cambridge University Press, 1996.

Porten, B., and A. Yardeni. *Textbook of Aramaic Documents from Ancient Egypt*. Vol. 2, *Contracts*. Winona Lake, IN: Eisenbrauns, 1989.

Prawer, Joshua. "The Autobiography of Obadiah the Norman, a Convert to Judaism at the Time of the First Crusade." *Studies in Medieval Jewish History and Literature* 1 (1979): 110–34.

Preisendanz, K. *Papyri Graecae Magicae: Die griechischen Zauberpapyri*. 2nd edition. Stuttgart: Teubner, 1973–4.

Pucci Ben Zeev, M. *Diaspora Judaism in Turmoil, 116/117 CE: Ancient Sources and Modern Insights*. Leuven: Peeters, 2005.

Qafiḥ, Yosef (ed.). *Mishnah with Commentary of Maimonides*. Jerusalem, Mossad ha-Rav Kook, 1963. [In Hebrew.]

Quatremère, Étienne (ed.). *Les Prolégomènes d'Ebn-Khaldoun*. Translated by M. De Slane. Paris: Imprimerie Impériale, 1873. Original French edition, Paris: Typographie de Firmin Didot, 1858.

Ragib, Yusuf. "Lettres nouvelles de Qurra b. Šarīk." *Journal of Near Eastern Studies* 40 (1981): 175–6.

Rajak, T., and D. Noy. "*Archisynagogoi*: Office, Title and Social Status in the Greco-Jewish Synagogue." *Journal of Roman Studies* 83 (1993): 75–93.

Rapoport, Yossef. "Matrimonial Gifts in Early Islamic Egypt." *Islamic Law and Society* 7 (2000): 1–36.

Reiner, Elhanan. "Hanhagat ha-kehila be-Yerushalayim be-shalḥey ha-tequfa ha-Mamlukit: Teʿudot u-verurim be-shuley parashat ha-zekenim" [Jewish Community Leadership in late Mamluke Jerusalem]. *Shalem* 6 (1992): 23–81. [In Hebrew.]

Reiner, Rami. "A Proselyte—Is He Really Your Brother? The Issue of Proselytes' Status in Jewish Communities of Ashkenaz and Zarfat in the 11th–13th Centuries." In *Ta-Shema: Studies in Judaica in Memory of Israel M. Ta-Shema*, vol. 2, edited by Avraham Reiner et al., 747–69. Alon Shevut: Tevunot Press, 2012.

Richards, Donald S. "Dhimmi Problems in Fifteenth-Century Cairo: Reconsideration of a Court Document." In *Studies in Muslim-Jewish Relations*, vol. 1, edited by Ronald L. Nettler, 127–63. Chur: Harwood Academic Publishers, in cooperation with the Oxford Centre for Postgraduate Hebrew Studies, 1993.

Rivlin, Joseph. *Bills and Contracts from Lucena (1020-1025 CE)*. Ramat Gan: Bar Ilan University Press, 1994. [In Hebrew.]

________. *Inheritance and Wills in Jewish Law*. Ramat-Gan: Bar Ilan University Press, 1999. [In Hebrew.]

Robert, C. H. *The Antinoopolis Papyri*, vol. 1. London: Egypt Exploration Society, 1950.

Roberts, Simon. "The Study of Dispute: Anthropological Perspectives." In *Disputes and Settlements: Law and Human Relations in the West*, edited by John Bossy, 1–24. Cambridge: Cambridge University Press, 1983.

Röhricht, Reinhold, and Heinrich Meisner (eds.). *Ein Niederrheinischer Bericht über den Orient.* Berlin: n.p., 1887.

Rosen, Lawrence. *Anthropology of Justice: Law as Culture in Islamic Society.* Cambridge: Cambridge University Press, 1989.

Rosenbaum, Gabriel. "The Arabic Dialect of Jews in Modern Egypt." *Bulletin of the Israeli Academic Center in Cairo* 25 (2002): 35–46.

Rosenblatt, Samuel. *The High Ways to Perfection of Abraham Maimonides*, vol. 2. Baltimore: The Johns Hopkins Press, 1938.

Russ-Fishbane, Elisha. "The Maimonidean Legacy in the East: A Study of Father and Son." *JQR* 102 (2012): 190–223.

________. "Respectful Rival: Abraham Maimonides on Islam." In *A History of Jewish-Muslim Relations: From the Origins to the Present Day,* edited by A. Meddeb and B. Stora, 858–9. Princeton, NJ: Princeton University Press, 2013.

________. *Judaism, Sufism and the Pietists of Medieval Egypt.* Oxford: Oxford University Press, 2015.

________. "Fellowship and Fraternity in Jewish Pietism of Medieval Egypt." In *Ethics and Spirituality in Islam: Sufi adab,* edited by Francesco Chiabotti et al. Leiden: Brill, 2016.

________. "The Legacy of the Prophets and the Prophetic Path in Medieval Sufism and Egyptian Jewish Pietism." *Pe'amim* 148 (2017): 59–86. [In Hebrew.]

Rustow, Marina. *Heresy and the Politics of Community: The Jews of the Fatimid Caliphate.* Ithaca and London: Cornell University Press, 2008.

________. "At the Limits of Communal Autonomy: Jewish Bids for Intervention from the Mamluk State." *MSR* 13 (2009): 133–59.

________. "The Diplomatics of Leadership: Administrative Documents in Hebrew Scripts from the Geniza." In *Jews, Christians and Muslims in Medieval and Early Modern Times: A Festschrift in Honor of Mark R. Cohen,* edited by Arnold Franklin et al., 306–51. Leiden: Brill, 2014.

________. "Patronage in the Context of Solidarity and Reciprocity: Two Paradigms of Social Cohesion in the Premodern Mediterranean." In *Patronage, Production and Transmission of Texts in Medieval and Early Modern Jewish Cultures,* edited by Esperanza Alfonso and Jonathan Decter, 33–4. Turnhout: Brepols, 2014.

________. *The Lost Archive: Traces of a Caliphate in a Cairo Syngogue.* Princeton, NJ: Princeton University Press, 2020.

Sa'adia Ga'on, *Ha-'Egron: Kitāb 'Uṣul al-Shi'r al-'Ibrānī.* Edited by N. Allony. Jerusalem: Academy of Hebrew Language, 1969.

Sabatino Lopez, Robert. *The Commercial Revolution of the Middle Ages, 950–1350.* Englewood Cliffs, NJ: Prentice-Hall, 1971.

Sadan, Joseph. "What does *Manhaj al-Ṣawāb* Want from the Jews?" In *Adaptations and Innovations: Studies on the Interaction between Jewish and Islamic Thought and Literature from the Early Middle Ages to the Late Twentieth Century, dedicated to Professor Joel L. Kraemer,* edited by Y. Langermann and J. Stern, 315–30. Paris: Peeters, 2007.

Sagi, Avi, and Zvi Zohar. *Transforming Identity: The Ritual Transformation from Gentile to Jew—Structure and Meaning.* New York: Continuum, 2007.

Ṣalāḥ al-Dīn ibn Yūsuf al-Kaḥḥāl al-Ḥamawī. *Nūr al-ʿuyūn wa-jāmiʿ al-funūn.* Riyadh: Markaz al-Malik Fayṣal li-l-Buḥūth wa-l-Dirāsāt al-Islāmiyya, 1987.

Salzman, Marcus (trans.). *The Chronicle of Ahimaaz.* New York: Columbia University Press, 1924.

Samir, Khalil. "Abd al-Masih al-Israʾili al-Raqqi." *The Coptic Encyclopedia,* 5b–7a.

Savran, Scott. *Arabs and Iranians in the Islamic Conquest Narrative.* London: Routledge, 2016.

Sawirus ibn Al-Mukaffa. *History of the Patriarchs of the Egyptian Church Known as The History of the Holy Church.* Translated by Antoine Khater and O. H. E. KHS-Burmester. Cairo: Imprimérie de l'Institut Français d'Archéologie Orientale, 1943–76.

Schacht, J. "Fiḳh." In *Encyclopedia of Islam,* vol. 2, edited by Clifford E. Bosworth et al., 886–91. Leiden: Brill, 1995.

Schäfer, P. *Judeophobia: Attitudes toward the Jews in the Ancient World.* Cambridge, MA: Harvard University Press, 1997.

Schäfer, P., and S. Shaked (eds.). *Magische Texte aus der Kairoer Geniza.* Tübingen: Mohr Siebeck, 1994–9.

Scheiber, Alexander. "A Fragment from the Dīwān of Eleazar ha-Kohen." *Sinai* 35 (1954): 183–6. [In Hebrew.]

________. "New Poems from the Kauffmann Collection." In *Ḥayyim (Jefim) Schirmann Jubilee Volume,* edited by Shraga Abramson and Aaron Mirsky, 393–411. Jerusalem: Schocken, 1970. [In Hebrew.]

________. "A Letter of Recommendation on behalf of the Proselyte Mevorakh from the Geniza." *American Academy for Jewish Research Proceedings* 2 (1980): 491–4.

Schippers, Arie. "Some Remarks on Judaeo-Arabic Poetical Works: An Arabic Poem by Moses Darʿī." In *Studies in Medieval Jewish Poetry,* edited by Alessandro Guetta and Masha Itzhaki, 141–56. Leiden: Brill, 2009.

________. *Spanish Hebrew Poetry and the Arabic Literary Tradition: Arabic Themes in Hebrew Andalusian Poetry.* Leiden: Brill, 1994.

Schirmann, Ḥayyim (Jefim). "Laments for the Persecutions in Palestine, Africa, Spain, Germany, and France." *Qovetz ʿal Yad* 3/13 (1940): 23–74. [In Hebrew.]

________. "Poets Contemporary with Mose [sic] ibn Ezra and Yehudah ha-Levi (III)." *Studies of the Research Institute for Hebrew Poetry in Jerusalem* 6 (1946): 249–339. [In Hebrew.]

________. *Hebrew Poetry in Spain and Provence.* Jerusalem: Mosad Bialik, 1959. [In Hebrew.]

________. *New Poems from the Geniza.* Jerusalem: Israel Academy of Sciences and Humanities, 1966. [In Hebrew.]

________. *Studies in the History of Hebrew Poetry and Drama.* Jerusalem: Mosad Bialik, 1979. [In Hebrew.]

________. *The History of Hebrew Poetry in Christian Spain and Southern France,* edited and annotated by Ezra Fleischer. Jerusalem: Mechon Ben-Zvi, 1997. [In Hebrew.]

Schlossberg, Eliezer. "Maimonides's Attitude to Islam." *Peʿamim* 42 (1990): 38–60. [In Hebrew.]

Schwarb, Gregor. "ʿAlī ibn Ṭaybughā's Commentary on Maimonides' Mishneh Torah, Sefer ha-Maddaʿ, Hilkhot Yesodei ha-Torah I–IV: A Philosophical 'Encyclopaedia' of the 14th Century." Forthcoming.

Schwartz, Michael (trans. and ed.). *Maimonides: The Guide of the Perplexed, Hebrew Translation from the Arabic, Annotations, Appendices, and Indices.* Tel Aviv: Tel Aviv University, 2002. [In Hebrew.]

Sebba, Mark, Shahrzad Mahootian, and Carla Johnsson (eds.). *Language Mixing and Code-Switching in Writing: Approaches to Mixed-Language Written Discourse.* London: Routledge, 2011.

Sela, Shulamit. "The Head of the Rabbanite, Karaite, and Samaritan Jews: On the History of a Title." *Bulletin of the School of Oriental and African Studies (BSOAS)* 57 (1994): 255–67.

Shahar, Ido. "Theme Issue: Shifting Perspectives in the Study of Shariʿa Courts: Methodologies and Paradigms: Introduction." *Islamic Law and Society* 15 (2008): 1–19.

Shaked, Shaul. "An Early Karaite Document in Judeo Persian." *Tarbiz* 41 (1971): 49–58. [In Hebrew.]

Sharma, Devyani. "Style Repertoire and Social Change in British Asian English." *Journal for Sociolinguistics* 15, no. 4 (2011): 464–92.

Shatzmiller, Maya. *Labour in the Medieval Islamic World.* Leiden and New York: Brill, 1994.

________. "Marriage, Family, and the Faith: Women's Conversion to Islam." *Journal of Family History* 21 (1996): 235–66.

Shailat, Yitzhak (ed.). *The Letters and Essays of Moses Maimonides.* Maʿale Adummim: Sailat, 1995. [In Hebrew.]

Sheynin, Hayim Vitaly Yehudah. *An Introduction to the Poetry of Joseph Ben Tanhum Ha-Yerushalmi and to the History of its Research: A Study Based Primarily upon Manuscripts from the Cairo Genizah.* PhD diss., University of Pennsylvania, 1988.

Shihāb al-Dīn Aḥmad al-Nuwayrī. *Nihāyat al-Arab fī Funūn al-Adab.* Cairo: *al-Hayʾa* al- Miṣriyya al-ʿAmma lil-Kitāb, 1992–8.

Shihāb al-Dīn Aḥmad ibn ʿAlī al-Qalqashandī. *Ṣubḥ al-Aʿshā fī Ṣināʿat al-Inshāʾ*. Edited by Muḥammad Ḥusayn Shams al-Dīn. Beirut: Dār al-Kutub al-ʿIlmiyya, 1987.

Shayzari, ʿAbd al-Rahman ibn Nasr. *The Book of the Islamic Market Inspector: Nihayat Al-Rutba Fi Talab Al-Hisba (The Utmost Authority in the Pursuit of Hisba).* Translated by R. P. Buckley. Oxford: Oxford University Press, 1999.

Shilo, Shmuel, and Menachem Elon. "Ones." *Encyclopedia Judaica*, 15:428–9.

Shochetman, Eliav. *Civil Procedure in Jewish Law.* Jerusalem: Library of Jewish Law, 1988. [In Hebrew.]

Shohat, Ella. "The Question of Judaeo-Arabic." *Arab Studies Journal* 23, no. 1 (2015): 14–76.

Shoshan, Boaz. *Popular Culture in Medieval Cairo.* Ithaca: Cornell UP, 1993.

Shtober, Shimon. "Questions Posed to R. Abraham b. Maimonides." *Shenaton ha-Mishpat ha-ʿIvri* 14–15 (1988–9): 245–81. [In Hebrew.]

Simonsohn, Uriel. *A Common Justice: The Legal Allegiances of Christians and Jews under Early Islam.* Philadelphia: University of Pennsylvania Press, 2011.

Sinai, Yuval. *The Judge and the Judicial Process in Jewish Law.* n.p.: Nevo, 2010. [In Hebrew.]

Sirat, C. *Les papyrus en charactères hébraïques trouvés en Égypte.* Paris: Éditions du CNRS, 1985.

Sirat, C., P. Cauderlier, M. Dukan, and M. A. Friedman, *La Ketouba de Cologne: Un contrat de mariage juif à Antinopolis*, vol. 12 of *Papyrologica Coloniensia.* Opladen: Westdeutschen Verlag, 1986.

Sklare, David. "Are the Gentiles Obligated to Observe the Torah? The Discussion concerning the Universality of the Torah in the East in the Tenth and Eleventh Centuries." In *Be'erot Yitzhak: Studies in Memory of Isadore Twersky*, edited by J. M. Harris, 311–46. Cambridge, MA: Harvard University Press, Center for Jewish Studies, 2005.

Smail, Daniel Lord. *The Consumption of Justice: Emotions, Publicity, and Legal Culture in Marseille, 1264–1423.* Ithaca: Cornell University Press, 2003.

de Smet, D. (ed. and trans.). *Les Épîtres sacrées des Druzes*, vol. 3 of *Récit sur les juifs et les chrétiens.* Leuven: Peeters, 2007.

Sokoloff, M., and J. Yahalom. *Jewish Palestinian Aramaic Poetry from Late Antiquity: Critical Edition with Introduction and Commentary.* Jerusalem: Israel Academy of Sciences and Humanities, 1999.

Soloveitchik, Haym. *The Use of Responsa as Historical Source: A Methodological Introduction.* Jerusalem: Zalman Shazar Center, 1990. [In Hebrew.]

Stampfer, Y. Zvi. "Responsa." In *Encyclopedia of Jews in the Islamic World*, vol. 4, edited by Norman Stillman, 159–67. Leiden: Brill, 2010.

Steinschneider, Moritz. "Hebräische Papyrus-Fragmente aus dem Fayyûm." *Magazin für die Wissenschaft des Judenthums* 6 (1879): 250–4.

________. *Die Hebraeischen Übersetzungen des Mittelalters und die Juden als Dolmetscher.* Berlin: Kommissionsverlag des Bibliographischen Bureaus, 1893.

Stern, Samuel Miklós. "A Twelfth-Century Circle of Hebrew Poets in Sicily." *Journal of Jewish Studies* 5 (1954): 60–79.

________. *Fāṭimid Decrees: Original Documents from the Fatimid Chancery.* London: Faber and Faber, 1964.

Stern, M. *Greek and Latin Authors on Jews and Judaism.* Vol. 2. Jerusalem: Israel Academy of Sciences and Humanities, 1980.

Stillman, Norman A. *The Jews of Arab Lands: A History and Source Book.* Philadelphia: Jewish Publication Society of America, 1979.

________. "The Non-Muslim Communities: The Jewish Community." In *The Cambridge History of Egypt.* Vol. 1, *Islamic Egypt 640–1517*, edited by Carl F. Petry, 198–210. Cambridge: Cambridge University Press, 1998.

________. "The Eleventh-Century Merchant House of Ibn ʿAwkal (a Geniza Study)." *JESHO* 15, no. 1 (1973): 15–88.

Stilt, Kristen. *Islamic Law in Action: Authority, Discretion, and Everyday Experiences in Mamluk Egypt.* Oxford: Oxford University Press, 2012.

Stroumsa, Sarah. "On Jewish Intellectuals who Converted in the Early Middle Ages." In *The Jews of Medieval Islam: Community, Society and Identity*, edited by Daniel Frank, 179–97. Leiden and Boston: Brill, 1995.

Sussmann, Y. "Oral Law Literally." In *Talmudic Studies Dedicated to the Memory of Professor Ephraim E. Urbach*, edited by Y. Sussmann and D. Rosenthal, 209–384. Jerusalem: Magness Press, 2005. [In Hebrew.]

Taqī al-Dīn Aḥmad ibn ʿAlī al-Maqrīzī. *al-Mawāʿiẓ wa-l-iʿtibār bi-dhikr al-khiṭaṭ wa-l-āthār fī Miṣr wa-l-Qāhira.* Cairo: Bulaq, 1854.

________. *al-Sulūk li-maʿrifat duwal al-mulūk.* Edited by M. M. Ziyāda. Cairo: Matbaʿat Dār al-Kutub, 1934-73.

Taylor, Christopher S. *In the Vicinity of the Righteous: Ziyara and the Veneration of Muslim Saints.* Leiden: Brill, 1999.

Tcherikover, V. (ed.). "Prolegomena: The Late Roman and the Byzantine Period." In *Corpus Papyrorum Judaicarum*, vol. 1, edited by A. Fuks and M. Stern, 93–111. Cambridge, MA: Harvard University Press, 1957.

Teshuvot ha-Rambam. Edited by Joshua Blau. Vol 1. Jerusalem: Mekize Nirdamim, 1957.

Tillier, Mathieu. "The Qāḍīs of Fusṭāṭ-Miṣr under the Ṭūlūnids and the Ikhshīdids: The Judiciary and Egyptian Autonomy." *Journal of the American Oriental Society* 131/2 (2011): 207–22.

________. "The Mazalim in Historiography." In *The Oxford Handbook of Islamic Law*, edited by Anver M. Emon and Rumee Ahmed, 357–80. Oxford: Oxford University Press, 2018.

Tillier, Mathieu (ed.). *Arbitrage et conciliation dans l'Islam médiéval et modern*, special issue of *Revue des Mondes musulmans et de la Méditerranée* 140 (2016): 13–226.

Timm, Erika. *Historische jiddische Semantik. Die Bibelübersetzungssprache als Faktor der Auseinanderentwicklung des jiddischen und des deutschen Wortschatzes.* Tübingen: Niemeyer, 2005.

Toch, Michael. "Jews and Commerce: Modern Fancies and Medieval Realities." In *Il Ruolo Economico delle Minoranze in Europa. Secc. XIII-XVIII (Atti della XXXI Settimana di Studi, Istituto Francesco Datini, Prato)*, edited by S. Cavaciocchi, 43–58. Florence: Istituto Francesco Datini, 2000.

________. "The Economic Activity of German Jews in the 10th–12th Centuries: Between Historiography and History (Hebrew)." In *Facing the Cross: The Persecutions of 1096 in History and Historiography*, edited by Y-T. Assis et al., 32–54. Jerusalem: Magness Press, 2000.

Toledano, Baruch (ed.). *Sefer al-Murshad al-Kāfī by R. Tanḥum ben Joseph the Jerusalemite.* Tel Aviv: Aḥdut, 1961. [In Arabic and Hebrew.]

Tov, E. *Textual Criticism of the Hebrew Bible.* 3rd edition, revised and expanded. Minneapolis: Fortress Press, 2012.

Treadwell, Luke. "The Numismatic Evidence for the Reign of Aḥmad b. Ṭūlūn (254–270/868–883)." *Al-ʿUṣūr al-Wusṭā* 25 (2017): 14–40.

Tritton, A. S. *The Caliphs and Their Non-Muslim Subjects: A Critical Study of the Covenant of ʿUmar.* London: H. Milford and Oxford University Press, 1930.

Tsugitaka, Sato. *State and Rural Society in Medieval Islam: Sultans, Muqta 's and Fallahun*. Leiden: Brill, 1997.

Tyan, Emile. "Juridical Organization." In *Law in the Middle East*, edited by Majid Khadduri and Herbert J. Liebesny, 236–78. Washington: The Middle East Institute, 1955.

________. *Histoire de l'organisation judiciaire en pays d'Islam*. 2nd edition. Leiden: Brill, 1960.

Udovitch, Avram L. "Merchants and Amirs: Government and Trade in Eleventh-Century Egypt." *Asian and African Studies* 22 (1988): 53–72.

Van Doosselaere, Quentin. *Commercial Agreements and Social Dynamics in Medieval Genoa*. Cambridge: Cambridge University Press, 2009.

Van Minnen, P., and Traianos Gagos. *Settling a Dispute: Toward a Legal Anthropology of Late Antique Egypt*. Ann Arbor: University of Michigan Press, 1994.

Verburg, Jelle, Tal Ilan, and Jan Joosten. "Four Fragments of the Hebrew Bible from Antinoopolis, *P.Ant.* 47—50*." *Journal of Egypt Archaeology 106 (2020) 1-8.*

Vilensky, Michael (ed.). *Sefer ha-riqma of R. Yonah ibn Janāḥ*. 2nd edition. Jerusalem: Academy of the Hebrew Language, 1964. [In Hebrew.]

Voyages d'Ibn Batoutah. Edited and translated by C. Defrémery and B. R. Sanguinetti. Paris: n.p., 1853.

"Waḳf." In *Encyclopedia of Islam*, vol. 11, edited by Bernard Lewis et al., 59ff; vol. 12, 823–28. Leiden: Brill, 1965.

Wagner, Esther-Miriam. *Linguistic Variety of Judaeo-Arabic in Letters from the Cairo Genizah*. Leiden: Brill, 2010.

________. "Challenges of Multiglossia: the Emergence of Substandard Judaeo-Arabic Registers." In *Scribes as Agents of Language Change*, edited by Esther-Miriam Wagner, Ben Outhwaite, and Bettina Beinhoff, 259–73. Berlin: de Gruyter-Mouton, 2013.

________. "Scribal Practice in the Jewish Community of Medieval Egypt." In *Scribal Practices and the Social Construction of Knowledge in Antiquity, Late Antiquity and Medieval Islam*, edited by Myriam Wissa, 91–110. Leuven: Peeters, 2017.

________. "The Socio-Linguistics of Judaeo-Arabic Mercantile Writing." In *Merchants of innovation. The Languages of Traders*, edited by Esther-Miriam Wagner, Bettina Beinhoff, and Ben Outhwaite, 68–86. Berlin: de Gruyter-Mouton. 2017.

________. "A Matter of Script?" In *Muslim-Jewish Relations in Past and Present: A Kaleidoscopic View*, edited by Yousef Meri and Camilla Adang, 115–36. Leiden: Brill, 2017.

________. "Judaeo-Arabic Language or Jewish Arabic Sociolect? Linguistic Terminology between Linguistics and Ideology." In *Jewish Languages in Historical Perspective*, edited by Lily Khan and Mark Geller, 189–207. Leiden: Brill, 2018.

________. "Script-Switching between Hebrew and Arabic Script in Letters from the Cairo Genizah." *Allographic Traditions*, special issue of *Intellectual History of the Islamic World*, edited by George Kiraz and Sabine Schmidtke (forthcoming).

Wagner, Esther-Miriam, and Bettina Beinhoff. "Merchants of Innovation: the Language of Traders." In *Merchants of Innovation. The languages of Traders*, edited by Esther-

Miriam Wagner, Bettina Beinhoff and Ben Outhwaite, 3–16. Berlin: de Gruyter-Mouton, 2017.

Wagner, Esther-Miriam, Bettina Beinhoff, and Ben Outhwaite (eds.). *Merchants of Innovation. The Languages of Traders*. Berlin: de Gruyter-Mouton, 2017.

Wagner, Esther-Miriam, and Magdalen Connolly. "Code-Switching in Judeo-Arabic Documents from the Cairo Geniza." *Multilingua* 36, no. 4 (2017): 1–23.

Wagner, Esther-Miriam, and Henrike Kühnert. "Codeswitching in Yiddish and Judaeo-Arabic." In *Dat ih dir in nu in huldi gibu*, edited by Sergio Neri, Roland Schuhmann, and Susanne Zeilfelder, 495–504. Wiesbaden: Reichert, 2016.

Wagner, Esther-Miriam, Ben Outhwaite, and Bettina Beinhoff. „Scribes and Language Change." In *Scribes as Agents of Language Change*, edited by Esther-Miriam Wagner, Ben Outhwaite, and Bettina Beinhoff, 3–18. Berlin: de Gruyter-Mouton, 2013.

Walker, Paul Ernest *Exploring an Islamic Empire: Fatimid History and Its Sources*. London: I.B. Tauris, 2002.

Weinberger, Leon J. *Jewish Poet in Fatimid Egypt: Moses Dar'i's Hebrew Collection*. Tuscaloosa: University of Alabama, 1988. [In Hebrew.]

Weiss, Gershon. "Documents Written by Hillel Ben Eli: A Study in the Diplomatics of the Cairo Geniza Documents." MA diss., University of Pennsylvania, 1967.

________. "Legal Documents Written by the Court Clerk Halfon Ben Manasse." PhD diss., University of Pennsylvania, 1970.

________. "Formularies (Shetarot) Reconstructed from the Cairo Geniza." *Gratz College Annual of Jewish Studies* 2 (1973): 29–42, 3 (1974): 63–76, 4 (1975): 69–76.

——— [as Gershom Weiss]. "Shetar Herem—Excommunication Formulary: Five Documents from the Cairo Geniza." *Gratz College Annual of Jewish Studies* 6 (1977): 98–120.

Weitz, Lev. "Islamic Law on the Provincial Margins: Christian Patrons and Muslim Notaries in Upper Egypt, 2nd–5th/8th–11th Centuries." *Islamic Law and Society* 26 (2019): 1–48.

Wexler, Paul. "Jewish Interlinguistics: Facts and Conceptual Framework." *Language* 57, no. 1 (1981): 99–149.

Worman, Ernest James. "Notes on the Jews in Fustat from Cambridge Genizah Documents." *JQR* 18 (1905): 13–15.

Würth, Anna. "A Sana'a Court: The Family and the Ability to Negotiate." *Islamic Law and Society* 2 (1995): 321.

Wright, Thomas (ed.). *Early Travelers in Palestine*. New York: Ktav Publishing House, 1968.

Yarbrough, Luke B. *Friends of the Emir. Non-Muslim State Officials in Premodern Islamic Thought*. Cambridge: Cambridge University Press, 2019.

Yagur, Moshe. "The Donor and the Gravedigger: Converts to Judaism in the Cairo Geniza Documents." In *Contesting Inter-Religious Conversion in the Medieval World*, edited by Yaniv Fox and Yosi Yisraeli, 115–34. London and New York: Routledge, 2017.

________. "Religious Identity and Communal Boundaries in Genizah Society (10th–13th centuries): Proselytes, Slaves, Apostates." PhD diss., The Hebrew University of Jerusalem, 2017.

Yahalom, Joseph. "'Ezel Moshe'—According to the Berlin Papyrus," *Tarbiz* 47 (1978): 173–84. [In Hebrew.]

________. "The Origin of Precise Scanning in Hebrew Poetry—Syllabic Metre." *Leshonenu* 47 (1983): 25–61. [In Hebrew.]

________. "The Temple and the City in Hebrew Liturgical Poetry." In *The History of Jerusalem: The Early Islamic Period (638–1099)*, edited by Joshua Prawer, 215–35. Jerusalem: Yad Izhak Ben-Zvi, 1987. [In Hebrew.]

________. *Palestinian Vocalised Piyyut Manuscripts in the Cambridge Genizah Collections.* Cambridge: Cambridge University Press, 1997.

________. "A Romance Maqāma: The Place of the 'Speech of Tuvia ben Tzedeqiah' in the History of Hebrew Maqāma." *Hispania Judaica* 14 (2010), Hebrew section, 113–28. [In Hebrew.]

________. "Qedushat Zakhor by Ya'aqov: a Palestinian Pronunciation as Reflected in Unique Babylonian and Tiberian Pointing Systems." *Ginzei Qedem* 12 (2016): 89–111. [In Hebrew.]

________. "A *Piyyut*-Papyrus for the Winter Holidays: And Its Significance for the History of the Settlement at the End of the Byzantine Period." *Cathedra* 162 (2017): 8–34. [In Hebrew.]

Yahalom, Joseph (ed.). *Libbavtini: Love Stories from the Middle Ages.* Jerusalem: Carmel, 2009. [In Hebrew.]

________. "Arabic and Hebrew as Poetic Languages within Muslim and Jewish Society: Judah Alḥarizi, between East and West." *Leshonenu* 74 (2012): 305–21.

Yahalom, Joseph, and Naoya Katsumata (eds.). *Taḥkemoni, or the Tales of Heman the Ezraḥite.* Jerusalem, Mechon Ben-Zvi, 2010. [In Hebrew.]

________. *The Yotzerot of R. Samuel the Third.* Jerusalem: The Ben-Zvi Institute , 2014. [In Hebrew.]

Yahalom, Joseph, and Michael Sokoloff (eds.). *Jewish Palestinian Aramaic Poetry from Late Antiquity (Shirat Bené Ma'arava).* Jerusalem: Israel Academy of Sciences and Humanities, 1999. [In Hebrew.]

Yarbrough, Luke, "'A Rather Small Genre': Arabic Works against Non-Muslim State Officials," *Der Islam* 93, 1 (2016), 139–69.

Yarbrough, Luke, "Did ʿUmar b. ʿAbd al-ʿAzīz Issue an Edict concerning Non-Muslim Officials?" in Antoine Borrut and Fred M. Donner, eds., *Christians and Others in the Umayyad State* (Chicago, 2016).

Yardeni, A., and G. Bohak. "A Pregnancy Amulet for Marian, Daughter of Esther." *Eretz-Israel* 32: *The Joseph Naveh Memorial Volume* (2016): 100–107. [In Hebrew.]

Yardeni, A., and B. Levine (with Y. Yadin and J. Greenfield). *The Documents from the Bar-Kokhba Period in the Cave of Letters: Hebrew, Aramaic and Nabatean-Aramaic Papyri.* Jerusalem: Israel Exploration Society, 2002.

Yehudah ha-Barzeloni, *Sefer ha-Sheṭarot.* Edited by Joseph Rivlin. Bene Beraq: Sefunim, 2014.

Yellin, David (ed.). *Gan ha-Meshalim veha-Ḥidoth: Dīwān of Don Todros son of Yehudah Abu-l-ʿĀfiah.* Jerusalem: Ha-Sefer, 1931-5. [In Hebrew.]

Yeshaya, Joachim J. M. S. *Medieval Hebrew Poetry in Muslim Egypt: The Secular Poetry of the Karaite Poet Moses ben Abraham Darʿī.* Leiden: Brill, 2011.

________. "In the Name of God: Judaeo-Arabic Language and Literature." In *Scripts beyond Borders. A Survey of Allographic Traditions in the Euro-Mediterranean World,* edited by Johannes den Heijer, Andrea Schmidt and Tamara Pataridze, 527–38. Louvain: Peeters, 2014.

________. *Poetry and Memory in Karaite Prayer: The Liturgical Poetry of the Karaite Poet Moses ben Abraham Darʿī.* Leiden: Brill, 2014.

Yosef, Koby. "Mamluks and Their Relatives in the Period of the Mamluk Sultanate (1250–1517)." *Mamluk Studies Review* 16 (2012): 55–69.

Zeʾevi, Dror. "The Use of Ottoman Shariʿa Court Records as a Source for Middle Eastern Social History: A Reappraisal." *Islamic Law and Society* 5 (1998): 35–56.

Zeitlin, Solomon. "Mumar and Meshumad." *JQR* 54 (1963): 84–6.

Ziadeh, Farhat J. "Integrity (*ʿAdālah*) in Classical Islamic Law." In *Islamic Studies and Jurisprudence: Studies in Honor of Farhat J. Ziadeh,* 73–93. Seattle: University of Washington Press, 1990.

Zinger, Oded. "Long-Distance Marriage in the Cairo Geniza." *Peʿamim* 121 (2009): 7–66. [In Hebrew.]

________. "'What Sort of Sermon is This?' Leadership, Resistance, and Gender in a Communal Conflict." In *Jews, Christians and Muslims in Medieval and Early Modern Times: A Festschrift in Honor of Mark R. Cohen,* edited by Arnold Franklin et al. Leiden: Brill, 2014.

________. "Women, Gender and Law: Marital Disputes according to Documents from the Cairo Geniza." PhD diss., Princeton University, 2014.

________. "A Karaite-Rabbanite Court Session in Mid-Eleventh Century Egypt." *Ginzei Qedem: Genizah Research Annual* 13 (2017): 98*–102*.

________. "'She Aims to Harass Him': Jewish Women in Muslim Legal Venues in Medieval Egypt." *AJS Review* 42 (2018): 168–69.

________. "'One Hour He Is a Christian and the Next He Is a Muslim!' A Family Dispute from the Cairo Geniza." *al-Masāq* 31 (2019): 20–34.

________. "Jewish Women in Muslim Legal Venues in Medieval Egypt: Seven Documents from the Cairo Geniza." In *Language, Gender and Law in the Judaeo-Islamic Milieu,* edited by Zvi Stampfer and Amir Ashur. Leiden: Brill, 2020.

________. "Social Embeddedness in the Legal Arena according to Geniza Letters." In *From Qom to Barcelona: Aramaic, South Arabian, Coptic, Arabic and Judeo-Arabic Documents,* edited by Andreas Kaplony and Daniel Potthast. Leiden: Brill, forthcoming.

Zulay, Menahem. "Liturgical Poems on Various Historical Events." *Studies of the Research Institute for Hebrew Poetry* 3 (1936): 151–83. [In Hebrew.]

________. *The Liturgical Poetry of Saʿadya Gaʾon and his School.* Jerusalem: Schocken, 1962. [In Hebrew.]

Index

A
Abbasid period, viii, 25, 29
Abbasids, 28, 31, 35
act of acquisition. *See* qinyān
ʿAbd Allāh al-Mahdī, 30
ʿAbd Allāh ibn Ṭāhir, 26
Abraham ha-Kohen, xii, 217-18
Abraham ha-Kohen b. Isaac ben Furāt, 221
Abraham ibn Abī al-Rabīʿ, 189
Abraham Maimuni, vii, xi-xii, xiv. *See also* Maimonides Abraham
Abrahamic religions, 175
Abū al-Fakhr, 63, 70
Abū al-Ḥasan al-Bakrī, 45
Abū al-Qāsim al-Mustaʿālī, 35
Abū al-Maʿāli Uziel, 152
Abū Ḥāmid al-Ghazālī, 176, 252
Abu ʾl-Ḥasan al-Shādhilī, 176
Abū Manṣūr, 149
Abū Manṣūr Nizār, 35
Abū Naṣr (Ḥesed) al-Tustarī, 149
Abu Saʿd (Abraham) al-Tustarī, 149
acquisition clause, 101
Acre, 39, 240-41
adolescent(s), 170-72, 194
adolescent girls, 171
adulthood, 151, 170, 174
agriculture, 130, 135-36
agricultural estates, 137
Africa, 41
Aharon ibn al-ʿAmmānī, xii, 227-31
ahavah poems, 226
Ahimaatz ben Paltiel, 28
ahl (family), 146, 164, 170. *See also* *ʿāʾila; ʿashīra; ʿitra; mishpaḥa*
Aḥmad ibn Ṭūlūn, 27, 29
ʿāʾila (family), 146, 164. *See also ahl; ʿashīra; ʿitra; mishpaḥa*
Aleppo, 36, 46, 52
Alexander the Great (Iskandar), 44
Alexandria, Egypt, vii, 2-3, 5, 22-23, 28, 31-32, 39, 65, 67, 76-77, 80, 84, 92, 108, 118, 134, 153, 160, 176, 236, 238, 248-49, 261, 267
Almohad tribes, 238
Alms lists, 149
Alp Takīn, 213
ʿamidah prayer, 216, 218, 224
al-Amin, 26
amīr. See military governor
amīr al-juyūsh (commander of the armies), 35
ʿAmr ibn al-ʿAṣ, 35
amulet, 12, 18, 120n137
Anatoli ben Joseph, 236-38
Andalus, 65, 139n33, 210, 221n25, 222, 224-27
anti-*dhimmī* laws, xiii, 256, 261, 268
anti-Semitism, 1
Antinoopolis, 5-6, 13, 15
apostasy, 48
apostate, ix, 65-66, 68, 70
apothecaries, 196
apprenticeship, 150, 171
Arab-Islamic conquest of Egypt (639–42), viii
Arabic calligraphy, 194
Arabic poetry, 209-210, 221, 237
Aramaic language, xii-xiii, 3, 5, 13-21, 35, 101, 106n77, 192-93, 197, 199, 201-2, 208, 219
Arians, 2-3
artisanal sectors, 139
artisanal work, 134, 136, 140
artisans, 130, 137-38, 144, 148, 248
aṣabiyya (group solidarity), 84
Asad al-Dīn Shīrkūh, 36
Ascalon/ʿAsaqlān (Ashqelon), 36, 131
ascetics, 188

ʿashīra, 146. *See also ahl; ʿāʾila; ʿitra; mishpaḥa*
Ashot, King of the Armenians, 213
Ashtor, 45
al-ʿAskar, 25
Athenaios, Bishop of Alexandria, 2
ʿatīq. *See* manumitted person
Atsiz ibn Uwaq the Turkman, 223
aunt, 69, 161-62
av bet din (president of the court), 80, 91-92, 95
Ayyubid sultan, 37-38, 114, 245n4
Ayyubid (1171–1250) period, viii, 175
Azerbaijan, 246

B
Babylon, 17
Babylonia, viii, 20, 73
Babylonian community, 51, 215-16
Babylonian courts, 92n19
Babylonian *geʾonim*, 73, 81
Babylonian synagogue, Fusṭāṭ, 60, 78, 92n19, 189
Badr al-Jamālī, 35, 75, 222
Baḥrī, 245, 257n40
Baḥriyya, 38-39, 245n4
al-Bakrī. *See* Abū al-Ḥasan al-Bakrī
al-Balawī, 29
banker's lists, 125
baqqashah (supplicatory prayer), 225
Bareket, Elinoar, 78
Barqūq, 262
Barsbāy, 259
Baybars, 42, 45, 256, 264
bayt. *See* private chamber
Baghdad, 23, 26, 34, 36, 52, 56, 73, 205-6
Balkans, 22
Bashmurite revolt, 26
bath [*hammām*], 251, 257, 259
beadle (*khādim*), 84, 92n19, 99
bedding, 150
bee-keeping, 136
Ben Ezra synagogue, vii
Ben Nissim family, 148
bene ha-neviʾim. *See* disciples of the prophets
Benjamin of Tudela, 76, 248-49
bet din. *See* court
bet genizah, vii
bet midrash, 171
betrothals, 153-55, 159
bidʿa. *See* innovation
bureaucracy (*qalimiyya*), 27, 33, 42, 111, 143, 259, 266
Bible, the, vii, 1, 12-13, 82, 194, 199
Bible commentaries, 192
Black Death (1348–52), 40, 42, 45, 247, 251
Black Sea, 40-41
Blau, Joshua, 205
biblical scrolls, 20
bill of divorce (*geṭ*), 54n20, 107, 164, 168
conditional bill of divorce, 164
bill of manumission, 58, 60, 62
bill of release (*bara'a*), 168
bill of repudiation, 163, 168
bogeret, 153-54
Book of Esther, 216, 218
Book of Gifts and Rarities, Ibn al-Zubayr, 34
book of records. *See* court notebook
bride, 16, 101, 118, 151-57, 160, 166
brother, 52, 147-49, 166, 172-73
Burjī, 245
Byzantine Empire, 22
Byzantine period, viii, 3, 6, 8, 10-11
Byzantium, 31, 53
C
cadastral surveys, 43
Cairo (al-Qāhira), 14, 23, 29, 31-32, 34, 40-43, 44, 46, 49-50, 75, 126, 148, 176, 206, 209, 223, 244-45, 248-50, 254, 256, 260-61, 263, 266-67
Cairo Genizah, the, vii-viii, x, 1-2, 5, 12-13, 15-16, 19-21, 31, 33, 34-37, 49, 51-55, 58, 60, 64, 66, 70n78, 72-74, 76-80, 82-93, 99, 100n55, 103, 105-6, 108, 111n92, 113, 114nn107-8, 116, 119-21, 123-31, 133n18, 134-36, 139-41, 143-44, 146-47, 149, 151-54, 157, 167-70, 172-76, 188, 191-94, 196-98, 200-201, 203, 206n47, 210, 224, 225n35, 231, 248, 252, 255
cancellation of notifications, 101
cantor (*ḥazzan*), 73, 80, 84, 95, 102n67, 117, 132n15, 146, 164, 231
capital, 23, 41, 125, 129n7, 134, 137-40, 224, 248, 250
Caracalla, 8
Carnarvon, Wales, 18
Catholic Church, 2
Catholics, 3
Cavafy, Constantine, vii
census (*taʿdīl*), 24
Ceuta, Morocco, 238

Chalcedon schism, 22
charity, 54, 58, 79, 84, 111, 125, 127n5, 134, 140, 144-45, 147, 163, 176, 187
charity chest (*quppa*), 118
charity lists, 52, 54, 169
recipients of charity, 125, 140
child marriage, 154
childbirth. 169
childhood, 52, 170
children, xi, 10, 36, 47-48, 60, 62-63, 68, 69, 83, 95n31, 97n41, 111, 138n31, 143-44, 146, 149-50, 161, 164, 170, 172, 190, 194-95, 219, 223, 241, 252, 263
China, 40
Christianity, ix, 2-3, 7, 49, 52, 63, 69, 257
Christians, ix, 8, 18, 38, 45, 50, 69, 128, 205, 214, 240, 251, 255-56, 258, 261, 265
circumcision, 60, 92n19
City of Death (*qarāfa*), 44
civil service, 13
clerking, 139
clothing, 83, 150-51, 156, 159, 166, 168, 222, 255, 257n40, 259, 265
clothing restrictions, 262n65. *See also* discriminatory clothes
code-switching, 199-200, 202
codex, 103
cohabitation, 147
Cohen, Mark, ix
commerce, 31, 37-38, 122, 124, 136, 138n31, 140, 144, 150, 171
commercial letters, 125
communal ban, 120
communal endowments, 93, 104n69
communal judges, 73
concubines, 41, 60, 150
conjugal relations, 60, 62, 166
Constantinople, 22, 133
conversion, 26, 38, 48-49, 51-55, 57-58, 60, 62-64, 66-67, 69-71, 150, 257, 263-66
convert(s), ix, 48, 50, 52-54, 56-58, 63-66, 68-71, 261, 266. *See also poshe ʿa*
cooked food, 134
Coptic Church, 23, 75
Coptic language, 18, 29, 35, 63
Copts, ix, 22, 25-26, 204, 263, 265-66
copying, 139, 173, 197, 203n36
copyist of books (nāsiḫ), 196-97
Cordoba (Cordova), 129, 224, 227
correspondence, 104, 120-21, 125-26, 138, 147, 160, 162, 192-95, 198-99, 201-3, 22, 231
cotton textiles, 37
court (Jewish), x, 9,124. *See also* Muslim court
court clerk, 59, 90, 95-96, 99, 101n62, 104, 106-7, 160, 197
court notebook (book of records; Heb. *shimush*, Ar. *maḥḍar*), 99, 103-7
court of the Palestinian synagogue, 92n19
court records, 88n7, 92, 160
court scribe. *See* court clerk
courtiers (Jewish), 139, 128n6
courtyard houses, 128
craftspeople, 137
credit, 136-37, 141, 144
Crusaders, 36, 39, 45, 246, 255

D

da ʿwa, 30
ḍamān al-darak. *See* warranty clause
Damascus, 23, 27, 35-36, 52-53, 70, 75, 251, 253, 256, 266
Damietta, 66
Dammūh, 184, 265
Daniel b. ʿAzarya, 74-75, 200
dār. *See* marital household
daughter, 154, 161-63, 169-70
David ben Abraham ben Moses Maimonides, 240
David ben Daniel, 61, 80
David ben Joshua, 253
David ha- Nasi, 75
dayyan, 80, 92, 236-37, 254, 267. *See also* Jewish Judge
deed (Heb. *sheṭar*, pl. *sheṭarot*), 62, 91n16, 100-7, 113n100, 115, 122, 202
deed of debt (Heb. *sheṭar ḥov*), 100
deed of quittance, 102
marriage deed (Heb. *sheṭar ketubbah*), 100
Delta. *See* Nile Delta
demography, 127, 137, 142-43
dhimma, dhimmīs, 33, 38, 48, 247, 248n7, 251, 255-59, 261-64, 266
Dhū al-Nūn al-Miṣrī, 30
disciples of the prophets (*bene ha-nevi ʾim*), 184
discriminatory clothes, 256. *See also* clothing restrictions

divorce, 16, 73, 80, 105n74, 111-12, 117-18, 155-57, 166-68, 202
divorce bill(s), bill of divorce (Heb. *geṭ*), 54n21, 105n74, 107, 118, 164
divorce deeds, 192
divorce settlements, 105n74, 113
dīwān (a collection of poetry), 209, 228-34, 237, 240
dīwān (administrative department), 33
diwān al-mawārith [office of inheritance], 115
domestic work, 134n22
Domnos the physician, 2
dowry, (*nedunyā, jahāz, shuwār*), 118, 150, 155-60, 168-69, 171
dowry list (Ar. *taqwīm*), 105, 125
dukhūl. See wedding
Dunash ben Labrāṭ, 220
dyers, 134

E
economic mobility, xi, 137, 139, 145
economic respectability, 144
Edfu, 6, 9
Edomites, 214, 228. *See also* Seʿir
educated professions, 130
education, xii, 83, 127, 139, 140n35, 170-71, 194-96, 198, 203, 206, 208, 235, 241
Egyptian Scroll, *Megillat Mitzraim*, 33, 216
elders, (Heb. zeqenim; Arab. shuyūkh), 78, 80, 85
Eleʿazar ha-Kohen ben Khalfūn, xii, 231-33
ʿEli ben ʿAmram, 220-22
Elijah ha-Kohen ben Solomon, 74
Elephantine, 6, 16
Elḥanan ben Shemarya, 74, 81-82, 84, 215, 220
employment, 130, 134
emporias Ioudaion, 9
endogamy, 151
engagement (*shiddukhin*), 153-55
engagement contract, 158-59, 167
Ephraim b. Shemarya, 78, 81
esqivtar, 213
Eutychios, 3
evil rumors (Ar. shanāʿa), 119
excommunication (Heb. *nidduy*), 70, 93, 122, 163
exilarch, 56, 61, 73, 76, 85
exile, 75, 85, 179-80, 184-85, 226
expulsion from Spain, xiii, 267
extended family, 156-58, 170
exterior commandments (*al-miṣvot al-ẓāhirah*), 182

F
father, 151, 153-54, 158, 162-65, 169-70, 172-73, 219
family and communal correspondence, 125
farmers, 25, 43, 136-37, 211
farming, 24, 26, 37, 42-43, 84, 136
faṣl, 102n66
Fatimid caliph, 32, 36, 73, 80, 114, 213, 255
Fatimid period (969–1171), viii
Fatimids, 30-32, 35, 140, 194, 213
fatwā, 81
Fayyum, 6, 9-10, 12-13
female domestic labor, 134n22
Fez, 129
fiancée, 155
flax, 135, 136n25, 140
food security, 136
formularies, 106-7
Franks, 36
freed persons, 58-60
Frenkel, Miriam, xi
Frenkel, Yehoshua, viii
funeral eulogies, 234
Furniture, 156, 168
Fusṭāṭ, 17, 23, 25, 31, 50-51, 54, 59-60, 66-67, 75-77, 83-84, 91-93, 108, 118, 121, 126, 130, 148, 160, 189, 206, 215, 220, 223-24, 230, 249-50, 265

G
Gaonate, 73-75, 82
Garcin, 46
Gardner-Chloros, Penelope, 199
Garshuni, 195
gaʾon, ix, 55-56, 72-73, 75-76, 80, 85, 91, 212, 224
genealogical lists, 147
Genizah. *See* Cairo Genizah
ger. See proselyte
geṭ. See divorce bill
geʾulla [salvation] poems, 210
al-Ghazālī. *See* Abū Ḥāmid al-Ghazālī
Ghāzī Ibn al-Wāsiṭī, 258
Gibeonites, 55
gilit-dialects. 204
Goitein, Shelomo Dov, 88-89, 96-99, 124, 195
Goldberg, Jessica, x
gold, 31, 135

goldsmiths, 134, 207
grain, 22, 131, 140, 143
grain shortages, 136
groom, 62, 100, 151, 153, 155-57
guard of the quarter (*ṣāḥib al-rubʿ*), 114
guild, xi, 10, 133-34
Gujarat, 34

H

al-Ḥākim bi-Amr Allāh, 33, 216, 255
halakhic queries. *See* responsum
Ḥalfon ben Manasse, 196-97, 201
ḥalitza, 167
al-Ḥallāj. *See* Manṣūr al-Ḥallāj
hammām. See bath
Ḥananel ben Samuel, 189
ḥanna (kindness), 165
Hārūn al-Rashīd, 26
ḥaruz mavriaḥ, 221
ḥasidim (pietists), 252
ḥasidut (pietism), 175. *See also* pietism
Ḥasidut Mitzraim, xi-xii
ḥaver, ḥaverim (fellows of the *Yeshivah*), 78, 79n27, 80, 92, 118
hayba, 76
Hayya Gaʾon, 55, 154
hazaj meter, 223n30
ḥazzan. See cantor
Head of the Jews (*raʾīs al-yahūd*), ix, 9-10, 47, 50, 75-76, 78-82, 85, 91-92, 108n81, 111-12, 122, 176-77, 181, 189, 257
Head of the Synagogue. *See rosh ha-keneset*
Hebrew language, vii, xii-xiii, 3-6, 13, 15, 17-21, 64, 79, 85, 101, 146, 192-202, 207-8, 213, 221, 226, 233, 234n58, 236-237, 240-41, 243
Hebrew poetry, xii, xiv, 209, 221, 240-42
Hermopolis, 6, 9
Hellenistic period, 3, 12
Hellenistic Judaism, 2
heqdesh. See pious trust
Heraclius, Byzantine emperor, 22
Herders, 136
herding, 7, 136
ḥerem (ban), 73, 76, 93, 112, 120, 187
ḥerem setam (anonymous ban), 93n23
hides, 135
high court (*bet din gadol*), 61, 75, 80, 255
Hillel ben ʿEli, 197
ḥizb (party), 84
ḥisba, 114n108
Horn of Africa, 40
House of David, 56
household economy, 134, 150
household goods, 150
husband, 16, 83, 111, 113, 117, 118, 119n135, 121, 147, 150, 153, 155-71
ḥuqqot ha-goyim, 187

I

Ibn ʿAbd al-Ḥakam, 29
Ibn al-ʿAmmānī. *See* Aharon ibn al-ʿAmmānī
Ibn Janāḥ. *See* Yonah ibn Janāḥ
Ibn Ṭāhir. *See* ʿAbd Allāh ibn Ṭāhir
Ibn al-Zubayr, 34
Ibn al-Mudabbir, 27
Ibn al-Nābulsī, 32
Ibn al-Rifāʿa, 258
Ibn ʿAwkal family, 148
Ibn Khaldun, 41
Ibn Qayyim al-Jawziyya, 258
Ibn Taymiyya Taqī al-Dīn, 258
Ibn Ṭūlūn. *See* Aḥmad ibn Ṭūlūn
Ibn al-Wāsiṭī. *See* Ghāzī Ibn al-Wāsiṭī
iftidāʾ. *See* ransom
Iḥyā ʿulūm al-dīn (Revival of Religious Sciences), Abū Ḥāmid al-Ghazālī, 176
Ikhmīm, 30
Ikhshidid (935–68) period, viii
Ilan, Tal, viii
ʿilm, 32
imām, 31-36, 85
immigration, 101n62, 152, 206
India, 30-31, 34, 36-37, 40-41, 165
India traders, 166
Indian Ocean, x-xi, 31, 127, 129, 172
industries, xi, 126, 135
inheritance, 59, 112, 120, 138n31, 142n41, 202, 229, 257, 263
innovation (*bidʿa*), 185
ioudaikos telesma. See Jewish tax
iqṭāʿ, 37, 42-43, 45, 179
Iraq, 28, 34, 56, 246
Iran, 30, 34, 246
Isaac ben Samuel, the Spaniard, 82
Isaac ibn Mar Shaʾul of Lucena, 210
Isaac Sholel, 266
Islam, ix, 4, 32, 38, 42, 45-46, 48-49, 57, 63, 66, 72, 83, 125, 175, 179, 185-87, 246, 256, 265
Islamic Caliphate, viii-ix
Islamic canonical law (sharīʿa), 42
Islamic guilds, 133n18
islamization, 25-26, 45

Ismāʿīlī, 30, 32-33, 35-37, 40, 255
Ismāʿīlī al-Qāḍī al-Nuʿmān, 49
Ismāʿīliyya, 30
Italian merchants, 28, 32
Italy, 28
ʿitra [family], 146. *See also ahl; ʿāʾila; mishpaḥa*
ittiṣāl, 152

J

jahāz. See dowry
Jaqmaq, 259
jamāʿa (community) 77. *See also qahal*
Jawhar al-Ṣaqlabī, 31
Jeremiah, 179
Jerusalem, 35-36, 46, 74, 83, 214, 223, 253-54
Jerusalem yeshiva, 147
jewelry, 150
Jewish judge, 80-81, 93, 95n32, 115, 120n137, 123. *See also dayyan*
Jewish papyri, 3, 6, 8
Jewish Sufism, xi, 175, 252
Jewish tax (*ioudaikos telesma*), 9-10
jihad, 28, 42
jizy. See poll tax
John Tzimiskes, 213
Joseph al-Lebdī, 34
Joseph ben Khalīfa, 253
Joseph ben Tanḥum the Jerusalemite, 240-41
Joseph ha-Maʿaravi, 238-39, 241
Joseph ibn Abitur, xii, 224-227
Judah al-Ḥarīzī, xii, 224, 239, 241-43
Judah ben Joseph, 67
Judah ben Saadya, 75
Judah ben Moses ibn Sughmār, 152
Judah ha-Kohen ben Joseph, 82
Judah ha-Levi, 54, 65, 227-30, 233, 235
Judah ha-Melammed, 231
Judah ibn Shabbetai, 239
Judaism, ix, 4, 8, 48-50, 52-54, 60, 63-64, 68-70, 175, 185, 192
Judean Desert, 13, 16
Judeo-Arabic language, xiii-xiv, 101, 106n77, 191-202, 205, 207-8, 230n47, 235-36
Judeo-Armenian language, 192
Judeo-Greek language, 192
Judeo-Persian language, 192

K

Kāfūr, 30
Karaite courts, 92
Karaite deeds, 101
Karaite legal documents, 101n64
Karaite synagogue, 77, 250, 256, 265
Karaites, 77, 198-99, 233, 249, 253, 267
Karanis, 9-10
kātibs (government clerks), 77, 196, 213
kephalaiotes Ioudaion (head of the Jews), 10
ketubbah, 5, 15-16, 103, 105, 107, 117, 155-56
khādim. See beadle
al-Khāḍir, 45
khalwa [pietist solitary retreat], 184
khānqāh. See sufi convents
kharāj (annual taxation based on produce), 24
Khushqadam, 259
Kifāyat al-ʿābidīn (Compendium for the Servants of God), Abraham Maimonides, 176, 180
al-Kindī, 29
kinnus. See wedding
kinship, xi, 121, 146-49, 151
kosher, 58, 69, 73
Krakowski, Eve, 147
Kyrillos, bishop of Alexandria, 2

L

Labov, William, 203
Labraṭ ben Moses ben Sughmār, 149
Ladino, 192
Latin Kingdom of Jerusalem, 35-36
Layth ibn Saʿd, 29
learning institution. *See madrasa*
legal act of acquisition. *See qinyan*
legal documents, 80-81, 87-91, 96, 99-101, 106, 113n102, 120, 147, 168, 191, 193, 196-97, 199, 201-2, 264
legal opinions. *See* responsum
letter of recommendation, 50, 53
letters of petition, 125, 131, 140
legal queries. *See* responsum
Levant, ix
levirate marriage (*yibum*), 166-67
Libyan desert, 31
Life of the Prophet, Abū al-Ḥasan al-Bakrī, 45
lists of communal donors, 125
lists of donors to charity, 54
lists of recipients of charity, 125
literacy, 191, 193, 194n6, 201-2
liturgical poems (*yotzerot*), 13, 82, 210, 215-16, 224, 231, 240
locusts, 211
long-distance merchants, 88, 125
long-distance trade, 31, 37, 124, 138n30

love, 165, 170, 172-73, 226-27, 232, 237-38, 240-41
love poetry, 165, 238
Lunel, 236
luxuries, 135
luxury textiles, 34

M

ma ʿamad, 224
al-Maʾmūn, 26
ma ʿtūq. *See* manumitted person
madrasa, 37, 246. *See also* learning institution
Maghreb, 66, 68
magic papyri, 18
al-Maḥalla, 118
al-mahdī, 32
al-Mahdiyya, 31, 34
al-Maqrīzī, 38, 265
al-Muʾayyad Shaykh, 259
al-Muqaddasī, 25
al-Muʿaẓẓam Turān Shāh, 39
al-Muʿizz, 34, 213
al-Mustanṣir, 34-35
al-Muʿtaṣim, 26
al-Mutawakkil, 27
maḥḍar. *See* court notebook
al-Mahdī. *See* ʿAbd Allāh al-Mahdī
Maimonides, Abraham (1186-1237), 57-60, 63, 69-70, 76, 82, 118, 176-79, 181-89, 252, 254
Maimonides, Moses, (1138–1204), vii, xi-xii, 56-57, 60-62, 68, 76, 82, 118, 152, 159, 162, 167, 192, 232, 235, 253. *See also* Abraham Maimuni
market inspector, 141
market inspectors' manuals, 133n18, 141
market price, 140
marriage, xi, 5, 15-16, 54, 59, 61-62, 73, 80, 91n16, 92n19, 100, 105, 118, 119n135, 121-22, 150-59, 164, 166-68, 171-73, 192, 202, 238
 marriage contracts, viii, 15-16, 101n63, 150, 155, 157-58, 166, 171, 192
 marital gift, 155-56, 160, 166
 delayed marriage gift (*me ʿuḥar*), 105, 118, 157, 167-68
 early marriage gift (muqdam), 156
 nuptial gift (*mohar*), 155
Marj Dabiq, 46
Marseille, 236
Maslak [path in Egyptian pietism], 184
Mālikī law, 49
Mamluk period, 40, 43, 45, 196, 244, 246-53, 255, 260, 264
Mamluk Sultanate, viii, xiii, 39-41, 46, 245-47, 251-53, 258, 262, 265-66
Manṣūr al-Ḥallāj, 176
manufacturing, 129-30, 137, 139
manumission, 10-11, 58-63, 150
manumitted person (Heb. *meshuḥrar*, Ar. *ʿatīq*, J.-Ar. *ma ʿtūq*), 58-60
maqāma, 238
marital household (*dār*), 156,158
Maṣliaḥ ha-Kohen ben Solomon, 75-76
mastūr, 144
maternal kinship, 147
matrimony, 151, 165, 174
mawlā (client), 59
maẓālim (a special venue of justice meant to redress wrongs), 114n106
Mazor, Amir, xiii
Mediterranean, 34, 40, 127
Megillat Mitzraim. *See* Egyptian Scroll
merchants, x, 10, 28, 31-32, 40-41, 59, 79, 81, 89n7, 95, 125, 126n3, 127-30, 135, 136n25, 137-40, 143, 148, 174, 198, 202, 248, 267
meshuḥrar. *See* manumitted person
Meshullam of Volterra, 249, 253-54, 267
meshūmad, 64
messianic redemption, xi, 175, 184
metals, 43, 129n10, 140
me ʿuḥar. *See* marriage: delayed marriage gift
Mevorakh ben Nathan, 96
Mevorakh b. Saadya, 75-76, 80
middling sort, 128, 130, 134, 142
migration, 29, 70, 137, 205
military aristocracy (*sayfiyya*), 42, 41-43, 195
military equipment, 140
military governor (Ar. *amīr*, *wālī*), 114
Milroy, Jim, 203
Milroy, Lesley, 203
Mishaʾel ben Isaiah ha-Levi al-Shaykh al-Thiqa, 152
Mishnah, 57, 167, 192, 235, 244
Mishneh Torah, 157, 252
mishpaḥa (family), 146. *See also* *ahl*; *ʿāʾila*; *ʿashīra*; *ʿitra*
mohar. *See* marriage: nuptial gift
Mongol Il-Khans of Iran, 39
mongols, 39, 44
moredet. *See* rebellious wife
Moses ben Ḥanokh, 227

Moses ben Mevorakh, 75
Moses Darʿī, 233-35
Moses ha-Levi ben Levi, 47
muḍāraba (kind of partnership), 138
muftī, 81, 82, 113, 264
Muḥammad, the prophet, 32
Muḥammad ibn Ṭughj, 28
muḥtasib. *See* supervisor of the markets
munāẓarāt. *See* theological disputations
muqaddam, 47, 78-80, 92, 112
muqdam. *See* marriage: early marriage gift
musk, 37
Muslim court, 62, 112-13, 115, 116n117, 118, 120, 264
Muslim religious scholars. *See ʿulamāʾ*
Muslims, ix, 24, 35, 44, 65, 73, 76, 128, 178, 251-52, 257, 261
al-Mustaʿālī. *See* Abū al-Qāsim al-Mustaʿālī
mustaʿrib Jews, 254, 267
mutaʿamimūn [religious establishment, men of the turban], 42-43
Myers-Scotton, Carol, 199

N

Nagid, 50, 75-76, 118, 176, 179-82, 184-86, 188-89, 222, 230, 232, 240, 253-54, 257, 266
Nagidate, ix, xiii, 76, 79n28, 189, 253
nāʾib, 76, 79, 114
Nahray ben Nissim, 82
nāʾib (deputy), 76, 79, 114
Najm al-Dīn al-Malik al-Ṣāliḥ, 38
nāqūs, 56
nasīb, 222
nāsiḫ. *See* copyist of books
al-Nāṣir Muḥammad, Qāitbāy's son, 260
Nāṣir-i Khuṣraw, 31
Nathan ben Abraham, 74
Nathan ben Solomon, 197
Nathan ben Samuel, 197
Nathan (Jonathan) ha-Kohen Sholel, 254
nedunyā. *See* dowry
neʾeman bet din. *See* trustee of the court
Neoplatonism, 32
nephew, 147
nidduy. *See* excommunication
Nile, 31-32, 34, 38-39, 41, 43, 184, 238, 245n4, 251
Nile Delta, 25, 26n10, 36, 39, 42, 59, 118, 205-6, 227
Nile valley, viii, 22-23, 26-29, 31, 34, 37, 42, 46
Nishmat Kol Ḥai (prayer), 226
Nizār. *See* Abū Manṣūr Nizār
nuptial gift (*mohar*). *See* marriage: nuptial gift
Nūr al-Dīn, 36

O

oaths (Heb. shevuʿa, Ar. yamīn), 107n78
Obadiah the Norman, 52-53, 56-57
Obadiah of Bertinoro, 244, 249, 267
ʿofan [kind of liturgical poem], 210
olive oil, 135
orchards, 136
Ottoman rule, xiv
Ottomans, 46, 246
Oxyrhynchos, 6-7, 9-12, 15, 17-18
oysterers, 134

P

pagarchs (officials Gk.), x, 24, 78, 83-84, 95, 118, 126-27, 142n40, 152, 251, 258, 262, 266
Palermo, 129
Pact of ʿUmar, xiii, 142n43, 253, 255-57, 259, 264
Palestine, viii, 4, 8, 11, 20, 28, 34, 74, 91, 152, 212, 224, 240, 245, 254
Palestinian community, 67, 215, 218, 220, 224
Palestinian synagogue, 91, 92n19, 93, 181
Palestinian Talmud, 57
Palestinian *yeshivah*, ix, 72-75, 78, 81, 85, 91, 126, 210, 212, 222, 224, 254
papyri. *See* Jewish papyri; magic papyri
paper, 20, 76, 103, 127
parchment, 12-13, 103
parents, xi, 146, 149, 153, 157-58, 171-72, 219
parnas, parnasim, 83-84, 95, 121
paternal lineage, 147
partnership, 32, 129, 134, 142, 202
    family partnerships, 148
    cross-confessional partnerships, 145
    partnership contracts, 125
    interconfessional partnership contracts, 141
    partnership workshops, xi, 134
patriarchy, 148
patrilineal cousins, 151, 152n22
Pax Mongolica, 40
pedophilia, 155
peoples of the book, 132
perfumers, 134
Persian period, vii, 6

personal letters, viii, 16-17, 20, 108n81, 151
pesiqa. See pledge
petition, 33, 73, 76, 79n27, 80, 108n81, 111, 114, 122, 125, 131, 140, 149, 198
petitioning, 110, 111nn92-93, 113
Petrie, Flinders, 15
Philo of Alexandria, 1
physicians, 38, 75, 139, 152, 164, 196, 252, 253n27, 254-55, 259-61, 266
pietism, xii, 175-77, 181, 183n18, 184n25, 185, 189-90. *See also ḥasidut*
pious endowments (*waqf, pl. awqāf*), 37, 43, 83, 263-64
pious trust (*qodesh* or *heqdesh*), 83
piyyut (Jewish liturgical poems), 13-15, 20-21, 217
pledge (*pesiqa*), 83
polemics, 70, 176-78, 186, 266
police (*shurṭā*), 114, 263
poll tax, x, 83, 112, 140, 142n42, 144-45, 149, 248n7, 259
polygyny, xi, 156, 166-67, 174
poor of Jerusalem, the, 83
popular music, 44
potters, 134
poverty, 54, 125, 127n5, 160
poshe ʿa (convert), 64. *See also* convert(s)
practical kin, 149, 174
pragmatic literacy, 202
preachers, 73
precious metals, 43
prenuptial agreements, 166
private chamber (*bayt*), 146, 158
professional witnesses. *See* ʿudūl
profit-making, 134
property seizure, 142
prophets, 178, 183, 186
proselyte (*ger*), 50-59, 66, 69-70
proseuche, 11
prostates, prostatin, 11-12
protected people, 33. *See also dhimma, dhimmīs*
proto-Genizah community, 20
Ptolemaic period, vii, 6
pupils, 146, 171
Purim, 218, 223

Q

qāḍī [supreme judge], 24, 81
qahal (community), 77. *See also jamāʿa*
al-Qāhira. See Cairo
al-Qāʾim, 30
Qāitbāy, 259, 262, 266
Qānṣūh al-Ghūrī, 259, 262, 266
Qalāwun, 40, 256
qalimiyya. See bureaucracy
qarāfa. See City of Death
qaṣida, 217, 222, 229, 237-38
Qayrawan-al-Mahdiyya, 129, 153
qedushah, 218
qedushta, 218-220
qeltu-dialects, 204-5
qerovah, 218, 224-25
qibla, 183
qinyān, x, 86-87, 90-91, 97
qiyyūm. See validation clause
qiraḍ, 138
qodesh. *See* pious trust
quittances, 125
Qumran, 13
Qurʾān, 32
Quṣayr al-Qadīm, 37

R

raʾīs, 79
raʾīs al-yahūd. See Head of the Jews
raʿiyya (consideration), 165
al-Rāḍī, 28
Ramla, 74
ransom (*iftidāʾ*), 117-18, 167-68
rav, 81-82
real estate, 83, 96, 103, 134, 138
rebellious wife (*moredet*), 167
Red Sea, 40
redeeming (Jewish) captives, 11
reforms, 177, 180-83, 185-87, 189, 254n32
pietist reforms, 182
rental properties, 138
reʾshut poems, 225
responsum, 55, 61-62, 81, 95n30, 108-110, 118, 125, 141,160, 173
ribāṭ. See Sufi convents
righteous elders (Heb. *ziqne kosher va-yosher*), 96, 98
ritual bath, 58, 60
Roman Empire, 11
Roman law, 8
Roman period, vii, 3
romances, 238
Rome, 22
rosh ha-keneset (Head of the Synagogue), 79
Rosh ha-Qahal [leader of the community], 79-80

Rosh ha-Qehillot [president of the congregation], 79
Rūmī, 53
Russ-Fishbane, Elisha, xi-xii

S

Saʿadia Gaʾon, 13, 56
Sabbath, 50, 58, 141, 165-66, 210, 219, 226, 233, 235
Sahara, 31
ṣāḥib al-rubʿ. *See* guard of the quarter
ṣāḥib al-shurṭa [officer in charge of public order], 24
Ṣafī al-Dīn ibn Abī l-Manṣūr, 177
sayfiyya. *See* military aristocracy
ṣāḥib al-rubʿ. *See* guard of the quarter
Saladin, 36-37, 246
Salāmiyya, 30
Ṣāliḥ ibn ʿAlī al-ʿAbbāsī, 25
Salim, sultan, 46
Samaritans, 249, 253, 256, 261, 267
Samuel ben Hoshaʿna, xii, 210-217
Samuel ha-Nagid, 223
Sar Shalom ha-Levi, 47
Sasanian invasion of Egypt, 2
scholarly elite, 139
scholars, 29, 74, 81-84, 88, 89n9, 129, 152-53, 164, 175, 188, 207, 221, 233, 251, 254, 260
scribes, xiii, 102n67, 127, 146, 195-98, 201, 207, 266. *See also* court clerk
scribing, 139
script switching, xiii, 199-201, 208
seclusion, 171, 178
seder ʿavodah, 217n19
Seʿir (Esau/Edom), 214
seliḥah poems, 226, 231, 233
Seljuq Sultanate, 35
Seljuqs (Seljuq Turks), 35, 74-75
Sephardi, xiii
services, 83, 126, 130, 134, 137, 144
settlements of marital discord, 160
al-Shādhilī. *See* Abu ʾl-Ḥasan al-Shādhilī
Shādhiliyya, 176
shahāda, 67, 258
al-Shāfiʿī, 37
Shāfiʿī school of law, 48
Shajar al-Durr, 39
Shemarya ben Elḥanan, 74, 81, 215
Shafaqa [tenderness], 165
Shāfiʿī school, 48
sheṭar, pl. *sheṭarot*. *See* deed
sheṭar ḥov. *See* deed of debt
sheṭar ketubbah. *See* deed: marriage deed
Shīʿa, 30
Shiʿī, 32, 49, 246
shiddukhin. *See* engagement
shilṭon, malkhūt [state authoriy], 113
shimūsh. *See* court notebook
shofet [judge], 92n20
shop-keeper's bills, 125
shopping lists, 125, 165
shurtā. *See* police
shuwār. *See* dowry
siblings, xi, 149, 172-73
Sicily, 153, 236
sidra [order], 219
silk dealer, 139
Sinai, 37, 40
Sinai desert, 36
sister, 69, 163, 173
sister-in-law, 166, 173
Sitt Ghazāl, 160-62
slaughterers of kosher meat, 73
slave girls, 150, 166-67, 257
slave markets, 41
slaves, ix, 11, 31, 33, 35, 41, 48, 57-63, 70, 95n31, 141, 143, 149-51, 156, 174, 255, 257
manumitted slaves, ix, 57, 59
slavery, 57, 60, 70, 134, 149, 245-46
sleeping partner, 138-39
soap, 135
social mobility, 139
sociological conversion, 63
Sokrates, the Church historian, 2
Solomon ben Judah, 55, 74
Solomon ha-Kohen ben Joseph, 222-24
Solomon ben Elijah, 160-62
son, 169-172
firstborn son, 172
sororate, 167
Spain, 14, 31, 152, 238
spices, 135, 229
spreading rumors, 120
St. Louis, 39
story-telling, 44
ṣūf. *See* wool
Sufi, 30, 44, 185
Sufis, 42-43, 177-78, 252
Sufi convent (*khānqāh, ribāṭ, zāwiyya*), 246
Sufi rites, xii, 175
Sufism, 42, 44, 176, 252
sulṭān (state authority), 113-114
sulūk [path in Egyptian pietism], 184

sulūk khāṣṣ [the particular way in Egyptian pietism], 182
sulūk ʿāmm [the general way in Egyptian pietism, 182, 186
supervisor of the markets (*muḥtasib*), 114
synagogue, 10-13, 15, 17, 20-21, 60, 76-80, 83-84, 91, 92n19, 93, 95, 99, 117, 125-26, 138, 163, 181-186, 189, 193-94, 220, 232, 241, 243, 250, 256, 257n40, 259-60, 263-65
synagogue building accounts, 125
Syria, 22, 28, 32, 34-35, 40, 85, 244, 246-47
Syriac language, 195, 211n3

T

taʿdīl. *See* census
tailored garments, 134
tailoring, 134
Talmud, 57, 72, 82, 173
Tamerlane (Timur Lang), 40, 246
Tanḥum son of Papa, 4
Taqanna, 116n117
taqwīm. *See* dowry list
tax collector, 10, 65
Tcherikover, Victor, 2-4, 6-9
teshuvot. *See* responsum
thaghr, thughūr [port city], 40
theater, 44
theological disputations *[munāẓarāt]*, 251
Theophilus, Emperor, 133
Tel el-Amarna, 18
textile industry, 134
timber, 131, 140, 143
ṭofes, 101
Torah, 21, 54n22, 58, 82, 94n27, 151, 173, 180, 187, 210-11, 216, 226-27, 233-35, 238-39
    Torah scholars, 169
    Torah scrolls, 13, 20n58
    Torah study, 169, 153
toref, 101
transit trade, 125
transport economy, 131
transportation, 130
Tripoli, 129
troubadours, 238
trustee of the court (neʾeman bet din), 73, 83, 93, 96
Tughril Bak (Beg), 35
Tulunid period (868–905), viii
Tūmām Bāy, 46
Tunisia, 31
al-Tustarī. *See* Abū Naṣr (Ḥesed) al-Tustarī, Abu Saʿd (Abraham) al-Tustarī
Tyre, 74-75

U

ʿudūl (professional witnesses), 94. *See also* witnesses
ʿulamāʾ, 132n16, 143, 252, 255, 257-59
Umayyad period (657–749), viii, 23, 25

V

validation clause (Heb. *qiyyūm*), 91n16, 102
Venetians, 40
Vespasian, 9
viziers, 114, 136, 221
violence, 2, 39, 111, 118, 142-43, 159-60, 162, 211, 214

W

wage labor, 134
Wagner, Esther-Miriam, xii
wālī. *See* military governor
waqf. *See* pious endowments
warranty clause (Ar. *ḍamān al-darak*), 101
weapons, 131
weaver, 6, 65, 134
wedding (*dukhūl, kinnus, zifāf*), 155, 160, 237-38, 247
wedding songs, 165, 234
welfare officials. *See parnas*
well-known clause, 166
widow, 169, 171
wife, 111, 117-19, 134n22, 147, 151-52, 155-70, 173
second wife, 156, 166
wills, 59
witnesses, 13, 61-62, 67, 91, 94, 97, 101-2, 141, 155, 168. *See also* ʿudūl
women's inheritance, 112
workshops, xi, 135, 137, 145
    interconfessional workshops, 142
    cross-confessional workshops, 145
wool (ṣūf), 184
wuṣūl [arrival of inner illumination], 184

Y

Yagur, Moshe, ix
Yahalom, Joseph, xii, 14-15
al-Yahūdiyya (language), 199
Yehosef, son of Samuel ha-Nagid, 222
Yehudai Gaʾon, 159
Yemen, 30, 37, 40, 66

yibūm. *See* levirate marriage
Yiddish, 192, 194n4, 199, 202n33
Yom Kippur, 217n19, 224-25
Yonah ibn Janāḥ, 210
yeshivah. *See* Palestinian *yeshivah*
Yeshuʿah ben Nathan, xii, 218-20
Yosi ben Yosi, 14
yotzerot. *See* liturgical poems
Yusūf ibn Ayyūb (Ṣalāḥ al-Dīn, Saladin) *see* Saladin

Z

al-Ẓāhir, 34
Zakkay of Alexandria, 4
Zāwiyya. *See* Sufi convent
Zifāf. *See* wedding
ziqne kosher va-yosher. *See* righteous elders
Zinger, Oded, x
zunnār [distinctive belt], 255

www.ingramcontent.com/pod-product-compliance
Lightning Source LLC
Chambersburg PA
CBHW051109230426
43667CB00014B/2504
* 9 7 8 1 6 1 8 1 1 7 4 7 2 *